Russian and American Poetry of Experiment

Avant-Garde Critical Studies

Founding Editors

Ferd Drijkoningen†
Klaus Beekman

Series Editors

Paula Barreiro López
Hubert van den Berg
Günter Berghaus
Sascha Bru
Andrea Giunta
Agata Jakubowska

International Advisory Board

Henri Béhar – Sophie Berrebi – Ralf Grüttemeier –
Hilde Heynen – Leigh Landy – Ben Rebel – Jan de Vries –
Willem G. Weststeijn

VOLUME 34

The titles published in this series are listed at *brill.com/agcs*

Russian and American Poetry of Experiment

The Linguistic Avant-Garde

By

Vladimir Feshchenko

BRILL

LEIDEN | BOSTON

Grant of Russian Science Foundation (project no. 19-18-00040, carried out at the Institute of Linguistics, Russian Academy of Sciences, 2019–2023).
Grant of DFG Kolleg-Forschungsgruppe FOR 2603 (project 'Lyrik in Transition', carried out at University of Trier, 2017–2021).

The Library of Congress Cataloging-in-Publication Data is available online at https://catalog.loc.gov
LC record available at https://lccn.loc.gov/2023024817

Typeface for the Latin, Greek, and Cyrillic scripts: "Brill". See and download: brill.com/brill-typeface.

ISSN 1387-3008
ISBN 978-90-04-52625-9 (hardback)
ISBN 978-90-04-52630-3 (e-book)

Copyright 2023 by Koninklijke Brill NV, Leiden, The Netherlands.
Koninklijke Brill NV incorporates the imprints Brill, Brill Nijhoff, Brill Hotei, Brill Schöningh, Brill Fink, Brill mentis, Vandenhoeck & Ruprecht, Böhlau, V&R unipress and Wageningen Academic.
All rights reserved. No part of this publication may be reproduced, translated, stored in a retrieval system, or transmitted in any form or by any means, electronic, mechanical, photocopying, recording or otherwise, without prior written permission from the publisher. Requests for re-use and/or translations must be addressed to Koninklijke Brill NV via brill.com or copyright.com.

This book is printed on acid-free paper and produced in a sustainable manner.

You Russians and we Americans—our countries so distant, so unlike at first glance—such a difference in social and political conditions, and our respective methods of moral and practical development the last hundred years; and yet in certain features, and vastest ones, so resembling each other.
WALT WHITMAN

• • •

Who wants to travel from Moscow to Kiev by way of New York? And yet what phrase from contemporary literary language is free from such detours? And all because there exists no science of word creation.
VELIMIR KHLEBNIKOV

Contents

Aims, Scope and Acknowledgments XI
List of Illustrations XV

Intro: The Linguistic Twists and Turns of the Literary Avant-Garde 1

PART 1
Revolutions of the Word: From Symbolist to Late Avant-Garde Russian Poetry

1   *Energeia*, Not *Ergon*: Humboldtian Linguistics in Russian Poetry 19
    1   Wilhelm von Humboldt's *Energeia*: Poetic Speech as Activity 19
    2   The Humboldtian Spirit-and-Letter in the Poetic Systems of Russian Symbolism and Futurism 23

2   *Zvukoslovie*: Verbal Magic as Poetic Action in Russian Symbolism 31
    1   'The Magic of Language' in the Poetics of Russian Symbolism 32
    2   Glossolalia as a Special Case of Verbal Magic: Andrey Bely and the Poetry of Language 37

3   Futurist *Glossolalias* and *Grapholalias* 45

4   *A Breakthrough into Languages*: Velimir Khlebnikov's *Yazykovodstvo* 57
    1   Khlebnikov's Language Experiment and Philosophy of Language 57
    2   The Futurian as Linguae Constructor 64

5   Wassily Kandinsky and the Birth of the Languages of Art 71
    1   Verse 72
    2   Self-Commentaries to Paintings 77
    3   Theory of Art 79

Transition 1: Experiments with Time and Language: Alexander Vvedensky's and Gertrude Stein's Poetic Grammar 82
    1   Alexander Vvedensky's 'Chinarian' Language 84
    2   Discontinuity of Time, Mind, and Language in Stein's and Vvedensky's Poetics 87

3　Repetition in Poetry: the Serial Grammar of Time　89
　　　4　Verbs and Other Tense Forms: Tools of (Non-)Understanding Time　92

PART 2
A Turn to Language in American Modernist and Avant-Garde Writing

6　Language Arts: the Early American Avant-Garde in Verbal Art　99
　　　1　Ezra Pound: a Few Don'ts by a Language Innovator　101
　　　2　Gertrude Stein: an Impelling Language　102
　　　3　Language Arts of the American Dada　104

7　*Poempictures*: E. E. Cummings' Performative Language　112

8　Heteroglossia and Hybridisation in E.E. Cummings' *Eimi: a Journey through Soviet Russia*　124
　　　1　*Eimi* or *I Am*: Travel Notes, Travelogue or Novel?　129
　　　2　'Comrade K' in the 'Marxist Unworld': Narrative – Composition – Characters – Motives　132
　　　3　Linguistic Hybridisation in *Eimi*　134
　　　4　Dystopia vs Factuality: Yevgeny Zamyatin's *We* and E.E. Cummings' *Eimi*　138

9　Revolution of Language and Eugene Jolas　143
　　　1　Multilingualism, Polyglotism, and 'Revolutionary Tendencies' in Avant-Garde Literature　144
　　　2　The 'Revolution of Language' According to Eugene Jolas　146
　　　3　'Vertical Poetry' as a 'Revolutionary Approach to the Word'　149
　　　4　The Transatlantic 'Universal Language'　150
　　　5　Origins of the 'Universal Language'　153

　　Transition 2: Linguistics and Poetics: Roman Jakobson's Opening and Closing Statements　158

PART 3
Post-Modernism, Neo-Avant-Garde: Russian and American Poetries of Language after WWII

10　From Babel to Babble: the New Russian Poetic Avant-Garde after the Loss of Speech　169

11 American and Russian Conceptualisms: How to Do Verse with Concepts   180
    1   The Concept in Western Thought   181
    2   Concept Art in America   182
    3   The Concept in Russian Philosophy   184
    4   Moscow Conceptualist Art and Poetry   186
    5   Conceptual Analysis of Language in Russian Linguistics and Semiotics   200

12 Language Writing: American-Russian Poetic Transfers   205

13 Object-Oriented Languages: American Objectivism and Contemporary Russian Poetry   220

14 Poetry beyond Language Barriers: Contemporary 'Trans-Language' Writing in Russia and USA   232
    1   Elizaveta Mnatsakanova's Translingualism   233
    2   Contemporary Russo-Anglophone 'Trans-Language' Writing   246

Outro. Lab(-)oratory of the Logos   254
Bibliography   260
Index of Names   285
Index of Terms   291

Aims, Scope and Acknowledgments

Russian and American Poetry of Experiment: The Linguistic Avant-Garde addresses several cases of linguistically eccentric and language-oriented literary writing in Russia and the United States over the last century. It is only in the late Perestroika years, when the Language poets visited Soviet Leningrad, that Russian and American experimental writers first came together to collaborate between and across the two great literary traditions of avant-garde poetry. Before that, the two national traditions had developed independently, yet with a common orientation towards artistic and linguistic experimentation. The chapters of this book focus on major literary 'breakthroughs into language', starting with Andrey Bely, Velimir Khlebnikov, Ilia Zdanevich and Alexander Vvedensky, on the Russian side, and Gertrude Stein, E.E. Cummings, and Eugene Jolas, on the American side. In addition, the book examines post-WWII examples of Russian and American conceptualist art and poetry, language writing, as well as the linguistically challenging poetics of Gennady Aygi, Elizaveta Mnatsakanova, Arkadii Dragomoshchenko, Vladimir Aristov, and some others.[1]

The **aim** of this study is to present the Russian poetics of language experiment in juxtaposition with what would seem like very distant analogs from the other side of the Atlantic and Pacific –North American experimental literature. Comparative studies of Russian and American literatures are scarce. Jacob Edmond (2012) explores aspects of commonness and strangeness by juxtaposing late-Soviet underground writers (Dmitry Prigov and Arkadii Dragomoshchenko) with American counterparts representing Language writing (Charles Bernstein and Lyn Hejinian). A similar but expanded comparison of Russian Conceptualism and Metarealism vs. American conceptual and Language writing is the subject of Albena Lutzkanova-Vassileva's (2015) book-length study. Ian Probstein's monograph (2017b) tackles aspects of time, space and language in Russian and Anglo-American modernist and contemporary writing. Apart from these valuable contributions, there have been no major comparative studies of these two innovative national literary traditions. My study explores language-oriented poetries in the two countries from the perspective

---

[1] The editors of the recent Oxford *A History of Russian Literature* (Kahn et al., 2018) aptly titled the section dedicated to avant-garde and neo-avant-garde Russian poetry of the 20th century 'The Poetics of Language,' and included a survey of different kinds of formal experimentation, from Velimir Khlebnikov to contemporary post-conceptual writings. My study adheres to the same periodisation and is aimed at elucidating the specific strategies of language-oriented poetics carried out by Russian and American authors within the context of linguistic theories of their times.

of language theories and the linguistic turn in the humanities. It contributes, I hope, to Russian-American comparative poetics, the theory of the avant-garde, and to the history of linguistic ideas.

The research for this book was carried out at the junction of literary studies (a comparative and contrastive analysis of Russian and American language-oriented writing of the 20th century) and linguistic historiography (literary inventions are analysed from the perspective of the linguistic theories and paradigms underlying the experimental techniques used in poetic texts). The **central question** of this study is how experimenting with language is linked to evolving ideas about language in linguistic scholarship. I use the term 'language experiment' to denote the various manifestations of the avant-garde's verbal creativity across disciplines.

Situated in a domain shared by both language and literature studies, this book draws on a field of research that Roman Jakobson once called 'linguistic poetics'. Starting in the first decade of the 20th century, Russian scholarship – the context for Jakobson's linguopoetic ideas – was particularly interested in the close connection between discussions by language and literature scholars and concepts developed by experimental poets. Jakobson's 1960 essay 'Linguistics and Poetics' made an appeal for a renewed understanding of the role of language in literature. His 'statement' was controversial in American and Western-European literary criticism and linguistic theory. Yet in Russian scholarship in both the Soviet and post-Soviet periods, Jakobson's communicative and semiotic approach to poetic language set the stage for the development of a specific philological discipline, which acquired the name *lingvisticheskaja poetika* (linguistic poetics). Scholars working in this field have been investigating how poetry – and literature more generally – transform everyday language through a specific kind of *poetic discourse*.[2] My study aims to reconstruct the *historical linguo-poetics* of Russian and American experimental literature of the past century. The main thesis of this book is, then, that the idea of language as such and language as an object of linguistic inquiry has been proliferating with equal force in Russian and in American experimental literary writing of the 20th century, in ways both convergent and divergent. The chapters of this book address, in chronological order, authors from Russian and US literature whose experimental poetics is informed by linguistic meta-reflection, from

---

2 Roman Jakobson's writings on linguistic poetics are collected in Jakobson, 1987. Drawing on Jakobson's observations, another major scholar of linguistic theory, Emile Benveniste, was working in the 1960s on what he called *discours poétique*, analysing Charles Baudelaire's poetic language. These studies remained in Benveniste's archive and were only published in 2011 (see Benveniste, 2011). Joseph Graham (2010) analyses linguistic theories and models as applied to the language of literature, terming this field of study 'onomatopoetics' (a poetics of naming).

Walt Whitman's odes to language to contemporary 'trans-language' poets working with Russian *and* English within the same texts.

The overall scholarly **methodology** behind this study is trifold. First, avant-garde creativity is seen as a specific model of creative behaviour that can appear in diverse fields of practice or theory. It makes its way across multiple artistic and cultural disciplines, even including scientific scholarship. This is what makes this study **transdisciplinary**. Second, this study takes up the **transnational** aspect of avant-garde cultural creation. My analysis encompasses these two cultural contexts from the perspective of experimental writing as a method of avant-garde performativity, however diverse these practices may be within and across national and linguistic contexts. Lastly, my study is **transhistorical** – in addition to the 'historical avant-garde', it analyses a later 'post-' and 'neo-avant-garde' in the second half of the century. This three-fold approach situates my research within global avant-garde and modernism studies.

This methodology explains the rationale behind the monograph's structure. The first two parts deal with language-oriented arts, poetries and theories of the historical avant-garde – Russian and American, with all their similarities and differences, commonalities and variabilities. The third part is devoted to neo-avant-garde conceptions of language writing, which developed separately in Russia and the United States starting in the 1950s and first came into direct contact in the late 1980s, united in their common pursuit of the poetic function of language. The introductory chapter, together with two transitional chapters that break up the main sections of the book, lay out the various contexts – historical, cultural, philosophical and scientific – for innovative developments in poetry and the study of language in both Russia and the US. While my analysis focuses mainly on linguo-poetic and linguo-philosophical facets of experimental writing, I provide socio-political contextualisation for the linguistic philosophy of certain authors. For example, the Russian Futurists' 'revolutionised language' is unthinkable without the social upheavals following 1917, and OBERIU's linguistic apophaticism of the 1930s-40s was to a large degree a reaction against the Soviet regime of totalitarian representation, as were – in a different manner – the language-focused poetic practices of the post-WWII Russian neo-avant-garde. For E.E. Cummings, the reality of the Stalinist state mirrored his own linguistic weirdness in *EIMI*; similarly, Eugene Jolas's macaronic 'transatlantic language' was a way to transcend international crises; and for the Language poets of the 1970s, poetic disourse was a critique of the Vietnam War.

For some structural elements of the book, I use terms from contemporary music (*intro, transition, outro*) rather than conventional academic designations in order to dynamise the reader's perception of the material discussed. After all, this book is about *resonances* – between Russian and American poetic traditions, between linguistic knowledge and literary practice, between language and creativity. This monograph will, I hope, be useful for specialists and students in language and literature studies – Slavic, Anglo-American, comparative, and general – and inspire further research of transnational, transdisciplinary and transhistorical aspects of avant-garde creativity.

I worked on the final version of this book during what is probably the most difficult period in the history of Russian-American (political) relations, aggravated by the war of the Russian regime against Ukraine. At the same time, in the realm of culture, poetry and academia, my friendly and professional bonds with Russian, Ukrainian, American, and European colleagues have inspired and helped me at this final stage of writing. I am deeply thankful to Brill Publishers for including my book in the renowned Avant-Garde Critical Studies series, and to my colleagues from The European Network for Avant-Garde and Modernism Studies (EAM) for their commitment to avant-garde scholarship. Some chapters in this book emerged from papers I have delivered at EAM conferences over the past dozen years. The research behind this monograph was funded by a grant from the Russian Science Foundation (project no. 19-18-00040, carried out at the Institute of Linguistics, Russian Academy of Sciences). The book has been approved for publication by the Academic Board of my native institution – Institute of Linguistics of the Russian Academy of Sciences. I thank Olga Iriskhanova, Timur Radbil and Denis Akhapkin for their valuable reviews. I am equally grateful to the German DFG Foundation for supporting my research at Trier University as part of the project 'Lyrik in Transition'. My colleagues from the Institute of Linguistics (Moscow, Russia), Trier University (Germany), University of Belgrade (Serbia), and Smolny College of Liberal Arts and Sciences (Saint-Petersburg, Russia) have been immensely helpful at various stages of this book's making. The friendly and unfailingly kind exchanges I've had with American Language poets – Barrett Watten, Charles Bernstein, Lyn Hejinian – were highly important for my understanding of American-Russian poetic connections. I am equally indebted to Marjorie Perloff, Mikhail Epstein, and Eugene Ostashevsky for their valuable comments at the last stage of the book's making. Without Maria Vassileva's thorough copyediting this text would read as a piece of wooden language. The last stages of the book's submission, review process, and production would have been impossible without the kind professional help and advice of Brill members Masja Horn, Iulia Ivana, and the anonymous reviewers. A massive thank you to my dear friend Dennis Ioffe (Université Libre de Bruxelles, Belgium) who was instrumental in proposing the book for publication in Brill. And finally, *mille grazie* to my dearest wife Olga Sokolova, for her care, encouragement, and support in all things, including our shared interest in American and Russian poetries of the linguistic avant-garde.

Illustrations

1	Ilia Zdanevich. 'GAROLAND'	53
2	Marius de Zayas. 'Mental Reactions'	105
3	Francis Picabia. 'Voilà ELLE' (right) and Marius de Zayas. 'Femme' (left)	105
4	Bob Brown. A visual poem from *The Blind Man*	106
5	Abraham Lincoln Gillespie. 'Readie-Soundpiece'	107
6	Abraham Lincoln Gillespie. A visual poem	108
7	Fragment from Jackson Mac Low's 'H U N G E R S T r i kE'	109
8	Francis Picabia. 'Thoughts without language'	110
9	E.E. Cummings. 'r-p-o-p-h-e-s-s-a-g-r'	115
10	Max Nänny. A graph of E.E. Cummings' poem	116
11	Eugene Jolas. 'Atomica'	152
12	Dmitry Prigov. Versogram	194
13–18	Andrei Monastyrski. From *Elementary Poetry*	195–199
19–20	Elizaveta Mnatsakanova. From *Beim Tode zugast*	235–236
21–26	Elizaveta Mnatsakanova. From *Das Buch Sabeth*	237–242
27–29	Elizaveta Mnatsakanova. From 'Jelmoli'	244–245
30	Fragment from Ivan Sokolov's poem 'And night took night and illumined the night'	253

INTRO

The Linguistic Twists and Turns of the Literary Avant-Garde

> Can there be a discourse that, without being a metalanguage or sinking into the unsayable, says language itself and exposes its limits?
> GIORGIO AGAMBEN

∴

1   Linguistic Turn or Linguistic Turns?

The turn of the 20th century marked a radical shift in all areas of scholarly and creative pursuits. One of the most significant cultural trends was the 'linguistic turn' which affected the humanities, philosophy, and artistic endeavors.[1] The linguistic turn was first announced retrospectively on the pages of the collected volume *Linguistic Turn: Essays in Philosophical Method* (1967), edited by the American philosopher Richard Rorty, in reference to logical and philosophical concepts from the first half of the 20th century in works by Ludwig Wittgenstein, Martin Heidegger and Walter Benjamin, among others, which sought either to reform language, or to ontologise it to solve philosophical problems.

Wittgenstein, who would become a major source of inspiration for later language poetries, was the first philosopher to focus on the functioning of language in the natural conditions of communication, and to identify a special logic of this functioning. The very linking of life processes and speech activity – linguistic forms with forms of life – by the Austrian-British philosopher and logician signaled a pronounced change in ideas about the status of language and the transition from philosophising about life to philosophising about language. Thus, a 'linguistic bias' manifested itself in philosophy: a search for linguistic structures, their identification, and analysis. In the intellectual culture of the early 20th century, a similarly major role was played by linguistics as well as semiotics, the science of sign systems. Language theory oscillated between Ferdinand de Saussure's positivist focus on 'language

---

1   The term was coined by the Austrian philosopher of science Gustav Bergmann.

studied in and for itself' and Wittgenstein's mystical, and at times apophatic, take on language summarised in a remark from *Zettel*: 'The concept of a living being has the same indeterminacy as that of a language' (1967: 60e).

While Wittgenstein, as well as his teachers George Moore and Bertrand Russell, were primarily interested in the laws and norms with which everyday language and everyday consciousness operate, Martin Heidegger's philosophical thought leaned towards poetic thinking from the very beginning, both as a method and as subject matter. Reflecting on how the experience of human existence relates to the experience of human thought, instead of asking *What should we do?* Heidegger ponders *How must we think*? In the spirit of linguistic philosophy, in his essay 'The Turning' ('Die Kehre') he declares (1977: 40–41):

> For thinking is genuine activity, genuine taking a hand, if to take a hand means to lend a hand to the essence, the coming to presence, of Being. This means: to prepare (build) for the coming to presence of Being that abode in the midst of whatever is into which Being brings itself and its essence to utterance in language. Language first gives to every purposeful deliberation its ways and its byways. Without language, there would be lacking to every doing every dimension in which it could bestir itself and be effective.

In this examination of linguistic problems specifically through the problematics of poetic language, the German philosopher sees an essential 'turn' in the thought and philosophy of his time.

In the domain of philosophy, the term 'linguistic turn' is clearly defined and covers a specific range of directions in philosophical research.[2] However, recent studies indicate that the linguistic turn itself was part of a broader, transdisciplinary trend in the culture and science of the 20th century, which can more generally be called the *turn to language*.[3] In science, a turn means an interdisciplinary focus on a certain set of phenomena, connections and

---

2   The different stages of the linguistic turn in philosophy are set out in Losonsky (2006); in the context of social theories – in Hirschkop (2019); in hermeneutic philosophy – in Lafont (1999). Ken Hirschkop talks about a series of 'linguistic *turns*' that were going on from the late 19th to the mid-20th centuries, in which intellectuals in Europe 'both reorganized their intellectual fields around language and argued for a new understanding of language itself' (2019: 1). These turns are looked at 'in concert, as a whole, as a comprehensive reconceptualisation and revaluation of language in the modernist moment' (Ibidem).

3   The linguistic turn in historiography, for example, is discussed in Clark (2004). A turn to 'language' is an expression used by the American Language poet Barrett Watten (2002) in relation to the 1960s. The linguistic turn continues to spark discussions in various domains such as performative studies (Nealon 2021) and new materiality (Ihde 2021).

processes, increased attention to these problems in a certain historical period. A *turn* is different from a *scientific revolution* in that it does not signify a dramatic change in world views and may cover several scientific paradigms at once.[4] A scientific revolution constitutes 'changing the world view' and 'changing the conceptual grid', according to a classical definition by Thomas Kuhn (1962). A consistent transition from one paradigm to another is carried out through revolutions. In contrast, the notion of a *turn* is understood as a kind of gradual transition of knowledge from one state to another, or from one cultural area to another.

The 'turn to language' was expressed, above all, in the emergence of theoretical linguistics (as laid out in Ferdinand de Saussure's *Course*), that is, in the establishment of linguistics and semiotics as independent sciences. The turn towards language also manifested itself in such areas as logic, theology, art history, literary criticism, and even in the natural sciences.[5] Take physics – in his 1942 treatise 'Reality and its Order', Werner Heisenberg speaks of the language of poetry as a specific language for describing reality. Moreover, the 'turn to language' has been studied alongside later *turns* of intellectual thought, such as the cultural, performative, iconic, interpretive, translational turn, etc., by Bachmann-Medick (2016). Thus, the linguistic turn was part of a ramified process in the evolution of science and culture of the last century, associated with an orientation towards language.[6]

---

4   On the phenomenon of the 'turn' in the culture of the twentieth century, see Savchuk (2013). Valery Demyankov clarifies that the English term *turn* and the German *Wende* (in such phrases as *linguistic turn, pragmatic turn, cognitive turn, interpretive turn*, etc.), as well as the similar term *wave* (for example, the *new wave*) are 'deprived of the drama brought about by the term *revolution* and refer to an interval of time rather than a point. After all, the turn is noticed only after it has taken place, and it is not always possible to return back' (2016: 76).
5   In American philosophy, a similar tendency towards a turn, yet not so much towards language as towards 'sign' and 'meaning', took the form of 'pragmatism' in the first decades of the twentieth century (Charles S. Peirce, William James, John Dewey, Charles H. Morris, and others).
6   Giorgio Agamben has famously challenged the concept of Language as an Idea persistent in philosophical inquiry. In a chapter of his book *Potentialities*, titled 'The Idea of Language', he speaks about philosophy as *revelation* through language: 'Philosophy considers not merely what is revealed through language, but also the revelation of language itself. A philosophical presentation is thus one that, regardless of what it speaks about, must also take into account the fact that it speaks of it; it must first of all say language itself' (1999: 25). The philosophical *idea* as such, he claims, is 'not a word (a metalanguage), nor is it a vision of an object outside language (there is no such object, no such unsayable thing); it is a vision of language itself' (Idem: 27).

2 *The Return of Language* at the Turn of the Century: Philosophy, Linguistics, Poetry

Russian intellectual culture of the early twentieth century did not lag behind the global trend of 'turning towards language'. However, in the Russian philosophical and philological traditions, the linguistic turn took the form of a *turn to the Logos*. The ancient Greek concept of *logos* became relevant again in the context of the Russian religious Renaissance, and was rethought both within the framework of the Christian tradition and under the influence of the 'philosophy of the name', represented by Pavel Florensky, Sergey Bulgakov, Alexei Losev, and some others. Just as in ancient Greece, the concept of Logos stood for a certain synthetic phenomenon, combining the meanings of word, speech, utterance, sentence, meaning, sign, concept, judgment, reason, and consciousness.

According to a summary by Russian cultural scholar Sergey Averintsev, 'logos is altogether an immediately and objectively given content for which the mind must "provide an account", an "accounting" activity of the mind and, finally, a recurrent semantic ordering of being and consciousness; it is the opposite of everything that is irresponsible and wordless, unrequited and irresponsible, meaningless and formless in the world and in man' (2000: 114). A significant influence on this logocentric tradition was exerted by Sergey Trubetskoy's book *The Doctrine of the Logos and its History* (1900, publ. 1906) and Vladimir Ern's book *The Struggle for Logos* (1911). In Russian logocentric philosophy, two opposing lines were established: Orthodox-oriented theology (Ern, Florensky), on the one hand, and rationalistic scientism oriented towards Western philosophy (Yakovenko, Bely, Stepun), on the other.

As Thomas Seifrid (2005) indicates, these concepts from the first decades of the twentieth century represent 'Russia's culture of the Logos'. At the same time, the concept of the Logos in this new cultural context incorporates not only a general philosophical meaning, but also more specific linguistic and poetic interpretations. On a larger scale, this linguo-aesthetic 'turn to the Logos' was characteristic of the work and poetics of Russian poet and theorist Andrey Bely. Bely's philosophy of language applies the Logos concept to broader anthropomorphic descriptions of language, focusing on themes such as incarnation, death, and the resurrection of language. Although devoid of distinctly religious meanings, they nevertheless have explicit connections with the doctrine of the incarnation of Christ, which is at the center of the Christian concept of the Logos.

This fusion of religious and linguistic thinking can be seen in the title of the programmatic manifesto of the Russian Formalist school, 'Resurrection of the

Word' by Viktor Shklovsky, as well as in various metaphors about 'living' and 'dead' words in Russian discourse about language in the first decades of the 20th century. Steven Cassedy (1990: 104) points out that due to the ambiguous nature of the logos and the word, which fluctuates between theological and other (scientific and artistic) meanings, the philosophy of language in Russia has always, and especially in the early 20th century, been explicitly or implicitly intertwined with theology and Orthodox *logology*.[7]

Linguophilosophical and logological conceptions of language as a creative process and Logos as a creative verbal principle of thinking marked the Russian variant of the 'linguistic turn', and also paved the way for the innovative literature of the first half of the 20th century. 'New literature', 'revolution of language', 'decomposition of the word', 're-creation of grammar', 'word creation' and 'language creation', 'poetic critique of reason' – these designations of that linguistic turn and logosophical revolution accompanied the diverse manifestations of the Russian avant-garde experiment. Ideas introduced by Wilhelm von Humboldt, Karl Vossler, Alexander Potebnja, Gustav Shpet, Valery Bryusov, Andrey Bely, Vyacheslav Ivanov, Osip Mandelstam, Velimir Khlebnikov, Vladimir Mayakovsky, and others informed a view of language as (a) an effective *tool* of artistic and scientific creativity; (b) an intrinsic *object* and *material* of artistic experience; and (c) a new *scientific object* that required approaches using methods from various disciplines.

The avant-garde experiment aspired to look beyond the limits of human experience and comprehend the hidden structural laws of the world. The language experiment as a constituent of avant-garde creativity attempts to reach beyond the boundaries of language and toward the abyss of reality hidden behind it. The mystery of the Logos hidden behind the veil of language is what enthralled a whole generation of experimenters, practitioners, and theorists of the 'laboratory of the Logos'.

A variety of linguistic and semiotic categories underwent experimental treatment in avant-garde literature. In the early stages of Russian Symbolism and Futurism, it is the individual word (*word-symbol, word as such,* or *word-creation,* as it was variously named) that was challenged. At a later stage, the focus shifted to language as a universal system of signs (in concepts such as *language-creation, language of the stars,* or *alphabet of the mind* etc.). By the 1930s, in the last years of the Russian historical avant-garde, the very ability of language to convey the content of the world was 'besieged' and discredited, and the very mechanisms of meaning-formation were called into question

---

7 For a discussion of the *logocentrism* of Russian culture of this time, see Hansen-Löve (2008).

(in concepts such as *nonsense, dumb language,* or *the absurd*). Meanwhile, the Anglo-American avant-garde was represented by two major poles – one that could be called maximalist (the Babel poetics of James Joyce, Ezra Pound and Eugene Jolas), and the other minimalist (e.g., Gertrude Stein, E.E. Cummings, Marcel Duchamp).[8] Each of these writers foregrounded a particular level of linguistic experimentation in their work. All of them sought to reconsider the categories of linguistic expressiveness.[9]

Linguistic scholarship of that period revealed a similar tendency towards making language a full-fledged and independent object of study. In 1923, the Russian linguist Lev Shcherba complained that modern linguistics 'has lost sight of language as a living system of signs that express our thoughts and feelings' (1974: 100). Hence the increased interest of linguists in 'living language as a phenomenon given in experience, in the living process of speech, in syntax and semantics' (Idem: 102). This interest was evident not only in specific linguistic studies, but also in institutionalised forms of research. For example, 1918 saw the establishment of the Institute of the Living Word in Petrograd, a collective venture dedicated to the 'living word' as a new object of scientific research and 'living speech' as a subject of reflection in the Russian avant-garde.[10]

The individualisation of language as an object of study brought about new principles of linguistic research. For instance, a new approach to interpreting texts from antiquity comes to the fore. As Michel Foucault notes in *The Order of Things* about this 'episteme', the new criticism 'has devoted itself to a strange kind of commentary, since it does not proceed from the observation that there is language towards the discovery of what that language means, but from the deployment of manifest discourse towards a revelation of language in its crude being' (1970: 298). All new major conceptions of language of the 19th century are marked by a similar goal: from Humboldt with his search for the 'spirit of language' to the interpretation of anagrams in ancient texts by Saussure.

In the context of this book on language poetries, another point by Foucault is notable, which concerns the specific circumstances of the 'turn to language'. Experimental art and avant-garde literature ('writing degree zero', as Roland Barthes (1967) periphrastically calls it) emerges as an offshoot of a new

---

8 Marjorie Perloff's recent book (2021) explores 'infrathin possibilities of poetic language within what she calls the 'micropoetics' of minimalist writing.
9 Nicholas Birns (2017) distinguishes between three phases of the linguistic turn and their corresponding literary manifestations over the 20th century: the logical positivist, or aesthetically formalist; the semantic, or new criticist; and the deconstructivist.
10 For an overview of the broad range of its activities see the collected volume by Feshchenko (2015).

linguistic epistemology, Foucault claims. However, he traces the origins of this movement back to the early 19th century, when the concept of 'literature' first emerged (Idem: 300):

> This is because at the beginning of the 19th century, at a time when language was burying itself with its own density as an object and allowing itself to be traversed, through and through, by knowledge, it was also reconstituting itself elsewhere, in an independent form, difficult of access, folded back upon the enigma of its own origin and existing wholly in reference to the pure act of writing. Literature is the contestation of philology (of which it is nevertheless the twin figure: it leads language back from grammar to the naked power of speech, and there it encounters the untamed, imperious being of words.

A similar turn in the post-revolutionary Russian context is attested by the Russian scholar Shcherba (1974: 102):

> Poets for whom language is a material began to relate to it more or less consciously; they were followed by young literary historians who felt it impossible to understand many literary phenomena without a linguistic approach; finally, people in theater, for whom a living spoken language is the alpha and omega of their art, perhaps more than anyone else contributed to the awakening of an interest in language in society.

The poetic work of Stéphane Mallarmé clearly suggests that as early as the late 19th century, literature developed a concern with its own linguistic depth. The French poet's 'Notes on Language' dwell upon the 'Results of the acquaintance of the Idea of Science and the Idea of Language', as he puts it. He predicted a future era of language-centered thinking: 'Science, having in Language found a confirmation of itself, must now become a *confirmation* of Language' and 'derive an epoch of the reflection of language' (cit. in Stark, 2020). Literature after Mallarmé, according to Foucault, 'breaks with the whole definition of genres as forms adapted to an order of representations and becomes merely a manifestation of language which has no other law than that of affirming – in opposition to any other forms of discourse – its own precipitous existence' (1970: 300). Thus, the essence of the new literature is 'to curve back in a perpetual return upon itself, as if its discourse could have no other content than the expression of its own form; it addresses itself to itself as a writing subjectivity, or seeks to re-apprehend the essence of all literature in the movement that brought it into being' (Ibidem). What is significant is that Foucault calls this process 'the return of language'. Compared to 'linguistic turn', the advantage of this term is that it suggests the most important quality of this 'turn' in the modernist era, namely, the 'turning to oneself', 'returning the language to itself and upon itself', or what would later be called in linguistics the self-reference of language.[11]

At the turn of the century, philosophical, scientific, and artistic thought made a pivot to language; language, in its turn, pivoted to its own essence in these new linguistic conceptions. Language, Foucault notes, 'appeared in a multiplicity of modes of being' (Idem: 304). A focal question arose: 'What is language? How can we find a way round it in order to make it appear in itself, in all its plenitude?' (Idem: 306). The 'return of language', which manifested itself in a variety of disciplines and approaches, served as the background against which experiments in poetic language creativity became possible. The epoch of the historical avant-garde thus coincided with the era of the 'linguistic turn', both sharing a common orientation towards experimentation – with language as much as with artistic experience per se. In a broader aesthetic context, this orientation towards the language of art was part of a global and fundamental shift of what Jacques Rancière calls the 'aesthetic regime of art'. Writing about several 'scenes' from such a shift (specifically, about Russian avant-garde cinema), Rancière elucidates 'how a performance or an object is felt and thought not only as art, but also as a singular artistic proposition and a source of artistic emotion, as novelty and revolution in art - even as a means for art to find a way out of itself' (2013: XI). In the cases analysed in my book, language becomes a means for literature to find a way out of itself – and a way back into itself – in a revolutionised aesthetic regime of poetry.

This book discusses several concepts which have the word 'revolution' in them, such as 'revolution of language', 'revolution of the word' and the like. Indeed, the idea of revolution is inherent to what we know as the 'avant-garde' in art. This was evident for early Russian Futurists, as well as for the French Surrealists. According to Peter Bürger, the avant-gardiste intention 'to revolutionize life by returning art to its praxis turns into a revolutionizing of art' (1984: 113). Even before Bürger, the French intellectual and essayist André Malraux (1957) associated avant-garde art of the early 20th century

---

11   Expanding on Foucault's vision, Gerald Bruns' ground-breaking book (1974) is a seminal study of modern poetry through the prism of linguistic theories, tracing back the origins of this idea to Romanticism. Trevor Stark's recent contribution to this field (2020) is an insightful reappraisal of the role of language in avant-garde arts and literature from Mallarmé to Duchamp.

with 'aesthetic revolution'.[12] Another philosopher and social theorist, Herbert Marcuse, pointed out in his book *The Aesthetic Dimension* that revolutions in art may foreshadow social revolutions or follow them: 'Art can be called revolutionary in several senses. In a narrow sense, art may be revolutionary if it represents a radical change in style and technique. Such change may be the achievement of a genuine avant-garde, anticipating or reflecting substantial changes in the society at large' (1978: xi). The aesthetic and linguistic revolution in the early avant-gardes went hand in hand with the political, social, and scientific experimentation with language and languages.

3 The Dizzying Mephisto Waltz of Experimentation

The English word *experiment* is etymologically related to the concept of 'experience', meaning 'life experience', 'test', 'trial', or 'examination'. Taking the concept of 'experiment' as a basic term for my study, I mean to emphasise the interrelation of poetic and scientific experimentation with life experience. This relationship announced itself most decisively in the era of the historical avant-garde, when artists began to consciously conduct direct experiments on reality – on language, everyday life, the social environment, etc. Literature started to test, examine, and investigate language. Experiment as a method in poetry and poetics was aimed at a transformation of primary linguistic materials with a view to creating new forms of conscious experience and a new system of life relationships. As Kazimir Malevich stated in his treatise '1/42. Non-Objectiveness', 'Man has found himself in new circumstances and must build a new form of new relationships' (2003: 132). Of course, 'revolutions of life' and 'revolutions of language' carried different degrees of risk for their leaders. This meaning of *risk* is, furthermore, inherent to the original Latin word *experimentum*.

The relationship between experiment and literature was first explored by the German Romantics. In his *Notes for a Romantic Encyclopedia* (*Das Allgemeine Brouillon*), Novalis associated 'true poetry' with 'the art of experimentation': 'Experimenting with images and concepts in the faculty of representation in

---

12 On aesthetic revolutions, see Raunig (2007); Erjavec (2015). For Jacques Rancière (2009), 'aesthetic revolution' is a radical change of relationships between knowledge and action, simultaneously a revolutionary transformation of aesthetics and an aesthetic avatar of political revolution.

a way entirely analogous to physical experimenting' (Novalis, 2007: 162).[13] In the late 19th century, the idea of literary experiment reemerged within the framework of Emile Zola's theory and practice of the Experimental Novel. In Russian literature, Fyodor Dostoevsky was hailed by contemporary critics as one of the first literary experimenters,[14] as were Nikolai Gogol and Anton Chekhov.[15] However, in these discussions about *experiment in literature*, critics were not yet talking about a full-fledged *experimental literature*. The latter is usually understood to mean the later art of the avant-garde, as well as processes associated with this art in the linguistic aspects of artistic creation.

The rapprochement of science and art introduced by Romanticism and later deployed in fin-de-siècle positivism was also explored, in the 1900–1910s, in the theoretical works of the Russian Symbolist poet and critic Andrey Bely. In search of the foundations for what he called 'formal aesthetics', he turned to the concept of 'experiment' in his article 'The principle of form in aesthetics'. He also devoted a separate article, 'Lyrical Poetry and Experiment' (publ. 1910), to justifying the need for a science of 'experimental aesthetics'. From the very beginning, Bely emphasises the new role of linguistics in experimental poetics: 'the study of words and their arrangement comes into contact with philology and linguistics' (1910: 240). Therefore, he claims, 'the problem of language, reduced to more complex problems of experiment, has an essential meaning in lyrical poetry; language, as such, is, indeed, a form of creativity' (Idem: 571–572). Following this logic, he refers to the linguistic theories of Humboldt, Wundt, Steinthal, Vossler, Potebnja and others in his experimental studies of poetic speech – and arrives at an important conclusion: 'This shows how closely the particular problems of experimental aesthetics are intertwined with the most general problems of linguistics; and vice versa: problems of poetry enter linguistics as parts of a whole' (Ibidem).

Bely's treatment of 'experiment' has three basic features. Firstly, for him, it entails the principle of experimental and purposeful handling of language

---

13   On the origins of literary experimentation, see Krause et al. (2005), Gamper (2010), Grimstad (2015).
14   According to Nikolai Berdyaev, all of Dostoevsky's work is about 'anthropological experiments': 'Dostoevsky is not a realist artist, he is an experimentor, a creator of an experimental metaphysics of human nature' (1918: http).
15   The literary scholar Dmitry Ovsyaniko-Kulikovsky devoted his essay 'Observational and Experimental Methods in Art' (1914) to 'experiments on reality' carried out by the two writers. This Russian academic was an ardent proponent of the Humboldtian linguistics of *energeia* (see Simonato, 2005), at the same time developing positivist and physicalist approaches to literary creativity. This synthesis of Romanticism and Experimentalism would later on be taken up by the Russian Formalists.

material. He implements this principle superbly in his studies of the 'comparative morphology' of verse and 'rhythm' patterns in Russian poets and prose writers, most brilliantly in a reading of Gogol. Secondly, he adopts Novalis' idea that the formal, and sometimes functional, features of scientific experiments can merge with artistic experiments, e.g., when a poet works with linguistic material in the same way as an experienced researcher: 'In addition to a finely developed vision, which makes it possible to deeply penetrate all reality (this or another), the poet is, above all, an artist of form; for this he must also be an experienced experimenter; many features of an artistic experiment are strangely reminiscent of a scientific experiment, although the methods of experimentation here are sui generis' (Idem: 597). And thirdly, his conception of experiment focuses on recreating language in the aftermath of a poetic revolution.

Another outstanding Russian poet, Osip Mandelstam – a great admirer of Bely's work – reached a similar understanding of literary experiment in his book-length essay *Conversation about Dante*. In Dante's approach to verbal and mythological material, he argues, all elements of 'passionate experimentation' are on display: 'These include the creation of specially contrived conditions for the experiment, the use of instruments of such precision that there is no reason to doubt their validity, and clear verification of the results' (Mandelstam, 2001: 70). Addressing the issue of artistic experiment was both a sign of the times and an example of a new outlook on the world. It is this new view, through the eyes of Dante, that the Acmeist poet implemented in his essay, yielding to what he calls 'the dizzying Mephisto Waltz of experimentation'.

Concurrently with the literary experiments of Bely, Mandelstam and the Russian Cubo-Futurists, the principle of linguistic experiment was introduced into Russian linguistics. Lev Shcherba was one of the first to do this in his classic article 'On the threefold aspect of linguistic phenomena and on experiment in linguistics'. Criticising the neogrammatical methods of working with linguistic material, he called for studying living languages in all their qualitative diversity: 'A scholar of living languages must do otherwise. Of course, he must also proceed from linguistic material understood in one way or another. But, having built an abstract system from the facts of this material, it is necessary to check it against new facts, i.e., see if the facts deduced from it correspond to reality. Thus, the principle of experiment is introduced into linguistics' (Shcherba, 1974: 33). 'Negative linguistic material' should be an integral part of the linguistic experiment, he claims. By 'negative material' he means 'unsuccessful statements marked with "don't say this"'. Shcherba would later produce as an example of this principle the artificial phrase 'glokaja kuzdra shteko budlanula bokra i kudrjachit bokrenka', which is a special case of a lexical experiment that obeys grammatical rules.

In the cultural context of the 1910s, experimentation with language became a scientific method that was intrinsically valuable to many fields in the humanities and, as this book will show, also for many currents of the literary avant-garde. Collaborations between scholars and poets of the avant-garde stimulated the development of academic poetics and linguistics. Roman Jakobson later recalled: 'The road to a new experimental art and the road to a new science called to us equally – they called to us precisely because both were based on shared invariants' (Jakobson, 1999: 80). Diverse cognitive models converged and research in the natural sciences and the humanities revealed similar concerns and results in artistic discourse. According to Theodor Adorno's *Aesthetic Theory* (1984), 'the idea of experimentation' consists in the transfer of the methods of science to the methods of art. This process takes place at the linguistic level of a literary work. The key term 'language experiment' which appears throughout my book, therefore, encompasses both the phenomena in poetry (Symbolism, Futurism, Absurdism) and theoretical concepts aimed at understanding these phenomena (scientific poetics, experimental linguistics, aesthetic philosophy).

4   Language Experiment and Experimental Writing: from Whitman to the Russian Avant-Garde

Experimental writing in the United States has always been deeply rooted in the poetry of Walt Whitman.[16] In the chapters that follow, it is hard to name a single American author who was not in some way inspired by *Leaves of Grass*, a herald of free verse, modernist poetics, and avant-garde mentality. Whitman was also a language reformer, who anticipated the revolution in poetic language in the following century.

Commenting on his magnum opus, Whitman embraces the concept of language experiment, making an implicit call for innovation in poetry: 'This subject of language interests me – I never quite get it out of my mind. I sometimes think the Leaves is only a *language experiment* ...' (1904: viii–ix, *emphasis mine – V.F.*). In the same statement, as if anticipating Futurist logic, he claims that 'new words' in poetry contain 'new potentialities of speech' (Ibidem). The same futuristic stance appears in a remark from his essay 'Our Language and Literature' about 'wording the future with indissuadable words' (cit. in Warren, 1990: 10). As James Warren's book suggests, Whitman was an ardent reader of

---

16   Alan Marshall (2009) considers Whitman the originator of 'American experimental literature' in his study of the nature of democratic thought.

contemporary linguistic theory. Most notable is his interest in Wilhelm von Humboldt's theory of language – language seen both as a creative activity and an expression of the national spirit. According to Warren, 'Whitman's vision of language is so fundamental to his vision of his own poetry, and vice versa, that the poems are as "theoretical" as they are "practical", just as Whitman's pronouncements concerning language are as performative and rhetorical as the poems' (1990: 4). We can see this in an ode to language from his 'Preface' to *Leaves of Grass*, cited in Warren's study (Idem: 35), which sounds like a poem and a theoretical essay at the same time:

> Language-using controls the rest;
> Wonderful is language!
> Wondrous the English language, language of live men,
> Language of ensemble, powerful language of resistance,
> Language of a proud and melancholy stock, and of all who aspire,
> Language of growth, faith, self-esteem, rudeness, justice, friendliness, prudence, decision, exactitude, courage,
> Language to well-nigh express the unexpressible,
> Language for the modern, language for America.

Whitman's free and democratic verse arises as a poetry of the creative energy of the word, a poetry of language that well predates poetry's serious engagement with language experiments per se. For over a century now, the two national traditions of language-oriented avant-garde, the American and the Russian, have been similarly persistent in revolutionising the poetic language.

A comparative study of Russian and American poetry could not begin with anyone other than Walt Whitman. And this book, indeed, does just that – with an epigraph from the poet's heartfelt letter, dated 1881, about the differences and similarities between Russians and Americans. Now, almost a century and a half after this appeal to Russia, we can appreciate the perspicacity of Whitman's insight about the two countries and cultures, 'so distant, so unlike at first glance ... yet in certain features, and vastest ones, so resembling each other' (cit. in Ball, 2003: 15).[17]

Russian literature has been greatly influenced by the American premodernist classic. In the 19th century, he was translated into Russian by Ivan Turgenev and Leo Tolstoy. But the most significant reception of Whitman's work occurred in the Silver Age of Russian poetry. He was not just translated

---

17   Russian and American models of creativity and experimentation have been the subject of a transcultural analysis in Berry et al. (1999).

by several poets[18] – including such aesthetically dissimilar ones as Konstantin Balmont and Korney Chukovsky[19] – but his verse reform contributed in many ways to the Futurist revolution of the word in the works of Velimir Khlebnikov and Vladimir Mayakovsky.[20] Another Futurian, Benedikt Livshits, called Whitman the creator of the poetic language of modernity: 'Possessing a cosmic consciousness, Whitman, like all carriers of this higher form of consciousness, testifies to the impossibility of expressing the structure of the soul, incomprehensible to the intellect, using the language of concepts: "The words of my book nothing, the drift of it every thing"' (cit. in Novikov, 1992: 147). Alexander Blok called him 'the star of New America' (cit. in Idem: 144). Beyond literature, the pioneers of Russian avant-garde cinema, Sergey Eisenstein and Dziga Vertov, were likewise inspired by Whitman's poetics.[21]

The Russian 'Whitmaniana' (as Korney Chukovsky called it) is perhaps comparable in scale to the reception of only one other representative of American literature – the Romantic and yet also pre-modernist Edgar Allan Poe. Poe had a particular impact on the older generation of Russian Symbolists, with their infatuation with the mystical word and verbal magic. Collections of his poems were published in translations by Valery Bryusov and Konstantin Balmont. For the latter, the American Romantic was especially attractive due to his views

---

18 For Whitman's Soviet-era translations, see Mendelson (1976).
19 See Polonsky (1997), Venediktova (1993) and Novikov (1992) for discussions of their different approaches to translating Whitman.
20 Aspects of Whitman's influence on Mayakovsky are touched upon in Peterson (1969) and Cavanagh (2010). The extensive topic of Whitman and Khlebnikov is still awaiting its researcher.
21 Jacques Rancière in his *Aisthesis* specifically points out Whitman's relevance for Vertov and Eisenstein: 'Later the propagandists of young Soviet Russia widely distributed Korney Chukovsky's translation, to the point of making fliers from it in order to boost the morale of the soldiers of the Russian army and the workers of the industrial reconstruction. But next to these poems transformed into propaganda tracts for combatants, there was the edition published in 1923 in Petrograd, with its futurist cover on which the Cyrillic letters making up Walt Whitman's name danced before a background of sky-scrapers, between the stars of the American flag and the accordion folds of the red flag. The spiritual and materialist poem of modern life is also the poem that abolishes the separation between the signs of speech and graphic images. [...] This explains why, more than once, the frenetic rhythms of Whitmanian lyricism would contaminate the rigorous constructions of the Soviet avant-garde directors who were working to make cinema the language of the dialectic. [...] the montage of *Man with a Movie Camera* which sweeps up the manicurist's gestures, magicians' tricks and miners' labour in the same accelerated rhythm owes more to *A Song of Occupations* or to the *Song of the Broad Axe*, than to *Capital*. And the dialectic of *The General Line* receives its demonstrative force only in the torrents of milk or the frenzy of reapers carried away by the Whitmanian rhythm' (2013: 73–74).

on the magic of language. In Poe's dramatic miniature 'The Power of Words', the angel Agathos asks: 'And while I thus spoke, did there not cross your mind some thought of the physical power of words? Is not every word an impulse on the air?' (1903: http). The idea of the physical power of words and the magical effects of language would become, as I will argue in later chapters, one of the overarching themes of Russian poetries of language in the 20th century. The Russian reception of Poe played a significant role in this orientation towards verbal magic.

Whitman and Poe were the most powerful sources of inspiration from the American continent for Russian experimental literature. Their reception bridged 19th century American pre-modernism and 20th century high Modernism and the radical avant-garde in the two countries 'so distant' from each other – notwithstanding their shared border and the fact that less than four kilometers separated them from each other across the Bering Strait in the Far East. After that, language experiments in the two cultures developed with practically no awareness of each other up until the Second World War.

Meanwhile, around 1912–1913, simultaneously and independently of each other, revolutionary calls for the liberation of poetic language sounded on both continents.

In pre-WWI Russia, the Futurists-'Gileians' proclaimed the right of poets 'to feel insurmountable hatred for the language that existed before their time' (in the 'Slap in the Face of Public Taste' manifesto), and announced 'the word as such' and 'the language of the future'. Velimir Khlebnikov prophesied a new science, the development of which 'would make it possible to think out all the wisdom of language' ('Teacher and Student'). At the Brodyachaya Sobaka cafe, Ilia Zdanevich performed a manifesto on the revolution in writing systems, calling for the freedom of 'a language suitable for art' ('On Writing and Orthography'). At the same venue, the future leader of the Formalist school, Viktor Shklovsky, made statements about the 'resurrection of the word', speaking of 'the place of Futurism in the history of language'.

On the other side of the Atlantic and the Pacific, Ezra Pound, founder of Imagism and Vorticism, urged readers to 'forget the old language of poetry' in the name of a new 'language of intuition'.[22] Gertrude Stein's first writings were

---

22   There was a brief encounter between the Russian and Anglo-American avant-gardes in 1915 when Zinaida Vengerova, a Russian literary critic close to Symbolist circles interviewed Ezra Pound. Vengerova, who often visited London and was considered the 'Russian correspondent' of Ezra Pound, published an essay titled 'English Futurists' in the first issue of the *Strelets* almanach (1915). In it, she recounts the contents of the first issue of *Blast* in some detail and publishes translations of two poems by Pound and Hilda Doolittle. It is likely that Vengerova's essay aroused interest in Vorticism among the

'setting the language in motion in order to induce new states of consciousness', as the literary critic Mabel Dodge characterised them. This is how the common turn of poetry towards language announced itself in completely different literary traditions – precisely at the turning points of these traditions.

The literary experiments of Stein and Pound became the two poles of experimentally oriented poetry in America.[23] One side gravitated towards the strategies of minimalism – Stein's writing works with minimal units of the language, the smallest shifts, and 'insistent' repetitiveness. The other side, led by Pound, is associated with the strategies of maximalism – working with a variety of linguistic means, compositional complexity, and the use of different languages and dialects. This polarity was also present in the social lives of these poets: Stein's calm solitude and literary simplicity, on the one hand, contrasted with Pound's political maximalism and literary expansionism. American experimental writing would oscillate between these two poles throughout the following century.

Russian Cubo-Futurists. For example, El Lissitzky later credited *Blast* magazine as one of the forerunners of the new typography of the 1920s. However, we do not know anything about further contacts between English/American and Russian avant-garde artists. Even the leader of Russian Futurism, David Burliuk, who emigrated to the US in the 1920s, did not manage to establish close contact with major literary or artistic figures in experimental art.

23 Scholars analysing currents in experimental literature originating with Stein and Pound have given this tradition designations such as 'the experimental school in American poetry' (Winters, 1937); an ongoing 'tradition of the new' (Rosenberg, 1959); 'disjunctive poetics' (Quartermain, 1992) and 'the language of rupture' (Perloff, 1986). For a discussion of this tradition see also Perloff (1985); Perelman (1994); Watten (2003); Bernstein (2016). One of the first uses of the term 'experimental writing' occurs in Laughlin (1947). Natalia Cecire (2019) has recently challenged the concept of 'experimental writing' in a bold critical revision of its historical roots. The collected volume edited by Georgina Colby (2021) proposes ways experimental writing can be read through a socio-political lens.

PART 1

Revolutions of the Word: From Symbolist to Late Avant-Garde Russian Poetry

∴

CHAPTER 1

Energeia, Not *Ergon*: Humboldtian Linguistics in Russian Poetry

> In that a people effects, from its inner freedom, the development of its language, as the instrument of every human activity within it, it seeks and simultaneously attains to the thing itself, that is, to something different and higher; and in that it gets on to the road of poetic creation and speculative thought, it simultaneously works back, in turn, upon language.
> WILHELM VON HUMBOLDT

∴

> Language is the fullest creativity possible for a person.
> ALEXANDER POTEBNJA

∴

> In the Word's word you are—a theologian:
> O, radiant Hosanna
> Of Matthew, Mark, and John—
> My tongue! . Leap high: by word mystery!
> ANDREY BELY

∴

1   Wilhelm von Humboldt's *Energeia*: Poetic Speech as Activity

As Steven Cassedy rightly points out with reference to Russian Humboldtianism, 'the Russian tradition that is central to the development of language theory in modern literary aesthetics begins precisely in the context of the transition that Cassirer identifies in the work of Humboldt' (1990: 38). Wilhelm von Humboldt's impact on Russian thought extends, crucially, to the formation of a new Russian poetry at the turn of the 20th century, on the developing theories of poetry and language, and on poetic language itself. A characteristic feature of Russian thought about language was the close contact between theoreticians and practitioners of the poetic word. It is common for Russian poets to advance, or keep up with, the literary theories and linguistic ideas of their time; this was especially true of the early twentieth century. Conversely, the influence of linguistics on poetic theory and practice is also a characteristic feature of the Russian 'turn to Logos' at the beginning of the 20th century, as part of the global 'linguistic turn'. The first chapter of the book will focus on this aspect of Russian thought, which treats the philosophy of language as an expression of creativity, emerges from the tradition of Wilhelm von Humboldt and Alexander Potebnja, and develops in the poetry and poetics of the Silver Age.

Humboldt first addresses the linguistic nature of poetry in the chapter 'Character of languages. Poetry and Prose' from his famous work *The Diversity of Human Language-Structure and its Influence on the Mental Development of Mankind* (*Ueber die Verschiedenheit des menschlichen Sprachbaues und ihren Einfluss auf die geistige Entwicklung des Menschengeschlechts*, 1827–1829); the chapter first considers particular aspects of interaction in language before moving on to more general ones. Considering the reciprocal influence of national character and language, he notes that there are two phenomena 'wherein not only do they all most decisively come together, but where the influence of the whole is also so far in evidence, that the very concept of the particular vanishes from the scene, namely *poetry* and *prose*' (1999: 168). Thus, he identifies poetry and prose as specific forms of the existence and functioning of language, in which the influence of the whole becomes the dominant tendency, i.e., their special organisation and specific goals. Humboldt calls poetry and prose 'phenomena of language', predetermined by its 'original disposition' and the constant impact of language on their development. Moreover, he considers a tendency towards poetry and prose the 'truly great' form of a particular language, evident in an 'equal development of both in regular proportion'. In the spirit of Romantic Idealism, he measures the richness and perfection of language by the development of precisely these two forms of language existence as well as the development of its 'intellectuality'. He associates the development of intellectuality with a variety of 'phenomena of language': 'The works of language can prosper only so long as they are carried upward by a mental ardour directed to the enlargement of its own culture, and to conjoining the world to its own essential nature' (Idem: 175). Poetry and prose, according to the German linguist, are the highest and most harmoniously organised manifestations of language.

Humboldt further establishes the following categories: ordinary speech, scientific speech, prosaic speech, and poetic speech. Unlike ordinary speech, prosaic and poetic speech ('ennobled speech', which later thinkers will refer to as 'artistic speech') have an inner formal cohesion ('inner form', as he puts it). At the same time, he notes, external artistic form is always essential for poetry. This dialectical unity eventually forms the basis of linguistic poetics and also, as I will show below, the principles of twentieth century poetry. However, Humboldt goes no further than a comparison of poetry and music and devotes his attention to the historical sources of prose and poetry, as well as to the differentiation of scientific, philosophical, and poetic style in the forms of language. This line of thought was taken up by his Russian follower Alexander Veselovsky in his work on 'historical poetics' and by Alexander Potebnja working on 'theoretical poetics', the study of 'poetic and prosaic thinking' (see Seifrid, 2005; Bartschat, 2006).

Poetry and prose, according to Potebnja, correspond to two 'states of thought, which are reflected in two states of the word' (Potebnja, 2006: 194). However, this leads him to blur the boundaries between the ordinary and the artistic in his thesis that 'the word itself should be called a poetic work'. The same trend later becomes characteristic of the Western tradition of 'aesthetic idealism' in linguistics (in works by Vossler, Croce, Schuchardt, etc.), which moves away from Humboldt in its aestheticisation of linguistic activity. At the same time, the key and most famous thesis of the German linguist is used extensively in their work – the distinction between language as a static system (*ergon*) and language as an activity (*energeia*). Let us examine in greater detail this aspect of Humboldt's linguistic theory.

It is important to consider in what context Humboldt expressed this famous idea. Biographical evidence suggests that the idea of 'language as an activity' was inspired, on the one hand, by his studies of the Basque language with its original ergative structure and, on the other, by his reading of Condillac and Diderot (Aarsleff, 2007: 202). In particular, he was influenced by Condillac's analysis of the changed word order in poetic texts (such as Horace's 'Odes'), which creates the aesthetic effect of 'energy'. The idea of energy in poetry was familiar to Enlightenment writers (Diderot writes about it); an entry for 'Energy' appeared in the *Encyclopédie méthodique. Grammaire et littérature* (1782) by the encyclopaedic linguist Nicolas Beauzée. Beauzée offers the following definition: 'Energie est cette quantité qui, dans un seul mot ou dans un petit nombre des mots, fait appercevoir ou sentir un grand nombre d'idées' (cit. in Aarsleff, 2007: 202). This concept of energy suggests the utmost saturation of the word with ideas.

The idea of energy was thus suggested to Humboldt by literary references such as Condillac's analyses. However, in his own texts, it acquires a more abstract and general character. At first it is expressed using the German terms *Erzeugtes* and *Erzeugung*: 'We must look upon *language*, not as a dead *product*, but far more as a *producing*' (Humboldt, 1999: 48). The antinomy is based on such binaries as 'constant/transitory', 'limited/infinite', 'finished/lasting', 'closed/open', 'dead/living', 'mummy-like state in writing / recreation in living speech'.

The *ergon-energeia* opposition is at the core of Humboldt's conception of language, as expressed in his famous formula that language 'in itself is no product (*Ergon*), but an activity (*Energeia*)' (Idem: 49). Despite the dialectical opposition, the emphasis is on *energy*. Humboldt's definition of language as energy refers primarily to its genetic plan, i.e., to language at the time of its making. His discussions of the origins of language show him to be a typical Romantic thinker. His thoughts on the dynamic and creative nature of the emergence of language correlate with other Romantic myths about language – for example, with the Rousseauean myth which also incorporates the category of energy. Jean-Jacques Rousseau also proposed the idea that language had 'energy': 'Words (voix), not sounds (sons), are written. Yet, in an inflected language, these are the sounds, the accents, and all sorts of modulations that are the main source of energy for a language, and that make a given phrase, otherwise quite ordinary, proper only to the place where it is' (cit. in Derrida, 1997: 280). Jacques Derrida further comments: 'Rousseau himself articulates this chain of significations (essence, origin, presence, birth, rebirth) on the classical metaphysics of the entity as energy, encompassing the relationships between being and time in terms of the now as being in action (energeia)' (Idem: 311). Yet, unlike Rousseau, Humboldt positions the driving force of language development not in nature, but in the human spirit.

Humboldt sees energy as a creative principle in language. In his view, language is 'created' by different aspects of humanity working together – its spirit, spiritual activity, consciousness, a certain universal principle, its forces and impulses. At the same time, language tends to 'create itself', through an unconscious process. Humboldt writes about an 'independent activity', arguing that the transformation of sound into articulation is when it becomes an independently creative principle. An individual can also be a creator since languages, being the creation of peoples, can be generated in an individual person. Things that are creative are associated with productive activity, the introduction of something new, while the non-creative is linked to passive, reproductive activity that reflects what is already present in a system. At the same time, Humboldt believes that creativity (generation, creation) is possible only while language is being invented: 'The creation, if it is to be a true and complete one, could hold good only of the original invention of language, and thus of a situation that we do not know about, but only presuppose as a necessary hypothesis' (Humboldt, 1999: 76). In other cases, he speaks of the 'transformation', or 'rebirth', of language. Thus, even as he postulates the creative principle in language, he also delimits areas and degrees of its presence. The same is not true of the majority of his followers, both in the West (e.g., Benedetto Croce) and in Russia (e.g., Alexander Pogodin or Dmitry Ovsyaniko-Kulikovsky), who believed that all of language is creativity.[1]

2 The Humboldtian Spirit-and-Letter in the Poetic Systems of Russian Symbolism and Futurism

The genealogy of Russian poetic Humboldtianism begins with the Russian Symbolist poet and language theorist Andrey Bely. His work is arguably an exceptional case in Russian literature; as a poet, he not only bases his creative principles on contemporary linguistic theory, but also contributes to the development of ideas about language.

Bely's first literary experiments, the *Symphonies*, showcase the paramount importance of language to his artistic endeavors. Alongside these early poetic experiments, Bely theorised a revolutionary turn in attitudes towards language. In the article 'Forms of Art' (1902) he reflects: 'The translation of reality into the *language of art* [...] is accompanied by some reworking. This process, in essence a kind of synthesis, leads to an analysis of the surrounding reality. The analysis of reality necessarily follows from the impossibility of conveying, through external methods, the completeness and variety of all elements of the surrounding reality' (Bely, 1994: 90, *emphasis mine – V.F.*). New forms of art called for a new attitude to language as an artistic medium, as he writes in a later autobiographical essay (Bely, 1988: 21):

> [H]ence the experiments with language taken as the making of new signs of communication (words); hence the interest in folk language, which preserves the virgin lands of life, hence the abundance of neologisms in my vocabulary, and the experience of rhythm as a principle that connects poetry with 'prose'; I saw the writer as an organizer of the linguistic aspirations of a people [...].

The need for new signs of artistic communication thus calls for both an in-depth study of language and its aesthetic processing.

---

1 See Bartschat (2006) for Humboldt's legacy in Russian linguistics; Feshchenko et al. (2014) for how the Humboldtian concept of linguistic creativity is reflected in the Russian philosophy of language.

More than any other writer of the Silver Age, Bely had an ear for linguistics. This is evidenced both by his deep knowledge of Humboldt's and Potebnja's works, and by the numerous references to linguistic theory in Bely's notes and self-commentaries. The following is a partial list of linguists he mentions: Dahl, Afanasyev, Buslaev, Ovsyaniko-Kulikovsky, Korsh, Zhirmunsky, Vinogradov, Brik, Müller, Noiret, Becker, Schleicher, Brugmann, Fabre d'Olivet, Vossler, Steinthal, Grimm, Curtius, Geise, Geiger, Marty, Mommsen, Wackernagel, Mautner. His affinity for the discipline allowed him to implement the main ideas of the scholarship he read within his own artistic and linguistic theory.

Andrey Bely's linguistic ideas were an integral part of his theory of Symbolism. In a later essay on Symbolism written in 1928, he posits that 'the studies of linguists, since they reveal a linguistic metaphor, inform the linguistic basis of the symbolic school [...] The symbolic school sees its linguistic genesis in the works of Wilhelm von Humboldt and Potebnja [...] But the symbolic school does not stop at Potebnja's ideas, it seeks to deepen them' (Bely, 1994: 446–447). In the same essay, he considers his own influence on the theory of language: 'A thorough dissection of the motto of the symbolic school about form and content gives new criteria for the analysis of linguistic forms, theory of the word, theory of styles, theory of myth, psychology, criticism, etc.' (Idem: 447). Bely's aesthetic principles were characterised by linguistic symbolism informed by a post-Humboldtian philosophy of language.

Language is important for Bely both as a medium for literary creation and as a cultural phenomenon in the philosophical sense. For Bely, language is just as pivotal as myth in its impact on the formation of spiritual culture. When it comes to poetic creativity, language creation is primary in relation to myth creation. In the article 'The Magic of Words' he writes that 'poetry is directly linked to the creation of language and obliquely linked to mythical creation' (Bely, 1985: 110). The purpose of poetry is 'the creation of language'; language, 'it must be borne in mind, is the creation of living relations' (Idem: 100–101). The 'cult of words' is important, and he considers it 'the active cause of new creation' (Idem: 99). Moreover, he emphasises the anthropological and theurgical significance of linguistic creation. In this, Bely differs from other Symbolists; for Vyacheslav Ivanov, for example, the mythological-theurgical component of poetry is more important, for Valery Bryusov – the figurative-metaphorical one. However, all three leading poets of Russian Symbolism were influenced by the principles formulated by Humboldt and Russian Humboldtians of their time.

The 1900s were the heyday of Symbolism and, particularly for Bely, a formative time for Symbolist theory and philosophy of language. The articles included in the book *Symbolism*, as well as the 1910 treatise 'Thought and Language. A. Potebnja's Philosophy of language' all deal with questions of linguistics. Bely builds upon Humboldt's ideas as refracted in Potebnja's work (Bely, 2006a: 201–202):

> From the point of view of Humboldt and Potebnja, language is individual creativity, turning into individual-collective creativity and striving to expand universally; language is the creation of the 'indivisible', but it presupposes the creativity of a multitude of generations and depends on its refraction by others; language is the struggle of the sum of neologisms against the petrified heritage of the past; the theory of language as activity involuntarily comes up against an understanding of this activity in a kind of tragic collision (1) between the individual creations of the collective, (2) between future activity caused by prior motives and the sum of the products of all past creativity. The 'Dionysian' (Nietzschean) side of language as energy, and the Apollonian completeness of what was historically formed lead to the formation of the tragedy of language through antinomies. Potebnja warns against understanding Humboldt's antinomies as logical errors: 'To solve the question of the origin of language and its relation to thought,' he says together with Humboldt, 'means to reconcile the contradictions that exist in language' (p. 40). The metaphysical concepts of the organism and their various analogies cannot reconcile these contradictions. Humboldt traces spirit and language (understanding and speech) to a higher principle; the dualism of language is not predetermined by this unity. This is where further research ends according to Humboldt; this is where Potebnja's original theory begins.

This essay by Bely is significant because it establishes a direct evolutionary connection between Potebnja's theory of literature and Humboldt's theory of language. Bely identifies the importance of Potebnja as including grammar and linguistics within the field of aesthetics. Thus, according to Bely, verbal values enter the ranks of cultural values. At the same time, the essay emphasises the importance of Potebnja for the theory of Symbolism, the theory of creativity, and the theory of knowledge.

Bely's main argument – that 'the word itself is an aesthetic phenomenon' (Idem: 205) – is clearly influenced by Potebnja. The poet was a very attentive reader of the Kharkiv scholar. He takes up the idea of language as a bearer of continuous creativity of thought from Potebnja's work. By placing this Potebnian idea within his own aesthetic framework, Bely provided a certain empirical proof for it. However, after declaring the autonomy of the word-symbol, Bely takes another theoretical step: 'from the unification of external form and content, the unity of form and content is proclaimed in both the verbal and artistic symbol' (Idem: 207). The Symbolist poet reactualises Potebnja's theory, inscribing it directly into the context of new artistic and linguistic practices. According to Bely, in the works of Potebnja, new poetry can find 'answers to the most burning questions concerning the origin and meaning of language, mythical and poetic creativity' (Idem: 199).

Language and the word continued to be the main focus of Bely's theoretical writings and poetic texts throughout his life. In 1917, he published 'Aaron's Rod', a long treatise 'about the word in poetry' which laid out the principles of a new literature (*'новая словесность'*) based on the 'living word' (*'живое слово'*). The new word, Bely believed, would be born from the unity of philosophy and poetry, the reconciliation of conceptual logic and sonic aestheticism. In the early post-revolutionary period, the poet lectured extensively on what he called 'the theory of the word', with lecture titles such as 'The Living Word', 'Theory of the artistic word. Creativity of speech', 'On artistic language', 'Word as an organ of creativity', and 'On the word' – all of which were published in the recent collection mentioned earlier (Bely 2018).

In 1922, Bely published a book titled *Poetry of the Word*, in which he analysed lyric texts by other Russian poets using an experimental methodology outlined in his earlier article 'Lyrical Poetry and Experiment' (1910). The word as such becomes the object of experimental philology. Experimenting with the word begins with a description of the verbal material: 'Studying the structure of the verbal cuts on these verbal trunks strengthens our consciousness in the hope that there is still a root [...] to realise the juices of the leaves: to give birth to the Word in ourselves, for the first time to see the tops of your own words, where wind storms run and lightning bolts of meanings hitherto hidden from us are flashing [...]' (Bely, 1917: 208). Thus, verbal experimentation can reveal semantic laws unobservable on the surface of a text (at the material level of language). Humboldt's idea of the inner form of language, further developed by Potebnja in his theory of the inner form of the word, plays a crucial role in Bely's conception of the 'inner word' (*'внутреннее слово'*), as well as in his own 'poetry of language'.

Andrey Bely's peer, the Symbolist poet Vyacheslav Ivanov, also considered Potebnja the first theoretician of Symbolism and a 'powerful ally' of the Symbolist poets. For Ivanov, the 'linguocreative symbolism' present in Potebnja's analysis of the nature of the word was highly valuable. In his 1918 article 'Our Language', the poet also directly refers to Humboldt's work (Ivanov, 1986: 119):

> It is Wilhelm Humboldt's profound insight that language is simultaneously a deed and an active force (ergon and energeia), a communal

medium that is constantly being created by everyone in concert, and that anticipates and brings about any creative act in the very cradle of its conception; the antinomial cohabitation of necessity and freedom, of the divine and the human; the creation of the popular spirit and God's gift to the people.

Ivanov turned to Humboldtianism late in his formative years as a writer (after the Revolution of 1917). He made use of Humboldt's ideas about the creative spirit of language and the initial organic nature of language as guiding principles for a Symbolist philosophy of language.

Another pillar of Russian Symbolism, Valery Bryusov, applied the Humboldtian doctrine to his theory of 'synthetic poetry'. Noting that art is an act of cognition, he saw in cognition the ultimate goal of art, which coincides with the goal of science (Bryusov, 1925: 9):

> In relation to poetry, this is revealed (by the school of Wilhelm Humboldt) from an analogy between poetry and linguistic creativity. The creation of language was and remains a cognitive process. The word is the primary method of cognition. Primitive man meant by the word an object or a group of objects; he named them in order to distinguish them from the incoherent chaos of impressions – visual, auditory, tactile and others – and thus to know them. To name something is to recognise it, and therefore to know it. The process of creating a poetic work, artistic poetry, is entirely parallel, analogous to this.

Bryusov, the founder of 'academic Symbolism' in poetry, refers to Humboldt in his treatise on scientific poetry (Bryusov, 1955: 209):

> A. Potebnja, continuing the work of W. Humboldt, drew attention to the remarkable parallelism between the creativity of language and the creativity of the artist. Language, according to the findings of W. Humboldt, arose primarily not as a means of communication, but as a means of cognition. Primitive man gave names to objects in order to distinguish them from others and through that to know them. Similarly, the artist creating an artistic image seeks to comprehend something, to grasp it. The image of Othello is artistic knowledge of jealousy. All art is a special method of cognition.

For Bryusov, much as for Bely and Ivanov, the concept of language as creativity was the most significant idea borrowed from Humboldt's writings and their later appropriations in Russian philology.

A literary theorist and major proponent of Russian Futurism, Viktor Shklovsky, had his own accounts to settle with Humboldtian legacies. In what would become the manifesto of Russian Formalism, 'Resurrection of the Word', he seeks to distance himself from the poetics of Symbolism and, simultaneously, from the Potebnian approach to understanding language in poetry. The strategic goal of this démarche was to make a case for the new avant-garde movement, but Shklovsky's actual thinking adopts the principles of the 'energetic' philosophy of language that he formally denied. Shklovsky's concept of 'the word's resurrection' echoes Humboldt's idea about the 'revival of language'. Shklovsky and Formalism were dependent on Humboldtianism, much as the Futurists were dependent on Pushkin and Dostoevsky, whom they metaphorically 'threw overboard from the ship of modernity'.[2]

Meanwhile, Humboldt's idea of energy as a creative and inventive principle in language flourished in the writings of Futurist poets, most impressively in the work of Velimir Khlebnikov. His philosophy of language will be presented in greater detail in a later chapter of this book. Here, I will merely outline the poet's Humboldtian themes.

The central element of Khlebnikov's version of Futurist poetics was the so-called 'self-contained word', or 'the word as such' ('самовитое слово', 'слово как таковое'), which was an extension of Andrey Bely's Symbolist concept of the 'autonomous word'. This poetic concept is in line with one of Humboldt's main ideas, that of the 'independent power of language' ('Selbsttätigkeit'), according to which language draws its resources and capabilities from itself, especially at the moments of its formation. Khlebnikov's linguistic project represents a poetic reconstruction of language at the time of its emergence, i.e., primordial creation, to use Humboldt's terms. The Humboldtian idea of 'linguistic creativity' takes on a more concrete meaning in Khlebnikov's poetic conception – it is not merely creativity *in* language, but the creativity *of* language (and languages) – even though the poet is dealing with invented languages created for purely aesthetic purposes.

Khlebnikov's creative attitude to the word is summed up in his formula 'The word is an embroidery hoop, the word is flax, the word is fabric'. Translated into the language of linguistics, this formula could be restated as follows: the word is not only a finished product of historical development or something produced by someone and intended for use ('fabric'), not only material for poetic and other transformations ('flax'), but also a tool for these transformations ('hoop'). Characteristically, the latter, creative conception of the word is listed

---

2 See Holquist et al. (2005) for how Shklovsky's concept of estrangement can be linked to Humboldtian linguistics.

first. 'The word being born' is the subject of most of Khlebnikov's poetry and theory. Humboldt's argument that 'language is "energy", not "ergon" (activity, not a product)' 'finds a significant development in the poet's stance, as well as a specification that considers the evolution of language as a tool of imaginative thought, with special attention to the word as the most important means of proper poetic activity and any creative attitude to language' (Grigoryev, 2000: 66–67).[3] Interestingly, in spite of his pronounced orientation toward Leibniz, Khlebnikov's Humboldtianism, which is less obvious at first sight, was quite evident to his closest literary contemporaries. The Futurist Benedikt Livshits argued: 'Humboldt's understanding of language as an art found its most eloquent confirmation in the works of Khlebnikov, with the one stunning proviso that a process that was still understood as a function of the collective consciousness of an entire people, was embodied in the work of a single person' (2000: 368–369).

The Futurists' word-creation, interpreted in Humboldtian terms, can be seen in Pavel Florensky's concept of the antinomy of language (Faryno, 1995). According to the Russian religious philosopher Florensky, the antinomy of language is the balance of two principles, *ergon* and *energeia*, which must be observed in linguistic creativity. Florensky viewed avant-garde experiments as a crisis in the evolution of language. He critisised the artificial languages that were being created in large numbers around that time. The pathos of these philosophical languages is rationality, and thus opposed to the nature of the Logos: 'The attempt to create a language when it is not created, but composed, decomposes the antinomy of language. Living contradiction is dissociated; then either the ergon side or the energeia side gains the upper hand' (Florensky, 2000: 153–154). Another way of 'spoiling language', from Florensky's point of view, can stem from the energetic nature of language (Idem: 155):

> Language is spontaneous, therefore unreasonable, and therefore it is necessary to compose your own language, a reasonable one, as the disbelievers in the reasonableness of the Word would have it; language is reasonable, therefore lifeless and meaningless, and therefore it is necessary to exterminate from the depths a new language, internal, essential, transrational, as the disbelievers in the Essence of the Word demand.

Florensky's polemic targets the linguistic innovation of Futurists who subjected the word to laboratory experiments in search of a new, more perfect language.

---

3 See also Bukhshtab (2008).

What is interesting here is not Florensky's negative attitude to experimental linguistic processes, but the very fact of the theologian and philosopher's understanding of avant-garde poetic creativity.

Wilhelm von Humboldt's idea of *energeia*, or *language as creativity*, can be traced through the Russian linguistic and linguopoetic conceptions of the early twentieth century. It infiltrated the theoretical thought and poetic practice of Russian Symbolism and Futurism, appearing as a relevant conceptual field for philosophy of language (e.g., Gustav Shpet) and the theologically oriented philosophy of the name (e.g., Pavel Florensky). The latter not only drew upon Humboldtian thought, but also made use of the energetic concept of language for polemical purposes when discussing the Futurists' linguistic creativity. This, in turn, brings us to another major idea advanced in early 20th century Russian culture, by scholars and poets alike – the magic power of words to transform reality.

CHAPTER 2

Zvukoslovie: Verbal Magic as Poetic Action in Russian Symbolism

My tongue! ... Leap high: by word mystery!
ANDREY BELY

∴

O inhuman magic, create!
through the suffering words, perform your creation!
[...]
O, crucifixion-like magic,
create and create now!
VLADIMIR MAYAKOVSKY

∴

Interest in verbal magic emerged in Russian poetry at the turn of the 20th century at the intersection of three cultural traditions: firstly, folklore, associated with incantatory formulas and folk magical practices; secondly, Symbolism, dating back to European mysticism in the field of poetry; thirdly, linguistic inquiries into the sound shape of language, from Wilhelm von Humboldt through Alexander Potebnja to Roman Jakobson. A number of general works on the occult tradition in Russian literature (Rosenthal, 1997; Ryan, 1999; Bogomolov, 1999; Epstein, 2006; Gilchrist, 2009) explore some aspects of the first influence. The paths of the second influence –the Symbolist poetics of the 'secret word' – have not been thoroughly studied (since the classic yet quite dated book (Donchin 1958), this topic has not received much attention). The third line was discussed in the previous chapter of this book and will be touched upon here in some other respects.

Verbal magic, in the general sense, connotes the incantatory function of language in poetic speech, an emphasis on the primacy of sound in its repetitions and variations. The magic of the word can manifest in charms, glossolalia, *zaum*, nonsense, muttering, interlingual experiments, and other forms of suggestive sound and sound symbolism. Russian poetry of the twentieth century demonstrates a special interest in the 'magic', 'secret' and 'sonic' side of the poetic word.

In his influential book *The Structure of Modern Poetry*, the German literary critic Hugo Friedrich foregrounds 'the magic of language' as a key concept of modern lyric poetry. He associates the magic powers inherent to the word with the primacy of sound in poetic speech, and the suggestive power of the poetic form. The magical view of the poetic word is associated with the presumption of 'mystery', the idea of the 'hiddenness' of content in form: 'The poem was given the opportunity to arise from combinatorics governing the tonalities and rhythmic elements of language, as if by magic formulas [...] The lyricist turned into a magic operator' (Friedrich, 2010: 60). Friedrich traces the origins of the relationship between poetry and magic to Novalis' idea about the union of magic and mathematics in poetry, as well as to Edgar Allan Poe's theory of form as the poem's primary entity. The change from Classicist clarity to the Symbolist 'obscurity' and 'mysteriousness' of the word marked the transfer of the magical function of sound from ritual to modern poetry, which Charles Baudelaire expressed in the following statement: 'There is something sacred in the word, and therefore one should not play with it by chance. An artistically understood language is a kind of magic spells' (Idem: 62–63). The French Symbolist Stéphane Mallarmé discussed the 'sacredness' of the poetic form in his reflections on the 'mystery in letters'.[1] In this way, he laid the foundation for the principles of Russian poetic Symbolism at the beginning of the 20th century.

1 'The Magic of Language' in the Poetics of Russian Symbolism

In 1906, the major Symbolist lyric poet, Alexander Blok, wrote an essay titled 'Poetry of Spells and Incantations', which was published soon after in a textbook on the history of Russian literature. Drawing on a wide range of folkloric material extracted from collections of Russian folk magic, he proposed the idea of a 'recreation' of 'magic action' and 'the magic word' in 'the paper poetry of books'. Confident in the practical applications of charms and incantations, Blok finds them interesting not just for 'psychological' and 'historical' reasons, but also 'aesthetic' ones. His knowledge of academic literature on folk magic is striking: the essay is replete with examples of 'ritual incantations'

---

1   See Mallarmé's programmatic essay (1896), as well as his poem 'Magic' from the *Divagations* collection, in which the poet is called 'a mystagogue of letters and syllables' whose task is 'in deliberate darkness to spell hidden things through allusions' (cit. in Friedrich, 2010: 167).

from a large number of philological sources, from Sakharov and Afanasyev to Potebnja and Anichkov.[2] Among them is an example 'consisting of incomprehensible words': 'Ay, ay, shiharda kavda! / Shivda, vnoza, motta, lampreys, / Kalaidi, indie, yakutashma bitash, / Okutomi mi nuffan, zidima ...' (Blok, 1962: 57). This incantation for 'charming away mermaids' enchanted the Symbolist poet with its transrational melodiousness. Although Blok himself stopped short of pure sound poetry, this fascination with folk glossolalia was soon taken up in the poetic practice of the next generation of Russian poets.

The next example of comparing magical practices and the language of poetry in Russian literature was Andrey Bely's essay 'The Magic of Words' from his book *Symbolism* (1910). He wrote it simultaneously with his novel *The Silver Dove*, in which word play acquires a special role (see Beyer, 1978). In 'The Magic of Words', Bely writes the first draft of what would become his philosophy of language. The emphasis here is on the recognition of language as 'the most powerful instrument of creativity'.[3] According to this view, language operates along two sides of the verbal sign: the explicit and the hidden. It is the second, 'innermost' and 'secret' side that manifests itself in poetry and creates the 'world of sound symbols' (Bely, 1985: 94). Using attributes such as 'secret' and 'hidden' to describe poetic language, Bely increasingly borrows theoretical vocabulary from the field of magic and esoteric knowledge.

Bely's occult theory of language in 'The Magic of Words' is based on two principles: (1) 'every *word* is a *sound* before it is anything else' (*emphasis original – V.F.*); (2) 'every word is a charm' (Ibidem). The process of the poetic naming of things is a process of incantation: 'by charming a given phenomenon I am in essence subjugating it. Thus, connections between words, grammatical forms, and figures of speech are in essence charms' (Idem: 94–95). By pronouncing the onomatopoeic Russian word '*гром*', we charm the very phenomenon behind the word. Bely then turns to the initial stages of human language (which also help his later meditations on the topic of the word and language), in which speech functions as 'continuous magic'. In support of his theory, he brings up the French mystical philosopher Antoine Fabre D'Olivet, who in 1815 published a book about the Hebrew sacred dialect Zenzar, a 'magic language' said to exist in antiquity, which acted through the sheer force of the sound-letter. As Irina Gutkin (1997: 230) points out, Bely might have picked up information about this text from *The Secret Doctrine* by Helena Blavatsky. However, in a comment about the essay, Bely provides a direct reference to the work of the French occultist as well as other texts on magic and hermeticism. In

---

2 On Blok's sources in the said essay, see Toporkov et al. (2021).
3 On Bely's linguistic views, see Kustova (1999) and Feshchenko et al. (2014: 157–168).

addition to Zenzar, he mentions Vedanta (in connection with the 'magic word' *Om*), legends about Hermes Trismegistus and Thoth, the Christian doctrine of the Logos (as he puts it, the 'word as a magical, or theurgic, spell'), as well as Kabbalah ('the magicians' alphabet where each letter corresponds to a number and an image', in his words) (Bely, 2010: 457–462). With these references to ancient magic and esoteric knowledge, Bely provides multiple arguments in defence of his theory of the word.

Remarkably, unlike other Russian occultists of his time who dealt with verbal magic, Bely, much like his fellow poet Blok, also seeks justification for his arguments in scholarly literature on folklore. His reading list included titles by major philologists such as Potebnja, Afanasyev and Veselovsky. 'The Magic of Words' contains multiple excerpts from Potebnja's works on metaphor in folklore texts.[4] In an essay written that same year, 'Thought and Language (The Philosophy of Language by A.A. Potebnja)', discussed in my previous chapter, Bely shifts his analysis of verbal symbolism from esoteric doctrines to analytical data on linguistic creativity. He concludes that Humboldt's and Potebnja's approaches to language accord with the Romantic poets' search for 'an ineffable, fluid, instantaneous and rationally inexpressible meaning, as if shining from the depths of every word'. Here, Bely again addresses the verbal magic present at the initial stages of language development: 'underneath the everyday meaning, the word conceals a primitive-elemental, spellbindingly effective force' (2006: 206). In order to convince his reader of this new doctrine of the word, he alludes to Potebnja, a scholar, to Fabre d'Olivet, a mystic, and to Mallarmé, a poet whom he sympathetically calls the 'most insane of the Symbolists'. The idea of a magic word-symbol thus crystallises at the intersection of three different areas: linguistics, philosophical mysticism, and the mystical poetry of the German Romantics and the French Symbolists. As the literary critic Konstantin Mochulsky put it, Bely's 'religion of the artistic word' transforms Romantic 'magical idealism' into his own kind of 'magical verbalism' (1997: 314).

Bely's theory of 'the magical word' did not receive much attention from his contemporaries, yet he continued to develop it at later stages of his life. Ideas about the 'magic of language' continued to emerge, with or without Bely's direct influence, among other authors both close to the Russian Symbolists and in opposition to them. On the subject of Symbolist circles, we should also mention Konstantin Balmont and his book *Poetry as Magic* (1915). Like Bely six years earlier, the older Symbolist appealed to the potency of verbal

---

4 About the influence of Potebnja on Bely, see Weststeijn (1979), Cassedy (1990), Khan (1991), Seifrid (2005), Aumüller (2005).

magic to substantiate the principles of his art. Edgar Allan Poe's philosophical tale 'The Power of Words' played a crucial role in inspiring Balmont's 'fairy-tale' style in general and his ideas about 'the creative magic of the word' in particular.[5] Departing from Poe's formula about the 'physical power of words', Balmont brings together several mythological texts from ancient cultures. The text abounds with quotations from Vedanta (on 'magic words'), Edda (on the 'magical power of the melodious word'), the *Kalevala* (on 'sonic mystery' and 'spell words and letters'), and Egyptian mythology (on 'magic spells'). All those references contribute his theory of poetry as akin to Music, which in itself is a spell: 'verse in general is magical in its essence, and each letter in it is magic'. The essay sets forth a theory, according to which symbolic meanings are assigned to certain sounds of the alphabet (similar to what Arthur Rimbaud called the 'alchemy of the word' a few decades earlier).

Balmont's romantic fantasies about verbal magic were categorically rejected by the more radical camp of literary theorists, represented by the emerging 'formal school'. One of the leading Formalist scholars, Boris Eikhenbaum, was quick to blast the Symbolist discourse on magic in a review of *Poetry as Magic*. According to the young critic, Balmont self-indulgently believes 'faithfully in the power of a separate sound, a separate letter'. If 'every letter is magic', then Balmont's attitude to the word can lead to a rupture of the whole, living organism of language, complains the critic. Eikhenbaum's later career was built precisely on the assertion of the primacy of form in a literary work, and Futurist performances would push the adherents of the Formal school to assert an even more radical alienation of meaning from sound. Eikhenbaum's ironic reproach to Symbolist 'verbal witchcraft' also reads as a prophecy about the future paths of experimental poetry: 'Another step – and the sound will be superfluous; a separate letter or a separate punctuation mark will replace the "sounding symbol"' (Eikhenbaum, 1987: 324). This is exactly what formal poetry arrived at just a few years after Eikhenbaum's attack on the Symbolist 'magic of letters and sounds'.

It seems even more surprising that, the same year that Eikhenbaum's review was published, Dmitry Filosofov, a Symbolist literary critic whose views were much more moderate than those of the Formalists, expressed support for the new trend in literary studies, titling his review of OPOYAZ's first collective publication 'The Magic of the Word'. While Eikhenbaum criticised Balmont's 'magical attitude to sounds', the prominent 'miriskussnik'[6] saw magic precisely in Futurism and its literary theory. According to Filosofov, the Futurists and OPOYAZ members were 're-examining the mysterious combination of sound

---

5   On E.A. Poe's reception in Silver Age Russia, see Polonsky (1998: 97–114).
6   Filosofov was member of the early 1900s Mir Iskusstva circle of artists, critics, and writers.

and representation': 'all their attention has been focused on sound. In the end they found out that sound, even if "inarticulate", would give birth to representation. They talk about the magic of sound, the magic of the word' (1916: 2). Shklovsky's reasoning about 'zaum poetry' and 'sectarian glossolalia' (addressed in the next chapter of my book), which emphasised the 'magical role of the sound image', in poetry earned special praise from Filosofov. The incursion of magic into poetic speech, and of the very term 'magic' into the discourse of Russian literary criticism, contributed to the ongoing polemics about the essence of sound and meaning, or form and content, in the pre-revolutionary years – a debate over language between opposing schools of thought.

A few years later, the topic of verbal magic became so trendy that the prominent Russian philosopher and theologian Pavel Florensky felt the need to clarify what was meant by 'magic' and how it should be treated. In his essay, also titled 'The Magic of the Word', he argued against the official version of Orthodox Christianity, which banned all magical practices and rituals. Magic, Florensky claims, is a dialectical phenomenon that has both positive and negative effects on the world and mankind. He argues for a magical attitude to the word in cases where the magic in question is a source of positive energy. Verbal magic allows one to perceive the word as a whole beyond the limits of rationality. The philosopher discusses examples of the physical magnetism of sound as an analogy for the 'magical effect' of a word in the spiritual realm. Sound carries the word's energy, its 'magical power' (Florensky, 2000: 230–249). According to this view, magic manifests itself above all in the *personal name* as a collection of different meanings and spiritual energies.

The Russian Church disapproved of Florensky's views, to the extent that his fellow religious thinker Alexei Losev had to stand up for him. As Losev argued, Florensky's magic means something broader than simple divination: 'Unity, the connection of a living person with living nature, is magic' (2000: 249). This understanding of magic is not at odds with canonical Christianity, he adds. Magic, according to the religious philosophy of the name, is a property deeply inherent in the word.[7] Such treatment of verbal magic was, indeed, quite far from both the thought of Andrey Bely (Florensky makes no reference to his essay 'Magic of Words'), and the phonic glossolalia of the Futurist Formalists (Florensky deliberately dwells on this difference in another article, 'The Antinomy of Language'). However, the diverse spectrum of opinions on the magical nature of the word in Russian culture of the 1910s testifies to an important moment of cultural transfer, when the concept of 'magic' and the magical practices of speaking and writing converged and diverged all at the same time.

---

7   On discussions about the 'magic of the word' among the Imiaslavites, see Kuße et al. (1995) and Ioffe (2007).

These debates were echoed much later by Roman Jakobson's idea of the 'magic function of language', introduced in his 'Linguistics and Poetics' statement (Jakobson 1960: 355):

> The magic, incantatory function is chiefly some kind of conversion of an absent or inanimate "third person" into an addressee of a conative message. "May this sty dry up, tfu, tfu, tfu, tfu" (Lithuanian spell). "Water, queen river, daybreak! Send grief beyond the 7 blue sea, to the sea bottom, like a gray stone never to rise from the sea bottom, may grief never come to burden the light heart of God's servant, may grief be removed and sink away" (North Russian incantation). "Sun, stand thou still upon Gibeon; and 8 thou, Moon, in the valley of Aj-a-lon. And the sun stood still, and the moon stayed". (Joshua 10.12)

Jakobson attributes this idea to Charles Ogden and Ian Richards' book *The Meaning of Meaning* (1923) and, more particularly, to Bronisław Malinowski's article appended to that book, which mentions the 'phatic' function of speech in ritual formulas. Another possible influence could have been Toshihiko Izutsu's (1956) book on a related topic. Jakobson might have also been revisiting his own earlier idea, from the essay on Velimir Khlebnikov's incantatory poetry and its connection to folklore. The linguist would later return to the topic of the 'magical function' in his final book, co-authored with Linda Waugh (1989), exploring these poetic-mystical ties in more detail. Even before Jakobson's first forays into this topic, the German critic Walter Benjamin, in 1916, addressed the subject of magic as a type of verbal communication in his early writings on the philosophy of language, claiming that 'mediation which is the immediacy of all mental communication, is the fundamental problem of linguistic theory, and if one chooses to call this immediacy magic, then the primary problem of language is its magic. ... The incomparable feature of human language is that its magical community with things is immaterial and purely mental, and the symbol of this is sound' (1996: 64). However, it is very unlikely that any of the Russians writing on verbal magic in the 1910s or later would have been aware of Benjamin's essays, which were not well known in his time.

2 Glossolalia as a Special Case of Verbal Magic: Andrey Bely and the Poetry of Language

After several years of travelling around Europe with his spiritual teacher, Rudolf Steiner, Andrey Bely revisited the practice of verbal magic at this new, anthroposophical stage of his career. In 1916, while in Dornach, Switzerland, he sketched the first drafts of his 'poem about sound' *Glossolalia*, his most experimental piece of writing. A fragment of the poem was first published in 1921 in Moscow, and the poem in its entirety was published in 1922 in Berlin. This poem, which resembles a poetic treatise, proved a mysterious and incomprehensible text for Bely's contemporaries. On the one hand, many themes and techniques of Bely's other literary experiments are clearly evident here; on the other hand, we are dealing with a work that does not fit within the framework of traditional literary genres or the entire oeuvre of the Russian Symbolist. In a preface to the reader, the author says that he considers it his 'most successful poem', on par with his two other major poems 'The First Encounter' and 'Christ is Risen', and that 'criticising from a scholarly point of view is absolutely ridiculous' in his view (Bely, 1994: 4). Yet critics seemed to ignore his objection. The Humboldtian scholar Alexander Gornfeld labelled *Glossolalia* 'mystical linguistics', 'linguistic mysticism', 'playful linguistics' and 'glossolalic ventriloquism' (Gornfeld, 1927), while the Formalist-oriented Grigory Vinokur criticised it from the standpoint of scholarly poetics (Vinokur, 1976).

While claiming that *Glossolalia* is more poetry than theory – an 'improvisation on several sonic themes', by his own definition – Bely also acknowledges that it contains a certain extrapoetic meaning (be it philosophical, gnoseological or theoretical) more characteristic of treatises. He calls 'Aaron's Rod', his other major work similar to *Glossolalia*, a 'treatise' about 'the word in poetry'. How to perceive this complex synthetic text and how to interpret it within the framework of traditional literary criticism and linguistic poetics remains a mystery and a challenge (see Beyer, 1995).

In her memoir *On the Banks of the Neva*, Irina Odoevtseva, who knew Bely personally, describes the way he would become agitated while speaking: 'And suddenly, as if pulling himself again by an invisible thread, he jerked, jerked, everything turned into movement and "sound-word"' (1967: 370). 'Sound-word' ('звукословие') is a neologism coined by Bely in *Glossolalia* to describe a particular kind of writing he elsewhere calls 'sound writing' ('звукопись') (Bely 2003: http):

> Once upon a time we lived in ancient Airia, in "Air", as sounds; and the sounds live to this day; we express them with a sound-word.
> [...]
> Sound is imageless, incomprehensible, but – meaningful; if it had developed a meaning unrelated to the given meanings of the concepts, – beyond the falling leaves of words we would be able, as we penetrate the written word, to penetrate to the bottom inside of ourselves: we would

be able to view our own concealed essence; and the sound-word is – an attempt; in the sound-word the universe is restored.
[...]
In ancient-ancient Aeria, in Aer, once upon a time we lived – sound-people; and there we were sounds of exhaled lights: the sounds of lights live silently in us; and sometimes we express them by a sound-word, by *glossolalia*.

The terms 'glossolalia' and 'zvukoslovie' are used synonymously here. Bely interprets the biblical idea of 'speaking in tongues' (Greek *glossas lalein*) in his own way, calling language 'the dancer of the world'. In the Bible, the idea of 'speaking in tongues' arises in connection with the miracle of Pentecost, the descent of the Holy Spirit, which took place in the Upper Room of Zion in Jerusalem. In the Acts of the Apostles, the gift of new languages (*glossolalia*) is equated with the ability of prophecy and is characterised as a secret language, inaccessible to ordinary understanding, and often associated with the language of birds and with angelic speech. The idea of 'speaking in tongues' is presented as a reversal of the Babel myth and is treated as such in Holy Scripture. The perfect mutual understanding and single universal language of the Tower of Babel is regarded as false pride, whereas in the gift of Pentecost, new languages incomprehensible to people but serving as a communion with God are hailed as overcoming the Babylonian catastrophe. The Russian religious thinker Sergey Bulgakov comments on this in his book *Philosophy of the Name*, noting that the miracle of Pentecost allowed the defeat of multilingualism that followed the Babylonian mixing of languages: 'How should we understand this wonderful gift of languages from the nature of language itself? It only means that its disease, the blurring of meaning, was healed, and its natural, or primordial, transparency and unity, which were its characteristics from Adam to the Babylonian confusion, were revived. As a result, the veil of multilingualism was removed' (1999: 54–55).

Pavel Florensky also writes about the reciprocity of the Babylonian and the Pentecostal myths, as well as about the gift of tongues as a consequence of the descent of the Holy Spirit. This gift of tongues signals 'the reunification of humanity in mutual understanding' which is 'analogous to, but directed backwards from, the event of the fragmentation of humanity in the confusion of language' (Florensky, 2000: 197). These languages, Florensky notes, are marked by transparency for the speaker (but not for an outside observer) and a striving for the original creativity of the primal language, which was lost by humanity in Babylon.

The correlation between the myths of Babylon and Pentecost can be visualised through the metaphors of 'the tower' and 'the pit' using the French words *tour* and *trou*. When the Tower of Babel (*Tour de Babel*) is turned upside down, it transforms into the Pit of Babel (*Trou de Babel*).[8] The unfinished construction of a single artificial language collapses into a crater with the inaccessible deposits of the human proto-language at its bottom. This imagery is also present in Andrey Bely's *Glossolalia*: sound is a 'gesture of lost content', and 'memories of the sound of an ancient meaning'. Improvisations on sonic themes appear here as 'models for the expression of a mimicry of sounds that we have lost'. One such 'figurative improvisation' is the interpretation of the biblical phrase in German 'Am Anfang schuf Gott Himmel und Erden'. Bely departs from his reading of Jakob Böhme, citing his words (Bely 2003: http):

> You have to look precisely at these words, what they signify; because the word **Am** collects itself in the heart, and approaches the lips, here it is captured, and soundingly returns back to its point of departure ... This signifies ..., that the sound departed from the heart of God and embraced the whole space of this world; but as soon as it turned out to be evil, then the sound again retreated back. Here is vividly depicted the soulful (spiritual) quality of the movement of the vowel "a", and the giving up of the sound with "m": the gestures of "m" are a giving forth from the lips into the realm of the orifice – lower and more forward in relationship to the "n" ... The word **An** explodes from the heart to the lips, and leaves a long trace; when it is pronounced, then it closes the circle in the center on its throne by means of the upper palate and remains half on the outside and half on the inside... (Here once again the vowel "a" is directly connected with the heart; and the "n" permitting a stream of exhalation through the nose, leaves behind its own impression: "*half on the outside and half on the inside*".) ... This signifies, that the heart of God conceived an aversion to the damaged and turned away from itself the damaged being ...

Throughout the pages of his book *Aurora*, Jakob Böhme 'draws gradations of gestures from sound', Bely claims, and adds to this his own further 'delving into sound' (Ibidem):

> In the sounds mentioned is represented "*am-an-an*" (Am *Anfang*); it is interesting, that "m" and "n" are semivowels, or sonants; "am-an" or "*man*"

---

8 Franz Kafka (1961: 34–35) suggested a similar metaphor in an enigmatic note: ' – What are you building? – I want to dig a subterranean passage. Some progress must be made. My station up there is much too high. We are digging the pit of Babel'.

are – the sounds of thought; actually: – *man*-yti is "to comprehend" (*ponimat'*) (in Lithuanian), *man-am* (in Armenian) is also this; in *Zendic thought is* – *mana; and in Sanskrit thought* is – *manah*, prayer is – both *man*-ma, and *man*-tra, mind is – *mana-s*; had in mind is – *mamn-ate* ; "mn" are – sounds of thought: Russian *mn*-it' is *me think* and *mn*-enie is *my opinion*; *min-eti* is to "*have in mind*" (imet' na ume) (in Lithuanian); mind is – *menos*, both *men-s* and *men-me* (Irish) are – mind. Now we can be mindful of these sounds. – "Am Anfang" – in them is the combination of "am-an-an", which is transformed into (a)mana(n); – "am Anfang" ("in the beginning") announces with the sound of the words, that "*in the beginning there was a reasoning mind*". The very beginning is a reasoning mind: "In the beginning was the word".

The *Evangelist John* is inscribed with sounds.

Thus the Jewish "bereshit" and the German "Anfang" give two pictures: a world aflame with gleamings; and – the *Elohim* beneath it; this was revealed by Rudolf Steiner... And the cosmic man "*Adam Kadmon*" (ad-ad-am-on) (in the divine thought of God, in "Mana", sounds in German; "In the beginning of it all").

The sound "aman" contains the thought of a reasoning mind (*mana*), of love (*ame*), of the bridegroom (*Mann*); the Beginning came together with the End; Judaism with Christianity; the pictures and sounds are different: the gesture of meaning is – one and the same.

Bely illustrates the Babylonian imagery visually, in drawings included into *Glossolalia*. The oral cavity is drawn as an inverted triangle – a microcosm – inscribed into the large triangle of the head-macrocosm, and is explained thusly (Ibidem):

> the cavity of the mouth – the microcosm; the macrocosm is arranged, as if a triangle; the upper point of the summit lies at the place of the "I" (between the arcs of the eyebrows); the lower points of the angles are supported on the shoulders; and the microcosm (or the mouth) is inscribed in the same triangle; it lies in an inverted view: the larynx and two extreme points, lying in the cavity of the mouth; thus in the paysage arising in the mouth, the paysage of our thoughts is turned upside down; the mouth is – a camera obscura of cosmic thoughts: of the head.

Isn't this the same image of the inverted tower from the Pentecostal myth? Another drawing depicts a similar motif – a bowl turned into the oral cavity, the base of which emanates from the center of the head, with the walls abutting the front and back palates. Sounds flow along the walls of the bowl, rushing out through the lips. A sound generation model based on a mythological symbol is also part of the image – a fire-breathing serpent which represents the motif of the 'burning tongue'.

The utopian idea of a primordial language fascinated many philosophers, poets, and linguists from Romanticism to Modernism. The search for a 'universal', 'perfect', 'original', or 'fantastic' language has accompanied the history of human culture (Yaguello, 1984; Auroux et al., 1985; Olender, 1989). Philosophical ideas – for example, those of Jean-Jacques Rousseau or Giambattista Vico – about the origins of human language echoed the mystical and poetic revelations of Böhme, Novalis or Hölderlin about the 'speech of nature', 'pure speech' and 'absolute language'. Aside from biblical contexts, we see evidence of glossolalic speech in a wide variety of traditional cultures, both Christian and non-Christian (for example, in shamanism and various sects).[9] This topic rose to prominence at the turn of the 20th century, both as a practice and in terms of theoretical approaches to it. Since the first decade of the 20th century, glossolalia was represented by three main currents: religious-mystical, psychopathological, and poetic, or ludic, all of which intertwine. Sigmund Freud's *Studies on Hysteria* drew the attention of psychologists to aphasia and pathological speech production. The disintegration of articulation was associated with mental mechanisms and transformations of the deep self. The emerging study of the psychology of religious experience, the foundations of which were laid in the United States by William James, used the findings of psychopathologists and applied them to spiritual mediums. The Swiss psychologist Théodore Flournoy, a student of James, embarked on an unprecedented adventure when he participated in the seances held by his compatriot, the clairvoyant Hélène Smith. As a result of these sessions, Flournoy published the scholarly monograph *From India to the Planet Mars: A Case Study of Somnambulism and Glossolalia* (1899), in which he presented a detailed analysis of the protocols of these psychic sessions. For the first time in history, a *glossolalist* (a practitioner of glossolalia) and a *glossologist* (an interpreter of glossolalia) joined forces to undertake 'fieldwork' that was both visionary and scientifically sound.

This is the global cultural context Bely's glossolalic writings were part of, in addition to the Russian tradition of verbal magic they adhered to. Yet Bely was the first to turn glossolalia into a poetic experiment. His experiment proved incomprehensible to his contemporaries. Despite Bely's own description of *Glossolalia* as his 'most successful' poem, the poetic significance of this text was not acknowledged by anyone in his time – except, perhaps, for a rather

---

9 See Lombard (1910), Goodman (1972), and especially Pozzo (2013).

tepid response from Vera Lurie (cit. in Beyer, 1995) and a later remark by the Russian philosopher Vladimir Ilyin: 'Glossolalia, and especially symbolic glossolalia, is an invariable companion of the true art of the word. This is due to the essential, immortal contribution of Andrey Bely, both in theoretical terms and in terms of artistic realisation' (1997: 276–277).

Eventually, in Bely's lifetime, most of his contemporaries saw *Glossolalia* as an exposition of the author's anthroposophical and cabalistic interests (represented, respectively, by Steiner and Böhme), which seemed at odds with their place and time. Perhaps, had the poem been printed five years earlier, in 1917, and not in Berlin, the reaction might have been quite different. However, back in 1917, Bely used the word *glossolalia* with rather negative connotations when discussing the zaum poetry of Futurism, claiming that the latter separates form from content, or sound from meaning: 'the glossolalia of Futurists' sounds is picking the fruit off the tree of words, or the tree of meanings, for the selfish, carnivorous eating of the matter of sound' (Bely, 2006: 416). Glossolalia stands here for the separation of the material shell of sound (phonetics) from the conceptual core (semantics). This critique of 'Futurist glossolalia' might have been due to a confrontation between Andrey Bely and Viktor Shklovsky. In his manifestos on zaum language, the Formalist drew upon a rather influential book by Dmitry Konovalov, philologist and historian of religion, titled *Religious Ecstasy in Russian Mystic Sectarianism* (1908) which analyses cases of 'speaking in tongues' in the Khlyst sects.

It is likely that Bely had also read Konovalov's book, from which he probably borrowed the concept of 'glossolalia'. Another source for this could have been Mikhail Fiveysky's work *Spiritual Endowments in the Original Christian Church* (1907), which lays out a glossolalic theory that likens apostolic speaking in tongues to the Pythagorean 'series of cosmic sounds'. In his turn, the Orthodox writer Fiveysky refers to an even earlier theological work on glossolalia by Mitrofan Muretov, *Prophecy and Tongue Speaking (Glossolalia) as Signs for Believers and Unbelievers* (1904). Beyond that, Bely might have also been aware of Vladimir Soloviev's practice of glossolalia as a kind of automatic writing (see Titarenko, 2007). Another source might have been the 1913 book *Language as Creativity* by Alexander Pogodin, a proponent of Humboldtian linguistics. Characteristically for this Russian philological context, Pogodin associates pure linguistic creativity (language as *energeia*) with cases of religious or mystical speaking in tongues – a chapter of his book is titled 'The role of language in mystical enthusiasm and night dreams'.

Andrey Bely's poetic theory implies a total symbolisation of language – and not only of language. Russian thought about language, from Potebnja on, has always been focused on the symbolic nature of language. Bely pushes this tendency to its limit by employing a poetic language that is pansymbolic and panhistorical. This, of course, is already a rather distant departure from the biblical roots of glossolalia, but such is the unique experience of Bely's poetic mystery. In terms of Ferdinand de Saussure's linguistic theory, religious glossolalia gravitates towards the pole of speech, whereas Bely's poetic glossolalia gravitates towards language – a universal language that goes back to the potentialities of symbolic meaning hidden in history. However, these two types of glossolalia also have common typological features. Both cases concern a conscious or unconscious search for meaning in what is meaningless. The glossolalist is convinced of the truth of his prophecies and poetic revelations. One must possess a special gift (prophetic, mediumistic, or poetic) for speaking in tongues. In all cases of glossolalia, language is seen in the process of its birth – implicitly, as in religious practices, or explicitly, as in poetry. Glossolalia is language being reborn – the existing but unfamiliar language of religious examples, or the non-existent but reconstructed language of Bely's poetic and meta-poetic writings.[10]

At the same time, there is one property that distinguishes poetic glossolalia from the religious one – the ability of a person to produce this kind of speech and also interpret it, which we see so clearly in Bely. The author here is both a glossolalist and a glossologist, for the act of speaking in tongues is not only performed, but also theoretically examined. One of Marina Tsvetaeva's notebooks contains a telling misprint: 'You will be curious to know that Bely wrote *Glossology* (?) <Sic! – V.F.> after my *Parting*'.[11] For Tsvetaeva, who understood Bely better than most of his fellow poets and contemporaries, the poet's *glossolalia* is at the same time his *glossologia*. Bely's theory of sound in poetry paved the way for a new generation of Russian avant-garde poetry. The next chapter of this book is devoted to utopias of sound in the poetry of Russian Post-Symbolism.

---

10 Andrey Bely's theoretical writings on language, rhythm, and glossolalia have recently been collected in (Bely, 2018).
11 http://tsvetaeva.lit-info.ru/tsvetaeva/proza/tetradi/tetrad-1-6.htm (last accessed 27.02.23).

CHAPTER 3

Futurist *Glossolalias* and *Grapholalias*

> There will come a time in verse when poets will be interested only in sounds.
>
> JULIUSZ SŁOWACKI

∴

> Mankind will be able to reclaim a pure word. When sound writing kills the existing writing systems, a new era of mankind will come … In the era of sound writing, the word will be fixed but orally and free from rest. We, its prophets, begin this era.
>
> ILIA ZDANEVICH

∴

Fragments from Andrey Bely's poem *Glossolalia* were first published in 1921 in the *Drakon* literary almanac together with Osip Mandelstam's essay 'The Word and Culture'. In this essay, Mandelstam discusses contemporary poetry, invoking, as does Bely, the concept of glossolalia: 'in sacred frenzy, poets speak in the language of all times, all cultures'. Poetic glossolalia, in the poet's view, plays the role of uniting different cultures through poetic language: 'In glossolalia the most striking thing is that the speaker does not know the language in which he speaks. He speaks in a totally obscure tongue. And to everyone, and to him, too, it seems he's talking Greek or Babylonian. It is something quite the reverse of erudition' (Mandelstam, 1977: 53). Due to this 'speaking in tongues' (not the unifying multilingualism of Babel, but the unique Pentecostal gift of tongues), the word becomes a 'thousand-stop reed', in which each voice is free in its expression, and the Logos-Psyche freely chooses its meanings and objects: 'The living word does not signify an object, but freely chooses, as though for a dwelling place, this or that objective significance, materiality, some beloved body', the essay suggests (Idem: 52). Like Bely, Mandelstam prophesies that a new, 'living' word coming out of obscure glossolalia would revolutionise poetic language, and eventually, human culture.[1]

Bely's *Glossolalia* would probably have been met with interest by Velimir Khlebnikov, had he read it before he died in 1922. That same year saw the publication of his super-saga *Zangezi*, in many respects reminiscent of Bely's experimental poem about sound. Pure glossolalia is present in Khlebnikov's text in the form of what he calls 'the language of the gods', in the section titled 'Plane 11' (1989: 350):

> Hahahaha hehhehheh!
> Grakahata grororo
> Leelee eghee, lyap, lyap, bem.
> Leebeebebee neeraro
> Seenoahno tseetseereets.
> Heeyu hmapa, heer zen, chench
> Zhooree keeka, seen sonegha
> Hahoteeree ess esseh
> Yunchee, enchee, ook!
> Yunchee, enchee, peepoka.
> Klyam! Klyam! Eps!

Glossolalia also appears in Khlebnikov's early texts. In 'Night in Galicia', for example, it is likened to spells that the poet draws not only from Ivan Sakharov's collections, but also from Alexander Blok's essay on the poetry of folk spells mentioned earlier (Idem: 92):

> Io ia tsolk,
> Io ia tsolk.
> Pits, pats, patsu.
> Pits, pats, patsa.
> Io ia tsolk, io ia tsolk,
> Copotsamo, minogamo, pintso, pintso, pintso!
>
> Witches
>
> Shagadam, magadam, vykadam.
> Chukh, chukh, chukh.
> Chukh.

---

[1] On the interaction of different languages in Mandelstam's poetry, see Levinton (1979), Uspensky (2014). For Mandelstam's theory of words, see Glazova (2019).

Andrey Bely's wife Klavdia Bugaeva wrote in her memoir that, in the last years of his life, he aspired to conceive a new language based on the sounds of nature. She cites him as saying: 'there is something in the voices and rhythms of nature that, like a fermenting agent, must enter human speech in order to transform it, make it concrete and strong again' (Bugaeva, 2001: 113). Interestingly, she immediately refers to Khlebnikov, admitting that 'Khlebnikov's experiments are going in a different direction' and that Bely 'found something interesting in these experiments, but treated them with restraint' and 'did not have much sympathy for them' (Ibidem). Nevertheless, Khlebnikov's 'звукопись' ('sound painting') and Bely's 'звукословие' ('sound writing') are similar ways of treating sound in poetry.[2] What is striking is their synchronous coinage of the same neologism 'звуко-люди' ('sound people'), which Bely introduces in *Glossolalia* and Khlebnikov in his long poem 'The Scratch on the Sky', cf.: 'In ancient-ancient Aeria, in Aer, once upon a time we lived – **sound-people**; and there we were sounds of exhaled lights: the sounds of lights live silently in us; and sometimes we express them by a sound-word, by *glossolalia*" (Bely, 2003: http, *emphasis mine – V.F.*); "Come learn to play on the frets / Of war without the wild screeching of death – / We are **soundpeople**! / Batu and Pi! The violin is on my shoulder" (Khlebnikov, 2002: 269, *emphasis mine – V.F.*).

In its essence, Khlebnikov's utopian glossolalic project epitomises the idea of an inverted Babel, or 'pit of Babel', where he excavates layers of existing languages in order to find a proto-language comprehensible to all who have the creative gift of understanding. Linguistic diversity, according to Khlebnikov, emerged because the primordial universal language was forgotten. It should be noted, however, that Khlebnikov's glossolalia functions differently than its biblical and mystical equivalents. His utopia aims to recreate the pre-Babel unified language by reconstructing meaning through the sound characteristics of many languages.[3]

An experiment strangely analogous to Khlebnikov's 'imaginary' proto-language studies was Nikolai Marr's linguistic reveries, as part of his 'new doctrine of language', imagining a single human proto-language which emerged as a result of the 'sonic revolution' of 'labour shouts'. According to Marr's theory, these shouts were initially nonsensical and had a magical function but were later reduced to four basic sound combinations: SAL, BER, YON, ROSH.[4] Although this theory was later deemed pseudoscientific, Khlebnikov

---

2 On Khlebnikov's 'magic of the word' in connection with Balmont and Bely, see Gofman (1936).
3 The next chapter will give a detailed overview of Khlebnikov's language projects.
4 See Alpatov (1991), Velmezova (2007), Grechko (2010). Katerina Clark (1995) calls Marr's studies of this proto-language a 'Promethean linguistics', juxtaposing it with avant-garde poetic projects.

and Marr had in common a pursuit of artistic and scholarly reconstruction of the proto-language. This commonality is even more striking given the fact that Nikolai Marr's own son, Yuri Marr, was a poet working with zaum poetry as well as a scholar of Caucasian and Oriental languages. His zaum verse often echoes the phonetics of Georgian, Persian, and other languages, as in this 1919 poem (Marr 2018: 43):

> Kr br tr
> mukulba
> samakani
> f zh zzh r r
> Tumuk mumuk kumuk
> Baka ski
> lllllllllll
> Victory over a girl's heart
> cr r cr r crr
> mukalaki
> ghoul puli
> br r brr brr
> saki paki
> mulmuli

Associations of trans-sense language with Christian glossolalia also manifested themselves in the writings of Alexander Tufanov. A Futurist poet from a younger generation, a follower of Khlebnikov and a self-proclaimed 'Chairman of Global Trans-sense', he brought up speaking in tongues in a comment about his poem 'Spring': 'In the process of transrational creativity, these simple morphemes are cut down and simple sound complexes, fragments of English, Chinese, Russian and other words are obtained. It is a kind of "descent of the holy spirit" (of nature) upon us, and we acquire the gift of speaking in all languages' (Tufanov, 1924: 12).[5] In the poem itself, a variation of glossolalic speech appears, written in what the poet calls 'transcriptional scientific alphabet', using Latin script (Idem: 13):

> S'iin' soon   s'ii selle   soong s'e
> Siing s'eelf   s'iik signal   seel' s'in'
>
> L'ii l'eviš   l'aak l'ajs'iin'l'uk
> L'aa luglet   l'aa vlil'iinled

---

5 On Futurist glossolalia and zaum, see Grechko (1997).

Saas'iin'	soo sajl'ens	saajset
Suut siik	soon rosin	saablen
L'aadl'ubson	l'iil'i l'aasl'ub	
Sool'onse	serve seelib.	

As Tufanov notes, this sample of 'phonic music' is composed of English morphemes. However, when written in Cyrillic – which he does on the same page – the cross-linguistic effect is amplified by the interaction between the two writing systems. Something of this kind, with an even greater number of languages involved, was carried out by Tufanov's fellow Futurist poet Vassily Kamensky, in his poem 'The Babel of Phonetics'. It was written in the early 1920s, like Tufanov's book *Towards Zaum* (1924) cited above. The text consists of improvised phrases and sound combinations from several languages– Russian, French, English, German, Polish, Japanese, Italian, Hindi, etc. It starts with distinguishable fragments in foreign languages, and towards the end resembles pure glossolalia[6] (Kamensky, 2016: 27, 30):

Браба'.
Федерасион фонетик интернасиональ.
Жантиль э ронти.
Травайй, травайй.
Воль-плянэ. Финаль.
Вон труа. Ассэ. Ава.
Сюр ля пляс Исси-ле-Мулажи
[...]
Гамавата апаи оуш
Бгава аши жайи
Амоа
Хивата джоуш
Шкайи
Агуа
Шайма галайн уа.
Юма майи
Вэа аво моа тайн.
Браба'.
Айоц.

---

6 There is no point in providing the English translation or transliteration, as it would lose its imitative effect.

Another, perhaps even more radical, strategy of 'language revival' through poetic glossolalia was proposed by the Futurist and Dadaist poet Ilia Zdanevich. As early as 1912, his performances at various debates, and his exhibitions and publications, proved to be more radical and left-wing compared to the Cubo-Futurist wing of the movement. This radicalism is especially evident in Zdanevich's writings about language.

The Zdanevich fund (OR RM, f. 177) at the State Russian Museum, Saint-Petersburg, contains many documents that have not yet been published – manuscripts of his talks from the 1910s, drafts of manifestos and declarations, treatises, drafts of poems and plays, personal records, and correspondence. Some of these texts have been collected in two volumes under the heading 'Futurism and Vsyochestvo' (2014). Yet Zdanevich's manuscripts related to language and writing systems remain unpublished. The ideas contained in them are comparable to Viktor Shklovsky's more famous theory of the zaum language. The materials in the archive give us a sense of the linguistic ideas that guided Zdanevich in his poetic theory.[7]

The earliest documents from this archive related to Zdanevich's theory of language are three manuscripts dated 1913, devoted to the topic of orthography and writing systems. Apparently, Zdanevich wrote the first of these texts – a draft of the talk 'On Writing and Orthography' – in July 1913, while living in his native city of Tiflis in Georgia, for a Futurist event at Brodyachaya Sobaka, a Petersburg literary cabaret. This draft would later turn into his 'Manifesto on Orthography' and, finally, into a lengthy essay with the same title 'On Writing and Orthography'. His brother Kirill Zdanevich testifies to Ilia's early interest in linguistics, mentioning his student notebooks (Zdanevich, 1998b). It is difficult to determine which books on this subject he was reading at that time, but the topic of orthography was obviously a response to the spelling reform in the Russian language, which was widely discussed in the 1910s. In 1911, leading linguists at the Academy of Sciences passed a resolution on the development of a reform, and the eventual resolution was published in 1912. It seems that Zdanevich was reacting to this event, pursuing his creative and radical goals of changing and abolishing orthography.

The manuscript opens with the statement: 'Writing does not need history' (13, 1). The Futurist poet bemoans the modern context, in which orthography conserves long-dead processes in word formation, the 'dying word' (10, 98). He demands that new poetry exploit new means of capturing the flow of speech, or 'storing the word' (10, 93), as Zdanevich calls this task. A 'fight' against

---

7 Hereafter, in citing materials from this fund, the number of the storage unit is indicated in brackets and the number of the sheet or sheets is separated by a comma.

the 'evil of writing' (10, 98) is in order. Modern spelling is 'optional'; it needs 'freedom' (10, 99). The existing spelling system is arbitrary and unjustified; it deadens the word, dismembering it into inanimate signs. Zdanevich calls for new 'lettering' that ensures the freedom of 'a language suitable for art' (10, 98). His dreams of a new, 'pure' writing anticipated Khlebnikov's 'language of the stars' and Tufanov's 'phonic music'.

With a view to overthrowing the current spelling principles, Zdanevich undertakes an inquiry into the 'history of the Russian alphabet and the principles of the Russian writing system', considering other 'possible systems' and 'classification of letters' (10, 99). Among the principles of spelling, he singles out the 'auditory', the 'morphological', the 'semasiological', and the 'historical' (Ibidem). The 'phonetic' and 'semasiological' aspects of the word should be connected in a new way, he believes.

The terminology Zdanevich uses in these manuscripts allows us to trace his acquaintance with, and knowledge of, linguistic bibliography. Judging by the statements he proposes, the direct source for these ideas was the book *On the Relationship of Russian Writing to the Russian Language* (1912) by the Polish-Russian linguist Jan Baudouin de Courtenay.[8] It is very likely that the Futurist rebel drew on that book for his insights on the spoken and written forms of language. And it is precisely these principles that he opposes in his argumentation. It also seems plausible that he was familiar with another popular book by Baudouin de Courtenay, *A Collection of Problems for the Introduction to Linguistics, Primarily Applied to the Russian Language* (1912), in which the scholar proposes searching for words in nonsensical combinations of letters, such as: *permisat, myrgamat, myrmylet, sudumakhaloka, friktamani, pulp, molmoshota, levkorat, muskalet, gundukir, purnet, pursit, purcha, korgolgo, purkalban, molkoryt, kultutrduurd, kuruch, uproot, salinity, sumpurkul, kulekur.*

It seems likely that Baudouin de Courtenay himself was familiar with Zdanevich's talks on the topic of spelling; this later resulted in a dispute between the Futurists and the famous Petersburg linguist. Viktor Shklovsky recalls that, in 1914, Baudouin presented a talk titled 'On the Living Word', in which he urged poets not to separate the word from its meaning (Shklovsky, 1966: 100–101).[9] Zdanevich may have attended this debate, and he would undoubtedly have had a response to the venerable professor. In his opinion, it is precisely modern orthography that separates the word from its meaning

---

8 Alexander Tufanov also used this book to substantiate his theory of zaum (1924).
9 In the same year, Baudouin would publish two polemical newspaper articles about the Futurists' denial of conventional language: Baudouin de Courtenay 1914a and Baudouin de Courtenay 1914b.

since it does not attach importance to the living connection between sound and content. 'The word is dynamic, writing is static' (13, 10b), he declares in the manifesto. He proposes the concept of 'sound writing' ('звукопись') against 'sign writing' ('знакопись') as a conventional way of recording the word. He calls 'sound writing' 'a method of writing, which consists of creating stable traces for the direct reproduction of speech' (13, 36). He also expresses his high hopes for the phonograph as a new device for recording and storing poetic speech. He would later use the phonograph to record group readings by his fellow *zaumniki* (zaum poets).

The manuscript 'On Writing and Orthography' ends with a prophecy about a new era when mankind will be liberated by sound writing and sound recording, and 'the word will be fixed but orally, and free from rest' (13, 18). Thus, 'the fight against existing forms and methods of spelling' should not be limited to a mere spelling reform, but also aimed 'at re-educating the human psyche' (10, 93). Zdanevich's archive also preserves a student essay devoted to the psychology of art, titled 'The Development of Art and Its Impact'.

As we can see from these earlier theoretical writings, even before moving on to create pure zaum poetry, Zdanevich sought a linguistic basis for the transition to new spelling systems in poetry. At the next stage of his development, from 1914 on, these assertions would be put into poetic practice. In one of his first zaum poems, 'Garoland', published posthumously by Régis Gayraud (Figure 1, Zdanevich 1998a), the poet uses a graphic method of depicting elongated vowels and consonants in writing, as well as various diacritics, accents, apostrophes, and numbers over the words.

The very title of the poem is written in unusual typography, which the poet used extensively in his later 'zaum dramas': the letters *za* are printed in lower case, *ланд* as superscript, and *PO* in capital letters. Elsewhere in Zdanevich's experimental writings, this technique will mark syllables and letters that, when reproduced (read out loud), must be pronounced by several readers at the same time. In his essay 'Manifest Vsechestva. Mnogovaya poezia' (which can roughly be translated as 'The Toutisme Manifesto. Manifold Poetry') he describes a particular type of poetry recited by several performers at once: 'We are introducing polyphonic multi-theme creation and performance of verbal works' (22, 3). And again, there is an appeal to the phonograph as 'the liberator of language from the arrogant eye' (22, 70b). Apparently, this same principle of poetic reading ('orchestral poetry' as he calls it elsewhere) was used by Zdanevich in scoring and staging his 'zaumnye dra', as in the production of 'Yanko Krul Albanskay' in 1916 in St. Petersburg (Marzaduri, 1990).

Having already written the first examples of purely trans-sense texts, in 1918 Zdanevich gave a public talk 'On Zaum Poetry', the draft of which is preserved

гаРОланд (*длинный вариант*)

1888 индо-Китай отец адвокат джу̅нгли джу̅нгли охота на тигров коб-рррры жа̅лят павли̅ны си̅дя на де̅ревьях хво̀ст в вѐтр какао ааааo ррррах перелетают слоны̅ то̅пчат посевы парохоооoды прииистани китайцы негры англичане bonjour comment allez vous в европу у̅у̅у̅у̅у̅у̅у̅у̅у̅у̅у̅ 1910 парррриииииж кры̣ыылья пуска̅ют пропе̣̅ллер я то̣̅же. Сантос Дюмон[1] в Амѐрику Одема̀р Одемаааaaaр Барьеееес[2] назад Парррриииииж мадрѝт уууууулепетывай Ведри̅н[3] Пиринеи бородатый ягнятник кры̣ыылья погоня вы̅ше парррриииииж рѝм 4 сентября 1911 вы̅сота 3950 метров хоооооооoлодно браво Гаррò выыыше 6 сентября 1912 4960 метров браво Гаррò 11 декабря поля сте̅лятся фа̅брики кадят уууу ветр стая облаков ещо̣оооo солнце слепит океан слю̣юююони высота 5600 метров браво Гаррò браво Гарррррро РО-РО-РО РÒ-РÒ ррррум война̀ рòpòрò monsieur le ministre Гаррò Одема̀р Жильберррр

FIGURE 1   Ilia Zdanevich. "GAROLAND"

in the same archive (archive unit 35). This essay is a response to contemporaneous declarations by his fellow Futurists Alexei Kruchenykh and Velimir Khlebnikov, and, most likely, to Viktor Shklovsky's 1916 article 'On Poetry and Trans-Sense Language'. Zdanevich deems Kruchenykh's statements an insufficient liberation of language: 'The word as such and the word as medium – the terminology established by Kruchenykh and taken up by Nikolai Kul'bin – is essentially incorrect. It is an insufficient analysis of the word' (35, 1–2). However, this declaration does not go any further than these refutations. Its other statements are quite consistent with Shklovsky's interpretation of zaum language, the only difference being that, in the case of the latter, we are dealing with a philologist's theory distinguishing between poetic and everyday language, while Zdanevich's position is the theory of an avant-garde poet, for whom the entire human language must be transformed, both in its poetic and practical manifestations.

The points made by both Futurist theorists are, indeed, similar. Zdanevich speaks about the word beyond content and concept: 'It is possible to evoke coloured emotions beyond the subject matter along two aspects of the word: […] the sonorous and trans-sense. […] The word is a sound, or a combination of sounds familiar in themselves. Trans-sense in the word is the excitement of emotions by a word beyond its subject matter' (35, 1). Shklovsky writes about more or less the same thing, citing examples from classical and modern literature, where nonsense is present in its pure form: 'Some people assert that they can best express their emotion by a particular sound-language which often has no definite meaning but acts outside of or separately from meaning, immediately upon the emotions of people around' (1985: 5–6). He corroborates this statement by citing both Symbolist poets and psychologists. Incidentally, he finds nonsense in its purest form only in the language of mystical sectarians, with reference to the above-mentioned book by Dmitry Konovalov, published in 1908. Zdanevich uses the same sources and arguments when referring to the phenomena of glossolalia: 'The absolute expressiveness and excitability of emotions by the trans-sense side of words' (35, 6). However, unlike Shklovsky, Zdanevich distinguishes the 'glossolalia of zaum poetry' from 'sound ornamentation'.[10] In his opinion, Symbolism had reached a dead end, and trans-sense poetry in its pure form was inevitable. Shklovsky merely wonders if real poetry is possible in a purely trans-sense language, and enthusiastically cites Juliusz Słowacki's prophecy that serves as the epigraph to this chapter. For Zdanevich, this time had already come; he moved beyond the sonic achievements of other Futurists, which led him to a stage that can be called *grapholalia*[11] – poetic glossolalia in writing and the sonic extremism of Dada and '41 degrees'.

We know a lot more about the Dadaist period of Ilia Zdanevich's career than about the early Petersburg-Tiflis period. Yet one text from the Paris (Dadaist) period deserves a closer look given my aim to examine the entire spectrum of language-oriented writing in the Russian avant-garde.[12] In 1922, Iliazd (Zdanevich's Parisian pen-name) delivered a 'talk at the Academy of Medicine', as he titled it; the text was only published posthumously (Iliazd, 1982).[13] Giving a talk on zaum poetry in a medical institution is quite the Surrealist or Dadaist act, characteristic of the Paris period of Iliazd's activities as part of the '41 degrees company' (itself a 'medical' name for a poetic movement).

---

10 In his talks and writings from the 1920s, Zdanevich attacked Andrey Bely's views on glossolalia, referring to the Symbolist's essay 'Aaron's Rod' and his poem *Glossolalia* as an 'epigonic imitation' of Zdanevich's own earlier ideas (see Zdanevich 2021).
11 From Greek *grapho* – to write, and *lalo* – to mutter.
12 See Tokarev (2015) on Zdanevich's zaum as an 'escape from utopia'.
13 Hereafter I will refer to pages of this publication in brackets.

The content of this talk is even more surreal than Zdanevich's early manifestos on writing and orthography. On behalf of himself, as well as his recent allies Kruchenykh, Khlebnikov and Terentiev, the author informs the readers that humanity suffers from a 'pearl disease' ('жемчужная болезнь'), a treatment for which is only offered by the company of doctors in '41 degrees'. This disease is associated with damage to the human language and manifests itself, according to Dr. Iliazd, 'in the form of hard grains in the folds of the body of a living language ("langage vivant")' (294). What follows in the text is an explanation of the causes of this disease. They are linked to the process of individualisation of the human language, its birth from the language of animals – in which sounds serve as 'an echo of the emotional states of animals' and are 'purposeless by nature' – into a state of purposefulness, in which sounds become 'carriers of thought particles' and serve the purpose of communication (295). But language can undergo an anomalous process – it occasionally returns to its pre-linguistic state. It was at that stage, according to Iliazd, that this 'pearl disease' first appeared. However, he claims, it can be turned into something good. Later in the text, it becomes clear that the treatment of this disease is a poetic task, and that all previous schools of poetic "medical science" have been unsuccessful in addressing it. The task of their new poetry 'is neither to completely isolate the pearls from the living language surrounding it, as the Parnassian school demanded, nor to yield to a one-sided outflow of pearly secretions into a healthy environment, according to the aesthetic school, nor to uniformly nourish it with the juices of a living language, as the realistic school taught' (295). It becomes clear that by 'pearls' Iliazd means 'sound writing', or the sounds of language in general, with trans-sense poetry being the only remedy for the 'pearl disease' of contemporary language.

Which methods of treatment does Iliazd propose for the above ailment? The school of Futurism, he notes, was the only one that 'approached the correct formulation of the question when it pointed out that a living language is an unsuitable environment for the progression of pearl disease and must be subjected to special processing' (296). The talk then turns to different types of languages and their suitability for such processing. At this point, Iliazd echoes his earlier declarations about the 'harm of writing systems as an alien appendix to language'. Once again, Zdanevich-Iliazd reaffirms his desire to introduce the phonetic principle into the modern language of poetry, to the detriment of all other principles such as the semasiological, ideographic, etc. To overcome existing writing systems is to liberate the 'phonic structure of a living language'. As a result of this, the 'pearl disease' of the 'living language' will transmute into what he calls a 'pearl language' ('жемчужный язык'). Instead of synonyms, this language operates with 'synophones' – homophonic sound units. These units constitute a particular kind of 'pearl thinking' ('жемчужное мышление') operating with 'synophones', analogous to how 'linguistic thinking' operates with synonyms. Among the analogues of such 'pearl language', Zdanevich lists dreams, insane delirium, babbling, and glossolalia. Finally, it becomes clear that this weird imagery restates Iliazd's earlier theories of zaum; the mysterious 'pearl language' is none other than zaum language itself.

Summing up his achievements in the field of trans-sense poetry, Iliazd concludes that, 'the discovery of zaum language' was his school's greatest victory. He is hopeful that 'every new year would bring new conquests' in the field of zaum and addresses those critics who consider zaum a matter of pure, meaningless sounds. Trans-sense zaum, he argues, 'is saturated with a particular content that peels off from sounds'. These elementary sounds carry in themselves 'a primary semantics, not crystallising into thought, but striving to evoke, through pearly associations, words filled with concepts, and thus attracting a new meaning'. After all, trans-sense language 'is a field of battle between instinct and the ever interfering thought' (304), the essay proclaims.

This later essay by Iliazd is interesting and important because it not only talks about the school of zaum poetry in an oddly allegorical way, but also expands the stipulations on trans-sense language introduced by Zdanevich ten years earlier about the content of zaum. The body of critical texts written by Zdanevich-Iliazd, both published and unpublished, dating from 1912 to the 1920s, reveal him to be one of the leading early theorists of Futurism and zaum poetry, whose role was no less significant than Shklovsky's in laying out the principles of new poetry and new poetic language.

Interestingly, Shklovsky himself was fully aware of this, maintaining ties with Iliazd both early on and later, in the 1920s, and considering him a member of the 'attack unit of explorers', those 'who are on the cutting razor's edge of art', though perhaps the only one 'who actually turned all his enormous talent into an artistic experiment' (Shklovsky, 1990: 150). In a letter to Zdanevich, Shklovsky specifically praises him for defending and affirming the phonic and articulatory aspects of the word: 'Zdanevich's zaum is not just the use of meaningless words. Zdanevich knows how to invoke halos of meaning with his meaningless words; meaningless words give rise to meanings'. This appraisal from the head of the Russian Formalist school confirms Ilia Zdanevich's position as a major theoretician of trans-sense language and practitioner of 'grapholalia', the poetry of sounding language. The only figure of the Russian avant-garde who surpasses him in significance and in the grandeur of his zaum ideas is, Velimir Khlebnikov – the self-proclaimed 'Futurian' and 'Chairman of the Earth' whom the Formalist literary critic Yuri Tynianov would designate 'the Lobachevsky of the Word'.

CHAPTER 4

A Breakthrough into Languages: Velimir Khlebnikov's *Yazykovodstvo*

> The word is an embroidery hoop; the word is flax, the word is fabric.
> VELIMIR KHLEBNIKOV

∴

> [Khlebnikov] did not think of himself as a scholar – he was a 'railwayman of artistic language'.
> YURI TYNIANOV

∴

1   Khlebnikov's Language Experiment and Philosophy of Language

Velimir Khlebnikov's declaration 'we want the word boldly to follow painting' marked a semiotic turn from modeling a word as a musical symbol towards modeling it as an iconic sign, in terms of Charles Peirce's classification. Meanwhile, I shall examine a still deeper transformation in the poet's creative semiotics. Underneath the word-as-icon principle lies another analogy crucial for the Futurian – the word-as-number. The numeric model of language constitutes the core of Khlebnikov's linguistic experimentation. The number is the real instrument in the hands of the poet-as-artist: 'The number as the sole clay in the fingers of an artist; with it we are willing to mould the deep-worldly face of time!' (*Tables of Fate. Fragment VII*).[1]

---

[1] In this chapter, most translations from Russian are mine, unless otherwise indicated and referred to. Of all versions of the title of Khlebnikov's Доски судьбы we adhere to Andrea Hacker's *Tables of Fate*. See her on-going critical, bilingual and annotated publication of the newly transcribed text in special issues of the journal *Russian Literature* (2008-), as well as her PhD thesis (2002). See also the collection of articles wholly concerned with *Tables of Fate* in Feshchenko et al. (2008).

Khlebnikov views the number and the word as interrelated 'constants of the world' ('постоянные мира'). There is good reason for these mathematical analogies in the theory of the word. Mathematics, or more precisely, cosmology was a generative model for the poet's language philosophy, where, as Rudolf Duganov argues, 'the cosmos of the word was regarded as quite similar to the cosmos of the world. The word is the expression of the world, and as a consequence it does not only tell about the world, but represents the world by its mere structure, it is isomorphic with the world. The word, as such, is the world itself in terms of its sensible expression' (1990: 143).[2]

A view of the universe as word and of the word as universe leads Khlebnikov to tease out the nature of human language as such. 'It is evident that language is as wise as nature, and only now with the growth of science are we discovering how to read it', he explains in the article 'Our Fundamentals' (Khlebnikov 1987: 378–379). At the basis of all his language experiments lies an original theory of art – mainly verbal art – as a means of understanding the world. I agree with Willem Weststeijn who noted that Khlebnikov's quest for new language forms never resolves itself into sheer word play (as in the case of Alexei Kruchenykh's *zaum*) but is always driven by an effort to reveal the hidden knowledge of the world through language and the knowledge of language in the world (Weststeijn, 1983: 18). This Futurist 'magician of language' ('тайновидец языка'), as the literary critic Viktor Gofman dubbed him, stated that 'the wisdom of language has advanced beyond the wisdom of science' (Khlebnikov, 1987: 379). In this respect, there is a clear parallel with Andrey Bely's study of 'the wise deeps of language', a similar search for the cognitive and creative potentialities of the artistic word.

Early Khlebnikov scholars already recognised the clearly evident language problematics in his poetics: 'One of the major problems associated with the name of Khlebnikov is the problem of language [...] Theoretically and practically Khlebnikov pointed a spotlight at the fact that the notorious issue of beyonsense constitutes a substantial part of the general issue of language' (Gofman 1936: 186).[3] The issue of language innovation was tackled as early as the 1920s. As the linguist Grigory Vinokur put it in a 1923 article 'Futuristy – stroiteli jazyka', 'the Futurists were the first to enter consciously

---

2 See also Lönnqvist (1979). Raymond Cooke (1987: 73–74) discusses the problem of the word and the world in Khlebnikov's texts.
3 Of all translations of the Russian term *zaum* we adhere to the most widely accepted *beyonsense* (Paul Schmidt's variant). However, other translations are also taken into account elsewhere to clarify the meaning of the term, as in the case of *transreason*, *transrational language* and *trans-sense*.

into language invention, to show the path of linguistic engineering' (1990: 18). Boris Bukhshtab, author of the most significant early works on Khlebnikov's linguistics, dating back to 1920s, firmly states that 'Khlebnikov's theory of language played too crucial a role in the history of Russian literature' (2008: 53). The scholar complains that, in the minds of contemporary linguists, Khlebnikov's image was obscure: either the poet's thinking about language is integrated into a consistent system of ideas, or it is reduced to a number of scattered thoughts recurring in different essays (Ibidem):

> Reading criticism of Khlebnikov, one clearly sees that critics are not sure about the key tenet of these essays: whether they contain an individual and autonomous handling of linguistic issues, or a range of figments indisputable to the author, who created them with the sole purpose of supporting the poetic experiment. Nor is it clear whether these are theories of language in general or of poetic language only. These questions are not clearly defined, and different views blend together. More importantly, Khlebnikov's principal thoughts, which recur in all his writings, that which could be named the core of his theories, are interpreted not differently but in dramatically opposite ways. Khlebnikov's standpoint is treated either as 'a turn against sense altogether, or the other way round: 'What really matters in his theory is that he shifted the center of gravity in poetry from issues of sound to the issue of sense. For him, there is no sound not coloured by sense'.

Arguing against such accounts, Bukhshtab endeavors to grasp the 'integrity of ideas' in the Futurian's philosophy of language, noting that 'Khlebnikov, on the contrary, did not doubt that it is possible to interfere in the life of language on the basis of theoretical findings, and for him there was no need for a bridge between "language studies" and "language husbandry" ("языководство", his proper term)' (Idem: 55).[4]

Khlebnikov's 'sublime language reveries', as Paul Celan (cit. in Enzensberger, 1967) poetically described them, his linguistic insights (Solivetti, 2004), language project (Kustova, 2002), theory of language (Kostetsky, 1975; Imposti, 1981), linguistic concept (Scholz, 1968; Lauhus, 1987; Tsivyan, 2004; Chernyakov, 2007), language utopia (Ivanovic, 2004; Baydin, 2007), and imaginary philology (Grigoryev, 2000), no matter how they are defined, were closely related to his literary activities.

---

4 Starkina provides a bibliography of Khlebnikov's linguistic ideas (2008) and an overview of the poet's linguistic theory of the elementary units of speech (2012).

In the meantime, the first Khlebnikov scholars brought to our attention the close link between his 'language mythology' and the Symbolist theory of language. As Viktor Gofman argues in his persuasive essay, 'Khlebnikov's language principles had more to do, strange as it may seem at first, with the principles of some Symbolists than those of other Futurists; with the latter, Khlebnikov has some formal points of convergence, in theory and in practice' (1936: 188). It appears that, of all the Symbolists, Andrey Bely was the closest to him in this respect. Indeed, Bely's creed that 'a work of art is an art of the word' is more than relevant for Khlebnikov, with its allusions both to the theory of language and to linguistic creativity. Gofman explains (Idem: 224):

> In general theoretical terms the link is evident: in both cases, there is an idealistic conception of a specific poetic language, 'the language of gods', set apart from 'the language of everyday'; both authors acknowledge the leading, independent role of the word as such in the creative experience of the world, and its transformation through philosophical and poetical intuition; in both cases, we find an understanding of the poet as magician and prophet, primarily a magician of language; in both cases, there is an attempt at a peculiar natural philosophy.

In spite of these parallels, the Khlebnikovian poetics of the word and language develops in a profoundly unique fashion. It is marked by a prevailing interest in linguistic technology in a broad sense, as Gofman remarks (Idem: 228):

> The Symbolists were devoutly concerned with language techniques, but not in themselves, rather as a means of materialisation, a disclosure of 'contacts with other worlds', as inevitably indirect, approximate, symbolic expression of the 'inner verb', the word-logos. Whereas for Khlebnikov, language techniques and means of expression coincide with the 'logic of inventions', the laws of grammar, the architecture of speech, as well as the laws of numbers, they 'precede the sciences' and govern any kind of cognition.

For one thing, the basic principle of Khlebnikov's language creativity is language analysis, much like number analysis in mathematics. Rational analysis in regard to language experiments is associated, again, with his penchant for numbers. Insights into verbal language, just as with the mathematical language of numbers, eventually acquire a pointedly rationalistic nature: 'Khlebnikov does not reject the "language of concepts", but in every way aims at reforming, "revising" and "reviving" it. His task is to make even a trans-rational word a "rational" one, that is, logically substantial' (Ibidem). Khlebnikov's word bypasses the Symbolist aporia of appearance and sense.

The Symbolist poetics of allusion, their praise of the unutterable, is contrasted here with a poetics of complete expressiveness and profound out-spokennness; the Symbolist claim for 'music before everything else' is contrasted with the number and the word in all their semantic intensity. Andrey Bely takes the sound as a unit of his language model, whereas Khlebnikov proceeds to the letter as such, that is, the 'visible sound' as the elementary constituent of poetic language. It is no wonder, as historically letters of the alphabet have often been assigned numeric value, and vice versa. Khlebnikov merely takes this practice to its creative limits. It is just here that his semiotic orientation towards the iconicity of the sign comes to the fore. In his manifesto 'To the Artists of the World', he sets out to 'create a common written language shared by all the peoples of this third satellite of the Sun, to invent written symbols that can be understood and accepted by our entire star, populated as it is with human beings, and lost here in the universe' (Khlebnikov, 1985: 146).[5]

This brings up the question of whether or not music, so precious to the Symbolists, meets the requirements of a 'language common to everyone'. It certainly does. But Khlebnikov goes still further to reach for the 'new ways of the word'. The new written language, to him, shall be composed of 'mute' signs: 'Mute graphic marks will reconcile the cacophony of languages' (1985: 147). It follows that expressly 'graphic' signs ought to lay the foundation of the desired 'universal language'. Whereas 'to the artists who work with ideas falls the task of creating an alphabet of concepts, a system of basic units of thought from which words may be constructed', it is 'the task of artists who work with paint' to 'provide graphic symbols for the basic units of your mental processes' (Ibidem). Therefore, the 'edifice of the word' is to be constructed from the 'alphabet of concepts', deduced, in turn, from the spatial vocabulary of graphic signs.[6]

Natalia Pertsova has published Khlebnikov's manuscript titled 'The Language of Marks' ('Значковый язык') (Pertsova, 2000: 372–382), which addresses the linguistic topic of the 'alphabet of thoughts', referring, on the one hand, to interlinguistic writings by 17th century philosophers, and on the other, to Khlebnikov's own studies of the 'mute language' of graphic signs.

---

5 According to Julia Kristeva, the work of Khlebnikov 'threaded through metaphor and metonymy a network of phonemes or phonic groups charged with instinctual drives and meaning, constituting what for the author was a numerical code, a ciphering, underlying the verbal sign' (Kristeva, 1980).
6 See Kostetsky (1975), Pertsova (2000), Perloff (2002).

The 'language of marks' shall contribute, according to him, to 'the creation of new concepts (units and points of thought, its echoes, sudden turns, beautiful movements)', and the benefit of this kind of writing system is that 'by establishing several new concepts we can substitute the great many particular concepts'. He proposes a principle of reducing all concepts 'to a few purely geometrical operations in the field of logic', which would bring about 'a lot of new dense meanings'. The attempt to create a 'language of marks' is, by the poet's own confession, only a test. However, as Pertsova rightly reasons, it also seemed to be an approach towards creating the 'language of the stars' ('звездный язык').

According to Khlebnikov's own theory (1985: 149),

> The simple bodies of a language – the sounds of the alphabet – are the names of various aspects of space, an enumeration of the events of its life. The alphabet common to a multitude of peoples is in fact a short dictionary of the spatial world that is of such concern to your art, painters, and to your brushes.
>
> Each individual word resembles a small workers' collective, where the first sound of the word is like the chairman of the collective who directs the whole set of sounds in the word. If we assemble all the words that begin with the same consonantal sound, we observe that, just as meteors often fall from one single point in the sky, all those words fly from the single point of a certain conceptualisation of space. And that point becomes the meaning of the sound of the alphabet, and its simplest name.

Here is one example he gives: 'After all, even in Sanskrit *vritti* means rotation, and in Egyptian as in Russian *khata* means hut' (Idem: 150). In the same essay, Khlebnikov proposes the first experiments in 'beyonsense language as the language of the future' (Idem: 150–151):

> Instead of saying:
> The Hunnic and Gothic hordes, having united and gathered themselves about Attila, full of warlike enthusiasm, progressed further together, but having been met and defeated by Aetius, the protector of Rome, they scattered into numerous bands and settled and remained peacefully on their own lands, having poured out into and filled up the emptiness of the steppes.
> Could we not say instead:
> SHa + So (Hunnic and Gothic hordes), Ve Attila, CHa Po, So Do, but Bo + Zo Aetius, KHo of Rome, So Mo Ve + Ka So, Lo SHa of the steppes + CHa.
> And that is what the first beyonsense story played upon the strings of the alphabet sounds like.

This example clearly demonstrates how Khlebnikov's language technique applies the logic of mathematical operations. Analysing words resembles the analysis of numbers or the decomposition of chemical elements. As he contends in the theoretical essay 'Our Fundamentals', 'the plentitude of language must be analysed in terms of fundamental units of "alphabetic verities", and then for these sound elements we may be able to construct something resembling Mendeleev's law or Moseley's law – the latest achievements of the science of chemistry' (Khlebnikov, 1987: 376). With this law, Khlebnikov seeks, among other things, to juxtapose concepts relating to the ethical world of man and the light phenomena of the world, based on the aforementioned principle of sound images ('alphabetic verities'):

The Other World	The Relative Principle
telo (body), *tusha* (carcass)	*ten'* (shade)
delo (act), *dusha* (soul)	*den'* (day)
tukhnut' (to go off, in the sense of go bad)	*tukhnut'* (to go off, in the sense of extinguish)
voskresat' (rise from the dead, rekindle the spark of life)	*kresalo i ognivo* (flint and steel, used to kindle a spark)
groznyi (threatening)	*groza* (thunder)
molodost' (youth), *molodets* (young man)	*molniia* (lightning)
solodka (sweetroot), *sladost'* (sweetening)	*solntse* (sun), *solniia* (sunning)
soi (klan), *sem'ia* (family), *syn* (son), *semia* (semen)	*siiat'* (to shine), *solntse* (sun)
temia (crown of the head), *tyl* (back, rear), *telo* (body)	*tiiat'* (to darken; by analogy with *siiat'*)
cherti (devils)	*chernyi tsvet* (colour black)
merzost' (abomination)	*merznut'* (to freeze)
styd (shame)	*stuzha* (severe frost)
kholostoi (unmarried)	*kholod* (cold)
zhit' (to live)	*zhech'* (to burn)
peklo (hellfire)	*pech'* (furnace, oven)
pylkii (ardent)	*plamia* (flame)
gore (sorrow, woe)	*goret'* (to burn)
grekh (sin)	*goret'*, *gret'* (to give off heat)
iasnyi um (a clear, lucid mind)	*iaski* (stars: dial.)
iarost' (fierceness, furor)	*iarkoe plamia* (fierce flame)
iskrennii (candid)	*iskra* (spark)
sviatoi (saint), "*svetik*" (darling)	*svet* (light)
zloi (wicked)	*zola* (ashes)

According to the poet, these two columns 'describe the lightning-like, luminous nature of man and, consequently, of the moral world' (Idem: 379–380). In this example, language is left to speak for itself, and Khlebnikov establishes a law of word correlations, by analogy with mathematical equations. Here, he claims, 'linguistics paves the way for the natural sciences and attempts to measure the moral world by treating it as a chapter in the study of rays of light' (Idem: 382):

> Word creation is hostile to the bookish petrification of language. It takes as its model the fact that in villages, by rivers and forests, language is being created to this very day; every minute sees the birth of words that either die or gain the right to immortality. Word creation transfers this right to the world of literary creativity [...]

This idea of a 'beyonsense language' largely contests the perceptions of *zaum* as 'sound speech devoid of sense' or as mere 'sound imagery'. Khlebnikov's *zvukopis'* is by no means at odds with sense. He speaks of 'sound imagery' as 'a nutrient from which a tree of the universal language can be grown'. The Futurian did not aspire to separate and isolate the sound and graphical aspects of language from sense (form from content), but quite the reverse, all his attention was directed to opposing the traditional gap between linguistic techniques of expression and the expressed meaning, between the sound form and the semantic contents of speech. As Viktor Gofman comments: 'In other words, Khlebnikov was mainly preoccupied with overcoming the "arbitrariness" of the linguistic sign, which for contemporary linguistic thought exists merely because of tradition, as a "conventional" form, while it is, in fact, genetically inseparable and intimately bound up with thinking, being neither "arbitrary" nor "conventional"' (1936: 197). This proves, in particular, that Khlebnikov's language experiment is of a formal-and-substantial nature, it is not purely formalistic.[7]

2   The Futurian as Linguae Constructor[8]

For Khlebnikov, the creation of a single universal language was the second approach to the subject of the word, the first being 'the self-sufficient word

---

7   On distinguishing between the two types of *zaum* – the sonoric and the sound-semantic – see Chernyakov (2008), Weststeijn (1983), Janecek (1996).
8   Here, I am adapting the title of Andrzej Drawicz's study of Khlebnikov, *Mundi Constructor* (2000).

that stands outside historical fact and everyday utility'. In an essay called 'Self-Statement', he describes in detail the embryonic stage of verbal creativity: 'I observed that the roots of words are only phantoms behind which stand the strings of the alphabet, and so my second approach to language was to find the unity of the world's languages in general, built from units of the alphabet. A path to a universal beyonsense language' (1987: 147). What, then, does 'beyonsense language' have to do with rational meaning? He gives an answer in 'Our Fundamentals' (Idem: 384):

> If we take any given word, say *chashka* (cup), we have no way of knowing what each separate sound means in terms of the whole word. But if we take every word that begins with the sound *ch* – *chasha, cherep, chan, chulok,* etc. (cup, skull, vat, stocking) – then the common meaning that all these words share will also be the meaning of *ch*, and the remaining letters in each word will cancel each other out. If we compare these words beginning with *ch*, we see that they all mean 'one body that encases or envelops another'; *ch* therefore means case or envelope.

Hence, 'beyonsense language' is based on two premises (Ibidem):
1. The initial consonant of a simple word governs all the rest – it commands the remaining letters.
2. Words that begin with an identical consonant share some identical meaning; it is as if they were drawn from various directions to a single point in the mind.

Further on, Khlebnikov quotes other words beginning with *ch*, reinforcing his argument that the letter *ch* is not merely a sound, but a name that conceals an image, being an 'indivisible unit of language'.

The next step of 'affirming the alphabet' implies operations with vowel sounds. Thus, about *o* and *y* he argues that 'their arrows of signification fly in opposite directions, and they impart opposite meanings to pairs of words (*voiti* (to enter) and *vyiti* (to leave); *soi* meaning clan and *syi* meaning individual, an indivisible entity; *bo* to express purpose and *by* to express volition, free will)' (Idem: 385–386). This method of vowel transformation is given the name of 'internal declension', or 'case declension by root', first introduced in the dialogical essay 'Teacher and Student' and later developed in some of his poetic writings. The relation of vowel sounds to consonants is presented in the following fashion: 'Language has two principles, and each consonant is a specific elementary world; vowels, which are conventional, relate these worlds to each other. Vowels are algebraic; they are values and numbers, whereas consonants are the pieces of space' (a manuscript note cit. in Pertsova, 2000).

Accordingly, phenomena like homonymy, sound similitude and identity of equivalent words are not just a particular means of equivocal expressiveness – characteristic of both traditional poetic speech and everyday humour – but a major semantic principle and law governing the movement of thought and revealing the essence of things, their hidden links and relations ('to destroy languages by besieging their secrets', as he appeals in 'A Letter to Two Japanese'). As Viktor Gofman correctly observes, the tools of Khlebnikov's language experiment are intended to 'turn language structure towards syntheticism in a particular way, to return to all its elements a new empirical specificity of meaning, a specificity that corresponded in its manner to the synthetic concreteness of primitive thought' (1936: 215). Paradoxically, by 'analysing the word', i.e., by its analysis in linguistic terms, the poet advocates for further syntheticisation of the Russian language in terms of its structure.

Khlebnikov's idea of the 'night reason' and 'day reason' of the word results in a theory of the 'language of the stars' as opposed to the 'ordinary' language of the 'everyday mind'. The 'language of the stars' is a language of 'world truths, close to both 'language of numbers' and 'language of vision'. As he postulates in 'Proposals' (an essay dated 1915–1916) (1987: 358).

> All the ideas of Planet Earth (there aren't that many), like the houses on the street, should be designated by individual numbers, and this visual code used to communicate and to exchange ideas. Designate the speeches of Cicero, Cato, Othello, and Demosthenes by numbers, and in the courts and other institutions, instead of imitation speeches that nobody needs, simply hang up a card marked with the number of an appropriate speech. This will become the first international language. This principle has already been partially introduced in legal code. Language will thus be left to the arts and freed from humiliating burdens.

The 'algebraic language' ('числоречи') consisting of 'number-words' ('числослова') is one possible 'language of the stars'. In Khlebnikov's words, 'the language of the stars relates to everyday language much like operations with algebraic values do to named numbers'. He calls the language of the future 'an algebra, as behind each sound an image of space is hidden'.

The idea of a 'language of the stars' developed gradually and took on its final form in the last period of Khlebnikov's life, when he was working on the supersaga *Zangezi*.[9] The 'language of the stars' is for him the 'highest degree

---

[9] The recent critical edition of *Zangezi* (Rossomakhin, 2021) collects all criticism and provides an extensive commentary to this major work. See also the bilingual Russian-English edition of *Zangezi* (Khlebnikov, 2020).

of synthesis' of all his probing insights and experiments. The poet associates it with his own personal ideal of overcoming the 'pluri-language' for the sake of an 'organic language living as a plant'. In 1921, he declares: 'You, those who ravel in languages, learn to think by movement'. There is a good reason why he associates the 'language of the stars' with cinema, in a note dated 1920: 'Script. Canvas. The word is marching – a row of infantrymen. The capital sound on horseback or aboard an airplane points the way with a saber, behind him the common sounds of the word are infantrymen. Two meanings of modern words'.

Approaches to creating the 'language of the stars' can be found as early as in the first of his experiments with words that begin with the same sound or syllable (see above).[10] Endowing particular sounds of the alphabet with units of thought ('epithets of world phenomena', as he calls them) turns out to be an attempt to outline the grammar of the 'language of the stars'.[11] For Khlebnikov, 'the word has a triple nature: related to hearing, the intellect, and a path to fate'. Thus, the poet singles out three main approaches for attaching meanings to sounds: (1) the immediate emotional perception of the sound, namely, its correlation with shape and colour; (2) a search for semantic similitude with alliterated Russian words ('poetic etymology', in Roman Jakobson's terms); (3) inquiry into the word as a 'path to fate' exemplified by the initial letters of historical proper and common names. Khlebnikov starts from the assumption that each consonant in the root of a word represents an image of a particular unit of the 'alphabet of the stars', a peculiar semantic focus: 'The language of the future is a language of viewing the point itself that illuminates things'. The list of elements of the 'language of the stars' is reconstructed in Pertsova (1995).

The theory and practice of the 'language of the stars' took its final shape in the supersaga *Zangezi*. In an explanatory 'Introduction' to the play, Khlebnikov remarks: 'A story is made of words, the way a building is made of construction units. Equivalent words, like minute building blocks, serve as the construction units of a story. A superstory, or supersaga, is made up out of independent sections, each with its own special god, its special faith, and its special rules' (1985: 191). In terms of linguistics, this note would mean that each part of the text ('plane of the word', using Khlebnikov's own term) is written in an individual language, each with its own grammar and poetics. It is a heteroglossia of invented poetic languages embedded into a single piece of writing. All 'language images' developed throughout the Futurian's oeuvre are represented here in a common, synthetic super-language. The 'language of the stars' is the

---

10　The French Symbolist poet Stéphane Mallarmé was the first to propose the idea of correspondence between a word's semantics and its initial letter, as, e.g., in his theoretical essay 'The English Words' ('Les Mots Anglais'), see Cassedy (1990) for this connection.
11　Here, I am guided by Natalia Pertsova's (2000) data.

particular focus of 'Plane VIII'. All stated principles of this 'world language' are put into use in the poem 'A Song in the language of the stars' as part of the supersaga. Right after this poetic fragment comes an exposition of the rules and laws of the 'language of the stars'.[12] The sage Zangezi is reading 'star-songs, where the algebra of words is muddled with yardsticks and clocks', interpreting them to the public (Khlebnikov 1985: 205):

> Have you heard all I've said. Heard my speech that frees you from the fetters of words? Speech is an edifice built out of blocks of space.
> Particles of speech. Parts of movement. Words do not exist; there are only movements in space and their parts – points and areas.
> You are now set free from your ancestral chains. The hammer of my voice has shattered them; your frenzied struggle against those chains has ended.
> Planes, the lines defining an area, the impact of points, the godlike circle, the angle of incidence, the fascicule of rays proceeding from a point or penetrating it – these are the secret building blocks of language. Scrape the surface of language, and you will behold interstellar space and the skin that encloses it.

Besides the 'language of the stars', Khlebnikov's *Zangezi* contains references to other types of 'languages', such as 'bird language', 'language of the gods', 'beyonsense language', 'analysing the word', 'sound painting', and 'absurd language'.

These examples make it clear that we are dealing not just with different speech styles, but fairly different languages. Each poetic world manifests itself in its specific language reality, and their manifoldness is implemented in the multitude of languages, in the heterogeneity of the word: 'Passing through these worlds, projecting from the past into the future, from reality to fantasy, from the micro-world to the mega-world, we encounter not only new subjects and characters, but surely each time a new language structure', Rudolf Duganov comments (1990: 188). A plurality of languages, a multiplicity of spatial and temporal schema, a multitude of events and meanings – such is the nature of Khlebnikov's language experiment. The 'image of language' here is multi-dimensional. The complete summary of the names of languages in Khlebnikov, drawn up by his first biographer Nikolai Stepanov and later greatly expanded by Viktor Grigoryev, amounts to 53 items – from the 'number-word' to 'roots conjunction' (Grigoryev, 2000).

---

12   See also Oraić-Tolić (1989).

Khlebnikov experiments not only with the word and poetic speech, as Andrey Bely, but also with language and languages, creating a sort of 'imaginary philology', as Grigoryev calls it. The Futurian's neology is closely related to the issue of language creation, not just word creation. The poet's treatment of the word and language is inspired to a substantial degree by his mathematical interests and his mathematical mindset. Yet it is difficult to agree with Vladimir Markov's critical judgment that 'Khlebnikov imposed his linguistics and, at times, mathematics, on poetry' (1954: 141). More accurately, in his poetic experiment he searched for correlations between mathematical and linguistic approaches. Using the methods of science and philosophy was not at all 'unlawful' for the poet, contrary to Markov's assessment; Khlebnikov's goal was to establish new laws on the basis of different scientific data, which eventually led to his 'laws of time' and 'laws of words'.

Treating the 'number' as a specific type of sign, Khlebnikov builds his poetics of language by analogy with the mathematical, or numerical, model. This model remains constitutive for his language mythology throughout his entire creative career. As early as 1913, he proposes research on 'words measurement' ('соизмер слов'): 'The task of this research shall be to discover the proto-units of language, the smallest sounding elements that have meaning, and to apply the laws of composition of these elements to the numbers of language' (a manuscript excerpt quoted in Pertsova, 2003: 21). Thus, the search for the 'numbers of language' is central to Khlebnikov's language project until his very last works. This 'linguistic metaphysics' (as Grigory Vinokur put it) was coupled organically and reciprocally with 'mathematical metaphysics'. However, the poet's 'theorism' was not an 'obstacle' to his creative development (as Vinokur unjustly claims), and even less so a 'creative tragedy' (1990: 209). Yuri Tynianov had a different opinion on the Futurian's scientific vision: 'Khlebnikov looks at things as phenomena – with the eye of a scientist examining their process and progress' (2002: 374). Indeed, Khlebnikov's linguistic and poetic experiment inaugurated a new kind of poetic-and-scientific discourse.

Khlebnikov's language experiment went through several stages that each corresponded to a particular 'principle of word creation' ('начало словотворчества'). Subsequent stages in no way negated preceding ones, but rather fulfilled their potential. That said, Khlebnikov's metaphorical formula 'The word is an embroidery hoop, the word is flax, the word is fabric' ('Слово—пяльцы, слово—лен, слово—ткань') persists throughout all of his creative development. It is characteristic that the central concern here is precisely the creative stance on the word. As the Symbolist literary critic Ivanov-Razumnik, a contemporary of Khlebnikov, pointed out, it was a strive for 'sensing in the painful stuttering a new force and the truth of the ever-nascent word'

(1922: 227). It is the 'nascent word' that enthralled both Khlebnikov and Bely in their theoretical and poetic work – the word as an object of laboratory testing, metaphysical inquiry, and, ultimately, life experience.

The issue of life-creation as it relates to word-creation was important to Khlebnikov interest from the beginning of his creative career. In a passage from the so-called '1908 Notebook', he prophesied: 'The sieve of the world's wills is in my hand. Lighten up, people, the making of belief […] the making of life and word' (cit. in Baran, 1993: 185). The topic of life and destiny appears as early as 1912, in a dialogue titled 'Teacher and Student' (Khlebnikov 1987: 280):

> Teacher: Anything else?
> Student: Anything else? Yes! You see, what I wanted was to read the writing traced by destiny on the scroll of human affairs.
> Teacher: And what exactly is that supposed to mean?
> Student: I wasn't concerned with the life of individuals; I wanted to be able to see the entire human race from a distance, like a ridge of clouds, like a distant mountain chain, and to find out if measure, order, and harmony were characteristics of the waves of its life.

Khlebnikov identifies sign-words and sign-affairs, attributing to them a common 'destiny' and a common 'life'. This idea not only laid the foundations for the poet's philosophy of destiny and philosophy of language, but also, specifically, predestined his own way of living and his creative exploration of all kinds of different languages. In a long poem titled 'The Scratch across the Sky', Khlebnikov uses the metaphor of a *breakthrough into languages* (прорыв в языки), which implies overcoming the barriers of consciousness and accessing different languages – the languages of culture and nature, arts and sciences, literature and painting, languages of numbers and languages of sounds. A similar breakthrough into the languages of poetry, painting, music, and philosophy was undertaken by Wassily Kandinsky, whose first poetic texts were published, alongside Khlebnikov's early works, in *A Slap in the Face of Public Taste*, a collective Futurist almanac published in 1912.

CHAPTER 5

Wassily Kandinsky and the Birth of the Languages of Art

> Painting as an art is not some vague projection into space but a power, so strong and full of purpose that it serves the refinement of the soul, (the movement of the triangle). It is its language which speaks to the soul.
> WASSILY KANDINSKY

∴

> The image is the poet's pigment; with that in mind you can go ahead and apply Kandinsky, you can transpose his chapter on the language of form and colour and apply it to the writing of verse.
> EZRA POUND

∴

Velimir Khlebnikov's slogan 'We want the word boldly to follow painting' inaugurated a whole new modernist aesthetics of uniting poetry and the visual arts, where word and image stood for two intertwined modes of artistic expression, the verbal and the visual. This chapter discusses Wassily Kandinsky's artistic strategy of bitextuality, which conveys artistic meanings through two media in parallel: the verbal text and the painted image. The poetries of verbal and visual languages make up the original art theory and practice of this major figure of the Russian and European avant-garde.

Bitextuality as a concurrent use of verbal and pictorial media can be viewed as a particular case of intermediality (Hansen-Löve, 1983). Building on this premise, I will consider the text of the artist as switching between two codes, the verbal and the visual, creating a two-fold, *bitextual* object. This issue was addressed using semiotics and communication theory by Roman Jakobson in his famous article 'On Linguistic Aspects of Translation', where he introduced the term *intersemiotic translation,* or *transmutation,* which he defines as the 'interpretation of verbal signs by means of nonverbal sign systems' (1959: 233).

However, in his definition of transmutation, the Russian-American linguist did not mention the reverse process, that is, the interpretation of nonverbal signs through the verbal sign system – a process defined in literature studies as *ekphrasis*. However, in this chapter, I intend to analyse a third type of intersemiotic recoding, which combines the two other types – the reciprocal translation of verbal signs into nonverbal and vice versa. I believe that these open transitions between different sign systems and different artistic media are an inherent feature of avant-garde creativity.

The choice of Wassily Kandinsky as a focus for this chapter is motivated by a number of reasons. Firstly, he was the one to introduce the term *text of the artist* in the title of his 1918 theoretical book *Steps. Text of the Artist* (originally published in German in 1913 under the title *Rückblicke*). Secondly, and more importantly, Kandinsky was one of the first, if not the first, in the history of the arts to consider verbal reasoning and theorising a key element of the artistic system. The central objective of his system was to present and define the grammar of his art, to compile the fundamentals, vocabulary and terminology of his own system of art. Lastly, and most essentially, Kandinsky was the first artist to theorise the language of his aesthetic experience.[1]

In his essay 'Little Articles on Big Questions' (1919) Kandinsky proclaims: 'A fundamental turning point is attained. Its fruit is *the birth of the language of art*' (1994: 425, *emphasis mine – V.F.*). The quest for the language of art correlates with the contemporaneous linguistic turn in philosophy and science. The painter himself calls it a 'spiritual turning-point', which in the sphere of the arts took the form of searching for an artistic method: one should study not *what* to paint, but *how* to paint.

All Kandinsky's reflections and writings about art involve reflections on verbal problematic. His texts can be divided into at least three different genres: poetry, self-commentary to his own paintings, and theory of abstract art.

1   Verse

Kandinsky's poetic oeuvre represents the first aspect of his bitextuality. In his short autobiography published in Germany in 1913, the artist recalls that in his youth he had written poetry which he subsequently destroyed.[2] Nevertheless, he continued to write verse and, whenever painting failed him, words became the preferred tool for self-expression and intersemiotic self-translation. At

---

1   The image/text problem in Kandinsky's abstract art is discussed in Podzemskaia (2009).
2   See Hahl-Koch (1999).

times, he writes in the same autobiography, the opposite would happen: the arising poetic sensations took a visual shape instead of a verbal one. Characteristically, his 1903 etching album was titled *Verses without Words*.

From 1909 to 1911, during his period of transition from figurative art to abstraction, Kandinsky composed a series of experimental poems, such as this untitled one:

> Ring the drop was falling
> It rang
> 'Ring' it rang
> A drop was falling.
> A heron spread its wings
> Rustling
> Wings rustling
> A grey heron[3]

As we can see, the painter searches for verbal analogies to his pictorial sensations. If we analyse this piece of poetry, which looks more like a sketch than a full-scale poem, we can observe the process of intermedial translation. It becomes clear how the object signified by the words of this text loses its objectiveness and materiality, while transforming into an abstract form.

Already in the first line of the poem, we find a certain move beyond the limits of the visible – *a drop was falling*. A drop of water can be imagined as an object of pictorial representation. However, it is more difficult to imagine the time-lapse process of it falling down on the canvas. Kandinsky no longer considers the material aspect of the drop of water but rather views it as a geometric shape moving in abstract space. Linguistically speaking, the past continuous of the verb *fall* (the past imperfect in Russian) highlights the dynamics of the subject in question. The whole first line *Ring the drop was falling* actualises the processual meaning of the 'sounding drop'. It rings – that is, it produces a prolonged sound effect. Introducing a lexical unit from the vocabulary of music, the author incorporates a different semiotic coding from the musical sign system. The third line reinforces the same process by a tautological device – *ring it rang*, depicting the reverberating nature of the sound while also reflecting upon the common inner form of the two different tense forms – *ring* and *rang*. The two words, in turn, previously appeared in the first and second lines, which creates a varied but repetitive abstract rhythm in the

---

3 Unpublished translation by Emily Wright. The Russian original is published in Hahl-Koch (1999: 124).

text. As a result of these first lines, the elementary pictorial image of the water drop acquires an abstract character, no longer related to material reality. The same principle is at work in the artist's 1905 painting 'Russian Beauty in a Landscape', which depicts a woman in a fairy-tale costume and setting. Spots and drops of tempera dematerialise the subject-matter of the canvas, transforming it into a rhythmical sequence of abstract patterns.

Regarding the issue of *rhythm*, Kandinsky wrote in *Concerning the Spiritual in Art* (1977: 15–16):

> The apt use of a word (in its poetical meaning), repetition of this word, twice, three times or even more frequently, according to the need of the poem, will not only tend to intensify the inner harmony but also bring to light unsuspected spiritual properties of the word itself. Further than that, the frequent repetition of a word [...] deprives the word of its original external meaning. Similarly, in drawing, the abstract message of the object drawn tends to be forgotten and its meaning lost.

Kandinsky makes use of the same technique in his later poetry, especially in his 1912 book *Sounds*, as well as in other poems from his archives, which have recently been published for the first time.[4] If we take a look at the titles of some of the poems from *Sounds*, we can clearly see a progression toward abstraction at the level of nominalisation: 'Open'; 'That'; 'Unchanged'; 'A Thing or Two'; 'Not'; 'Still?'; 'Why?'; 'In two'; 'Exit'; 'Later'; 'The break'; 'Different'; 'Softness'; 'Adventure'; 'Sight lightning'; 'Look'; 'Seeing'.[5]

Originally, Kandinsky wanted to call the whole album *The 'It' Series*, but he chose the more sensory yet abstract title *Sounds*. The predominance of abstract nouns, personal and indefinite pronouns, auxiliary words, and infinitive verbs contributes to the dematerialisation of meaning in the poetic text. The same linguistic principle is applied in Kandinsky's preference for giving works of art such abstract titles as 'Composition', 'Improvisation', the names of colours and shapes, etc. With this linguistic experimentation, akin to other avant-garde poetic strategies, he aimed to affirm a new mode of perceiving a work of art.

Of particular importance is the issue of Kandinsky's Russian-German bilingualism. The interlinguistic self-translation inherent to bilingualism is a particular case of the kind of intermedial self-translation that is bitextuality in

---

4 See Sokolov (2016).
5 See Kandinsky (1981). Another translation, by Tony Frazer, of *Sounds* into English was published in 2018 by Shearsman Books.

the broader aesthetic sense.[6] Kandinsky translated many of his own texts from German into Russian and vice versa, mainly theoretical essays and treatises. For our purposes, however, it is interesting to look at an example of Kandinsky's own translations of his poems. Before releasing the poetry album *Sounds* (*Klänge*) in 1912, Kandinsky tried to create analogs of his poetic miniatures in Russian. Russian versions of his poems were published only recently (2016), and they number at least twenty-six in total (twin versions written by the artist both in Russian and in German).

Here is an example of such a bilingual experiment – the humorous poem 'Song', which describes a person without eyes and ears who is listening to the sounds of the world around him and perceiving sounds through singing:

ПЕСНЯ	LIED
Вот человек	Es sitzt ein Mann
В кругу сидит,	Im engen Kreis,
В кругу сидит	Im engen Kreis
Стесненья.	Der Schmäle.
Доволен он.	Er ist vergnügt.
Он без ушей.	Er hat kein Ohr.
Без глаз он точно так же.	Und fehlen ihm die Augen.
И **солнцешара**	Des roten Schalls
Красный звук	Des **Sonnenballs**
Его не достигает.	Er findet keine Spuren.
Все что упало,	Was ist gestürzt,
Встанет вновь.	Das steht doch auf.
Все что молчало,	Und was nicht sprach,
Запоет.	Das singt ein Lied.
И человека	Es wird der Mann,
Без ушей	Der hat kein Ohr,
Без глаз – он точно также –	Dem fehlen auch die Augen
Тот солнцешара	Des roten Schalls
Красный звук	Des Sonnenballs
Уже его достигнет.	Empfinden feine Spuren
(Kandinsky, 2016)	(Kandinsky, 1912)[7]

---

6 See a chapter in Wanner (2020). Kandinsky's bilingual theoretical legacy is well represented in a recent two-volume critical edition (Kandinsky, 2020).

7 The contemporary Language poet Charles Bernstein translated this poem into English as follows: 'So sits a man / In tighter loop / In tighter loop / Encircling scents / What a fluke / He's

Kandinsky seeks to preserve both the rhythm and the vocabulary in both versions. However, there are minor differences in the interaction of syntax and metrics. In the line *Все что упало / Встанет вновь*, the clear syllabic articulation of the lines is broken. On the other hand, the line *Без глаз он точно также* has the same meter as its German equivalent. The neologism *Солнцешар*, which is a calque of the German *Sonnenball*, is also a result of the German-Russian linguistic transfer.

This kind of interlinguistic transfer is also apparent in the beginning of the poem 'Видеть/Sehen' ('See') in both the Russian and German versions (*emphasis mine – V.F.*):

> Синее, синее поднималось, поднималось и падало.
> Острое, тонкое свистело и втыкалось, но не протыкало.
> Во всех углах загремело.
> **Густокоричневое** повисло будто на все времена.
>   Будто. Будто.
> Шире расставь руки.
>   Шире. Шире. (Kandinsky, 2016)

> Blaues, Blaues hob sich und fiel.
> Spitzes, Dünnes pfiff und drängte sich ein, stach aber nicht durch
> An allen Ecken hat's gedröhnt
> **Dickbraunes** blieb hängen scheinbar auf alle Ewigkeiten.
> **Sch**einbar, **Sch**einbar.
> **B**reiter sollst Du deine Arme ausbreiten.
> **B**reiter, **B**reiter. (Kandinsky, 1912)

In addition to the nonce word *густокоричневый* ('thick-brown'), a calque from the German *Dickbraunes*, the verse creates sound echoes between the two versions: the sound *б* in the repeated word *будто* mirrors the sound *b* in the German word *breiter*, and the Russian *ш* in the word *шире* resonates with the German *sch* in *scheinbar*. There is interlingual paronymic attraction between these two twin texts by the bilingual poet. Kandinsky thinks simultaneously in two language systems, which makes for rather strange Russian

---

got no ear /Also missing eye. /Blush of sound / Sun goes round / Senses won't be found. / What's overthrown / Now stands as home. / No speech's tongued / The sung is song. / So it's the man / He's got no ear / Also missing eye / Flush of sound / Sun goes round / Senses finely ground'. (https://toddswift.blogspot.com/2013/08/new-charles-bernstein-poem.html, last accessed 27.02.23)

poetry. But what is the author trying to achieve? Certainly not a traditional translation between two languages; in both cases, the text tries for an abstract verse effect analogous to what Kandinsky is trying to achieve in painting. Kandinsky's poems have a clear purpose – they are exercises in synaesthesia between the language of poetry and the language of painting ('the language of colours', in the words of the artist himself). The self-translation that occurs here is a translation from the language of pictorial perception into verbal language, albeit in two different versions. This kind of correspondence in abstract poetry can be found in all of the artist's poetic sketches.[8]

Kandinsky's self-translations are an entry into the bilingual space which the Russian linguist Lev Shcherba called 'a common language with two forms'. In the most pronounced cases of such mixed bilingualism,

> when people are generally fluent in both languages, they create a peculiar form of language, in which each idea has two ways of expression, so that essentially a unified language is obtained, but with two forms. At the same time, people do not experience any difficulties in the transition from one language to another: both systems are correlated with each other to the last detail. In this case, a sometimes mutual, sometimes one-sided adaptation of the two languages to each other usually occurs.
> (Shcherba, 1974: 313)

In the case of poetic bilingualism, this interpenetration forms an even more pronounced synthetic bilateral form of language.

2 Self-Commentaries to Paintings

Kandinsky also wrote self-commentaries for his own paintings, which were published in exhibition catalogues. Most interesting is the text 'Composition VI', in which the famous painting of the same name undergoes structural analysis by its painter. Kandinsky notes that initially he painted a figurative image on glass titled 'Deluge' (1911). Later, he wished to revise this theme for a composition, but failed for quite some time, as he 'was still obedient to the expression of the Deluge, instead of heeding the expression of the w o r d "Deluge"' (Kandinsky, 1994: 385).

---

8 For a detailed analysis of Kandinsky's poetic work of various periods see Sokolov (2016: 161–288). On self-translation of poetry in general see Feshchenko (2018: 177–200) and Wanner (2020).

What did Kandinsky actually experience? The very word *deluge* looms large for him, and he wants to yield to its mood, that is, to the pure sensation of the inner sound and not to the external meaning of the word *deluge*. Unconsciously, he perceives the self-reflective nature of this word. The Russian word for deluge – *potop* – is a palindrome, a word that can be read in both directions. Abstracting himself from the meaning of the word and concentrating on its pure form, he projects this idea onto his own painting and is stunned by its composition and forms, without any reference to the denotation of 'deluge': 'This glass-painting had become detached from me' (Idem: 386), he comments. Finally, the 'Composition' was drawn as if by itself ('in two or three days', 'involuntarily'). The non-figurative sensation implies non-mimetism, a tension contained within itself, between its constituents. He sees the composition as an organic whole: '(1) on the left the delicate, rosy, somewhat blurred center, with weak, indefinite lines in the middle; (2) on the right (somewhat higher than the left) the crude, red-blue, rather discordant area, with sharp, rather evil, strong, very precise lines'. (Idem: 387) Between these two areas, there is a third, main one, which 'one only recognises subsequently as being the center, but is, in the end, the principal center'. The pink and white colours are foaming as if blotted out by a mist. A spectator looking at the painting, Kandinsky writes, is situated 'somewhere' in a place of constant search and balancing. Ultimately, he concludes, the initial theme of the picture (the deluge) was 'dissolved and transformed into an internal, purely pictorial, independent, and objective existence' (Idem: 388). Thus, by means of inner intersemiotic translation into verbal thinking, the artist creates a reciprocal effect with visual matter. The inner linguistic form transmutes into the inner plastic shape, existing in a parallel bitextual dimension.

Another significant example of Kandinsky's auto-ekphrastic technique is his essay 'Empty Canvas etc.' written for *Cahiers d'art* in 1935. It describes how an empty canvas starts filling with elementary abstractions: 'Empty canvas. In appearance: truly empty, keeping silent, indifferent. Almost doltish. In reality: filled with tensions, with a thousand low voices, full of expectation. A little frightened because it can be violated. But docile' (Idem: 780). Then it describes the formation of shapes – the line, the point, the circle – against the empty canvas. Kandinsky's shapes are self-organised and self-referential. They generate new life on the canvas, with shapes as living beings with voices. For example, the line is 'going of its own accord'. Each element speaks for itself: 'here I am!', 'listen, listen to my secret!'. These shapes endowed with voices function as performative propositions and speech acts that refer to themselves, in linguistic terms, or constitute self-contained abstract signs, in terms of visual semiotics.

3   Theory of Art

In contrast to his poetry, where Kandinsky experimented with applying the principles of his painting practice to words, in his essays about his artworks, verbal reasoning performed the role of *auto-ekphrasis*, translating the visual sensations expressed in the paintings back into words. In addition to these two types of verbal-visual interactivity, Kandinsky's writings include a third, more important type of textual product: theoretical treatises that substantiate his artistic vision. I am referring primarily to three major books – *Concerning the Spiritual in Art* (1912), *Steps. Text of the Artist* (1918) and *Point and Line to Plane* (1926) – which lay the foundations for Kandinsky's aesthetic doctrine.

The core of Kandinsky's artistic system is the principle of 'inner necessity'. A work of art, according to him, consists of an inner and outer element. The combination of form and content is necessary and indivisible. As he remarks: 'the relationships in art are not necessarily ones of outward form, but are founded on the inner sympathy of meaning' (Kandinsky, 1977: 2). Based on this guiding principle, he builds an integral system of 'basic elements of painting'. These elements constitute the language of art. One of his early writings is characteristically called 'Farbensprache' ('Language of Form and Colour', 1904–1909). Speaking of the 'deep kinship of the arts', he dwells upon the semantic indefiniteness of colours in painting, as opposed to shapes, which are definite and able to exist independently. Translating his reasoning on colours into verbal language, he notes (Idem: 3):

> A never-ending extent of red can only be seen in the mind; when the word red is heard, the colour is evoked without definite boundaries. If such are necessary, they have deliberately to be imagined. But red, such as it is seen in the mind and not by the eye, exercises at once a definite and an indefinite impression on the soul, and produces spiritual harmony. I say 'indefinite', because in itself it has no suggestion of warmth or cold, such attributes having to be imagined for it afterwards, as modifications of the original 'redness'. I say 'definite', because spiritual harmony exists without any need for such subsequent attributes of warmth or cold.

Indeed, from a linguistic point of view, terms such as *red, blue* or *yellow* are words with no definite referent. They refer not to objects, volumes or surfaces, but to perceptions, to certain transitions. According to Nelson Goodman's *grue/bleen* paradox 'emeralds, for example, are never blue, nor are they green, they are grue (1983: 74). Virginia Woolf describes this transition in a famous passage from her novel *Orlando*: 'Green in nature is one thing, green in literature another' (2000: 13). The painter or writer feels acutely the materiality and immateriality of colour, so that colour becomes a variable, whereas form remains constant. It is only through keen intuition that an artist can 'attain the artistic truth', according to Kandinsky. A picture for him is a phenomenon affecting the spectator using the inner meaning expressed by the totality of outer pictorial elements.

A good illustration of this principle is Kandinsky's analysis of the 'point to plane' as a basic artistic element in verbal-visual retranslations. The geometric point is a primary element of graphical language. The point, Kandinsky elucidates, represents an incorporeal, invisible concept, which, 'considered in terms of substance, equals zero' (1947: 25). However, this zero conceals various attributes of human nature. That is, the point has semantic content for us: 'We think of the geometric point in relation to the greatest possible brevity, i.e., to the highest degree of restraint, which, nevertheless, speaks' (Ibidem). Imagined as a union of silence and speech, the point is given its material form in writing. As a punctuation mark, the full stop belongs to language and signifies silence, a break in speech. Yet in writing, the point is merely a sign serving a useful purpose. As a rule, we do not attribute a particular inner meaning to the point.

Meanwhile, Kandinsky maintains, the point can be seen as a symbol with an 'inner sound'. Reconsidering the point in terms of artistic value, the artist actualises its inner properties and semantic potential. Kandinsky provides an example of intersemiotic recoding, or coding a narrative in musical terms (Idem: 27):

> 1. Let the point be moved out of its practical-useful situation into an impractical, that is, an illogical, position.
>
> Today I am going to the movies.
> Today I am going. To the movies
> Today I. Am going to the movies
>
> It is apparent that it is possible to view the transposition of the point in the second sentence still as a useful one with an emphasis on the destination, the stress on the intention, loud fanfare.
> In the third sentence the illogical, in pure form, is at work. This may be explained as a typographical error – the inner value of the point flashes forth for a moment and is immediately extinguished.
>
> 2. Let the point be moved so far out of its practical-useful situation that it loses its connection with the flow of the sentence.

Today I am going to the movies

•

In this case, the point must have considerable open space around it, so that its sound may have resonance. In spite of this, its sound remains delicate – overpowered by the sound of the print surrounding it.

Finally, Kandinsky's line of reasoning culminates in a typographical analogy (Idem: 28):

As the surrounding space and the size of the point are increased, the sound of the print is reduced and the sound of the point becomes clearer and more powerful.

•

Thus arises a double sound – print-point – besides the practical-useful association. It is a balancing of two worlds which can never meet or agree. This is a useless, revolutionary state of affairs – the print is shaken by a foreign body which cannot be brought into any relation to it.

This is how, according to Kandinsky, the world of abstract painting comes into being. The point as an elementary sense-distinctive sign, which in itself is full of potential meanings, serves as the starting point for building the alphabet of art. The point as a material and pragmatic sign falls short of its own materiality in favour of its symbolic *inner meaning* as a dematerialised unit of visual grammar. It then becomes rematerialised in Kandinsky's actual pictorial techniques, colliding with different types of materials and compositions.

By means of intersemiotic self-translation from verbal discourse into visual language and vice versa, the artist transmutes mental concepts into their inner plastic form, so that both exist in a common bitextual space. Thus, he seeks to revolutionise Gotthold Lessing's *Laocoon* model of the non-translatability of media in the arts. In Kandinsky's model, verbal and visual content become mutually recoded and transmuted. In line with the Futurist revolution of the word, the radical nature of the artistic revolution carried out by Kandinsky in the sphere of pictorial form was a *revolution of the sign*, primarily of the aesthetic sign as unity of form and content.

TRANSITION 1

Experiments with Time and Language: Alexander Vvedensky's and Gertrude Stein's Poetic Grammar

> It is understood by this time that everything is the same except composition and time, composition and the time of the composition and the time in the composition.
> GERTRUDE STEIN

∴

> Maiden:
> Do you even know what time means?
>
> Ef:
> I'm not acquainted with time.
> Will I see anyone wear it?
> I can't touch it or anything.
> It's fiction, it's an ideal.
> ALEXANDER VVEDENSKY

∵

Along with the linguistic turn of the 1910–30s, and the accompanying revolution in poetic language, there was also a seismic shift in how major metaphysical issues such as space and time were reconceptualised, particularly in their relation to linguistic representation. The first three decades of the 20th century were marked by a particular emphasis on time and temporality in literature and science. In 1908, the British philosopher J.M.E. McTaggart published the paper 'The Unreality of Time', which attracted much public attention with its ideas of the unreality, non-linearity, and self-inconsistency of time. This work had a huge impact on the philosophy of mind and language represented by the Cambridge school (Bertrand Russell, George Moore, Ludwig Wittgenstein) as well as on Modernist literature, particularly the Bloomsbury Group. Among the philosophers who reflected upon, and criticised the established notions of time were Henri Bergson, George H. Mead, Edmund Husserl, Martin Heidegger, and Alfred Whitehead. In 1927, the Irish engineer and natural philosopher John W. Dunne published the book *An Experiment with Time*, which contained his theory of the 'serial' perception of time. The same year saw the publication of a highly influential artistic essay by Wyndham Lewis, *Time and Western Man*. In addition to such famous Modernist prose narratives about temporality such as those of Marcel Proust, James Joyce or Thomas Mann, the concept of time found its way into the language of experimental avant-garde poetry. We have already discussed its importance for Khlebnikov's poetic philosophy and language project. Most interesting in this respect are the cases of two seemingly unrelated authors – the American writer Gertrude Stein and the Russian poet Alexander Vvedensky – whose poetry posed very similar challenges to language as a means of spatio-temporal perception and, consequently, to the representation of time and tense in poetic grammar.

The poetic legacy of Alexander Vvedensky, a major poet of the late Russian avant-garde, has not been studied in a broad international context. His collected poems were only published in English in 2013. Several attempts have been made to compare his poetry with the European drama of the absurd (Eugène Ionesco and Samuel Beckett) and French Surrealism (Henri Michaux, René Daumal and Tristan Tzara). However, these comparisons have only revealed the stark differences between Vvedensky's poetics and similar poetic techniques in Western European avant-gardes or have limited themselves to specific parallels in terms of the use of poetic devices. In this interim chapter, I will consider Vvedensky's poetics alongside the literary experiments of Gertrude Stein, a leading figure in experimental literature of the early 20th century, whose sustained engagement with the concept of time in poetry mirrors Vvedensky's.

There were no biographical or cultural contacts whatsoever between these two authors (except that they were contemporaries who shared much common knowledge about the philosophy of time of the early 20th century), so my analysis will not concern the issue of direct influence, but will rather propose a typological and contrastive investigation of both authors' poetic grammar. I will specifically address the issues of time and temporality, which figure prominently in the writing of both Vvedensky and Stein and have a radical effect on the language of their poetry. I will argue that the linguistic experimentation of their writings is largely dependent on their reconsideration of time as a philosophical category. By comparing the conceptions of time in these two authors who pushed poetic experimentation to the limits of linguistic expressibility, I will explore the common ground in the avant-garde's creative attitude towards temporality through the lens of human language.

1 Alexander Vvedensky's 'Chinarian' Language

The most radical of the Oberiuty circle of poets (who also called themselves the Chinari, the 'titled ones'),[1] Alexander Vvedensky progressed from the trans-sense glossolalia of his early poems in the 1920s to alogism and nonsense as a 'poetic critique of reason' in his later poetic oeuvre (1930s). His first poems followed the poetic model of Velimir Khlebnikov and Ilia Zdanevich, with zaum-like text fragments imitating children's speech, sectarian glossolalia, folk spells, cryptic writing, and foreign speech (see verse fragments such as: 'ны моя ны'; 'шопышин А шопышин А шопышин А шопышин а'; 'дошка дошечкА дошка'; 'ТАКУШТО каК ШИНКИЛЬ'; 'ИКРАЙБЕЛЫ'; 'ХНОК'; 'огл агнь пропе'). After 1926, glossolalic poetry gave way to what Vvedensky himself called 'a play of nonsense' ('игра в бессмыслицу'). The poem 'Shaved all together Rostislav', dedicated to fellow OBERIU writer Daniil Kharms, contains absurd questions like 'What do THESE SCRIPTURES mean?' or 'will the language invest?', and the characters 'do not say unnecessary words'. This is a work that wants to verify the real limits of language and meaning. What decomposes here is not the words themselves, but the connections between their meanings, just as the world surrounding the poet disintegrates into infinitesimal points of experience. The glossolalia as vocal utopia[2] beyond the *Logos* seen in the early avant-garde is taken over by *Alogism*, a secret weapon against the overly rational, totalising and totalitarian Logos of Stalinist Russia.

As a poet and thinker, Vvedensky takes as his premise the fact that human language is limited in its ability to convey the content of the world, just as it is unable to adequately express the essence of such processes as time, death, the human 'I', and the like. The play 'A Certain Quantity of Conversations' features what looks like a remark from the author: 'Consider the poverty of the language. Consider impoverished thoughts' (in Ostashevsky 2006: 29). Behind that 'poverty of language' Vvedensky sees the abyss of the meaningless (he calls it 'the star of meaninglessness' in the play 'God may be around': 'the star of meaninglessness shines, / it alone is fathomless') (2013: 65). It is 'fathomless' because it presupposes an infinitely contradictory, or as it were, 'bottomless' understanding. In ordinary communication contradictions are unacceptable – meaning must have a 'bottom'.

The Chinari conceived of language as a model for the world, echoing an argument made by Ludwig Wittgenstein (whose work they were hardly familiar

---

1 English translations of various works by OBERIU members are collected in Ostashevsky (2006).
2 Michel De Certeau (1996) conceptualises glossolalia in terms of voice phenomenology.

with) in his *Tractatus:* 'The boundaries of my language mean the boundaries of my world'. The Chinarian philosopher Yakov Druskin remarked: '[...] Language and the world converge'. 'What is language for, what is its function?', asks another OBERIU philosopher, Leonid Lipavsky, in his 'Conversations', and replies to himself: 'It cuts the world into pieces and, therefore, subjugates it' (2000: 188). The linguistic model of the world that arises from such 'cutting' is perceived as inconsistent with the incoherent world accessed through the senses.

Vvedensky's 'feeling of the incoherence of the world and the fragmentation of time' manifests itself in poetic language. The poetic (rhythmic) organisation of language is an aesthetic phenomenon. Rhythm in poetic speech expresses the laws of correlation, the alternation of linguistic elements. As with any poetic system, the system of language and the presence of rhythm in Vvedensky's verse have a sense-making function. However, in his poetry, the elements of language lead to the destruction of the system, rather than its organisation. Every structure is an anti-structure. Viktor Shklovsky's principle of estrangement is brought to its logical, or should we say *alogical*, limit, where language itself becomes estranged. The critic Alexander Skidan calls Vvedensky's poetic principle a 'trans-formation': 'Vvedensky's poetic machines are configured in such a way that they accelerate progress vertiginously, forcing language to act deliriously and to approach its very limits (producing asyntactical, agrammatical, asemantic enunciations)' (2015: http).

The word in Vvedensky's poetry acts as an empty sign. It does not condense the semantic features of the world (as, for example, in Khlebnikov's or Mandelstam's poetry), but rather 'cuts out' these features out of the world, leaving in their stead an empty space, pure potency. There is no associative principle at work here: words are connected to each other not by association, but through *dis*sociation, that is, the decomposition of meanings. For Mandelstam, 'familiarising words with each other' was the central poetic task. For Vvedensky, the principle of 'unfamiliarity of words with each other' is more significant. In Mandelstam's and Khlebnikov's verse, paronymic attraction brings lexically distant words together; in Vvedensky's poetry of the absurd, the paronymic attraction present at the formal level accentuates the lexical disunity of words, as in this excerpt from his play 'Frother':

> И если жизнь протянется,
> То скоро не останется
> Ни сокола ни волоска.
> Знать смерть близка.
> Знать глядь тоска (Vvedensky, 2010: 211)

> And should my life drag on,
> Neither a falcon, nor a tuft of hair
> Will remain anywhere.
> This means death is at hand.
> This means hello boredom (in Ostashevsky, 2006: 17)

The function of 'real art' ('реальное искусство'[3]), according to Vvedensky, is a return to a 'tongueless', 'languageless' state. Vvedensky's word is an empty and pure sign, not because it does not mean anything (as in the case of Kruchenykh's zaum[4]), but because it opens up a deep semantic dimension – an abyss without a bottom. Vvedensky's technique of poetic alogism is explained (to the extent that it can be explained) by Yakov Druskin in a reflection upon names that lack the attribute they denote: 'A word that does not mean what it means – that is, perhaps, the main thing, formally, eidetically, the main thing that is in common between us <i.e., Vvedensky and Druskin – V.F.)>. [...] This is a designation of what it signifies through the designation of what it does not signify – which is the object of linguistics, logic, gnoseology, theology, and poetry' (1999: 124). Vvedensky's poetry is precisely about this paradoxical semantic situation – a 'semiotic silence', as Druskin calls it. It is not the meaning that is significant, but the intervals and the boundaries between meanings. Semantic remoteness, or disunity, between two distant meanings of two adjacent words within the poetic line is more important than the semantic proximity, or unity, of these meanings: 'Will the stream run a long distance / from the word *understood* to the word *flower?*' (Vvedensky, 2013: 109)

As I have demonstrated, early Russian avant-garde experiments with language transformed the Christian idea of the creation of the world from nothing into the idea of the creation of the world from language (*creatio ex lingua*). The very concept of the *world* undergoes a transformation, and, as a result, the relation of language – or the word – to the world changes as well. Andrey Bely's word creates an imaginary 'third world' of symbols. Khlebnikov's revolution of the word is aimed at transfiguring reality. Alexander Vvedensky and his fellow OBERIU writers go even further, perceiving language as an obstacle to understanding – let alone to creating – the world. The creative potential of language is called into question. The Chinari's creative act amounts to, as it were, the 'de-creation' of language, the containment of its energetic mechanism, a 'struggle with meaning' and a 'poetic critique of reason', to quote Vvedensky's

---

[3] OBERIU stands for 'Association for Real Art'.
[4] On Kruchenykh's zaum within the context of conceptual poetry see Janecek (1996), Dworkin (2004), Chernyakov (2008).

notebook. But, oddly enough, language as *Logos* does not disappear even under such extreme poetic conditions. It is born again in the guise of nonsense, it is incarnated, according to Yakov Druskin's metaphysical overview of the Chinari group (1989: http):

> Nonsense is not relative. It is an absolute reality – it is the Logos made flesh. This personal Logos itself is illogical, just like His incarnation. But this nonsense became an understanding of my existence. It is impossible to understand nonsense: understood nonsense is no longer nonsense. Nor can we seek the meaning of nonsense; the meaning of nonsense is the same, or even worse, nonsense. 'The star of nonsense' is that which cannot be heard with the ears, seen with the eyes, understood with the mind.

2 Discontinuity of Time, Mind, and Language in Stein's and Vvedensky's Poetics

Scholars have noted that the concept of *time*, along with the concepts of *death* and *God*, are at the core of Vvedensky's linguistic experimentation.[5] Likewise, the interrelation of language and time in Gertrude Stein's writings is the subject of a valuable book by C.F. Copeland (1975). Beyond that, however, the issues of temporality and language in both authors have not been sufficiently elucidated, either in isolation or in comparison.

A recurrent theme in both Stein's and Vvedensky's poetry is the *transformation of objects* in time and in language. This topic is highlighted in Vvedensky's lines from his verse play 'God May Be Around': 'In our posthumous rotation / the one salvation is transformation' (2013: 61). It is not the things themselves that matter, but the changing of things into other things, the very act of metamorphosis – and this applies to both authors. This principle recalls the work of Bertrand Russell, a major philosophical influence on Stein, and his claim that 'the *world* consists of *events*, not of *things* that endure for a long time and have changing properties' (1963: 142–143). Similarly, in Stein's poetic vision, words do not describe reality, they *constitute* reality. Consider the following passage from *Tender Buttons*: 'A hurt mended stick, a hurt mended cup, a hurt mended article of exceptional relaxation and annoyance, a hurt mended, hurt and mended is so necessary that no mistake is intended' (Stein, 1984: 183). What is

---

5 See Revzina (1978) and Pavlov (2010).

important here is not the description of a *stick*, a *cup* or any other *object*, nor the fact of their presence, but the *events* that unfold in the grammatical world. The *stick* and the *cup* are as eventful as their properties –'hurtness', 'mendedness' etc.

Stein's experimental grammar is akin to Ludwig Wittgenstein's language games.[6] According to Wittgenstein, Russell's disciple in logical philosophy, the meaning of the word is its use. His 'grammar of utterances' studies the usage of words in different language games. For instance, in his response to Saint Augustine's question 'What is time?' (quite relevant for Gertrude Stein, too), Wittgenstein (1958: 26–27) proposes a purely grammatical analysis of the issue. He invites us to consider how the word time is actually used in language and speech. For instance, when somebody asks 'What time is it?', or when somebody exclaims 'O time transient!', or when somebody laments 'It's no use killing time!', the speaker is merely playing language games, and the word 'time' acquires a new meaning every time it is used.

The transformational and transient nature of Stein's and Vvedensky's grammatical logic corresponds to the transience of mind and thought in their vision. The focus on fluidity in Vvedensky's works correlates with Stein's focus on processuality. Here, we should consider the possibility of common influences on both authors – the philosophies of Henri Bergson, William James, and Alfred Whitehead, which conceptualise the world in terms of event, process and duration. For example, William James, Gertrude Stein's professor at Radcliffe College, claims that the mind is always in the process of perpetual change. No state of consciousness can be repeated or identified with any preceding state, in his view.

Vvedensky's and Stein's interest in issues of mind and cognition derives from their general gnoseological attitude toward language. Vvedensky aspired to a 'poetic critique of reason', according to his first critic Yakov Druskin, who called Vvedensky's method 'poetic gnoseology' (2000: 334). Similarly, Stein rejects the logic of scientific knowledge in favour of a new, poetic logic, musing in *Poetry and Grammar*: 'And so I went on with this exceeding struggle of knowing really knowing what a thing was really knowing it knowing anything I was seeing anything I was feeling so that its name could be something, by its name coming to be a thing in itself as it was but would not be anything just and only as a name' (1984: 145). The two poets raise the essential issue of the limits of language and consciousness. Meanwhile, the discontinuity of language and

---

6   See a detailed and insightful study of this topic in Perloff (1996).

time is tackled differently by Stein and Vvedensky. On this topic, Vvedensky writes in his *Gray Notebook* from 1932–33 (2009: 9):

> All that I am trying to write here about time is, strictly speaking, untrue. The reasons for this number two. (1) Any person who has not understood time at least a little bit – and only one who has not understood it has understood it at all – must cease to understand everything that exists. (2) Our human logic and our language do not in any way correspond to time, neither in its elementary, nor in its complex understanding. Our logic and our language skid along the surface of time.

Therefore, Vvedensky claims, there should be a new logic capable of describing the deeper layers of time. He endeavours to reconstruct time as such, independent of its linguistic denominations. Convinced that existing logical connections are invalid, he seeks new types of connections in his poetry. According to him, these should express his 'basic feeling of the world's incoherence and time's disintegration' (cit. in Lipavsky, 2000: 186).

Stein, too, is not satisfied by the popular 'journalistic' concept of time, being convinced of its 'falsity'. Time as a complex natural phenomenon plays a crucial role in her writing process, according to two 1925 essays ('Composition and Explanation' and 'Natural Phenomena'). However, she differs from Vvedensky in her preoccupation with the 'current moment' of thought and speech, which is as if statically suspended in the present. Hence the pronounced tautological nature of her poetry and prose: a verb is followed by another verb, but no action is taking place; only the static present moment is emphasised.

3   Repetition in Poetry: the Serial Grammar of Time

The issue of time is closely associated with the topic of memory. Vvedensky sceptically declares in *The Gray Notebook*: 'I do not put my trust in memory, nor in imagination. Time is the only thing that does not exist without us. It devours everything that exists outside us. Here falls the night of the mind. Time ascends above us like a star' (2009: 8). Likewise, in composing her poetic 'portraits', Gertrude Stein insists that the artist should not recollect the features of a model, landscape, or still life. Instead of the mechanisms of memory, a true artist should activate the mechanisms of oblivion, as she writes in *The Geographical History of America*: 'And so the human mind is like not being in danger but being killed, there is no remembering, no there is no remembering, and no forgetting because you have to remember to forget no there is none in any human mind' (Stein, 1998: 374). Stein tries to write as if there were no patterns of memory; poetic knowledge should be based exclusively on experiencing the 'present moment'. Freed from memory, logical contradictions are not resolved, as they either go unnoticed, or their two constituent parts 'do not remember each other', as in these lines from 'Portraits and Prayers': 'One is frightened in being one being living. One is not frightened in being one being living. One is frightened again. One is again and again not frightened' (Idem: 221). Memory, in Stein's vision, is an enemy of creative thought. In any moment free of memory, a person reveals their creative essence, she notes in her essay 'What Are Master-pieces and Why Are There So Few of Them': 'At any moment when you are you you are you without the memory of yourself because if you remember yourself while you are you you are not for purposes of creating you' (Stein, 1984: 149).

Stein and Vvedensky differ in their conception of memory. The former explains the falsity of memory by pointing to the state of things in the new reality and contemporary avant-garde art, whereas the latter denies the very possibility of art and the mind having anything in common with memory, due to the disintegration of time and the incoherence of things. As for memory, according to Vvedensky and Stein, it has no relevance to the process of writing poetry; repetition ceases to be tautological. The same word repeated twice is no longer the same word. Repetition plays a key role in Stein's writings, determining the specific poetic grammar of her texts. 'I believe in repetition. Yes. Always and always. Must write the eternal hymn of repetition', she notes in her diaries (cit. in Franken, 2000: 122). The repetition of the same element (phonological, graphical, morphological, or lexical) is not mechanical. The repeated element in a series always appears in a unique syntactical position, which cannot be repeated twice, as in this excerpt from a poem called 'An Elucidation' (cit. in Dydo, 1993: 431):

> A place for everything and everything in its place
> In place in place of everything, in a place
>
> Again search for me.
> She looked for me at me.
> May we seat.
> May we be having a seat
> May we be seated
> May I see
> May I see
> Martha

May I see Martha
May I see.

May I see.

Every little word occupies a particular 'place' in the line and in the poem. The phrase *May I see*, with its five repetition, occupies a unique place each time because its surroundings are different.

A similar kind of repetition can be found in Vvedensky's poetry, as in this poem dated 1934 called 'Rug Hydrangea' (2013: 113):

What scares me is that I move
not the way that do bugs that are beetles,
or butterflies and baby strollers
and not the way that do bugs that are spiders.

[...]

I'm frightened that I'm not the grass that is grass,
I'm frightened that I'm not a candle.
I'm frightened that I'm not the candle that is grass
to this I have answered,
and the trees sway back and forth in an instant.

The 'grass that is grass', which in the Russian original is the same word 'trava' reiterated twice, indicates that the first appearance of the word stands apart in time from the second. The moment the second word is pronounced, its meaning is already transformed due to the flow of time being interrupted every time meaning is perceived.[7]

This kind of repetition was of crucial significance to the Russian poet. According to his friend Yakov Druskin's memoirs, whenever he recited this poem, Vvedensky would accentuate the transposition of the words *candle* and *grass*. The poet himself later commented: 'There are many repetitions here, but I think I need them all, if you look carefully, they reiterate differently, as if giving an explanation. And the pairs 'candle that is grass' and 'grass that is candle' are very important for me personally' (cit. in Lipavsky, 2000: 204). The goal of these reiterated sequences is to fragment the perception of temporal sequences. The repeated elements are not functionally identical because they

---

7 On Vvedensky's repetitive patterns see Tsvigun et al. (2021).

occupy structurally different positions. This principle can also be illustrated by an example from Stein's *Ida: A novel*, where the word 'morning' is repeated three times and followed by the very similar 'mourning'. The repeated elements uncover the structural difference of parts of the poetic text, making it more evident (laid bare, as Shklovsky would put it), and the accumulation of repetitions results in the semantic diversity of the text (Stein, 1984: 404):

> The spider says
> Listen to me I, I am a spider, you must not mistake me for the sky, the sky red at night is a sailor's delight, the sky red in the morning is a sailor's warning, you must not mistake me for the sky, I am I, I am a spider and in the morning any morning I bring sadness and mourning and at night if they see me at night I bring them delight ...

Stein also proposed a specific kind of repetition that she called 'insistence'. By this, she meant cases where the repeated element undergoes a slight change, a minimal but marked difference in each new series. The structure of these repetitions suggests that in Stein's and Vvedensky's texts the logical connections are arranged not in a hierarchal, but in a serial way. William Carlos Williams, who in his 1930 essay called Stein's poetic technique 'iteration', highlighted a kind of repetition unique to her language (2000: 196) that could be termed 'seriality' in logic. In the field of philosophy, John W. Dunne (1927) examined the phenomena of arts and physics and discovered a special state that certain objects fall into – a state of perpetual and multidimensional process. A few decades later, in the 1960s, the American linguist John R. Ross (1970) analysed English sentences of the type 'I think that...'. He showed that such phrases can be reiterated infinitely. Stein made the same discovery in poetry, for example in her famous line from the poem 'Sacred Emily': 'Rose is a rose is a rose is a rose'. This series of words is potentially infinite in semantic terms. Such iteration is self-sufficient: each new predicate refers to the following or preceding one and requires no logical coherence. Stein's 'serial grammar in repetition' is thus analogous to Dunne's idea of a 'serial universe'.

4 Verbs and Other Tense Forms: Tools of (Non-)Understanding Time

Alexander Vvedensky and Gertrude Stein share a radical attitude towards the word as such. Stein prefers an abundance of meanings achieved with a minimum of words: 'It takes a tremendous amount of inner necessity to invent even one word' (1984: 142). She is passionate about the many meanings a word can acquire in slightly changed contexts. Vvedensky, meanwhile, respects what he calls the 'poverty of language',[8] its inability to express meanings. Every word for him is an obstacle to understanding, as the system of words comprising language prevents pure communication with the world. Another of Wittgenstein's ideas – that of the limits of language enclosing the limits of our world – is relevant to Vvedensky. For him, 'real art' opens up the possibility of 'positive non-understanding'. To understand such concepts as *time*, *death* and *god*, we need to start from non-understanding and question the ability of language to refer to the real world (Vvedensky, 2009: 7):

> Before every word I put the question: what does it mean, and over every word I place the mark of its tense. Where is my dear soul Masha, and where are her banal hands, and her eyes and other parts? Where does she wander murdered or alive? I haven't the strength. Who? I. What? haven't the strength. I'm alone as a candle. I'm seven minutes past five alone 8 minutes past five, as nine minutes past five a candle 10 minutes past five. A moment as if never. And four o'clock also. The window, also. But everything is the same.

As we can see from these reflections, temporality for Vvedensky interferes with the discontinuity inherent to the text, making the true meanings of the words unclear. The word 'candle', as in the example cited above, ceases to produce the same meaning as it did just a moment ago, once interrupted by the fragmentation of time. The word 'candle' is thus a solitary entity. Pronounced several times in a row, like the word 'rose' in Stein's famous iteration, it remains the same, but its meaning changes with the flow of time. Each new moment of perception makes it a new entity with no logical connection to the previous minute. The dramatic tension in the reader's non-understanding of a word takes place due to the rupture between the sameness of form and the difference of apprehension. However, this drama gives way to a 'deeper', 'generalised' and 'wild non-understanding', in Vvedensky's words. If we try to write something about time, he insists, or even the non-understanding of time, we can at least 'try to fix those few positions of our superficial experience of time'. 'Woe to us who ponder time', he laments. He then argues: 'with the growth of this non-understanding it will become clear to you and me that there is no woe,

---

8   A phrase from Vvedensky's poetic dialogue 'A Certain Amount of Conversations': 'Respect the circumstances of place. Respect what happens. But nothing takes place. Respect the poverty of language. Respect low thoughts', cited from the translation by Thomas Epstein (http).

neither to us, nor to those pondering, nor to time' (Vvedensky, 2009: 9). This is what he calls 'positive non-understanding', or the 'star of meaninglessness'.[9]

Going back to the question of grammar, we should ask ourselves: how are time and temporality categorised in a poetic world devoid of temporal discontinuity? The objects and properties expressed by nouns, pronouns and adjectives are no longer stable, their identity is falsified. The only trustworthy element remaining is perpetual movement – which is better conveyed by verbs. The most interesting shared feature of Vvedensky's and Stein's poetics is their treatment of the verb as a grammatical category.

According to Stein's essay 'Poetry and Grammar', one should avoid or reduce the use of nouns in poetry: 'Beside the nouns and the adjectives, there are verbs and adverbs' (1984: 126). The advantage of verbs over nouns is that the former are in 'constant movement' and express more intensely the dynamics of the present moment. Moreover, she explains, 'verbs and adverbs are more interesting. In the first place they have one very nice quality and that is that they can be so mistaken' (Ibidem). Mistakes in poetry are good because they open pathways for the endless production of meaning: 'Beside being able to be mistaken and to make mistakes verbs can change to look like themselves or to look like something else, they are, so to speak on the move and adverbs move with them and each of them find themselves not at all annoying but very often very much mistaken. That is the reason any one can like what verbs can do' (Idem: 127). Why, then, can verbs 'be mistaken'? Because they are better at challenging the law of logical connections, since names are more fixed in their meaning. It is not accidental that all scientific logic and rationality is based on the nominative lexicon of language. Verbs, on the other hand, are logically freer and less predictable.

Gerunds and participles are frequently used in Stein's writings, conveying grammatical meanings of 'movement' and 'continuity'. In her quest to capture movement in its indefiniteness, she radicalises the analytical nature of English grammar by amplifying gerundial derivatives (*meaning, liking, knowing*), and by distorting substantives to resemble verb forms (*loving* instead of *love*, *timing* instead of *time* etc.)

The present participle produces the effect of decelerating or extending syntactical rhythm. Almost the entirety of her novel *The Making of Americans* (1925) is based on the use of these forms, which correspond to the author's attitude towards 'present immediacy'. Gerunds, for example, are conceptualised as a kind of static movement, a momentary snapshot of a process. By

---

9   A phrase from Vvedensky's play 'God May Be Around': 'The star of meaninglessness shines, / it alone is fathomless' (2013: 113).

substantivising the process, the gerund encloses it in temporal brackets, like Husserl's *epoche,* and makes the process easier to perceive, as the following phrase from *The Making of Americans* demonstrates: 'Some slowly come to be repeating louder and more clearly the bottom being that makes them. Listening to repeating, knowing being in everyone who ever was or will be living slowly came to be in me a louder and louder pounding' (Stein, 1995: 700).

The preponderance of continuous tenses is aimed at reproducing the making of the text itself. Performing this in poetic writing, Stein fills semantic and grammatical gaps not available in everyday language. As Benjamin Whorf observed, in the Hopi language, time is represented as 'real time'. While English has regular forms such as 'summer', 'September', 'sunset' and other substantives denoting time, Hopi demonstrates the possibility of thinking the quality of 'becoming later and later'. Time is conceptualised as 'a cyclic phase similar to an earlier phase in that ever-later-becoming duration' (Whorf, 1956: 142). Thoughts and concepts expressed in Hopi, much like in Stein's writing, have a serial character. Reality is seen as a series of events, and grammar adequately reproduces this eventfulness.

As for Vvedensky, he also thought that verbs were more appropriate for his poetic vision: 'As we understand them, verbs exist as if all by themselves'. Besides, verbs are 'mobile', 'they are flowing' and thus they 'resemble something truly existing' (Vvedensky, 2009: 12). Meanwhile, even if verbs, according to Vvedensky, 'have time', they also are subject to capture by the intangible and elusive time (Idem: 6):

> I thought about why only verbs are
> subjugated to the hour, minute and year,
> while house, forest and sky, like Mongols of some kind,
> have suddenly been released from time.
> I thought about it and I understood. We all know it,
> that action becomes an insomniac China,
> the actions are dead, they stretch out like dead men,
> and now we decorate them with garlands.
> Their mobility is a lie, their density a swindle,
> and a dead fog devours them.

Thus, whereas for Stein verbs supercede nouns as a better and purer expression of the world, for Vvedensky even verbs that are much 'friendlier' to the movement of time 'live out their life in front of our eyes' (Idem: 12). He is sceptical about verbs because they claim to be a true reflection of time in the structure of language. Vvedensky's standpoint is that human logic and human language do not correspond to any known concept of time, and this is implemented in his poetry through various linguistic devices, for example, by the abnormal collocations of verbs and adverbial forms in these lines from 'An Invitation for Me to Think' (2013: 112):

> We're tickled by what is unknown,
> the inexplicable's our friend,
> we see the forest walking backward,
> yesterday stands all around today.

Actions in his poems are illogical and useless, they cannot be called actions anymore, because 'action' is a noun, and therefore does not exist. For example, the sentence 'A person put on a hat and walked outside' is not acceptable, according to Vvedensky. Instead, he considers the following sentence to be more appropriate and 'real': 'He put on his hat and it was getting light and the (blue) sky took off like an eagle'. In addition, he comments: 'Events do not coincide with time. Time has eaten the event. Not even the bones are left' (Vvedensky, 2009: 13).

Juxtaposing the two conceptions of time and language together with their realisation in the poetry of Alexander Vvedensky and Gertrude Stein demonstrates that the two independent poetic systems share an interest in temporality and the essential role of time in poetic experimentation. For both authors, time has to be conceptualised differently from its everyday understanding and scientific treatment. Their approaches differ in their degree of scepticism about the ordinary understanding of time. For Stein, time can be understood only in the form of 'present immediacy', whereas for Vvedensky, time is unknowable by means of logical language conceptualisation, and can only be non-understood. Stein's continuous conception of time is opposed to Vvedensky's discontinuous vision of temporality. What is common in these two authors, however, is a striving for a radical reconsideration of how language conceptualises time and the recognition that poetic grammar can be recreated in order to overcome ordinary language restraints in thinking about time. Several decades later, a specific poetic grammar and poetic language was the subject of scientific linguistic inquiry in the studies of the Russian-American scholar Roman Jakobson. I will address his theory in the next Transition chapter, right after I explore the specifically American tradition of revolutionising language in avant-garde poetry of the 1910–30s.

PART 2

A Turn to Language in American Modernist and Avant-Garde Writing

CHAPTER 6

Language Arts: the Early American Avant-Garde in Verbal Art

>
> Curie
> of the laboratory
>   of vocabulary
> she crushed
> the tonnage
> of consciousness
> congealed to phrases
>   to extract
> a radium of the word
>   MINA LOY[1]

∴

Words forming themselves in black on white –
A living language.
[…]
Life and death relax –
O silent melting language of eternity!
    MAN RAY

∴

---

1 This 1924 poem by Mina Loy, titled 'Gertrude Stein' and dedicated to her, bears a striking similarity to Vladimir Mayakovsky's language in his 'Talk with a Tax Collector about Poetry', written in 1926, with its images of 'crushing the tonnage of language' and 'extracting the radium of the word': 'Поэзия – / та же добыча радия. / В грамм добыча, / в год труды. / Изводишь / единого слова ради /тысячи тонн / словесной руды'. It is highly unlikely that the poets knew each other – Mayakovsky only came to the US in 1925. Yet the idea of the poetic word as radioactivity seems to have been in the air on both continents and in both literary traditions. This idea has continued to mesmerise experimental poets into the 21st century, as the title of Craig Dworkin's (2020) recent book suggests.

© KONINKLIJKE BRILL NV, LEIDEN, 2023 | DOI:10.1163/9789004526303_009

As a rule, the terms *avant-garde* and *avant-gardism* are used in relation to the innovative art of the interwar years (1910–1930s), and *neo-avant-garde* to postwar art (1950s and beyond). These terms are widely used with respect to the Russian avant-garde, which has become a widely known cultural period. However, these terms are less frequently used with regard to twentieth century American art. American literature of the first half of the century is more often associated with modernism,[2] and that of the second half with postmodernism. Indeed, such writers as Gertrude Stein and Ezra Pound are associated primarily with the tradition of Modernist prose and poetry, and William Burroughs and Allen Ginsberg with Postmodernist literature. But was there *an avant-garde* in the USA? Many researchers are skeptical, referring to the fact that the artistic and social radicalism characteristic of Russian or French art of the period was not as popular in countries of the English-speaking world. However, a deeper examination of the processes that took place in Anglo-American culture in the 1910–1930s, and, later, in the 1950–1970s, can lead us to a different conclusion.

If we consider the dominant feature of the avant-garde to be a socio-aesthetic challenge, a denial of the established laws of art as an institution, according to Peter Bürger (1984), or opposition to any conventional judgments, following Philippe Sers (2001), then it should be acknowledged that what happened in the transatlantic triangle London-New York-Paris between the wars was, indeed, an avant-garde.[3] At times, it even took on a very radical stance, as in the activities of the American magazines edited by Marcel Duchamp and Francis Picabia, or in the diverse activities of the Beat poets. A hallmark of the 'transatlantic' avant-garde was the revolutionisation of language in various ways – from Ezra Pound's Imagist appeal for poetic language to be a 'language of exploration' to the work of the Language School poets in the 1970s. It was the idea of reforming existing language and creating new artistic languages that made Americans keep pace with the European and Russian avant-gardes. At the same time, it was precisely the transatlantic poetics that gave rise to a special kind of migration of ideas between the two continents, building numerous bridges to create a Babelian melting pot of people, languages, and communities.[4]

---

2 See, e.g., Symons (1987).
3 Marjorie Perloff's numerous studies have persistently proved the same, cf. Perloff (2005).
4 See the collected volume in Russian on the 'Transatlantic Avant-gardes' and their theoretical writings: (Feshchenko, 2018). One of the rare examples of collecting American avant-garde poetry is Rothenberg's work (1974). Selected movements of the Anglo-American avant-garde are highlighted in the anthology by Caws (2001). On the 'transatlantic avant-gardes', see also White (2013), Lévy (2004), Murphet (2009). American avant-garde authors are among those

1   Ezra Pound: a Few Don'ts by a Language Innovator

In 1908, Ezra Weston Loomis Pound, a young professor of Romance languages and aspiring poet from Idaho, decided to leave America in search of a new life in the Old World. He arrived by transatlantic cargo ship at Gibraltar, then travelled to Venice and finally found refuge in London. These migrations coincide with the release of his first poetry collections, *A Lume Spento* and *A Quinzaine for This Yule*. Armed with this work, he entered the artistic life of the British capital and immediately launched into frenzied literary and social activity.

A beginner poet, Pound collaborated with leading literary magazines on both sides of the Atlantic – the British *English Review* and *New Age*, and Chicago's *Poetry* (as a foreign correspondent from London). In 1910, the Poets' Club in London enrolled another American member: Pound's friend Hilda Doolittle, who published under the pseudonym H. D. It was H.D.'s selection of poems that inspired Pound to transform the already fading Club into a new poetry group. In 1912, Pound published a new collection of poetry, *Ripostes*, which consisted entirely of free verse with novel imagery. At the same time, Pound, Doolittle, and Aldington began to work out their ideas about the language of new poetry. Over tea at the British Museum, they decided to inaugurate a 'movement' in poetry – Imagism. The unifying ideology for the new group, formulated by Pound at the request of Frank Stuart Flint, proposed three approaches to poetic language: '(1) Direct treatment of the "thing" whether subjective or objective. (2) To use absolutely no word that did not contribute to the presentation. (3) As regarding rhythm: to compose in sequence of the musical phrase, not in sequence of a metronome' (Flint, 1913: 199). Another manifesto-like text by Pound – 'A Few Don'ts by an Imagiste' – included a section titled 'Language'. This, it seems, is where American poetry fist became language-oriented. A few years later, in a memorial essay on Henri Gaudier-Brzeska (1916), Pound used the exact same concept that the Formalist Shklovsky had introduced before the Russian revolution – 'poetic language'.[5] Pound's Imagist and Vorticist poetry of language was, for innovative American literature, what Andrey Bely's and the Futurists' linguistic poetics was for Russian experimental writing.[6]

---

included in the anthology *Imagining Language* (Rasula et al., 1998), dedicated to language-related experiments in world literatures.

5   One of the greatest Russian influences on Pound was Wassily Kandinsky's early abstract painting. The first issue of the BLAST magazine (1914), where Pound authored a number of texts, published an essay on Kandinsky's principle of 'inner necessity', linking it to the Vorticists' principle of 'inner energy'. For Kandinsky-Pound resonances, see Brandabur (1973).

6   The author of an insightful book on Pound and linguistics, James Dowthwaite, points out that 'language is, for Pound, a multifaceted, creative process, always with the capacity to

2   Gertrude Stein: an Impelling Language

In 1917, Ezra Pound's friend, the major American modern art collector John Quinn, organised an exhibition of Vorticist artists in New York. Five years earlier, he had been one of the sponsors of the first significant exhibition of European Modernist art on the American continent – the Armory Show. This touring exhibition of European avant-garde painting and sculpture became a bridge between Paris and New York and introduced the new art of the twentieth century to America, setting in motion a literary and artistic avant-garde in the United States.

However, the first bells of the American literary avant-garde rang out before the opening of the Armory Show. They came from the pages of *Camera Work,* a magazine run by the photographer and art promoter Alfred Stieglitz. A native of New Jersey, Stieglitz travelled extensively between Europe and the United States, taking photographs that would later be considered pioneering for the art. One of his most famous photographs, titled 'The Steerage' and taken in 1907, shows the transatlantic ship that had carried the artist himself from New York to Paris. *Camera Work* published this photograph in 1911. The following year, the magazine devoted an entire issue to Henri Matisse and Pablo Picasso, whose paintings were on show at Stieglitz's 291 gallery on New York's Fifth Avenue. Alongside the images published in the issue, a strange text was printed, ostensibly an article about the two French artists, but in fact something closer to Cubism in writing than a critical essay about Cubism. The author of these extraordinary verbal portraits of Matisse and Picasso was Gertrude Stein, and that was one of her first published literary experiments. Long before she wrote literature, Stein had studied with William James and conducted experiments on the distribution of attention in the writing and speaking process. These laboratory analyses of verbal motor automatism would become a prototype for her own literary writing.

Just as in numerous other avant-garde literary experiments of the early 20th century, new movements in painting (Impressionism and Cubism) served as a model for new textualities. Gertrude Stein began creating verbal portraits after observing the painting techniques of Picasso and others in her

---

extend beyond itself. According to Pound, poetic language is, then, not an extension of ordinary speech, nor a privileged metalanguage intended to draw our attention to the function or disfunction of signs, but the ordering and patterning of images and melodies; its fundamental unit is not the word, but the image and mood to which the words refer' (2019: 73). For a comparison of Ezra Pound's and David Burliuk's poetics of the West and the East, see Oshukov (2017). On Pound's Russian contexts, see Meyers (1988), Probstein (2017a).

Paris salon. Therefore, it was not surprising that her portraits of Matisse and Picasso, in words rather than oil on canvas, appeared in Stiglitz's art magazine. Not long before, *Camera Work* had published fragments of Wassily Kandinsky's treatise *On the Spiritual in Art* discussed above, showing that the magazine's editors had a strong interest in verbal manifestations of the new art. Literary criticism also followed this trend. In 1911, Stein was introduced to a wealthy American woman, Mabel Dodge, who patronised new artists and ran a salon in Greenwich Village.

While at Dodge's villa in Italy, Stein decided to portray her new acquaintance in prose. Dodge was impressed and, upon returning to New York, ensured the publication of this 'portrait' in *Camera Work*. 'A Portrait of Mabel Dodge at the Villa Curonia' came out in 1912. The following year, Dodge herself published a critical essay entitled 'Speculations, or Post-Impressionism in Prose' in the journal *Arts and Decoration*. In it, Stein is hailed as 'the only woman in the world who has put the spirit of Post-Impressionism into prose' and a 'pioneer' in American literature. Doing with words what Picasso did with paint, she 'is impelling language to induce new states of consciousness, and in doing so language becomes with her a creative act rather than a mirror of history' (Dodge, 1913: 172). Many believe, Dodge writes, that Stein distorts the English language, but this distortion conveys the intrinsic nature of the figurativeness of language. In her 'portraits', the word is no longer tied to specific meanings, but is guided by an exquisite rhythm and cadence, which brings this literature closer to the 'pure sound of sensuous music', just as the figures in Picasso's paintings are abstracted from trivial meanings: 'In one part of her writing she made use of repetitions and the rearranging of certain words over and over, so that they became adjusted into a kind of incantation, and in listening one feels that from the combination of repeated sounds, varied ever so little, that there emerges gradually a perception of some meaning quite other than that of the contents of the phrases' (Idem: 174). Mabel Dodge's review was, in fact, a proclamation of Stein's literary style, even before the writer herself began to describe her language method in meditative essays and lectures. It is characteristic that the post-impressionist movement in painting provided Mabel Dodge with the vocabulary for describing new literary phenomena just like it had done in London for Ezra Pound, Roger Fry and Wyndham Lewis.[7]

---

7   For more on Gertrude Stein's other language experiments, see Feshchenko (2009: 277–314). On language issues in Stein's writings, see Dekoven (1983), Dydo (2003).

3 Language Arts of the American Dada

Starting in 1913, heralds of the European avant-garde began to move from Paris to New York. The first to arrive was the French-Cuban artist Francis Picabia, whose works were featured in the Armory Show. He got involved in discussions about contemporary art on the pages of *Camera Work*. His 'Amorphism Manifesto' ('Vers l'Amorphisme') declared nothing less than a 'War on form!'. Picabia convinced Stieglitz to start a new magazine, *291* (named after the gallery of the same name), where more space would be given to the interaction of painting, poetry, and essayism. The design of the magazine was supposed to be a futuristically bold verbal-visual synthesis. The publication of Guillaume Apollinaire's ideograms in the first issue from 1915 was a proclamation unifying the French and American avant-gardes. A certain Russian influence was realised through the publication of Wassily Kandinsky's theoretical essays in their first English translations.[8] It is here that Picabia printed his first machine drawings, accompanied by written comments and captions. Another young poet and graphic artist, the Mexican Marius de Zayas, published his visual poem 'Mental Reactions' (Figure 2) as a prelude to Picabia's images. The verbal outline of the poem was co-authored by the poet Agnes Ernst Meyer; together, they created what is believed to be the first visual poem in America. De Zayas also published a manifesto titled 'Simultanism', calling for a verbal expression of simultaneous thoughts and emotions. Just like the Russian Dadaist Ilia Zdanevich in the same years, he advocated for the phonograph as an appropriate device for recording new verbal art: "In literature the idea is expressed by the polyphony of simultaneous voices which say different things. Of course, printing is not an adequate medium, for succession in the medium is unavoidable and a phonograph is more suitable" (cit. in Tashjian, 1975: 33). However, De Zayas's visual poem demonstrated that the desired effect of non-linearity and alogism could be achieved on paper without the use of a phonograph. Another example of this is the 'explosive' poem 'Femme' by De Zayas, printed next to Picabia's 'talking' drawing 'Voilà ELLE' (Figure 3). The authors of *291* magazine were confident that they were 'discovering America' anew, this time through new art and new poetry, which no longer had to imitate their European counterparts.

Following the scandal surrounding the painting 'Nude Descending the Stairs', exhibited at the Armory Show, the French artist Marcel Duchamp, who had moved from Paris to New York, became perhaps the main 'discoverer'

---

8   For Kandinsky's role in the American literary avant-garde, see Levin (1979).

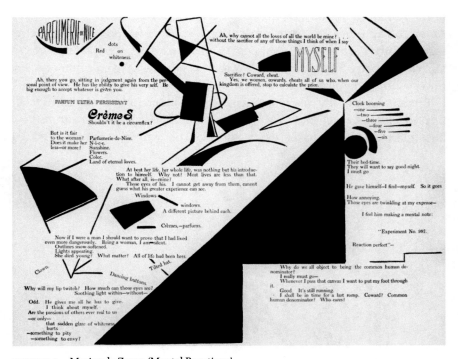

FIGURE 2   Marius de Zayas. 'Mental Reactions'

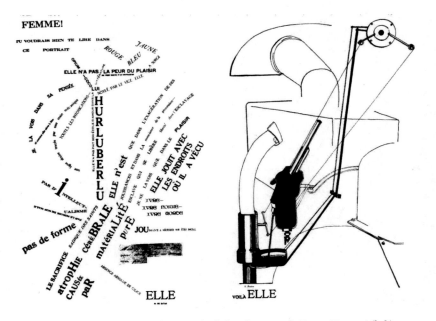

FIGURE 3   Francis Picabia. 'Voilà ELLE' (right) and Marius de Zayas. 'Femme' (left).

of the American avant-garde in the eyes of the progressive New York public. Among other things, Duchamp's magazine *The Blind Man* printed some of the first American proto-conceptual poems, reminiscent of much later concrete and visual poetry. Such, for example, was this verbo-visual comic miniature by the eccentric American writer Bob Brown (Figure 4).

Brown's eccentricity was apparent not only in his poetry, but also in his technical inventions. Much later, in a 1930 issue of the Parisian magazine *transition*, he published a manifesto-like user manual for the 'readies', machines invented

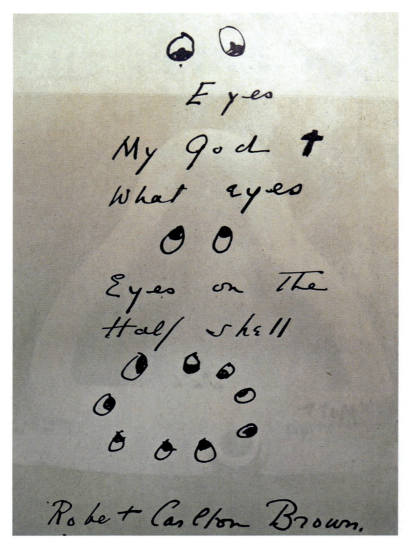

FIGURE 4   Bob Brown. A visual poem from *The Blind Man*.

for reading. With the help of a readie, a new way of writing and reading literature was conceived. It is not known for sure whether this 'reading machine' was only a project or if it was actually designed and put to use. Either way, in order to test such a 'machine', Brown published a collection of texts by fellow writers (among whom were Gertrude Stein, Ezra Pound, Eugene Jolas, and William Carlos Williams – the *crème de la crème* of the American avant-garde), written especially for this publication in a telegraphic avant-garde style.[9] The experiment, it appears, was not a success, but it remains an interesting utopian conceptual project for transforming the reader's perception of poetry. This style of writing poetry was taken up by some younger authors in *transition* magazine, such as Abraham Gillespie and Marius Lyle. The poems of the former are reminiscent of communication schemes in linguistics (see Figures 5 and 6 below). The latter is the author of an essay titled 'Scheme for Physical Improvement of Writers' Medium', also published in *transition*, which described all kinds of experiments with typographic writing.

Speaking of American linguistic experimentation in the pre-WWII period, and putting aside E.E. Cummings, whose poetry I will discuss in a subsequent chapter, a rare example of bold verbo-voco-visual extravaganza was Jackson Mac Low's 1938 poem 'H U N G E R S T r i kE'. A forerunner of the Language

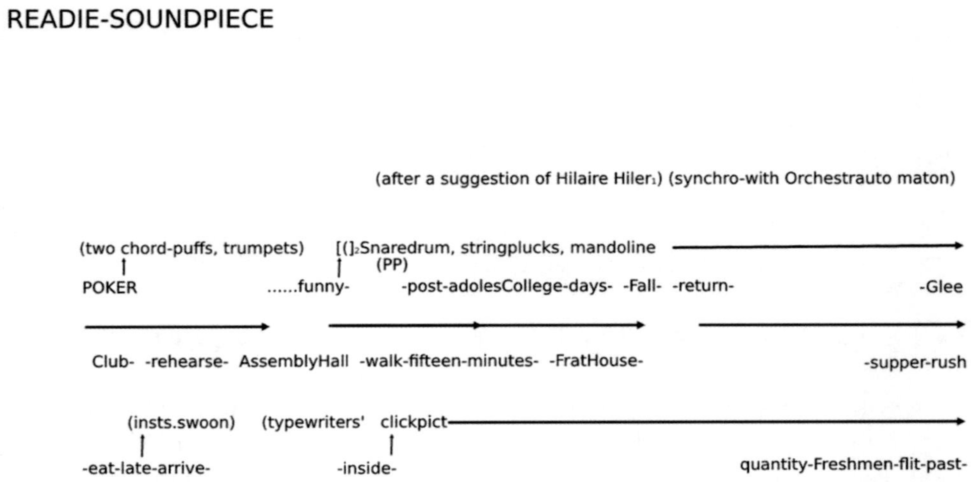

READIE-SOUNDPIECE

FIGURE 5   Abraham Lincoln Gillespie. 'Readie-Soundpiece'

---

9   Contemporary Bob Brown enthusiasts have re-created this technique on the Internet at http://www.readies.org. The authors of this project consider Brown to be the forerunner of the modern e-book.

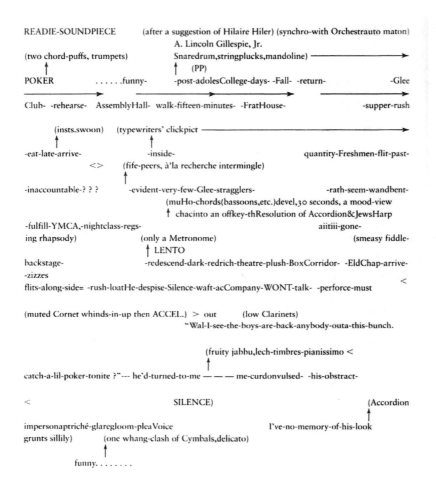

FIGURE 6   Abraham Lincoln Gillespie. A visual poem.

poets of the 1970s, Mac Low disintegrates the words on the page to reinforce the materiality of language units (2008: 6, Figure 7).

In all these poetic experiments, the interaction of the verbal and the visual elements anticipated the future conceptualism of post-WWII art. The verbal plane of a painting sometimes read like a manual for perceiving the object, as in the 'machine' paintings by Francis Picabia in the form of mechanical devices with verbal commentaries, such as the cover of his 1919 poetry book *Pensées sans language* ('Thoughts without language') (Figure 8), whose title contradicts the image: the picture does, indeed, contain words:

In Picabia's proto-conceptual experiments, the word invades the image. In Marcel Duchamp's readymades, the verbal description of an object becomes a concept and, most often, also an artistic object in itself. Before moving to New

Ğ   Ŏ   Ď

Go god go god go
   god   gogoD
                O   G O D

g ain   g a m e s   gain
        g a m es
gain   gay   gam e S
~~g ame~~   gain games

G o L l Y   god agog agog
gog gog goggog   g o g   gog gog gog

        G R O G

G R U C H   g r u c h   gruch
   g r a g   gr ag   grag

        g l u g

And the bathtub went down the drain
Ukraine
Cranium   U k r a i n i u m
      (Uranium)
  You   c r a n i u m   crane
Crane yum you crane
You crane Ukraine
Krake and krake and krake and krake and cake (krake)

FIGURE 7   Fragment from Jackson Mac Low's 'H U N G E R S T r i kE'.

York, Duchamp began to prepare his magnum opus 'The Large Glass'. He would collect notes, sketches, drawings and verbalise his ideas on the walls of his Paris studio. For the most part, these are strange verbal exercises, or language games ('texticles', as he would playfully call them himself), through which he seeks to get closer to what he thinks is a perfect work of art.[10] At first, it all looked like

---

10   Duchamp's linguistic games and strategies have been collected in Lyn Merrington's (2019) booklet.

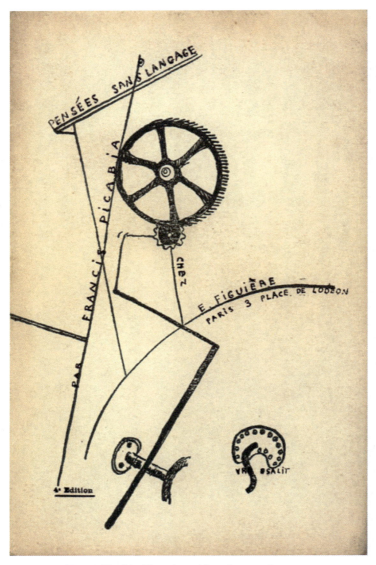

FIGURE 8 Francis Picabia. 'Thoughts without language'

an experimental prototype, preliminary documentation for a future creation. But soon he would conclude that the verbal design of the object was in itself a work in progress. Sketches of thoughts, sets of objects and images – these all counted as artistic activity. Before setting off for America, he collected these scattered notes in a box. They would later be published as *Box 1914* by Duchamp scholars.

For the artist himself, those notes were only a step towards the 'Large Glass', on which he began working in New York. While creating the 'Large Glass', he continued to keep notes, which, in his opinion, were intended to comment on the object itself, while also remaining works of verbal art in their own right. Some of these notes read as purely linguistic projects, such as this plan for the creation of a certain 'dictionary', or 'alphabet', from *A l'Infinitif* (Duchamp, 1967: 77):

> A Dictionary
> - of a language, in which each word would be translated into French order by several words, when necessary by a whole sentence,
> - of a language which one could translate **in its elements** into known languages but which would not reciprocally express the translation of French words or other, or of French or other sentences,
> - Make this dictionary by means of cards.
> - Find how to classify these cards (in alphabetical order, but which alphabet)
> Alphabet or rather a few elementary signs like a dot, line or circle etcetera (to be seen) which will vary, according to the position, etcetera.
> - The sound of this language, is it speakable? No.

The notes would be released much later under the titles *Green Box* and *A l'infinitif*. Duchamp's 'language art'[11] would be seen as a forerunner not only of Dadaism, with its rebellion against common sense in art, but of all conceptual art, with its passion for verbal duplication of images,[12] and specifically to language-oriented poetries in the USA. Another American pioneer of language experimentalism – Edward Estlin Cummings – deserves a separate chapter. Two chapters, in fact: one focusing on his poetry, the other on his prose. His is a special case for considering American avant-garde poetries of language in the Russian context and the other way round: Cummings had actually been to Russia and managed to catch a glimpse of the early Russian avant-garde, albeit when it was already starting to vanish.

---

11   As Jessica Prinz (2015) tends to call it.
12   Marjorie Perloff aptly calls Duchamp's notes 'proto-language poems' (2002: 86), relating them to Gertrude Stein's proto-language-writing techniques.

CHAPTER 7

Poempictures: E. E. Cummings' Performative Language

> Life is a series of Verbs.
> E.E. CUMMINGS

∴

> I am my writing.
> E.E. CUMMINGS

∴

In 1915, the young poet and artist E.E. Cummings spoke at the opening ceremony of the school year at Harvard, his alma mater. His talk, titled 'The New Art', referred to Amy Lowell's poem 'Grotesque' as an example of 'painting by sounds', as well as to Gertrude Stein's *Tender Buttons*, which had been published the previous year: 'Her art is the logic of literary sound painting carried to its extreme' (Cummings, 1965: 10). The future experimentalist in poetry had already found his aesthetic credo: sound and picture, poetry and painting would be inseparable companions. From then on, Cummings would call himself a 'poetandpainter', and his texts 'poempictures'. Music, the interaction of colour and sound, was just as important. Thanks to the Russian composer Alexander Skriabin, whom Cummings called 'the greatest theorist of modern music' in that same speech, modern poets 'may most readily pass from music to literature, through the medium of what has been called 'sense-transference', as exemplified by the colour music of the "Prometheus"' (Idem: 7). Cummings might have also known about another Russian pioneer of artistic synaesthesia, Wassily Kandinsky, who, as we saw in Part 1, was a painter and a poet with a strong interest in sound and music.

In this chapter I will propose an analysis of Cummings' poems using the concept of bodily deixis as applied to two semiotic systems – the verbal and the pictorial. In his book *Vision and Painting*, the art scholar Norman Bryson defines deixis in terms of corporeality: 'Deixis is an utterance in carnal form and points back directly (deiknonei) at the body of the speaker; self-reflexive, it marks the moment at which rhetoric becomes oratory' (1983: 88).[1] Cummings' poetry tends to move from the symbolic and the iconic planes of the artistic sign to the indexical plane and, therefore, to deictics and performativity. In doing so, his experimental verse anticipates later experiments in visual, concrete, and language-centered poetry.

Cummings was indeed a poet of the body and a follower of Walt Whitman who measured a poem in terms of bodily units of verse (as in his programmatic text 'I Sing the Body Electric'). Whitman was the first to pay attention to verse as a bodily form with a respiratory system. While Whitman extended the verse line to a new record in American poetry – perhaps even in world poetry – Cummings whittled it down to a minimum. Cummings' line can consist of one letter, a punctuation mark, a figure, or even a space.

How is Cummings' verse experiment related to his poetics of the body? The physical body is one of the most frequent topics of his poetry. Unlike the fellow American poet Emily Dickinson, for example, the body he praises is the material human body. His series of erotic poems accompanied by erotic drawings has been published as a separate volume (2010). But something else is more interesting about this aspect of Cummings' work – his attempts to move from the symbolic and iconic dimensions of the imagery to its indexality, and therefore, its deicticality through corporeality.

In Cummings' early poems, shifts in the poetic representation of the human body are already noticeable. In one of his most famous early poems, 'some ask praise of their fellows' (1926), instead of writing in symbols (as in the Symbolism or Aestheticism that preceded Cummings) or iconic signs (as, for example, in Futurism or Dada), he resorts to a different, indexical way of presenting the verse with the help of nouns denoting parts of the body (*emphasis mine – V.F.*) (292):

> some ask praise of their fellows
> but I being otherwise
> made compose curves
> and yellows, angles or silences
> (to a less erring end

---

1 The terms *bodily deixis* and visual deixis are used extensively by Mieke Bal, e.g., in her book *Endless Andness* (2013). For a semiotic account of voice deixis and bodily deixis, see Proskurin et al. (2019). On deixis in poetry, see Green (1992), Tsur (2008).

myself is sculptor of
your body's idiom:
the musician of your **wrists;**
the poet is afraid
only to mistranslate

a rhythm in your **hair,**
(your **fingertips**
the **way you move**)
                        the

painter of your **voice-**
beyond these **elements**

remarkably nothing is... therefore, lady
am I content should any
by me carven thing provoke
your **gesture** possibly or

any painting (for its own

reason) in your **lips**
slenderly should create one least **smile**
(shyly
if a poem should lift to
me the distinct country of your
eyes, gifted with green twilight)[2]

This poem, like many others by Cummings, is a verbal portrait of the beloved. But this portrait is bizarre. The indication of bodily features is not given in the traditional symbolic mode – the names of body parts do not refer to any sublime meanings. The semantics is materialised to the utmost in order to allow words to create an impromptu composition. The syntactic coherence of utterances is also violated – words and phrases are endowed with the ability to stand on their own and enter into nonlinear connections in the space of a verse (opening and closing brackets introduce multiple perspectives of

---

2 All poems by E.E. Cummings are cited from the most complete collection of his work (2013), the page number of this edition is given in brackets hereafter.

POEMPICTURES 115

the author's utterance). But in addition to shifts in semantics and syntactics, we also observe a pragmatic defocusing of poetic speech. The word begins to produce an event in the poetic text. The poem describes the process of creating the poem itself; similarly to the creation of a painting – instead of words, it is lines, colours, shapes and pauses that are created. The author molds the image of his lover's body through her words and her voice: 'myself is sculptor of your body's idiom: the painter of your voice-'. The poem performs the creation of the woman's portrait and remains as fragmentary as the face of the model as seen by the author. The lady's gestures literally manifest themselves in the verse space, avoiding rhetorical and stylistic decorations of speech.

To better understand the moment of transition from the symbolic and iconic means of signification to the indexical, or deictic, ones, let us look at his famous 'grasshopper poem' (1932, Figure 9).

Rather than writing a poem *about* a grasshopper, Cummings literally paints a grasshopper graphically on the page, as is schematically shown in this graph by Max Nänny in his article 'Iconic Dimensions in Poetry' (1985: 135, Figure 10):

```
                    r-p-o-p-h-e-s-s-a-g-r
              who
   a)s w(e loo)k
   upnowgath
              PPEGORHRASS
                                 eringint(o-
   aThe):l
           eA
             !p:
   S                                          a
                  (r
   rIvInG              .gRrEaPsPhOs)
                                        to
   rea(be)rran(com)gi(e)ngly
   ,grasshopper;
```

FIGURE 9   E.E. Cummings. 'r-p-o-p-h-e-s-s-a-g-r' (396)

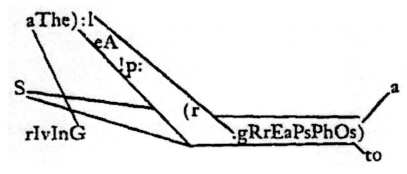

FIGURE 10   Max Nänny. A graph of E.E. Cummings' poem

But Cummings goes even further. To convey iconically the image of a grasshopper, it would be enough to confine the poem to this figurative and bodily portrayal. Cummings, however, conveys the activity of a grasshopper in writing, specifically by combining letters and sounds in verse. Indeed, the poem mimics the act of becoming and rearranging itself as a grasshopper in the movement of speech, in its articulations and dismemberments, in the abruptness of its leaps, and in the recomposition of its words by analogy with the body of the insect. The effect of this poem is not in its imitative or life-like nature, as would be characteristic of figurative painting, but in its transsemiotic performativity, where the very deployment of typographical signs creates an equivalent of the object of representation. As the Cummings scholar Norman Friedman noted, this poem models the process of reading and conveying meaning in poetry: 'the object is, for example, to loosen up the effect of a metrical line, to suggest the thing or idea spoken of, to alter and reinforce meanings, or to amplify and retard. His is a style of constant emphasis: since he relishes each phrase, word, and letter of a poem, he wants the reader to relish them too, and many of his devices are aimed simply at slowing down the reader's intake of the poem' (1960: 124). The poem ceases to be just a *poem*, instead transforming into *poiesis* as the event of the poem's creation.

In a later comment on this poem, Cummings pointed out that the poem lives like a human being: 'Like a particular humanbeing,& unlike mostpeople,a particular poem IS *im*measurably *alive*' (cit. in Webster, 2013: 138). The performativity of this text lies not in its sheer phonic and visual instrumentation, but in the *demonstratio ad oculos*, which Karl Bühler defined as the transfer from the indexical field of corporeality to the indexical field of language. The performativity of Cummings' verse differs both from the figurativeness and iconicity of visual and concrete poetry, and from the phonetic mimetism of sound poetry. It is noteworthy that Cummings refused to recite 'grasshopper' in his readings and audio recordings. The poem is created in such a way that it is silently performed as if by itself, by its very layout on the page. It is, in a sense, 'conceptual', i.e., it invites the reader to mentally perceive its own structure.

The performative nature of Cummings' word-pictures is related to his careful attention to subjectivity. Contemplating the transition from figurative to non-figurative painting, he writes in his notebooks that painting before Cézanne had to do with 'objective reality', whereas Cézanne introduced 'subjective actuality', where 'form is actually the expression of colour' (cit. in Cohen, 1987: 70–71). The same principle was later restated by Paul Klee with his idea that 'art does not reproduce the visible, rather, it makes visible'.

This principle manifests itself in poetry through the performativity of the act of writing and the indexicality of the word. Let us recall Franz Kafka's account of the same idea, as expressed in his notebooks: 'I have no literary interests, but am made of literature, I am nothing else and cannot be anything else'. Deixis of this kind turns up in E.E. Cummings, too, for example, in his expression 'I am my writing' (which became the title of Martin Heusser's (1997) book on Cummings' poetry). Similar ostensive performatives are present in many of his poems. By 'ostensive performative', I mean cases where the subject matter of a poem is enacted by the very means of writing. For example, the poem 'ecco a letter' (1940) is written as a direct address by the posted letter (504):

> ecco a letter starting'dearest we'
> unsigned:remarkably brief but covering
> one complete miracle of nearest far
>
> 'i cordially invite me to become
> noone except yourselves r s v p'

Subjectivity is transferred from the author to the message itself, which, in turn, opens up a multitude of possible subjective relationships. The concluding phrase 'r s v p' (French 'Répondez, s'il vous plaît') is addressed simultaneously to the recipient of the 'letter' and its sender ('I invite me'). Another poem, entitled 'since feeling is first' (1926), is about a death without 'parenthesis', which is performed in writing (291):

> we are for each other: then
> laugh, leaning back in my arms
> for life's not a paragraph
>
> And death i think is no parenthesis

There are many examples where ostensives are represented by silence as a suspension of speech, such as in a text dated 1963: 'enter no (silence is the blood whose flesh/is singing) silence:but unsinging'. The poetic text is constructed as a mathematical formula – from our present day it also looks rather like a line of programme code – in which brackets highlight the priority of the operation being performed (the definition of silence and singing), and the colon denotes the domain of definition and a set of meanings (silence is the absence of singing).

In a 1958 text, silence is defined by referring to the semantics of 'silent looking' and the 'turning edge of life' (712):

> silence
>
> .is
> a
> looking
>
> bird:the
>
> turn
> ing;edge,of
> life
>
> (inquiry before snow

Another means of indexicalisation and subjectivisation of writing are shifters, or egocentric words of all kinds. They come to the fore in Cummings' verse and often adopt the functions of other parts of speech. What stands out in the first instance, is the multiplicity of the 'I' peculiar to Cummings' poetics. This is explicitly stated in the first line of the poem 'so many selves:' (1950), dedicated to the multifaceted self-manifestations of the human essence, which an individual mind cannot keep track of: 'so many selves(so many fiends and gods'. Many consciousnesses can be hidden in one body ('most innocent(so deep's the mind of flesh'), and therefore, attempts to grasp the 'I' in its totality are limited for the rational mind: '—how should a fool that calls him 'I' presume/to comprehend not numerable whom?' (609) The pronoun 'I' is enclosed in quotation marks, for it is not a reliable carrier of innumerable subjectivities.

Cummings' subjectivity is also evident in the fact that the verb 'to be' in its singular forms 'is' and 'am' turns from a simple link word into a wholly meaningful concept. Instead of writing 'I have a feeling', Cummings writes 'I am feeling'. Shifters interpose into other words, subjectivising the stream of (at times) senseless speech, like the pronouns 'it', 'he', 'me', 'I', 'esse', and articles in this poem dated 1940 (488):

    fl

    a
    tt
    ene

    d d

    reaml
    essn
    esse

    s wa

    it
    sp
    i

    t)(t

    he
    s
    e

    f

    ooli
    sh sh
    apes

    ccocoucougcoughcoughi

    ng with me
    n more o
    n than in the

    m

In another famous late poem dated 1958, this kind of subjectivisation is at play on various semiotic levels (673):

l(a

le
af
fa

ll

s)
one
l

iness

This is a poem about the solitude of 'the Self', or 'the I', which is likened to the solitude of a leaf falling from a tree. 'I' is duplicated iconically as the figure '1', as the numeral 'one', as the French article 'le', and finally asserts itself in the neologism 'iness' in the last line. In other poems, we observe the materialisation of indefinite pronouns – for example, 'nobody' becomes 'no body' (*emphasis mine – V.F.*) (490):

nobody loved this
he)with its
of eye stuck
into a rock of

Forehead. **No**
Body
loved
big that quick
sharp
thick snake of a

voice these

root
like legs

or
feethands;

nobody
ever could ever

had love loved whose his
climbing shoulders queerly twilight
:never,**no**
(body.

Nothing

Other contexts show the indefinite pronouns functioning as appellatives, as in the first line of this poem: 'I am going to utter a tree, Nobody' (1922). The speaker in Cummings' verse is able to directly 'utter a tree' or other objects. In the poem 'look' (1920s), shifters are represented by the names of parts of the body – fingers, lips, hands, gestures perform the role of pronouns (*emphasis mine – V.F.*) (1002):

look
my **fingers**,which
touched you
and your warmth and crisp
littleness
—see?do not resemble my
fingers. My wrists **hands**
which held carefully the soft silence
of you(and your **body**
smile eyes feet **hands**)
are different
from what they were. My **arms**
in which all of you lay folded
quietly,like a
leaf or some flower
newly made by Spring
Herself,are not my
arms. I do not recognise
as myself this which i find before
me in a mirror. i do

not believe
i have ever seen these things;
someone whom you love
and who is slenderer
taller than
myself has entered and become such
lips as i use to talk with,
a new person is alive and
gestures with my
or it is perhaps you who
with my **voice**
are
playing.

Particularly interesting is Cummings' conceptualisation of the pronoun 'I', miscapitalised as the noun 'eye', as in this 1963 text (827):

i
never
guessed any
thing(even a
universe)might be
so not quite believab
ly smallest as perfect this
(almost invisible where of a there of a)here of a
rubythroat's home with its still
ness which really's herself
(and to think that she's
warming three worlds)
who's ama
zingly
Eye

From Cummings' standpoint, this conceptualisation reflects his orientation towards visual perception for both author and reader, which is peculiar to him as a 'poetandpainter'.

The visual poetry of E.E. Cummings epitomises a linguo-centric turn not only at the level of grammatical experiment, but also in the pragmatics, or deictics, of language. The iconicity of a linguistic sign begins to function as an index, indicating the metamorphosis of the subject in the poetic text. Cummings' experimental poetic discourse thereby opens the way for further language-oriented experiments with the performativity of verbal utterance in artistic practices of Post-Modernism and Conceptualism.

CHAPTER 8

Heteroglossia and Hybridisation in E.E. Cummings' *Eimi: a Journey through Soviet Russia*

> for any ruffian in the sky
> your kingbird doesn't give a damn –
> his royal warcry is I AM
> and he's the soul of chivalry
>
> E. E. CUMMINGS

∙∙∙

> The artistic representation of language is the goal of the novel's intentional hybridisation.
>
> MIKHAIL BAKHTIN

∙∙

E.E. Cummings was perhaps the only American experimental writer to gain first-hand[1] knowledge about the early years of the Soviet political and cultural experiment. His trip to Soviet Russia in 1931 and the subsequent publication of his experimental travelogue-cum-novel *Eimi* was a unique experiment in American-Russian ties carried out by an avant-garde writer. Before discussing the linguistic issues of Cummings' travel writing, it is worth outlining the circumstances surrounding this experimental text and highlighting the key moments in his adventurous journey into the totalitarian land of the Soviets.[2]

In the 1920–30s, Cummings travelled around the world, with frequent stops in Paris, where he participated in the life of the Parisian avant-garde. In the early

---

1 I thank Emily Wright for assisting me with the first version of this chapter.
2 A detailed description of the trip and the travelogue appears in the Russian volume by Feshchenko et al. (2013). The biographical reconstruction of Cummings' visit is to a certain extent a result of the translators' own 'decoding' of certain facts from the cryptic language of *Eimi*. Yet most of the decoding work had been done by Cummings scholars Norman Friedman and Michael Webster.

1920s, many American writers were living in the French capital: Hemingway, Fitzgerald, Pound, Barnes, MacLeish, Stein, Dos Passos, and others. Cummings entered into a friendly and creative relationship with the Parisian artistic and poetic bohemia. In 1922, he met Louis Aragon, one of the leaders of Dadaism and Surrealism in France at the time. They had a lot in common, both in terms of their left-wing political views and their passion for revolutionising the word in poetry. In 1930, Aragon, together with his Russian-born wife Elsa Triolet, made his first trip to the Soviet Union to participate in a conference of revolutionary writers in Kharkiv. Aragon talked a lot about this trip in the winter and spring of the following year, persuading his American comrade to make his own trip to the homeland of communism. Although the young Cummings had always been more interested in art – and the modernist revolution in art – rather than in politics, he became more and more drawn to Bolshevism, about which he argued a lot with his conservative father. In letters to his parents dated 1918–1920, he wrote enthusiastically about strikes and protests in New York and about reports from the Russian revolution.

Intrigued by the 'Soviet dream' stories from the Aragon-Triolet couple, as well as from Ilya Ehrenburg, Mikhail Larionov and Natalia Goncharova, who were living in Paris at that time, Cummings boarded the Paris-Moscow train all alone on May 10, 1931. Before the trip, Paris newspapers had reported that 'the writer and artist Cummings' was learning Russian and awaiting a visa to Soviet Russia. He took a typewriter and some gifts for Lilya Brik from her sister Elsa – magazines, ties, and perfume – with him. His suitcase also contained a manuscript of Louis Aragon's new poem, 'The Red Front', which Cummings had promised to translate into English. The scandal surrounding the publication of this propagandistic poem lay ahead, and for now the train was hurtling toward a wonderful tomorrow, and the American pilgrim was riding the 'red express train' to destination 'USSR'.

Armed with a notebook and a typewriter, Cummings started keeping a diary, carefully recording his movements and impressions from the 'Soviet Mecca'. Having passed Germany and Poland, on May 11, his train crossed the Russian border at the Negoreloye station. Many foreign intellectuals who came to the Soviet Union in those days were quite moved by the experience. According to Mikhail Ryklin, 'it was perceived not just as an entrance to another European country, but as a gateway to a new world' (2009: 40).[3] However, upon crossing the border, many experienced the opposite – for instance, passport checks caused nervous shock and confusion. As one traveller from Germany, the

---

3   See also Michael David-Fox's study of Western visitors to early Soviet Russia (2014), which, strangely enough, contains no mention of Cummings' visit.

writer Otto Friedlander, remarked, 'what seemed like heaven to one, seemed like hell to another' (Ibidem). Cummings seemed to have been gripped by the same feelings – he was carefully searched at the border. He understood straight away that he had gotten caught up in another world, which from the very first moments failed to meet his expectations. He had set off for a communist paradise – yet he found himself in something more like a hell. His travel notes began to dazzle with bestial language and infernal images. However, for the time being, the challenges were fueling the interest and curiosity of the misguided pilgrim.

On the next day, May 12, Cummings arrived in Moscow. By prior agreement with Ehrenburg, the Soviet playwright Vladimir Lidin was to meet him at the Belorussky railway station. However, they did not recognise each other on the train platform, and the American visitor had to contact the Intourist bureau, which directed him to the Metropol Hotel. A paradoxical circumstance, indeed – having arrived in the country of the victorious proletariat, he found himself in a luxurious hotel. However, he got lucky: the American professor Henry Dana, who was collecting materials on Soviet theater, also lived there, and would become his guide to the city. Dana took care of him showed him around Moscow – he arranged visits to proletarian theaters, writers' banquets, and various sights of the Soviet capital. At one of these dinners, the role of the individual in the Soviet system was being discussed. Cummings, champion of individualism and freedom of expression, was faced with a propagandistic tirade from his new friend praising the success of socialist labour. 'Long live IS!', Cummings exclaimed in response, alluding to his philosophy of poetry, in which the only possible forms of the verb 'to be' are the personal forms of the singular present tense in the first and third persons ('am' and 'is'). What he saw there, on the proletarian stage, was a strong denial of all things personal, singular, and present-tense – in favor of all things collective, mass-scale, and past-tense. In a dispute with Dana, Cummings spoke out against the violent Soviet experiment. His voice was way too loud, and someone unfamiliar appeared next to him – he had become an object of surveillance by the GPU. His further stay in Moscow would be carefully surveilled and he would have to encrypt his notes in the travel diary.

Cummings came to Moscow at a turning point in Russia's cultural politics – the 'Great Turn', as Stalin would name it. In May 1931, the Russian Association of Proletarian Writers adopted a resolution urging all proletarian writers to 'engage in artistic display of the heroes of the five-year plan'. Henceforth, only proletarian literature was allowed in the USSR. It was not surprising that, under these circumstances, the visiting writer's contacts were limited to proletarian circles (which he would call 'the circles of hell' in *EIMI*), even though he had arrived as a tourist. His American guides in Moscow, who were sympathetic to communism, strived to show him how real 'socialist literature' was made. He was constantly promised a meeting with Maksim Gorky, which never took place, and the Soviet writer ended up an 'invisible' ghost in Cummings' imagination. Cummings was taken to the circus – but the show was a costume agit-prop performance. He had seen a Russian ballet and his beloved Stravinsky in Paris, but at the Bolshoi Theater, he was subjected to a patriotic opera. Instead of an exhibition of contemporary art, he examined a 'model' Soviet prison. Instead of St. Basil's Cathedral, he ended up at the Museum of the Revolution, which housed a single icon, the passage to which was closed – just as everything else he approached appeared to be closed and locked.

Back in Paris, Cummings had been told a lot both about the early Russian avant-garde in art and about the new upsurge of the Soviet industrial arts in recent years. But here, too, a devastating disappointment awaited him – the only things he saw from that world were the canvases of Cézanne, Matisse, Van Gogh and Picasso, exhibited at the Museum of New Western Art as representative of a bygone culture, and a couple of sculptures by his Parisian Cubist friends. Instead of the Russian avant-garde, he was presented with the pyramid of the Lenin Mausoleum as the highest achievement of the Soviet spirit. In the eyes of the shocked pilgrim, the Leader's grave seemed like a temple of the cult of the Soviet man, and the dead deity lying in it – as the idol of the Soviet 'unworld', as he would persistently call it in his notes. Diabolical mythology continued to occupy the American traveller's imagination; his notes painted a terrifying picture of the promised land of communism.

Yet Cummings was lucky to have two or three important – and quite pleasant – appointments in Moscow. One of them was with Lilya Brik, whose sister Elsa Triolet had asked Cummings in Paris to bring her some gifts. Visiting the Briks' apartment, he was fascinated by the hospitality and charm of the muse of Mayakovsky, who had died just the year before. She was laughing 'not like all Marxists' whom he had met, he would note. She, like him, was in love with Paris, was fond of beautiful things; she wondered if she could read some of his books, persuading him to write about Russia for a newspaper and offering her help in Moscow. But here, too, the American guest was in for an embarrassment. Lilya's husband and Mayakovsky's life-long companion, Osip Brik, came in and decided to give their guest a lecture on the great goals of the Bolsheviks and the benefits of collectivisation. The guest barely escaped this indoctrination and, under the pretext of being late for another meeting, took his leave.

In his diaries, Cummings recollects yet another visit – to Vsevolod Meyerhold and his wife Zinaida Reich. During his stay in Moscow, he managed to see two performances at the acclaimed director's theater – Sergey Tretyakov's

1926 play 'Roar, China!' and Vsevolod Vishnevsky's 'The Last Decisive' (1931). Neither of the plays evoked any emotions in the American poet, except for laughter at the proletarian primitivism of dramatic propaganda. However, he was surprised by the design of the theater itself, which aroused his interest in the director. Cummings and Meyerhold had a mutual friend, the Parisian sculptor Ossip Zadkine, who had recommended the American poet visit the famous Soviet director. While visiting Meyerhold at his Moscow apartment, the two had a little talk about theater. Meyerhold privately complained to his American guest that the dictatorship established by the Proletkult in the theater was no good at all. Cummings followed along timidly, fearing another dose of socialist indoctrination. Later, he opened up and expressed his regrets in his diary. Indeed, Meyerhold seemed like no one else he had met in Moscow, one of a kind.

Had he stayed in Moscow a little longer, Cummings might have had some more interesting meetings – for example, with Boris Pasternak, who had just left Moscow on a production assignment; or with Valentin Stenich, a poet and translator, about whom Dos Passos had told him. At that time, Stenich was translating Joyce's *Ulysses*; there is evidence that he was also translating Cummings' poems into Russian. Alas, for some reason, Cummings could only meet with Stenich's wife, Lubov Fainberg.

If Cummings had arrived in Russia a year earlier, he would undoubtedly have met the person whom in *Eimi* he called 'comrade suicide' – Vladimir Mayakovsky. The American avant-gardist's trip to Russia could be seen as a mirror image of Mayakovsky's 'discovery of America' in 1926. Both poets published books with similar titles – *EIMI: I AM* (Cummings) and *I* (Mayakovsky).[4] Both poets embarked on their overseas trips motivated by a desire to explore a different political system and a different civilisation and culture.[5]

Meanwhile, the American pilgrim was already looking for all sorts of escape routes from the 'red hell'. After staying in Moscow for less than a month, he hastily applied for an exit visa and returned to Paris by train via Kyiv, Odessa, and Istanbul. He perceived crossing the borders back from Soviet Russia as a return to 'the World'. He left the Land of the Soviets as a 'disenchanted wanderer', and laid down his ideas about socialism in a diary which would soon be transformed into a book:

> I feel that whatever's been hitherto told or sung in song or story concerning Russia's revolution equals bunk. I feel that Russia was not once

---

4 Cf. also the title of Mayakovsky's polemical autobiography – *I myself*.
5 For more on the two authors in comparison, see Nikitina (2009).

upon a time, and what a time! any number of cringing peasants ruled by an autocratic puppet—Russia was any number of kings, so perfectly so immanently and so naturally royal that (with a single negligible exception or "Czar") they did royally disguise themselves as humblest slaves, lest the light of their royalty dazzle a foolish world. But a foolish world is more foolish than royalty can suppose. And what has been miscalled the Russian revolution surely is a more foolish than supposable world's attempt upon natural and upon immanent and upon perfect and upon kinghood; and attempt motivated by baseness and by jealousy and by hate and a slave's wish to substitute for the royal incognito of humility the ignoble affectation of equality. ... (255)[6]

1 *Eimi* or *I Am*: Travel Notes, Travelogue or Novel?

Two years later, in America, Cummings published a 432-page novel/travelogue about his Soviet adventures, which he called *Eimi, I Am*. The first chapters of his new work came out in instalments in the Harvard literary journal *Hound&Horn*. The birth of the novel was therefore similar to that of *Ulysses* ten years earlier, and Joyce's 'Fragments from *Work in Progress*', in 1924.[7]

Eimi is Cummings' longest and most experimental prose work. The difficulty of the language used and the scale of his conception surpass his first novel *The Enormous Room*, although there is continuity where style and poetics are concerned. Both books were published as 'novels' but neither of them conforms completely to the genre. They are both based on Cummings' own biographical

---

6   When referring to EIMI, I will hereafter give the bracketed page number from the latest edition (Cummings, 2007).

7   When he included *Eimi* in the canon of great Modernist novels such as Joyce's *Ulysses*, Ezra Pound was perhaps, for once, not exaggerating. In his correspondence with Cummings, he continued to praise what he called the 'great woik' of his young friend and fellow writer. The same cannot be said about other critics, who, even if they took notice of *Eimi* upon its publication in 1933, preferred to let the odd travelogue sink into oblivion for many years. Most reviews of *Eimi* that appeared at the time of its publication compared Cummings' 'long' prose to other 'long modernist novels', such as *Finnegans Wake* and 'long modernist poems', such as Pound's *Cantos*. Whereas similarities between *Eimi* and other works are obvious, Cummings' style differed from the others, mostly due to its exuberant burlesque word creation. One witty anonymous reviewer remarked, using Cummings' own language, that the author of the Soviet travelogue 'out-Joyces James Joyce and super-Steins Gertrude Stein'. In Russia, very few people or scholars seem to have known about *Eimi* before its translation in 2013. Among them, though, was Sergey Eisenstein, whose memorial house library preserved a copy of *Eimi*, which he most probably bought on his trip to America in the 1930s.

experience and the author is the main character in both cases. The lyrical 'I', so present in his poetry, dominates both narratives alongside visuality, musicality and experimentation, which are also reminiscent of his poetry.

Cummings turns his daily travel notes into an epic odyssey about the destiny of individuality within a totalitarian regime of pressure and violence. The title of the book states its main theme, the assertion of the individual (*I Am*). The Greek form for the first person of the verb 'to be' – 'eimi' – refers to the Bible's *Book of Exodus*, in which God tells Moses 'I am that I am'. According to Cummings' philosophy, the artist is independent from society and resists the impersonal masses. Cummings later compared his two novels, saying: 'EIMI is the individual again, a more complex individual, a more enormous room'.

The writer himself explained how to pronounce the title of his book in English – 'Aye' as in the indefinite article 'a', 'mee' as in the personal pronoun 'me', with an emphasis on 'me'. If we look closely at the graphic form of the word, we can see 'Me', 'I', and another 'I' inscribed in *EIMI*. 'ME', here, can be interpreted as a 'WE' turned upside down. The opposition between the *self* as an individualist poet and the Soviet communist *collective* is expressed in many linguistic ways to great effect in *Eimi* – for instance, the hybrid pronouns 'Ime', 'nonself', 'unI', 'unhe', 'selfhehim', 'selvesour', etc. Similarly, the name 'IweK' encrypts the initial letter of the author's surname in a sort of broken Russian ('Kemminkz'); together with his 'I,' K confronts the collective we of the Soviet system.[8] The abbreviation 'USSR' undergoes similar pronominal encoding. Cummings hints at the fact that Soviet people do not speak for themselves, for their 'I', but only for 'WE', 'YOU', or 'HE', 'THEY'. Hence his highlighting – within the 'USSR' – of 'You (es es) are', i.e., 'You are' and 'he (it) is' as opposed to 'I am'. The conflict between the artist's self-affirmation and an impersonal, 'commanding' and 'dictating' society becomes the central axis of good and evil in *Eimi*. This play on words and letters in Soviet names is exploited elsewhere in the book, as in the following line: 'USSR a USSR a night- USSR a nightmare USSR…' (432) As the narrator explains, 'USSR' is code for 'U for un- & S for self S for science and R for -reality' (Ibidem). The land of the Soviets, according to this sarcastic joke, represents a denial of personality in the name of science, elevated to the status of religion.

---

8   We should note a similar burlesque play on the Soviet 'WE' in the title of Cummings' 1933 humorous sketch 'Weligion is hashish', which refers to the famous Karl Marx phrase 'Religion is the opium of the people' (Cummings, 1965: 280–282). Further in this chapter I will compare Cummings' criticism of the *we*-philosophy with the image of 'We' in Yevgeny Zamyatin's dystopian novel of the same name.

From the moment of *Eimi*'s publication, critics argued about the genre of the text. Interestingly, the title of the first (1933) edition did not include a subtitle referring to Soviet Russia or any mention of the 'Journal'. Even the editor found it hard to tell what genre his author's work belonged to. As the commentary to the first edition explains, the text only seems like a travel diary at first glance. In fact, it should be understood as an epic narrative. It is not clear whether the commentary to the first edition was written by Cummings himself; either way, he was never forthcoming about the genre of his text. In drafts accompanying his manuscript, he distances himself from any sort of 'journalism and writing', considering any of its forms to be propaganda: 'Nothing, consequently, could be less like what mostpeople consider "writing" than eimi' (cit. in Oshukov, 2012: 198).[9]

It appears Cummings did not want his work to be considered a journalistic account on the subject of 'Returning from the USSR'. Contemporary literature was flooded with 'Russian diaries', such as those of his fellow citizens Theodore Dreiser and John Dos Passos; later examples include *Moscow Diary* by Walter Benjamin, *Retour de l'URSS* ('Return from USSR') by André Gide, and *Soviet Communism: A New Civilisation?* by English writer Beatrice Webb. Whether those accounts were positive or not, Cummings did not subscribe to this type of reportage or memoirist writing. As a poet and painter, he was far more interested in the artistic value of the adventures and feelings described.

At the same time, he refused to emphasise the fictional character of his work. In the commentaries to subsequent editions of *Eimi,* he was keen for his text to be read as a 'journal'. He considers the book identical to the notes he took during his journey. According to its author, 'not one word of Eimi is fiction'. Mikhail Oshukov, who studied Cummings' unpublished drafts, points out that the book and events described are the same thing in Cummings' understanding of his poetics: 'This book is what happened to me (not a record/not a mere record of what happened) from May 10 to June 14 1931)' (cit. in Oshukov, 2012: 199). Therefore, according to Oshukov, *Eimi* is 'not only non-fictional and not just identical to quick notes, taken on the spot, *Eimi* is the event and in that sense the text acquires an ontological status' (Ibidem). In this respect, the text does not belong to the 'literature of fact' tradition, which was established in the USSR not long before Cummings' arrival. Members of the LEF movement rejected fiction in favour of 'documentary' literature, which was to help build socialism. The American writer seemingly follows these guidelines, admitting, in *Eimi*, with reference to Mark Twain's witty aphorism, that

---

9 Mikhail Oshukov has worked with archival material pertaining to *Eimi*. His article contains unpublished notes by the writer.

'in describing an unfamiliar environment, it is always best to let facts speak for themselves. Truth is after all stranger than fiction' (114). But Soviet 'industrial literature' only served the propaganda he so despised, and thus did nothing but irritate him.

Interestingly, in the second and third editions of the book (published during Cummings' lifetime), the subtitle 'The Journal of a Trip to Russia' appears. Apparently, this was Cummings' way of answering his critics and opponents, who still doubted the documentary veracity of what was described in *Eimi*. On the other hand, it was clear to the writer's supporters how precious the book was from an artistic point of view. The publisher Pascal Covici claimed it was a novel right from the start. Cummings' close friend Ezra Pound reinforced this position by comparing the work to two other sizeable modernist novels: *Ulysses* by James Joyce and *The Apes of God* by Wyndham Lewis. The poet Marianne Moore went even further, calling *Eimi* 'a large poem' (1933). The most recent edition of the book was published in 2007, with the slightly different subtitle 'A Journey through Soviet Russia'. 'Journal' is replaced by 'Journey', moving the book from the autobiographical shelf to travel writing and presenting *Eimi* as a 'novelised travelogue', possibly to comply with commercial trends.[10]

Some researchers consider avant-garde and modernist autobiographical texts to be hybrid forms that are on the border between artistic and factual discourse. Literary critic Max Saunders (2010) introduced the term 'autobiografiction' to describe this genre. In *Eimi*, every chapter corresponds to one week of the writer's stay in Russia. But unlike Lewis Carroll's *The Russian Journal*, for instance, Cummings' work has many features of a literary text: the style of writing, the poetic language, the narrative system, the characters, etc.[11] If we were to determine the actual genre of this text, we could say it is a 'novel travelogue', both a novel and a travelogue, and a new (novel) type of travelogue.

2   'Comrade K' in the 'Marxist Unworld': Narrative – Composition – Characters – Motives

Upon opening *Eimi*, the reader may feel he is dealing with a fantasy novel, in which 'Comrade Joyce' and 'Comrade Dante' meet in Soviet Russia. But he is in

---

10   In his travel to Russia and in writing the Russian diary, Cummings may well have been inspired by Lewis Carroll's trip to the Russian Empire back in 1867. Carroll's *Russian Diary*, though, was only published in 1935, two years after *Eimi*'s publication. On this juxtaposition, see Welch (1999).

11   Likewise, Cummings' first novel, *The Enormous Room*, is a fusion of autobiographical prose and fictional memoir.

fact experiencing Soviet Russia through the eyes of an avant-garde poet, who has combined a Dantesque imaginary travelogue with Joycean prose. There is a reason why *La Divina Commedia* is behind Cummings' narrative. The protagonist encounters different characters along his way – among them, Virgil and Beatrice, guides to the infernal 'unworld'; celebrities of Soviet culture (Meyerhold, Brik, portraits of the dead Mayakovsky and Yesenin) disguised under pseudonyms; as well as living and inanimate beings inhabiting the Soviet inferno – busts of Lenin, the ghosts of Marx, the spirits of Gorky and millions of ordinary Soviet 'evil spirits' and 'non-humans'. Upon crossing the border of the Soviet Union, the traveller/author describes his descent into the 'land of Was': 'the subhuman communist superstate, where men are shadows & women are nonmen; the preindividual marxist unworld' (8).

The novel-cum-travelogue begins with the symbolic word 'SHUT' and ends just as symbolically with its antonym 'OPEN'. The metaphor of a locked space becomes plot-generating for the narration. In the train carriage heading to the Soviet capital, the narrator experiences a fit of claustrophobia, foreshadowing his subsequent wandering through the closed world of evil. The doors and windows of the carriage, which is likened to a coffin taking him to the afterlife, are sometimes locked, causing him to suffocate from 'SHUTNESS', which blocks the way of the pilgrim at every turn. Shutness surrounds and encloses the hero from all sides as soon as he enters the 'land of Was'. The stale air inside and outside, the clenched fists of the Soviet people, bolts on doors and barriers on the roads, fenced-in territories and spider-like, compressed people, restricted movement, and thwarted negotiations – all this intensifies the atmosphere of an inanimate world frozen out of time. The traveller finds himself in a ghostly cemetery, in which everything speaks of lifelessness and desolation, where 'nobody seems anything except lonesome; hideously lonesome in hideousness, in rundownness, in outatheelness, in neglected-ness, in strictly omnipotent whichnessandwhatness' (9).

The opposition between the living and the inanimate determines the author's attitude to what he contemplates and experiences. Soviet society is seen as an obstacle to all living beings and things. Therefore, everything that occurs along the way loses all signs of reality, becomes false and fake ('Pretend' is Cummings' word for that). People turn into 'nonpeople' – 'nonmen' and 'nonwomen', or 'wasmen' who have lost their humanity. Reality decays like a corpse. Everything becomes imaginary, superficial, being-denying. Like the 'Land of Nots' from Russian writer Sigizmund Krzhizhanovsky's 1922 fable,[12] the Land of Soviets centers around the omnipresent denial of existence. Everywhere the

---

12   See the story 'Страна нетов' in English translation in (Krzhizhanovsky, 2013).

narrator hears commanding and oppressive Soviet slogans like 'нет' ('no') and 'долой' ('down with'), sees signposts 'ХОДА НЕТ' ('no passing') and 'ЗАКРЫТО' ('closed'). The very word 'НЕТ' ('this hellword', as Cummings calls it) is repeatedly emphasised on the pages of *Eimi*, a marker of the prohibitiveness and shutness of Soviet society. Sometimes this wordplay takes on an avant-garde form, as in these lines, anagramming the 'hellish' keyword:

> then thennow thennowthen thennowthennow noW no N NOWT NOWTH NOWTHE nowTHENthenNOWing it
> there therehere thereherethere thereheretherehere here her he H HERET HERETH HERETHE HERETHER hereTHERE-there HEREing it wel

Intentionally or not, the Russian 'НЕТ' resonates orthographically with the English 'THE'. A faceless, indefinite mass expressing its attitude to life with a categorical 'NO' is contrasted with the definite and unique identifier 'THE'. Throughout the novel, the indefinite article 'A', together with an entire arsenal of indefinite and impersonal pronouns, signals an amorphous mass of faceless characters and under-characters inhabiting the Soviet 'kingdomless of spectres' (165). Negation governs everything in this 'cosmos of ofless not and nowless un-' (92). There is not even a 'world' here – Cummings exaggerates the metaphor by opposing the negative, inhuman 'isn't' and the affirmative human 'is'. This form of the verb 'to be' – along with its form 'I am' – is fundamental for Cummings; it expresses the creative act of the person who calls things into existence. He had written about this earlier in *The Enormous Room*, dwelling upon his philosophy of being: 'There are certain things in which one is unable to believe for the simple reason that he never ceases to feel them. Things of this sort which are always inside of us and in fact are us and which consequently will not be pushed off or away where we can begin thinking about them-are no longer things;they,and the us which they are,equals A Verb;an IS' (Cummings 1922: 231). His experiences in Soviet Russia further convinced Cummings of the primacy of the artist's vitality in the face of collective impersonal non-existence.

3 Linguistic Hybridisation in *Eimi*

According to the classic definition by Mikhail Bakhtin, *hybridisation* is a result of the 'mixture of two social languages within the limits of a single utterance, an encounter, within the arena of an utterance, between two different linguistic consciousnesses, separated from one another by an epoch, by social differentiation, or by some other factor' (1981: 358). In this sense, E.E. Cummings' *Eimi* is an exemplary hybrid in that it mixes two opposing linguistic forms of consciousness, the author's individualistic one and the collectivist Soviet one represented by the newspeak of the early Soviet era. Moreover, this mixing can literally appear within a single utterance – the author cites the catchphrases of Soviet citizens he meets, sarcastically playing up their absurdity in his authorial comments.

Eimi's hybridity is informed by multilingualism and heteroglossia. The author supplies his text with inserts from various languages – Russian, French, German, Italian, Polish, Turkish, Greek, Latin. He does so with a double purpose. Firstly, to document the dialogues that took place in different languages among the foreigners and Russians he observed in Soviet Moscow. Secondly, with the aim of interlingual play and puns. In this latter respect, *Eimi* is similar to Joyce's *Finnegans Wake* (fragments of which had already been published by the time of Cummings' Soviet trip). Although this formal similarity cannot be overlooked, the two novels are different in their use of hybrid words. Joyce's ironic multilingualism is aimed at ridiculing the entire human language. Its hybridisation is semiotic – the text juxtaposes visual and phonic imagery pertaining to different semiotic systems and different languages. Cummings does not share Joyce's universalism and panlingualism – his linguistic hybrids parody the language situation in the Soviet Union at the beginning of the 1930s. All of *Eimi*'s humour is based on the play between Soviet clichés and foreign language phraseology.

Cummings had already made extensive use of multilingual inserts in *The Enormous Room*. As a speaker of several languages, he took an interest in the multilingualism that surrounded him during his time in prison. His cellmates greeted him, according to his own calculations, in eleven different languages, and this made the prison cell a huge, monstrous repository of languages. It is there that Cummings got his first experience of the Babelian confusion of tongues. In the even more 'enormous room' of the Soviet underworld, the rumble of multilingualism haunted him with even greater force.

Not a page of *Eimi* goes by without hybrid words or expressions in different languages. There are overlaps between Russian and English[13] ('parody-koffyeh', 'parody-khleb', 'danodding', 'nyetimposscan't', 'tovarich-total-stranger',

---

13 Cummings studied Russian with a native speaker in Paris before coming to the USSR. The text of *EIMI* is foreworded by a small 'Russian-English' author's phrasebook, which includes key words and expressions used and played out in the novel. According to a notebook preserved in the Cummings archives at Harvard University, among the first words he learned to write in Russian are 'tovarich' and 'Kemminkz'.

'scarletnyetproletarian', 'rabotatically'), German and English ('Sie could have felled ich'; 'Trouble kapoot'), French and English ('bric-of-course-à-brac'; 'qui summons'; 'O say, does la régime soviétique hand all singularly ugly nonmales a break?'), Spanish and English ('mucho cautiously'), and Italian and English ('copyrightissimo', 'portraitissimo', 'americanissimo'). Sometimes four languages overlap at once (English, Latin, Italian and French): 'Looks like a million dollars – and which tastes like awful watered vino rosso à l'américain, N.Y. Eyetalian style, aetat nil'. Entire words from different languages are transcribed punnily: 'be-you-tifool' ('beautiful'), 'oo-Borneye-ah' ('уборная', restroom), 'boot-air-broat' ('бутерброт', sandwich); 'pair, rook, mah, care' ('парикмахер', hairdresser); 'spas-ee-bah' ('спасибо', thanks); or occasionally derived from different languages: 'Russianing', 'Germaning', 'nyezneyeyooing', 'peevohing', 'Frenchfully', 'nokomprennytablemate', etc. All these techniques of hybridisation playfully imitate certain forms of speech and the ideology of people encountered by Cummings on his trip.

A separate set of hybrid phrases used by Cummings could be called pidgin hybrids. These are cases when clumsy or incorrectly constructed phrases appear as a result of language transfer. Since the characters of *Eimi* speak different languages with each other, this confusion generates comedic dialogue. Thus, from the influence of German and French, comes the broken English greeting 'How goes it?'. In the seemingly gibberish phrase 'toykish kunsulit', one recognises the distorted English pronunciation of 'Turkish Consulate'. At the same time, foreign language words acquire new, most often ironic, meanings in the English text.

Speaking of *Eimi*'s avant-garde style and linguistic experimentation, we should note the connection of this unconventional language play with Cummings' experiments in poetry.[14] In his verse, as much as in his prose, morphemes with negative semantics and semantics of the past tense often play a central role. The use of negative formants in unusual combinations within and between words is a distinctive feature of his poetic language. In the opening scenes of *Eimi*, he calls Soviet Russia a 'Marxist unworld'. This 'unworld' creates its own language, consisting of continuous negations, signs of absence of anything human. Thus, the very word 'com**un**ism' seems to embed the negation 'un', as do all words containing the 'uni' formant, such as 'Soviet Union', '**un**iform', and the like. Hence the use of neologisms such as 'weremen', 'unmen', 'nonmen', which are used to denote the inhabitants of this 'unworld'. The addition of the prefixes 'un', 'non' or the suffix 'less' to any word indicates

---

14   For a survey of Cummings' experiments in grammar and lexis, see Fairley (1975).

a particular quality of objects in the Soviet world, used in estranging morphological hybrids such as 'unbanklike bank', 'unhuman smell', 'unimagination', 'untovarich', 'unmen', 'undeamon', 'unvalues', 'unvoice', 'unhe', 'unaliveness', 'unminnonutelesses', 'untheatre', 'unyouths', 'unfemale', 'unfunctioning'; 'nonmusic', 'nonunless', 'nonvolunteering', 'nonmale'; 'nowless', 'lifelessness', 'factless fact', 'Virde lessgilde comradeless Amerikanitz', dinnerless', 'systemless'. A similar neologism, 'withoutly', conveys the idea of non-existence and lack of things in the 'unworld'. A neologism can be fully composed of affixes, such as in 'nonunless'. In another example, we see a whole cluster of these negative forms: 'Very sleepfully thereat emerges young woman; yes, not a nonman (no, not unRussian – by her dazedness, and styleless style, and movingless moving, a subjectless subject of Old kingless King Karl'. This 'Kingless King Karl' is none other than Karl Marx, wandering like a ghost throughout the novel.

Hybrid compound words and phrases formed from English roots represent the largest group in *Eimi*. Words conjoin with no restrictions on grammatical selection or semantic valence. Some of these innovations encrypt real objects, often with visual coding involved, such as in 'barberpolemiracle-pineapple-prodigy', which stands in for the prominent Moscow landmark, St. Basil's Cathedral, whose domes resemble a pineapple and a barberpole at the same time, according to Cummings, who saw the cathedral several times on his visit.

Following this double encryption strategy, Cummings presents various objects using hybridised periphrasis: 'running mulmyritude change myrmultiad NowmultitudemyriadNow' stands for the train to Russia, 'a hyper2fisted supergogetting ultraredblooded certificate' for Aragon's notorious 'Red Front' poem. Some words are implanted into others, producing lexical hybrids: 'restaurperhapsant', 'disapnowpearing', 'optipessimism', 'Un (or possible) world', 'capvanitdalist', or 'comitalist caprade'.

Cummings' other characteristic technique is the ironic transcription or spelling of acronyms, especially Soviet ones. Thus, the seemingly German 'Volks' appears to encrypt the 'voks' ('вокс'), the Soviet Society for Cultural Foreign Relations, and the following example enciphers a whole series of polylingual abbreviations: 'You es es are es vee pee pee dee kyou kyou ee dee ay men (USSR RSVP PDQ QED Amen)'.[15] The compulsion to encrypt and decrypt letters in words – what Joyce called 'abced-mindedness' – allows Cummings to play with unexpected meanings in various layers of vocabulary. We have

---

15 USSR (Union of Soviet Socialist Republics, English); RSVP (Répondez s'il vous plaît, French); PDQ (Pretty Damn Quick, English slang); QED (Quod Erat Demonstrandum, Latin). 'Amen' might also be read as a typical Cummings neologism (a + men), suggesting the indefinite nature of people in the USSR.

already dwelt on possible 'literal' readings of the title *Eimi*. Other significant abbreviations undergo similar recompositions in the novel. For example, in a scene on the beach in Odessa, what seems an accidentally interspersed hyphenated word, 'G-A-Y', is followed, a few lines later, by the phrase 'et l'on paie', evidently in French, and, still further on, by an exclamation by one of the characters: 'ooooooooooo-noh!'. A naive reader could not possibly guess what lurks in this passage, but a competent reader could easily crack this mystery – these three scattered phrases spell out a hidden anagram, 'Gay-Pay-Oo' ('ГПУ'), which stands for the Soviet secret police ardently pursuing the hero right at the moment of narration. A similar authorial trick hides behind the word 'spas-ee-bah', encrypting Cummings' own initials, which he would often spell in lower case (e e cummings). It is no coincidence that both of Cummings' major prose works begin with the letter *e* (*The Enormous Room* and *Eimi*). As an advocate of Dr. Freud – who also features in *Eimi* as 'a gentleman from Vienna' – he would let language run riot in the cryptic mysteries of lexis and grammar.

The omnipresent hybridisation in Cummings' modernist/avant-garde novel-cum- travelogue is the result of a clash between two economic, political, creative, and linguistic worlds and their different, if not outright opposite, values. Hybridisation is used as the only possible means of depicting the confusion and agitation surrounding the stay of an American 'ME' in a Soviet 'WE'. Cummings' poetic 'I' undertakes an adventurous journey into Marxland and loses itself among the masses, in an infernal agglomeration of socialist figures. However, the 'I' triumphantly exits this inferno and finally has the chance to express itself in the vibrant manifesto of the 'I AM' – *Eimi*.

4   Dystopia vs Factuality: Yevgeny Zamyatin's *We* and E.E. Cummings' *Eimi*

Yevgeny Zamyatin's *We* is arguably the first example of a satirical futuristic dystopia, along with Jack London's *Iron Heel*. E.E. Cummings' *Eimi, A Journey through Soviet Russia* is a much less known book that also satirises Stalinist Russia but is written in a different, and original, form of novelised notes from a real journey. There are striking similarities in the subject matter and structure of both texts. I will argue that Cummings' anti-Soviet epic could have been inspired, if not by Zamyatin's novel itself, then at least by its main message and the conditions of its composition.

We was first conceived and drafted in 1919, soon after the October revolution. By 1921, the manuscript outline was finished and Zamyatin noted in a letter that 'he was completing a most bitter novel'. An announcement in Berlin's almanac *Zapiski mechtateley* advertised a novel 'portraying communist society in 800 years'. Though in the early 1920s, *We* was quite popular in Russian literary circles, all attempts to publish the novel in Russia failed, and in 1924 it was banned outright. It eventually was published that same year, not in Russia and not in Russian, but in English translation in the US. 1929 saw the French translation published under the title *Nous autres* by Gallimar publishers. These two editions had an influence on Aldous Huxley's *Brave New World*, published in 1931, and George Orwell's later dystopias. As a result, Zamyatin's dystopia first attained fame in America and Europe where it was widely distributed and read. A separate question is what the Western reader saw in the images of this futuristic utopia: a satire of Soviet society or a lampoon of the entire industrial capitalist world? The latter is more likely, as the Soviet Experiment was still alluring to Western intellectuals of the 1920s, especially in the years before the Great Depression, and was seen as an alternative to the deadlock of capitalist society.

Cummings's journey was inspired by, among other people, Ilya Ehrenburg, who had helped Zamyatin publish *We* in Paris some years earlier. It is likely that, as an acquaintance of both Zamyatin and Cummings, Ehrenburg might have told the American traveller to the Land of the Soviets about the 'most bitter' novel *We*. Although I there is no concrete evidence that Cummings knew of Zamyatin's *We*, we can assume that the overall atmosphere captured and described in *We* would also have had an influence on the American writer's experiences in Russia.

First, both texts viciously satirise early Soviet society. However, in Zamyatin's case, this takes the form of a dystopia showing the imaginary world of the One State. Curiously, the term 'Edinoe gosudarstvo' was translated in the later 1959 edition as 'United State', intentionally or not making a reference to the United States of America, though it is clear from the original text that Zamyatin meant a One State in a broader, utopian sense. In Cummings' *Eimi*, this One State is described using documentary evidence from the author's visit to 1931 Soviet Russia.

Furthermore, both texts are written in the form of a diary – Zamyatin's, or rather, his protagonist's, fictional 'records' parallel Cummings' real personal travel notes. In both cases, the diary form is meant to convey the individual and intimate nature of the utterance as opposed to the collective discourse of dictatorship. The diary as a literary form expresses the author's or protagonist's individual experience, the formation of his Self. But the fragmentary form of diary entries also reflects the disintegration of individual consciousness over time, standing in opposition the uniform opinion of the authoritarian WE. Both authors, Zamyatin and Cummings, draw on their Russian literary heroes – Dostoevsky with his *Diary of a Writer* and Gogol with his *Notes of a Madman* – in attributing to the diary the function of tracing a disrupted subjective consciousness. The Russian literary critic Lidiya Ginzburg (1971) called the diary 'a marginal kind of literature', a 'human document', registering the 'perpetual processing of life'. In both Modernist narratives, this function is reinforced and acts as an operator between the author's or hero's individual internal experience and the external discourse of the totalitarian regime.

This kind of collision is announced on the first pages of Zamyatin's novel. The first entry begins with an announcement in the State newspaper, which the protagonist D-503 'copies word for word'.[16] He opts to '[record] only the things he sees, the things he thinks, or to be more exact, the things *we* think. Yes, "we"; that is exactly what I mean, and We, therefore, shall be the title of my records'. However, he admits just here: 'It is I, and at the same time it is not I'. And indeed, the following entries emerge out of this conflict between *I-writer* and *We-writer*. With each new entry, D-503 thinks that his 'descriptions are not sufficiently clear', that he understands his own writings less and less. He notes: 'let this diary give the curve of the most imperceptible vibrations of my brain, like a precise seismograph, for at times such vibrations serve as forewarnings…' As the plot unfolds, the increasingly delirious I-writer completely represses the We-authority of his writing, and the entries grow into a chaotic stream of consciousness. Moreover, the protagonist has to hide his notes more and more carefully in fear of being punished by the Guardians and the Well-Doer. In effect, the novel *We* served as an omen of its author's fate – a few years after writing the novel, Zamyatin was banned from publishing under penalty of death.

Cummings was guided by similar feelings and considerations as those of Zamyatin's hero. *Eimi* is, indeed, a *roman à clef*. The encoding of well-known people and real-life situations actualises the symbolical figurality of proper names and provides an overview of historical and documentary facts and events. To a certain extent, Zamyatin's *We* can also be characterised as a *roman à clef*. The detailed commentary to the novel (Zamyatin 2011) suggests that Zamyatin's intention was to 'encrypt' Soviet realia in his hero's entries. On top of that, as the Russian dystopia scholar Leonid Heller notes (1981: 162), the 'fiercely political' and 'prophetic' *We* is a 'reflection on reality, a study of a particular historical situation and real historical process… His <Zamyatin's – V.F.> analysis proves to be true, and Stalin's state becomes so like the One State described in the novel *We*, that it is impossible to tell which is which'. This

---

16   I am quoting from the first English translation published in 1924, available online: https://gutenberg.org/cache/epub/61963/pg61963-images.html (last accessed 27.02.23).

argument becomes even more convincing if we assume that Cummings' *Eimi*, written ten years after *We*, entirely confirms Zamyatin's diagnosis and prognosis with documentary accuracy.

The same ironic attitude towards 'facts' is present in Zamyatin's *We*. In a bout of madness, D-503, the protagonist, writes in his diary: 'No more delirium, no absurd metaphors, no feelings – only facts'. Zamyatin depicts in his dystopia an imaginary 'paradise made of glass' and a 'better world of the future', though the hero suffers through spiritual hellfire, whereas in Cummings' book, the Soviet 'paradise', as it were, and the 'better world here and now' ('writer's paradise', as the narrator ironically calls it) in fact turns out to be an inferno. Both authors employ biblical metaphors and the motif of resurrection – for example, the resurrection of the American pilgrim on his return from 'hell', and the resurrection that Zamyatin's D-503 fails to achieve because resurrection is no longer possible in a world without good and evil; the world reverts to a paradise-like state of non-freedom. As for Cummings, he associates freedom with his own soul, the soul of an artist-creator under constant surveillance in the Soviet 'inferno'.

Another common motif in the two texts is the border between 'paradise' and 'hell', the 'world' and the 'unworld'. In Zamyatin, it is the image of the Green Wall, separating the One State from the rest of the world, which the protagonist fails to break through. In Cummings, this motif is repeated throughout *Eimi* in the image of 'Shutness'. There are other motifs that appear in both Zamyatin and Cummings: for example, the State as machine ('hatemachine' in *Eimi* – 'Well-Doer's' machine in *We*), new sexual norms and new family models in the Soviet regime, numbered people and innumerable crowds of comrades-tovariches, and so on. What was a work of imagination for Zamyatin became a true-to-life document about a dystopia that came true for Cummings. Both texts share similar linguistic techniques and devices. Among them are a cubistic perception of reality in narrative, disrupted narration that includes illogical combinations of words and letters, abrupt sentence structure, sudden leaps in narration, and a very characteristic stream of consciousness representing inner monologues and dialogues. Both *Eimi* and *We* are marked by conceptual neologisation and linguistic hybridisation.

Whether or not E.E. Cummings knew about Yevgeny Zamyatin's dystopia *We*, which had grown quite popular in the West, we can identify certain features common to both texts. Both were, to some degree, anti-proletarian works of literature. Both expressed their respective writers' reaction against totalitarian society in Leninist and later Stalinist Soviet Union. And both contain an ardent satire of that society. Furthermore, the two texts are quintessentially Modernist narratives that differ only in their genre (dystopia versus real-life travelogue). Reading these two texts now, almost a hundred years after their publication, we can clearly see how true and prophetic Zamyatin's *We* proved to be, and how grotesque Soviet reality looked as portrayed in *Eimi* through the eyes of an astonished American tourist. The experiment with language(s) and narration employed in Cummings' Soviet travelogue exemplifies the avant-garde quest to reconsider the literary text in terms of social revolt.

CHAPTER 9

Revolution of Language and Eugene Jolas

> We wanted to find the bridge to a reality where the nouveau homme surgira and where he will speak a new tongue.
> EUGENE JOLAS

∴

> So the jeunes joy with Jolas
> Book your berths: Après mot le déluge!
> JAMES JOYCE

∴

Aside from Ezra Pound's *Cantos* and E.E. Cummings' *Eimi*, American innovative literature of the early 20th century did not have many examples of multilingual experimentation within texts.[1] One of them was the theoretical and poetic oeuvre of Eugene Jolas, French-American trilingual poet, translator and literary critic, and founder of *transition*, an influential literary magazine which brought together diverse movements of the international avant-garde in the 1920–30s. As a writer and journalist, Jolas aspired to a new universal language that would make exchanges between national avant-gardes easier and bolder. On the pages of *transition*, he published poets, writers, artists, philosophers, psychologists, and literary critics in a kind of collaborative search for a new logos and a new mythos for the creative experiments of the inter-war period.[2]

---

[1] Parts of this chapter were written with the assistance of Olga Sokolova, whom I thank for the collaboration.

[2] Jolas' journal *transition* published works by several Russian authors. According to Neil Cornwell (1992), thanks to the efforts of a young Russian woman named Sofia Himmel, a steady stream of Russian Soviet (and sometimes older Russian) translated materials reached *transition*, especially in the early years of its existence. Among them were poems and short stories by Alexander Pushkin, Alexander Blok, Mikhail Zoshchenko, as well as articles by El Lissitzky and Sergey Eisenstein; articles about LEF and Soviet art by Alfred Barr, and art by Malevich and Kandinsky. However, despite Jolas' sympathy for Soviet proletarian literature and design, the magazine was almost unknown in Soviet Russia.

His was not a positivist investigation but a metaphysical quest, a tireless effort to transcend the borders of language, mind, communication, and artistic endeavor.

This chapter aims to reconstruct Eugene Jolas' conception of language as expressed in the essays published in *transition*. A self-styled 'man from Babel', Jolas advocated for a new international avant-garde of 'creative experiment' and 'orphic creation', for a 'laboratory of the word'. 'Quest' was a key word for Jolas, representing the metaphysical, mystical, and creative aspects of avant-garde work in literature, art, and philosophy. Jolas specifically stressed the role of language in the emerging forms of art and literature. He wrote a series of declarations about the 'revolution of language', which could be brought to life through the 'poetic state of language' and the creation of a 'hermetic language'. The result of such a revolution, he claimed, would be the 'universal word'. Using these premises as our point of departure, I will examine here the following issues: what were the different facets of language that Jolas revealed in his writings? What exactly did he mean by a 'revolution of language' and how did his theories and multilingual poetry contribute to the field of language-centered writing? How did Jolas progress from his 'vertical poetry' to the new conception of creative understanding among people that he called 'vertigralism'?

1   Multilingualism, Polyglotism, and 'Revolutionary Tendencies' in Avant-Garde Literature

According to Dougald McMillan's summary in his book on *transition* (1975), Jolas was searching for a shared language and experience beneath the superficial differences of individual national idioms as a way to compensate for the intercultural conflict that had plagued him since early childhood. The heterogeneity and polyglotism of the magazine were to a great extent the result of political and cultural circumstances – a series of crises, migrations, wars, and so forth. For Jolas, however, they were also a feature of his biography.

He was born in New Jersey, USA, but he was only two when his family moved to Elsass-Lothringen, then part of Germany (and now part of France) and the birthplace of Jolas' parents. The inhabitants of Forbach in Lorraine spoke German as well as French, so Jolas' grew up completely trilingual. He could easily shift among English, German, and French during the many transatlantic trips he took between France and the US over the course of his life. Jolas returned to America as a native-born immigrant in 1909. He lived in New York in the early 1920s and worked as a journalist, writing articles about Europe, and highlighting the Parisian literary scene in a series of profiles of writers and artists.

In addition to journalism, Jolas also took up experimental poetry. In two of his early poetry collections published in New York (*Ink*, 1924 and *Cinema*, 1926) one can see his first attempts at multilingual verse. Over the following two decades, he published about a dozen poetry books reflecting his macaronic striving for a universal language. Some of these books appeared courtesy of his own publishing houses, Editions Vertigral and Transition Press. Many of his avant-garde poems were published in *transition*, most often under the pen name Theo Rutra. Jolas was thus not only a proponent of a 'revolutionised' language, but also a quite original author of experimental verse. Poetry, he claimed, can be renewed through the 're-creation of the word' and the creation of a new 'verbal organism', which 'make it impossible that art be again and again the sycophant of reality' (Jolas, 2009: 245).[3]

Malicious contemporaries called Jolas a poetic epigone of the author of *Finnegans Wake*. But Jolas himself never made very much of his own contribution to experimental literature. What he cared about was the promotion of European and American avant-gardes in general and, most of all, the kind of linguistic experimentation that Joyce invented in his later writings. Jolas first met Joyce in 1926 through Sylvia Beach and the Shakespeare & Company bookshop. Jolas wanted to publish a fresh text by Joyce in the first issue of his journal *transition*. And he got it. The opening pages of *Work in Progress*, which would eventually grow into *Finnegans Wake*, appeared in the first issue of 1927. A year later, Jolas published an essay titled 'The Revolution of Language and James Joyce', in which *Work in Progress* is seen as heralding the new spirit of linguistic creativity of the 1920s.[4]

The essay begins with a powerful argument: 'The word presents the metaphysical problem today' (377). The problem is most clearly evident, according to Jolas, in the way modern poets operate with language. They break words apart for the purpose of reconstructing them on other planes. The new logos is engendered by a new mythos: 'Modern life with its changed mythos and transmuted concepts of beauty makes it imperative that words be given a new composition and relationship' (377). Jolas is making a point about the subversion of norms in modern literature. And it is here that he first speaks of revolution, activating its etymological meaning of 'turning around' or 'turning upside down'. In Joyce's new work, Jolas sees a 'revolutionary tendency' developed to its ultimate degree, whereby 'language is born anew before our

---

3   Hereafter in this chapter, the page number in brackets will refer to this collection of Jolas' writings.
4   See more on *transition* as a cultural phenomenon in McMillan (1975), Mansanti (2009), Setz (2019).

eyes' (377). But Joyce was not a solitary innovator. This revolutionary change in attitudes toward language encompasses all avant-garde literature in Europe and the Americas. In the same essay, Jolas gives examples of other poets and prose writers who 'deliberately worked in the laboratories of their various languages along new lines' (378–379): from Léon-Paul Fargue and Michel Leiris to Gertrude Stein and Hans Arp.

In performing a linguistic analysis of Joyce, Jolas refers to a scholarly work written by the French Jesuit and anthropologist Marcel Jousse. Just a couple of years before the Joyce essay, Jousse published a book called *Études de psychologie linguistique. Le style oral rythmique et mnémotechnique chez les verbomoteurs* (1925), positing a pan-ethnic origin of languages. According to Jousse, the rhythmical gesture is a universal element of verbal utterance and, moreover, a fundamental principle of any poetic act. To ground his findings, Jousse analyses 'parallel' examples from primitive languages and modernist poetry (Mallarmé, Péguy, etc.). But it is only in Joyce's writing, Jolas argues, that this commonality of linguistic origins is realised in a multilingual form: 'Whirling together the various languages, Mr. Joyce [...] creates a verbal dreamland of abstraction that may well be the language of the future' (381). In another manifesto, Jolas sees *Work in Progress* as 'the novel of the future' that will 'express the magic reality in a language that is non-imitative and evolutionary' (114) – just as language was at its origins, according to Jousse's theory.

2 The 'Revolution of Language' According to Eugene Jolas

Jolas's programmatic 1928 essay on Joyce's multilingualism was the first in a series of articles and other texts in *transition* dedicated to language issues. The magazine itself became a platform for creative inquiry into the nature of language in literature. By publishing various avant-garde writings translated from many languages into English, the editors of *transition* (or '*transocean*', as Joyce once rebaptised it) injected the spirit of Babel into the periodical.

In a 1929 issue of *transition*, wanting to give the journal a more avant-garde ethos, Jolas published a text called 'Proclamation'. It is likely that he wrote it himself, but it was cosigned by him and a number of his fellow writers. It has the structure of a typical avant-garde manifesto; it opens with the phrase 'We hereby declare' followed by a list of twelve declarations reminiscent of those found in Futurist pamphlets. What interests us here is the language metaphors and language problematic emerging from the manifesto. The 'Proclamation' appears right after the title of a section of the journal, 'Revolution of the Word', which is a slight modification of the phrase found in Jolas's earlier essay on Joyce ('Revolution of Language'). Jolas is referring in this new title to the Word-Logos, a complex and mysterious concept dating back to ancient Greek and early Christian conceptions of the divine Creative Word. This spiritual, even religious treatment of the Word by Jolas will remain relevant alongside its more typical meanings in ordinary usage. The question then arises: how is it that the Word, in this highly metaphysical sense, can undergo a 'revolution'? What is actually meant by the phrase 'revolution of the word'? Is it merely a pompous, strained metaphor, or does this formulation posit concrete changes in the properties of language in experimental literature?

The first declaration in Jolas' 'Proclamation' is straightforward and categorical: 'The revolution in the English language is an accomplished fact' (111). No evidence of this fact is provided, but we may suppose that, as Jolas demonstrated in a previous essay, the revolution was accomplished by James Joyce, and the proof of that revolution was the subversion of all linguistic norms in *Work in Progress*. For Jolas, then, the revolution of language was no mere metaphor. On the other hand, Jolas issues a caveat in his essay 'On the Quest', written at about the same time, about the use of the term revolution: 'It is true that we owe an incalculable amount of things to the influence of the Russian Revolution, but we cannot allow this conception to dominate us. The stimulus of the emancipation which we gain from the Cyclopean effort of the October rebels has been our constant encouragement, but not in its political, nor in its dialectic aspect' (246). As we can see from this remark, the notion of revolution interests Jolas as its purely spiritual value, even if the political term serves as a trigger. This double meaning requires further clarification in the context of the artistic avant-garde of the early 20th century.

In 1849, Richard Wagner wrote a long essay called 'Art and Revolution'. Inspired by revolutionary movements throughout Europe, the composer attempted to formulate how art relates to revolution. He does not draw a direct line between political action and artistic revolt, arguing instead that 'true Art is revolutionary because its very existence is opposed to the ruling spirit of the community'. According to Wagner, revolution in art is a revolution in itself, in the mind of an artist opposing society. The Russian Revolution reactualised this essay by Wagner and, indeed, inspired many Russian thinkers and writers in their thinking about 'revolution in art'. The Symbolist poet Alexander Blok, for instance, strove for a new 'artistic humanity', which would be brought about by the October Revolution. The experimental writer Andrey Bely, sometimes called the Russian James Joyce, saw a sacramental link between revolution and art. Although the direction of political and artistic revolutions may differ, they originate from a single epicenter which Bely calls 'the revolutionary volcano'. The energy of the revolutionary eruption gives birth to what Bely calls a 'revolution of spirit', which is quite similar to Jolas' formulation 'revolution of the soul'. For Bely, the revolution of spirit is a result of two further revolutions – a revolution of life and a revolution of creativity (cf. Jolas' motto that the creator's revolution 'aims at a complete metamorphosis of the world').

In the preface to an issue of *transition*, Jolas writes about experimentation in life and language. In this sense, both Andrey Bely and Eugene Jolas are truly avant-garde writers, if we apply Peter Bürger's principle that, for avant-garde art, the idea of revolution in life transforms itself into the idea of revolution in art. The concept of a 'revolution of spirit' was later widely referenced in the radical Russian avant-garde (by Vladimir Mayakovsky, Pavel Filonov, and others). In Futurist poetry, the revolution of spirit was accompanied by a revolution in language. It is quite unlikely that Jolas was aware of these Russian texts from the 1910–20s, but he certainly understood the atmosphere emanating from revolutionary Russia. Most likely, however, the concept of revolution was suggested to him by André Breton who, in 1924, founded the journal *La révolution surréaliste*. To a large degree, *transition* comprised texts written by Surrealists (some would even say that Jolas' journal was an organ of Surrealism). The title of Breton's journal, then, seems the most likely source for Jolas' formula 'Revolution of the word'. Jolas, however, repeatedly stated that the Surrealists had not in fact revolutionised language in the way that Joyce had.

In any case, as we have argued here, Jolas' concept of revolution was influenced by a whole array of political and artistic implications. And it seems that, for Jolas, there was no contradiction between the two basic meanings of the word revolution, as Gerald Raunig's book *Art and Revolution* (2007) suggests, that of 'revolt' and that of 'revolving' (as in 'revolving planets'). Jolas made use of both meanings. For him, a revolution of language was at the same time a break with conventions and a 'revolving' back to the primal stages of language evolution.

The poet's task, according to the 'Proclamation', is to 'disintegrate the primal matter of words' (246). Arthur Rimbaud's 'hallucination of the word' is evoked here to stress the rhythmic nature of this 'revolutionised' language. Some of Jolas' declarations may seem outdated and unoriginal, such as the appeal to 'disregard existing grammatical and syntactical laws' (112). Italian and Russian Futurists had already advocated for these principles twenty years earlier. Never before in the English language had the revolt against linguistic norms been as vigorously pursued as it was in the pages of *transition*. The primary feature of the revolution of language, according to Jolas, was free experiment and invention. It is this that allowed Jolas to speak of a revolution of language in Elizabethan theater in one of his essays.

3 'Vertical Poetry' as a 'Revolutionary Approach to the Word'

In his later *transition* essays, Eugene Jolas elucidated his revolutionary approach to the language of poetry – for example, in a series of texts about the 'vertical' dimension of poetry. In a 1932 manifesto titled 'Poetry is Vertical' (which was signed by Hans Arp and Samuel Beckett, among others), Jolas writes about the 'hermetic language' that is invented over the course of the creative act, an invention made possible 'by the use of a language which is a mantic instrument' and which 'adopts a revolutionary attitude toward word and syntax' (266–267). Poets create their own languages, Jolas claims. This assertion evokes the Russian Futurist poet Velimir Khlebnikov and his notion of a 'breakthrough into languages' discussed in Part 1 of this book. But Khlebnikov stresses that his 'language husbandry' does not violate the laws of language. Newly created languages breathe new life into existing national idioms: 'If contemporary man can restock the waters of exhausted rivers with fish, then language husbandry gives us the right to restock the impoverished streams of language with new life, with extinct or non-existent words' (Khlebnikov, 1987: 382). In contrast to Khlebnikov, Jolas calls for breaking the rules of grammar and lexis. Discussing the way language changes over the course of history, he points out that these changes often result from instinctual individual activity. Many linguists of his time would not have agreed with this statement; they would have claimed that linguistic change and linguistic creativity can occur only through the collective efforts of all speakers of a given language. But Jolas criticised such 'pedantic semasiologists', as he calls them: 'In seeking the flexibility of his language, [the poet] is at liberty to create his own laws' (182). The poet, then, has the power to break up the structure of syntax and morphology.

Jolas might have been aware of the latest trends in linguistics in the era of logical positivism, behaviourial descriptivism and grammatical structuralism. Most linguists of his time ignored the specificity of poetic language, the way it can constitute a sublanguage (or rather superlanguage) of its own. Jolas, in contrast, advocated for the special status of poetic linguistic experimentation. The photographic, utilitarian conception of the word did not satisfy him. Words in poetry possess a reality that dictionaries and grammar textbooks cannot know. He understood the need for a creative grammar, a revised language: 'Grammar is not a static thing', he writes. 'Modern poets foster the dynamics of an inner, alogical grammar' (164). Jolas' views on grammar are profoundly similar to Gertrude Stein's contemporaneous meditations on grammar. Where Stein uses the terms 'incantation' and 'insistence' to restore magic powers to reconstructed words, Jolas consistently emphasises the primal character of what he calls the 'orphic language of poetry' as a 'new symbolical language'. And again, he discusses it in terms of a spiritual revolution: 'The poet who gives back to language its pre-logical functions, who recreates it as an orphic sign, makes a spiritual revolt, which is the only revolt worth making today' (162). Language, he claims, must be given a mediumistic function; it must be charged with the mood of liturgy and litany. To give substance to his argument, Jolas refers to several important figures: (1) Novalis, who, in his *Fragments*, made the following enigmatic note: 'Language is Delphi', (2) Franz Baader, another German Romantic, who spoke of the 'language of dreams', and 3) Justinus Kerner, German poet and physician, who described in his *Die Seherin von Prevorst* a case of somnambulism (156). The turn of the 20th century saw a proliferation of glossolalic phenomena, as we have argued in Part 1 of the book. It is in this context that Jolas speaks of the 'malady of language', the idea that language is in a state of crisis and requires some sort of healing, a healing that poetry can provide.[5]

4   The Transatlantic 'Universal Language'

Eugene Jolas had a different idea for how to overcome this 'malady of language'. He finds a solution to the crisis in the creation of a universal language on the basis of a mixture of existing languages used on both sides of the Atlantic. The foundations for this language, he believed, had already been laid in his journal and in the linguistic revolution it proclaimed. The best examples of this 'interlanguage' were Joyce's work and, perhaps, Jolas's own interlinguistic experiments. In a long essay from 1932 titled 'The Language of Night', he summed up the evolution of multilingual poetry from Stéphane Mallarmé to Hans Arp. But it was only a few years before the Second World War broke out that he began to talk about the 'Euramerican', or 'transatlantic', language of the future as a language of creative expression and communication. He argued that linguistic reformation was already taking place in American society, referring to the journalist Henry L. Mencken's famous book *The American Language*. Jolas wanted to amplify and expand the trend via his conception of an 'Atlantic' or 'Crucible' language, resulting of the 'interracial synthesis' that he observed in the United States in the 1930s. He considered this new language an American form of English, building on Anglo-Saxon, but with additions and interferences from other tongues coming to, from and through America. This polyglotism is a characteristic feature of Jolas' own poems, too: 'I invented my own Atlantic language. I made the discovery of a multilingual form of poetry which corresponded to an inner need in me to express the linguistic monism which was my organic mode of thinking' (178).

---

5   A similar kind of reasoning can be found in the writings of Ilia Zdanevich about 'language revival' through poetic glossolalia (discussed in Chapter 3 of this book).

The 'Atlantic' language manifested itself in the co-presence of several languages in one poetic text (alternating lines in different languages, as in example 1 below), and in multilingual hybridisation (hybrid words from different languages, as in example 2), and in the sound synthesis of many languages, gravitating towards zaum, or trans-sense language (example 3):[6]

1.

XLVIII

The horizontal world is dying
We want to rise higher than the Andes
Higher than the empire state building
Higher than the world-tree
Voici venir l'ère de l'atlantide
Je vous salue inconnus pleins de grace
O vous qui revez un avenir de cristal
Que les anges vous gardent du tumulte
Des betes démoniaques qui se tapissent dans les caves pourries
The voyage goes upward
Veergulls drift farewells in foamrhythms
We stand in the conjuration of the lonely beings
Who wait for the ripple-chants of their redemption
The continent is incandescent
With the cries of the mutilated spirits
The vision of the new glass-age glisters
The boats are freighted with ecstatic men and women
We hear news from enormous epochs
Da die scheitelauegler sehnsuechtig in das weltall starrten
The moundbuilders are here
And the sky-storming creators
Join obsidian-swinging the migratory march
We enter a skyworld without horizon
We tear down the frontier-bars
We dream one tongue from alaska to tierra del fuego
We dream a new race visionary with the logos of God[7]

---

6 On Jolas' multilingual poetry see Perloff (1999), Kiefer (2002), Sokolova (2015), Kelbert (2015).
7 Eugene and Maria Jolas Papers. Beinecke Rare Book and Manuscript Library, New Haven, CT. Box 18.

2.

Mots-Frontiere: Polyvocables

malade de peacock-feathers
le sein blue des montagnes and the house strangled by rooks the tender entêtement des trees
the clouds sybilfly and the neumond brûleglisters ein wunder stuerzt ins tal with
eruptions of the abendfoehren et le torrentbruit qui charrie les gestes des enfants. [...][8]

3.

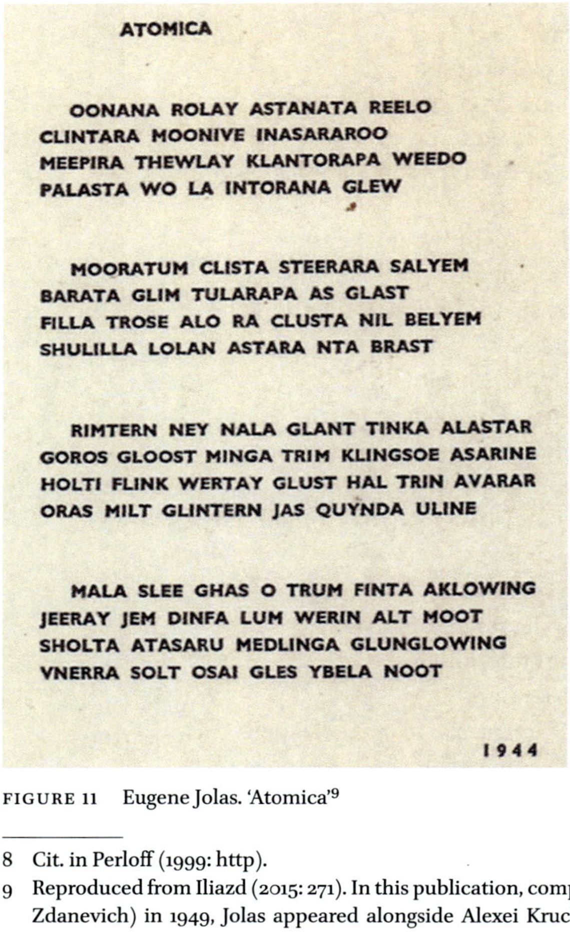

```
ATOMICA

OONANA ROLAY ASTANATA REELO
CLINTARA MOONIVE INASARAROO
MEEPIRA THEWLAY KLANTORAPA WEEDO
PALASTA WO LA INTORANA GLEW

  MOORATUM CLISTA STEERARA SALYEM
BARATA GLIM TULARAPA AS GLAST
FILLA TROSE ALO RA CLUSTA NIL BELYEM
SHULILLA LOLAN ASTARA NTA BRAST

  RIMTERN NEY NALA GLANT TINKA ALASTAR
GOROS GLOOST MINGA TRIM KLINGSOE ASARINE
HOLTI FLINK WERTAY GLUST HAL TRIN AVARAR
ORAS MILT GLINTERN JAS QUYNDA ULINE

  MALA SLEE GHAS O TRUM FINTA AKLOWING
JEERAY JEM DINFA LUM WERIN ALT MOOT
SHOLTA ATASARU MEDLINGA GLUNGLOWING
VNERRA SOLT OSAI GLES YBELA NOOT

                              1944
```

FIGURE 11   Eugene Jolas. 'Atomica'[9]

8 Cit. in Perloff (1999: http).
9 Reproduced from Iliazd (2015: 271). In this publication, compiled and published by Iliazd (Ilia Zdanevich) in 1949, Jolas appeared alongside Alexei Kruchenykh and Velimir Khlebnikov.

Among Jolas' manifestoes devoted to 'revolutions of language', the 'language of the night', and 'universal language', we find the following passage: 'The crisis in the communicative functions of language creates the intellectual chaos which characterises all human relations today' (141). In order to overcome this chaos, he suggested a new mode of communication based on a 'language of night' that 'will make the intercontinental synthesis of the inner and outer language'. That language 'will dance and sing, it will be a new vision of the "troisième œil" that will bind the races in the fabulous unity' (285). The manifesto-appeal 'Wanted: A New Communicative Language!' (1932) shows Jolas' endeavor to protest against modern 'language neurosis' and his belief that it is necessary to enhance the language capacity that developed in early humans and remains hidden in the brain as a 'universal language'.

Jolas' universal language is, firstly, a project aimed at a mixture, an 'interracial synthesis', of all languages 'being spoken in America today' (178); secondly, it is an 'intercontinental synthesis of the inner and outer language', able to express the collective unconscious of humanity' (285); thirdly, Jolas' universal language goes beyond the idea of multilingualism as an integration of languages, calling for a transformation of the very basis of language through the influence of diverse cultures;[10] fourthly, at the heart of that transformation lies Jolas' assertion of a poetic basis for the universal language as a 'mantic compost', constantly changing and developing on all linguistic levels; and, finally, the universal language not only activates various verbal layers, but also influences the speaker's mind by prompting creative linguistic activity and creating new communicative forms.

5   Origins of the 'Universal Language'

The Enlightenment era introduced two fundamental approaches to the idea of universal languages: René Descartes' belief in the significance of logical classification based on semantic definition of complicated concepts via more simple ones,[11] and Marin Mersenne's approach, whereby *a priori* evidence of language constituents are taken as the fundamental principle of a new 'artistic' language. Eugene Jolas certainly advocated for the second type of approach in his manifestoes devoted to the creation of a 'poetic state of language' and

---

Two traditions of experimental sound poetry – the Russian and the Euro-American – came together many decades after the first publications by these movements.
10   See Perloff (2002).
11   E.g., in Descartes' essay 'The Search After Truth by the Light of Nature'.

'hermetic language'. In 'The Language of Night', he stated that 'its primordial stratum is composed of images, the multiplicity of which is in exact ratio to the psychic potentiality of the possessor. Here an emotional conjuration occurs. The image seeks a new connection with another image. We observe the birth of the word as the symbol of the image' (158–159). On the one hand, Mersenne's idea of creating a new, organic language system based on *a priori* evidence of language constituents relates to Jolas' endeavor to renew the lost unity of word and image, in which art was 'primarily unity and synthesis' (155). Mersenne's language drew a direct correlation between the phonetic and semantic structures of a word. Jolas proposed rejecting conventional relations between signifier and signified. Those relations should always be discovered anew from the 'primordial stratum' in the 'vertigral' communication situation. This revival of a 'fossilised' word and its synaesthetic apprehension dates back to Jolas' longing for an Adamic language 'and the fulfilled experience of communication before the hubris of the tower of Babel' (130).

Economic globalisation and the concomitant growing need for international communication in the late 19th century stimulated the development of the so-called 'universal' or 'international auxiliary languages'. Thus, European and, in particular, Romance languages became the basis for Esperanto and Volapük, both invented in the 1880s. In the second half of the 1920 and the 1930s, with WWI still fresh in peoples' minds, and with widespread premonition that a new war was inevitable, universal languages were conceived as a means for avoiding new disasters. Driven by a desire to promote peace, British linguist Charles K. Ogden, creator of the International Auxiliary Language or Basic English, stated: 'The so-called national barriers of today are ultimately language barriers. The absence of a common medium of communication is the chief obstacle of international understanding, and therefore the chief underlying cause of war' (1931: 18).

Charles Ogden was familiar with Jolas' work. During his study of universal languages, the English linguist became interested in Joyce's experiments and even wrote a preface to an excerpt from *Finnegans Wake* in *transition*, containing his own translation of this fragment of the novel into Basic English (see Joyce, 1990).[12] In his idea for a universal language, the linguist saw the desire for 'debabelization'. In a book with the telling title *Debabelization* (1931), Ogden

---

12 See Sailer (1999) for more details.

admits that Joyce's multilingualism 'anticipated' his own project of language universalisation.[13]

In its turn, Basic English sparked interest among writers experimenting with language. For instance, Ezra Pound was enthusiastic about Ogden's artificial language and wrote that if a writer's work is tolerable when translated into Basic English, then there is a foundation to his style.[14] In contrast, the Objectivist poet Louis Zukofsky debated Ogden on the artistic merits of this auxiliary language. Zukofsky himself experimented with something similar in his early short novel *Thanks to the Dictionary*. The text is made up of excerpts and 'cut-ups' from randomly selected vocabulary entries and is drawn from a minimal set of improvised words. The strategies of this literary work resembled the linguistic methods of academic scholarship. Eugene Jolas' magazine was a platform for both.

The desire to express a dynamic new reality and to overcome the language barriers separating mankind was a stimulus for a number of philosophers and poets of the 20th century to create theories of international languages. These ideas informed the conception of a 'perfect language' proposed by Russian and American avant-garde artists, German Expressionists, the Portuguese poet Fernando Pessoa, and so forth. The philosophical concept of a 'pure language' proposed by Walter Benjamin in his 1923 essay 'The Task of the Translator' (1996) amounted to just that kind of 'perfect language' in the field of translation studies. Jolas paid particular attention to the artistic experiments of James Joyce,[15] Paul Éluard, Henri Michaux, Stefan George, and August Stramm. It was Jolas, however, together with the Russian Futurists,[16] who was most consistent in pursuing this goal.

Eugene Jolas' 'world revolution of language' developed along similar lines to other concepts for a reformed or revolutionised language in the 1920s and after. The so-called 'linguistic turn', which had actually begun in the late 19th-early 20th century had a major influence on European culture in the twentieth century. The interest of many *fin-de-siècle* intellectuals in languages and other sign systems was unprecedented. This was reflected in numerous experiments, both scientific and artistic, in language construction and language creativity. This linguistic turn reached its ultimate expression in Martin Heidegger's

---

13 Curiously, the same concept of 'debabelization' was used by the Russian literary critic Boris Bukhshtab in his article on Khlebnikov's language philosophy (Bukhshtab, 2008).
14 See more on Pound and Ogden in Dowthwaite (2019: 133–173).
15 About James Joyce's development of the 'universal language', see Israel (2017).
16 For more details on the commonalities between Velimir Khlebnikov's and Jolas' ideas about 'universal' language, see Sokolova (2015).

formula 'Language is the house of being' (from the opening page of his 1947 'Letter on Humanism'). Thus, a new mode of thinking and creativity arose, a mode determined by language.

War compelled serious adjustments to this linguistic turn. Jolas stresses this point in the introduction to his book of multilingual verse *Words from the Deluge*, published immediately after the outbreak of the Second World War, a war that affected all races and languages on the map of Europe and the world. After the trauma and catastrophe of WWII, Jolas could no longer speculate about a universal 'pan-logos'. In his eyes, the war had been the fall of the creative tower of Babel he had been building on the pages of *transition*. He was left with nothing but reminiscences of the *belle époque* of the interwar cultural renaissance in the global avant-gardes. Musing about the Babelian confusion of languages in contemporary literature, he wrote in his memoirs (Jolas, 1998: 271):

> I felt: as man wanders anguished through this valley of crises and convulsions, his language and languages wander with him. [...] In pre-war years we were a handful of poets who sensed it perhaps more than others, who passed through the pathological experience of diverse tongues, who found a progressive sclerosis in all of them. Some of us tried to find radical solutions. We tried to create a poetic and prose medium in which words were invented, in which the miraculous philology was posited. We were passionately interested in inter-linguistic experiments, in sound poetry as a musical or prosodical ersatz for desiccated word sequences, in phantasmatic deformations for deformation's sake. [...] We tried to redefine basic words in a semantic revolution, we tried to go back to primitive etymons. We tried to give voice to the sufferings of man by applying a liturgical exorcism in a mad verbalism.

In these musings, we see the metaphor of language as ocean, language as a huge space that divides continents but also ties them up into one transatlantic knot (Idem: 272–273):

> Language is in a fevered state today. It wanders about like the ocean washing the shores of the nations, depositing verbal sediments here and there, nibbling at the soil in foaming surges. Why should language not be channeled into a universal idiom? Seven years ago I called this potential tongue Atlantica, because I felt that it might bridge the continents and neutralise the curse of Babel. [...] Language, like man, is today engaged

in a vast migration. [...] The huge urban collectivities that are arising will forge the migratory and universal tongue in an exaltation of sacred and communal vocables, in a voyage without end.

These are the closing lines of Eugene Jolas' memoirs. These words round off the era of the transatlantic avant-garde whose active phase progressed between the two world wars, the era of the first experiments in language-oriented writing.

TRANSITION 2

Linguistics and Poetics: Roman Jakobson's Opening and Closing Statements

> Poetry is language in its aesthetic function.
> ROMAN JAKOBSON

∴

> The set (Einstellung) toward the message as such, focus on the message for its own sake, is the POETIC function of language.
> ROMAN JAKOBSON

∴

The Russian and American paths to linguistic revolutions in poetry seem to have begun intersecting in the 1960s, when information flows and intellectual migration between the USSR and the United States became possible after the difficult early years of the Cold War. A major figure involved in the transfer between these two avant-garde cultures was the linguist Roman Jakobson, who had been living and working in the US since 1941, carrying with him the legacy of Russian Formalist theory and Futurist poetics. From the 1960s on, Jakobson had a few opportunities to go back to his native country, once again acting as the missionary of cutting-edge ideas about poetry and language between the two otherwise antagonistic political worlds. In Khrushchev-era Soviet Russia, Jakobson would become a significant source of inspiration for Gennady Aygi, a Neo-Futurist poet; meanwhile, in America, his academic teachings would be very influential for the language innovator Michael Palmer.

Back in the first decades of the 20th century, Formalism – with its insistence on the 'resurrection of the word' (Viktor Shklovsky) and the description of living facts of verbal art – was guided by contemporary experimentation in artistic life. Roman Jakobson recollected: 'I was guided in my search by the experience of new poetry, quantum movement in the physics of our era and phenomenological ideas [...]' (1996: 181). The path to understanding the structure of language led through the avant-garde techniques of Picasso and

Braque, who 'attached importance not to things themselves, but rather to the connections between them' (Ibidem). A united front of science, art, and literature emerged, rich in new, as yet unexplored values of the future.[1]

The first uses of the terms 'poetic language', 'poetic utterance' and 'poetic function' appear in Roman Jakobson's analysis of Futurist texts by Filippo Tommaso Marinetti and Velimir Khlebnikov. In contrast to the public and scholarly consensus of his time, Jakobson singles out the work of the Russian 'Futurian' as the most representative language practice of the revolutionary period. Abnormal from the point of view of literary tradition and the diachronic view of Russian language, Khlebnikov's poems open up a new vision of their subject to the researcher of language (in Jakobson's pioneering 1921 essay on Khlebnikov). For the first time, linguistics referred not only to the facts of living language in their synchronous changes, but also to the language of contemporary literature, the 'poetic language of modernity', in Jakobson's formulation. Avant-garde poetics undergirds the revolution in linguistics. It is precisely in these analyses that the theory of linguistic functions (communicative, emotional, poetic, etc.), which later became paradigmatic in the functionalism of the Prague Linguistic School, comes to the fore. That which previous paradigm (represented by Jakobson's mentor Jan Baudouin de Courtenay) deemed extra-linguistic (for example, Futurist word creation) and harmful to a language's development, was seen as potentially productive for linguistic creativity in the linguistic paradigm.

In 1914, Baudouin de Courtenay published a critique of the theory of the word as such, which had been proclaimed by the Futurists Kruchenykh, Khlebnikov and Burliuk. One of the goals of their manifesto 'A slap in the face of public taste' was 'to enlarge the scope of the poet's vocabulary with arbitrary and derivative words (Word-novelty)' (Burliuk et al., 1988: 51). Futurists openly declared a rebellion against 'grammatical rules', a denial of spelling, a destruction of punctuation marks, and a declaration of a trans-sense language. Baudouin, who had published a book *On the Relationship of Russian Writing to the Russian Language* (1912), fiercely objected to the possibility of creating words from an arbitrary set of 'letters' and 'sounds'. He condemns such combinations as 'го existn кайт' and 'еуы' as anomalous and unacceptable in language, let alone in poetic language. The impossibility of such 'words' in language is caused, according to Baudouin, by the basic linguistic postulate that words do not consist of sounds or letters, but rather associations in the human psyche of certain representations of meanings. To him, *Bayachi*'s experiments

---

1   On the relationship between Russian Formalism and the avant-garde, see also Jakobson (2012), Pomorska (1968), Pomorska et al. (1987).

do not belong to the field of language (Baudouin de Courtenay, 1914a; 1914b). Curiously, Baudouin de Courtenay himself was able to generate anomalous combinations of words, such as these senseless sequences: 'Караменота селулабиха / Кеременута шёвелесула / Тиутамкунита чорчорпелита' (cit. in Biryukov, 2004: http). However, the senselessness of such combinations convinced him that language is not formed by pure sound combination.

Unlike Baudouin, Jakobson and the Futurist poets saw in these anomalies an embryonic state of poetic language. As is well known, Jakobson himself experimented with zaum. In the 1970s, he referred to these experiments as 'the sins of sixty years ago', but in 1915 they served as a model for the transition from Khlebnikov's 'samovitoe slovo' to 'poetic language as language set for expression': 'мзглыбжвуо йихъяньдрью чтлэщк хн фя съп скыполза / а Втаб-дклни тьяпра какайзчди евреец чернильница' (Jakobson, 2012: 190). In this distich, anomalies appear not only on the level of grammatical structure and lexical composition, but also on the level of the prosodical-phonetic system of Russian speech. These anomalies gave rise to a scientific breakthrough in linguistic poetics, making this discipline an important branch of research, especially for Russian linguistics of the twentieth century.

Apart from zaum verse, Jakobson took up what would later be called 'asemic writing'. In a letter to Khlebnikov dated 1914, he provides a 'sample of new poetry' composed of 'nodes of letters' ('сплёты букв'), reminiscent of musical chords. In the same letter, he suggests that such experiments could be a springboard for new ideas in art: 'These nodes cannot, then, be completely acceptable physically, but a share of unacceptability is a necessary prerequisite for new art' (Idem: 115). Considering Jakobson's later contribution to the theory of sign systems, these modest experiments with 'their unacceptability' (that is, anomality), indeed laid the groundwork for a new science – semiotics.

It seems that it was precisely such experiments with different levels of language that inspired another famous Russian linguist, Lev Shcherba, in his syntactic and morphological experiments with the creation of artificial phrases. In his famous example, 'Глокая куздра штеко будланула бокра и курдячит бокрёнка' (untranslatable into English), Shcherba sought to prove that even with an anomalous structure at one level (lexical), a statement can remain within the language framework at another level (grammar). At the same time, the virtuosity of this experimental text and its manner of creation made it a true hit in Russian and foreign linguistic literature. The scholar Fedor Dvinyatin (2003) even proposed that it be considered a poetic work similar to the transrational texts of Russian Futurists and called Shcherba a practitioner of the new Russian poetics. For Shcherba himself, this example emphasised the significance of the linguistic experiment and 'negative language material' not only for language teaching, but also for understanding the essence of language phenomena. In particular, this phrase illustrated the important thesis that abstract grammatical structures are always present in the speaker's mind, sometimes even without requiring lexically normal content.

We could cite more examples of this anomalousness from the texts of Russian Futurists, such as this text by Igor Terentiev dated 1918, consisting of non-existent yet grammatically coherent words (cit. in Karpov, 2012: 96):

Моснял мазами сено
Кутка неизверная
Тена фразам исчерна
Нерно прокатом
Окатом высокотом
Вуста уста стали
Сихи мелбормхаули
Мотма борма смений
Выборма вылисма вымотма
Выбормотался гений
Вот как.

Such verses may well have urged Shcherba to test his linguistic ideas using constructed expressions. Linguistic experiments served as support for his theory of 'speech activity' as a balance between the 'linguistic system' and 'linguistic material', which, in turn, was an elaboration of Ferdinand de Saussure's theory.[2] Shcherba's linguistic experiment, then, went hand in hand with the Futurist poetic experiment, and Russian linguistics has since paid serious attention to this affinity.

Several decades later, linguistic and poetic anomalies would once again spark scholarly discussion among prominent linguists. In the early 1960s, a debate took place between two friendly colleagues, Roman Jakobson and Noam Chomsky, which touched on a seemingly innocuous phrase that Chomsky composed and introduced into scientific discussions in the 1950s in his book *Syntactic Structures*. This constructed expression was given in two versions: 'Colorless green ideas sleep furiously' and 'Furiously sleep ideas green colorless' (Chomsky, 2002: 15). The American generative linguist was

---

2 In Anglo-American linguistics of the same time, the phrase 'The gostak distims the doshes', coined by the American school teacher Andrew Ingraham, garnered similar popularity. Charles Ogden and Ian Richards would later discuss it in their book *The Meaning of Meaning* (1924) within the linguistic context.

interested in the question of whether grammatically incorrect sentences relate to a particular language to the same extent as grammatically correct sentences. In addition, he raised questions about the boundaries of the correct and the meaningful (that is, bearing sense in the semantic sense). From his point of view, both of the above sentences are equally meaningless, but the latter is also grammatically incorrect, and therefore does not belong to the set of sentences that make up the English language. As for the first phrase, for all its semantic 'absurdity', he deems it syntactically correct, and, hence, fitting into the structure of the existing language. On these grounds, Chomsky elaborated his theory of degrees of grammaticalness.

Discussion of these artificial examples by Chomsky has led to many interpretations in the world of linguistics. However, we are particularly interested in Jakobson's polemics with Chomsky's reasoning. Jakobson responded to this discussion in an article dedicated to the anthropologist Franz Boas. Noting the general inventiveness of Chomsky's linguistic experiment in constructing a 'completely non-semantic theory of grammatical structure', the Russian-American linguist drew the opposite conclusions from the work by his American colleague. According to Jakobson, it is precisely anomalous phrases such as 'Colorless green ideas sleep furiously', that most vividly highlight the very meaningful categories of our consciousness. Right away he recalls some poetic tropes that resemble Chomsky's phrase: 'To a *green thought* in a *green shade*' by the poet Andrew Marvell and 'все тот же ужас, красный, белый, квадратный' by Leo Tolstoy. Why, then, can't 'ideas fall asleep'? Should we equate ontological unreality with meaninglessness? Jakobson objects to Chomsky's point that such expressions have 'a lower degree of grammaticality'.

For Jakobson, who emerged from the circles of Russian Futurism, both of Chomsky's phrases looked quite successful and meaningful in the context of the experiments of Mayakovsky, Khlebnikov and Kruchenykh. With all their semantic and syntactic anomaly, they still would be non-anomalous in any poetic context. As shown by Jakobson and much later by Boris Uspensky (2007), this phrase could be considered semantic and even syntactic in a poetic or folkloric context. This, in fact, proved to be true soon after their debate. Another American structural linguist, Dell Hymes, composed a poem using Chomsky's phrase as the title. The poem is a decoding of that phrase, which reads quite meaningfully here (cit. in Yaguello, 1998: 119):

'Colorless green ideas sleep furiously'

Hued ideas mock the brain
Notions of color not yet color

Of pure and touchless, branching pallor
Of an invading, essential green.

Ideas, now of inchoate color
Nest as if sleeping in the brain
Dormant, domesticated green,
As if had not come a dreaming pallor

Into the face, as if this green
Had not, seeping, simmered, its pallor
Seethed and washed throughout the brain,
Emptying sense of any color.

'Two for Max Zorn' 1957[3]

It is unlikely that Chomsky was specifically interested in the poetic context of his time (why would he be, we may ask), yet he could easily have found similar kinds of constructions in the work of American writers such as Gertrude Stein or E.E. Cummings. Chomsky wanted to demonstrate one of the core principles of his theory of language – namely, the inequivalence of grammaticality and meaningfulness. To dispute this view, Jakobson put forward an argument for the 'semantic value' of such alogical utterances, referring to the texts of Russian Futurists (1971, II, 495):

> In a comprehensive dictionary of Russian the adjective signifying "pregnant" was labeled *feminimum tantum* because – *beremennyj muzhchina nemyslim* 'a pregnant male is inconceivable'. This Russian sentence, however, uses the masculine form of the adjective, and the 'pregnant male' appears in folk legends, in newspaper hoaxes, and in David Burliuk's poem: *Mne nravitsja beremennyj muzhchina, prislonivshijsja k pamjatniku Pushkina* 'I like the pregnant man leaning against the Pushkin monument'.[4]

---

3   Another poetic use of Chomsky's composed sentences is in 'Poema Chomsky' (1979) by Italian neo-avant-garde poet Alfredo Giuliani, available on-line: https://www.babelmatrix.org/works/it/Giuliani%2C_Alfredo-1924/Poema_Chomsky?fbclid=IwAR01--J3BwFEwNWth-4lnEkrBmfbp-lD58BMdpfTJz1ShY8YaLWiFvNNsmg (last accessed 27.02.23). Yet another is the title of the book *Colourless green ideas sleep furiously* by contemporary Russian poet Pavel Arseniev.
4   An example from David Burliuk's poem 'The Fruit-Bearing' (1915).

Jakobson cites another example of this kind from E.E. Cummings' verse: 'silent not night by silently unday' (Cummings, 2013: 432). The American poet deliberately violates the rules of grammar. There is a good reason why Jakobson used these agrammatisms to counter Chomsky's argument about the 'meaninglessness' of constructed phrases.

As we can see from the Chomsky-Jakobson polemic, Chomsky's anomalous statement drew a line in the sand between two theories of language—the normative grammatical (generative) and the linguo-poetic. Jakobson's reflections about poetic 'irregularities' soon formed the basis for his fundamental 1960 article 'Linguistics and Poetics', which proposed a special 'poetic grammar' different from the standard grammar. Things that everyday speech deems a linguistic pathology or agrammatism can become a constructive principle in poetry, charged with the 'poetic function of language'.

As with his studies of Khlebnikov from the 1920s, Jakobson's theory of language and communication from the 1960s was based on anomalies in a poetic text. It is because of the proximity and transfers between poetry and linguistics that the Russian science of language developed a view of literature as a special language and a special communicative system. This trend is not characteristic of the Anglo-American linguistic tradition of the twentieth century, whose quintessential mid-20th century example was the theory of Noam Chomsky and his circle. We do not find any significant interest in poetic language in the work of Sapir, Whorf, or Bloomfield, to name but a few prominent US linguists. Similarly, the Anglo-Saxon current in the philosophy of language lacks interest in poetic texts. We find no mention of poetry in Wittgenstein, Russell, or Austin. In his pioneering work *How to Do Things with Words*, John Austin makes a characteristically critical remark about the essence of poetic utterance. Introducing his classification of 'performatives', he specifically stipulates that the 'poetic use of language' cannot be 'illocutive'. Moreover, Austin seems to mock attempts to interpret poetic utterances in terms of philosophy of language. Analysing the phrase 'Go and catch a falling star' (from a John Donne poem), he wonders how it is possible to perform this kind of action, 'to catch a falling star'. He then disparagingly calls it a 'parasitic, frivolous and abnormal use of language', leveling the same accusation at Walt Whitman, who fails to 'incite the eagle of liberty to soar' (Austin, 1962: 104). Austin's discussion of poetry stops there: a poetic statement for him is obviously anomalous, and therefore not capable of 'performing actions with the help of words'. Much of contemporary Anglo-American linguistics continues to be skeptical of Jakobson's postulates about poetic language. Most books on style would take issue with the Jakobsonian approach, as if he were a scapegoat of true language and literary scholarship.

Jakobson's major theoretical article 'Linguistics and Poetics' is programmatic, since it outlines a programme of research in the field of the language of literature (mainly poetic language), enlarging the scope of the field compared to the days of Russian Formalism and Prague structuralism. Jakobson never abandoned his study of linguistic poetics, present from his earliest student essays to his last book, co-authored with Linda Waugh, *The Sound Shape of Language* (1987). However, it was 'Linguistics and Poetics' – the 'Closing Statement', as he subtitled it – that became the impetus for new directions in the poetics of language after the 1960s, just as the 'opening statements' of his 1920s articles on Khlebnikov, Mayakovsky and other poets had triggered literary creativity and language innovation.

Jakobson devoted 'Linguistics and Poetics' to what he understood as 'poetics in its relation to linguistics', a relation which, in his opinion, should be studied more closely. The reasoning here aims to combine the methods of linguistics and literary studies within a single, linguopoetic approach (Jakobson, 1960: 350):

> Poetics deals primarily with the question, "What makes a verbal message a work of art?" Because the main subject of poetics is the differentia specifica of verbal art in relation to other arts and in relation to other kinds of verbal behaviour, poetics is entitled to the leading place in literary studies. Poetics deals with problems of verbal structure, just as the analysis of painting is concerned with pictorial structure. Since linguistics is the global science of verbal structure, poetics may be regarded as an integral part of linguistics.

The term 'linguistic poetics' does not appear in this article. However, in discussing his correspondence with Nikolai Trubetskoy, he later noted that he had systematically developed 'his own programme of linguistic poetics' in the 1950–60s (2004: 22). As a matter of fact, the expression 'linguistic poetics' was already used as early as the 1920s by another linguist, Vladimir Zhirmunsky (who called Jakobson an 'extreme representative' of this language-oriented poetics), but not in its terminological meaning. This notion would later – from the 1970s on – be developed in the terminological and disciplinary sense by Russian scholars following in the footsteps of both the earlier and the later Jakobson.

One of the earliest outlines of the principles of 'linguistic poetics' can be found in a book by Russian linguist Viktor Grigoryev (1979). This study draws to a large extent on Velimir Khlebnikov's poems and formulates an updated definition of poetic language as 'a language with an orientation toward creativity, and since all creativity is subject to an aesthetic assessment, this is a language with an orientation toward aesthetically significant creativity' (Grigoryev, 1979: 77–78). Worthy of note is the epithet 'aesthetically significant', which had often been neglected in early Formalist theories of poetic language.

Despite the fact that Roman Jakobson first published his 1960 linguopoetic manifesto in English (it was published in Russia fifteen years later), we can find no signs of solidarity with his programme in Anglo-American linguistics. The idea of poetic language as an individual object of research did not prove popular in the US. Generative linguistics studied language independently of its discourse variations, and therefore, showed no interest in the language of literature. The only exceptions, perhaps, were Theun Van Dijk's early studies on 'generative poetics' (see, e.g., Van Dijk, 1971; 1972) – some of them analysing Surrealist writings – and Morris Halle's and Paul Kiparski's work on the generative metrics of poetic speech.[5] However, these studies mainly concern the formal or genre aspects of literary language. Otherwise, since the 1970s, mainstream Anglo-American linguistics has been much more oriented towards stylistics, understood as the study of style in language.[6] The same, however, cannot be said of American language-oriented poetic *practice* of recent decades, which reveals a strong affinity with the Jakobsonian defence of poetic language as an extraordinary entity in itself, rather than just a functional style deviating from linguistic norms. I will comment on these affinities in a chapter on 'language writing' in Part 3 of the book, after discussing some post-WWII poetic conceptions of language in the Russian and American Neo-Avant-Garde.

---

5   Alexander Zholkovsky's generative 'poetics of expressiveness' (1984) was more influenced by the Russian Formalist school than by American transformational grammar.
6   Chomsky's idea of a universal 'linguistic creativity' seems to account for this lack of interest in poetic language in most Anglo-American theories of language. At best, the language of literature is viewed as a variation of everyday language.

PART 3

*Post-Modernism, Neo-Avant-Garde: Russian and
American Poetries of Language after* WWII

CHAPTER 10

From Babel to Babble: the New Russian Poetic Avant-Garde after the Loss of Speech

(For sure: it's time – no quotation marks. With a child's frankness – language-wards: bald-headed).
GENNADY AYGI

∴

The language of poetry is made up of millions of tiny cells, it is a conglomerate as complex as the human body, on the creation of which nature has spent thousands of years of time and innumerable efforts. And in both cases, the process is far from over.
ELIZAVETA MNATSAKANOVA

∴

As Irina Sandomirskaya showed in her illuminating study of violence and the blockade of the word under Stalinism, the pressure of totalitarian language accounted, among other things, for Oberiuty's withdrawals into silence, apophaticism and alogism. Paralysed by power and violence, the word 'seems to lose its corporeality, turning into "babble", into secret writing, into OBERIU's transcendental alchemy' (Sandomirskaya, 2013: 9). A formerly active, energetic word falls into a state when 'the patient, not the agent of speech, takes the place of the subject of speech – a "victim" of language [...] when the word no longer carries a meaning' (Ibidem). As Sandomirskaya suggests, all of Konstantin Vaginov's[1] novels were an example of that with their parody taking the form of dialogue. It appears that Alexander Vvedensky's poetry was one of the last convulsions of the agony of the poetic word in the era of political terror – the era when poetic utterance beyond the rational logos lost any chance of survival. The space for such poetry was eventually confined to the dimensions of Daniil Kharms' little locked suitcase holding the manuscripts of his fellow Chinari, which Yakov Druskin managed to preserve during the Leningrad

---

[1] A member of the OBERIU group of avant-garde writers.

blockade, the War and the persecutions that followed. Druskin himself had no choice but to withdraw into the apophatic asceticism of his diaries where he commented on Vvedensky's poems. The decomposition of logical connections in the language of poetry was forcibly halted, giving way to the radioactive decomposition of the atom at Soviet test sites.

The dissolution of language in a deformed speech environment as a result of catastrophic processes in history and society continued in the post-war period, in languages other than Russian, which were allowed no forms of utterance beyond the logos of Soviet poetic discourse. Allegorically, this era of poetic timelessness and fatigue, when 'big words' turn into 'screams' without finding a new language, is conveyed in a blockade-time poem by Oberiuty's successor Gennady Gor: 'The creek sick of speech / Told water it took no side. / The water sick of silence / At once began again to shriek' (2016: 29). After World War II, the work of Romanian-German poet Paul Celan became a successor to the poetic language of Bely, Khlebnikov, and Mandelstam. His concept of 'language mesh' ('Sprachgitter'), which implies that language could be a means of poetic communication during the prison regime of ideological violence, urged poetry to turn to the 'dumb', 'silent' and 'untold' zones of discourse about language. Against Heidegger's 'Gerede' and Benjamin's 'Geschwätz' of the masses, as they figure in the context of authoritarian language with Babel-like power, Celan opposes 'lallen', or inner 'muttering'.

In his poem 'Tübingen, January' Celan appeals to the glossolalia of the ancient prophets: 'Came, if there /came a man, / came a man to the world, today, with the patriarchs'/ light-beard: he could, / if he spoke of this / time, he / could / only babble and babble, / ever- ever- / moremore' (2012: http). In the German original, 'nur lallen und lallen' literally resonates with the ancient Greek 'glossas lalein' ('speaking in tongues'). At the end of the poem, the meaningless word 'Pallaksch' is repeated twice – a reference to Friedrich Hölderlin's glossolalia produced in a fit of poetic delirium, used here to convey the 'beyond-logos' experience repressed by authoritarian language.[2] The multilingualism and 'idle talk' of peoples is once again surmounted by the poet's dislalia, as in another verse by Celan: 'Eroded by / the beamwind of your speech / the gaudy chatter of the pseudo- / experienced—the hundred- / tongued perjury- / poem, the noem' (2013: http). The splitting of words into fragmented morphemes, the fragmentation of lexemes, the atomisation of prepositions, conjunctions and particles, characteristic of Celan's poetry – all these techniques inaugurate a new poetic turn in the deformation of an ossified and 'disenchanted' language.

Largely inspired by Paul Celan, the idea of the decomposition of the word is resuscitated in Russian Neo-Futurist poetry by Gennady Aygi[3] and Eliza-

---

2 For a close reading of this poem, see Weineck (1999).
3 For Aygi's role in the Russian and Soviet neo-avant-garde, see Valentine (2015), Sokolova (2019). Roman Jakobson called Aygi an 'extraordinary poet of the contemporary Russian

veta Mnatsakanova.[4] Aygi's free verse speaks to inaudible 'spaces of silence' ('However, muteness is a tribute – and for myself – silence',[5] in an early 1956 poem), mystical 'singing without words', 'places of no-thought', 'empty stages', 'long pauses' and 'tranquility of a vowel'. In Aygi's poetry, voices are orchestrated using multiple punctuation marks, or rather – marks of the 'cessation' of thought and speech (as, for instance, in his poem 'Island of Daisies in a Clearing'). The logos-sense is cleared by gaps between words and between morphemes. Alogism finds new spaces of expression: 'I notice one thing: something shaky-alogical, previously unfamiliar, becomes quite 'logical' in this work, as if I'm learning to speak some new language' (Aygi, 2001: 157). Aygi's silent poetry is a poetry 'speaking in a different way' (Idem: 158), 'with that essential Word in which the silence of the pre-Word is concealed' (Idem: 159). Glossolalia is present here both in its pure form, through the heritage of Chuvash shamanism,[6] and transformed as an interlingual transparency, as a 'hum of language' resonating in various national idioms. Thus, it transcends not only the uniformity of the 'Babelian confusion' of languages in favor of a unique translingual speech, but also the linguistic limitations of verse systems.[7]

Aygi and Mnatsakanova[8] share a particular musical sensibility, which guarantees the integrity of the linguistic structure of their verse despite the fragmentation and logical incoherence of its elements. The legacy of Anton Webern and the atonal musical tradition has a special significance for this kind of avant-garde poetics. This was already the case for the Chinari. Yakov Druskin noted the affinity of Alexander Vvedensky's poetics of nonsense with dodecaphonic musical techniques. Just as atonal music violates the principle of gravitation of sound pitch and sounds become significant by themselves in their position within a series, in poetry of the absurd, the principle of semantic connection is violated and words undergo desemantisation. Each line of

---

avant-garde' following in the footsteps of Khlebnikov's linguistic creativity. In his turn, Aygi professed his great respect for Jakobson, whom he met several times in Moscow: 'I greatly value the word of this great scholar. I consider 'avant-garde' my constant striving for the utmost sharpening of poetic language' (2001: 282).

4 Despite her prominent role in the evolution of unofficial Soviet poetry, studies and translations of her work are still scarce. See the special segment of the issue of the Russian journal NLO dedicated to Mnatsakanova's centenary (No. 5, 2022: https://nlobooks.ru/magazines/novoe_literaturnoe_obozrenie/177_nlo_5_2022/, last accessed 27.02.23). Among other things, Mnatsakanova translated some of Celan's poems into Russian.
5 Translated by Sarah Valentine in her own article (2007).
6 Aygi was of Chuvash origin and wrote poetry in both Russian and Chuvash.
7 Velimir Khlebnikov was in many respects the main inspiration for Aygi; on this topic, see Weststeijn (2016).
8 The two poets probably never met, but each expressed admiration for the other's work. Both had a profound passion for Khlebnikov's poetics of language. On Aygi's Futurist roots and his attitude to music, see Sandler (2016), Sokolova 2019).

Vvedensky's verse contains a main idea plus a 'drawback word' that displaces the logical structure of the poetic utterance.

Elizaveta Mnatsakanova's poetic speech moves along similar lines. Despite the seemingly static nature of the text on the printed page, Mnatsakanova's poetry demonstrates a freedom of language that is made possible by its musical elements. In her own words, this is a 'freed music', which 'encompasses everything and keeps in its depths an entire immeasurable ocean of performance' (Mnatsakanova, 2006: 151). However, her sound poetry cannot be categorised as a kind of zaum. Pure sound poetry is most often limited to the sonorous aspects of poetic language, bearing only a formal resemblance to music. Mnatsakanova's poetry employs the principles of musical composition; musical techniques structure the sounding stream to a much greater extent than in pure sonoric verse. Unlike pure zaum, this kind of poetry does not obscure or eliminate meaning – it enters into a free play of meanings. 'Free', however, does not mean 'whatever the reader wants'. The semantic frame of the text, fixed in its verbal score, sets a certain mood (what composers call 'Stimmung') – a topic or several topics that develop through free association as the process of reading or listening unfolds. Mnatsanakova's major poem 'Requiem', for example, employs key musical motifs such as 'death', 'doom', 'brotherhood', 'sisterhood', 'septenary', 'light', 'resurrection', etc.

In an essay about Anton Chekhov, Mnatsakanova reiterates the idea of the 'music of words', or 'music of speech'. A phrase from his classic play 'Seagull' – 'men and lions, eagles and partridges' – becomes a leitmotif, a 'musical sequence' giving the essay a kind of melodic unity. 'The secret music of the word', according to Mnatsakanova, is the actual subject matter of Chekhov's literary language: 'What kind of music is this, what is it about? … LISTENING to the text, catching and identifying the melody, that deep line that controls the mechanisms of speech movement' (Idem: 161). The melody of a language is deemed its most important characteristic. In the spirit of Stéphane Mallarmé, that seer of verbal music and verbal magic, she continues: 'So much the tighter are words bound with other music – not only phonic, audible, but also a secret one, hidden behind the text, behind all visible performance, behind the visible appearance of life' (Idem: 167–168). Music, almost a *doppelgänger* of language, forms a new unity – 'verbomusic'.[9] Musical intonation brings a new unity of sound and meaning, of voice and phenomenon, into language and into the realm of the decomposed Logos.

---

9   On Mnatsakanova's place in the tradition of musical verse, see Feshchenko et al. (2014: 263–282); on the musicality of her verse, see also Biryukov (2005), Janecek (2006).

Mnatsakanova wrote her magnum opus, 'Requiem', while staying at a 'hospital for the poor', which she calls a 'lazzaretto of innocent sisters'. The poem is an oratorio, a lab*oratory* of the word, where 'voices come to life in sounds and letters'.[10] According to later comments, 'Requiem' is 'a new model and a new word altogether'. In this poetry, words decompose like bodies in an infirmary over the course of a disease. Particles of words scattered across the page of the score are like disembodied senses, however, integrated through musical laws of composition. A poetic space of 'pain' is created when speech turns into rambling, while also striving to heal using the forces of a new graphic and phonic order:

Брат Септимус	*едва ли*	Brother Septimus
едва ли е два	*бо два ли*	only on ly
либо два	*бо три ли*	or two ly
ли два	*бо много*	or two
ли	*там бы*	or
бо два ли	*ло*	two or
бо три ли		three or
бо много там бы	*либо много*	many were the
	там бы	re
ло	*ло либо бы*	invisible
невидимых	*ло*	brothers
(Mnatsakanova 2003)		(tr. by Gerald Janecek, unpublished)[11]

Paul Celan's 'babble' and Andrey Bely's 'dark glossolalia' here acquire the force of a kind of medical conspiracy that magically transforms the verbal flow:

Бродит смерть в беде	brother after brother after fording will
братбродбраток	rove roving ford
Ходит снег тябрябродитбред	inbritherforoctober upto kneesfording
бродитбродбро	in woe brotherfordbrotheroc
По колено дитбраток	toberrovesraving rovesfordford
В дожде	ingbrotheroc
тябрябродитбратзабродомбрат	toberrovesbrotherafterfordingbrother
Бродит брат	afterbrotherbrotherafterbrotherr
забратомбратзабратомбратбро	oves
(Ibidem)	(tr. by Gerald Janecek, unpublished)

---

10   See Janecek (2003; 2000) for a more detailed account of Mnatsakanova's experiments.
11   I cordially thank Gerald Janecek for sharing his translation with me.

Mnatsakanova's 'Requiem', just like her earlier 'Little Requiem' from the book *Arcadia*, as well as Aygi's 'Presentiment of a Requiem' and Anna Akhmatova's classic 'Requiem', is also a liturgy for the primordial word, the ever-nascent word, the word through a child's perspective, which has not yet been dismembered into meanings. An example of such a word is 'звонкоиволга' from a children's song, which, together with the homophonic phrase 'и волк ягненка уволок' from Ivan Krylov's fable, becomes the main leitmotif of Mnatsakanova's book *Metamorphosen* (Netzkowa,[12] 1988). In an essay dedicated to verbal magic, she recalls Andrey Bely's glossolalic insights: 'The face is disguised, draped, curtained, covered with a veil painted with unseen, incomprehensible signs; these signs are fiery scriptures. The Invisible Magician sends his signals with the help of signs known only to him. But these signs have a mysterious, MAGIC power; constituting certain figures yet forming a straight line, they penetrate the depths and layers of times, centuries, AGES – and SPACES' (Mnatsakanova, 2004). For a poetry of language revived after the tragic losses of Stalinism, the magic of words, 'whose vague meaning remains unresolved', regained its power as an instrument for rehabilitating and 'rehealing' the traumatised Logos.

After leaving the country of her native language in 1975, Elizaveta Mnatsakanova wrote from within the foreign linguistic and cultural environment of Vienna, thereby making Russian a foreign language, as it were, for herself. Although she always preferred the hermitic life of a poet not involved in any movements, her early work had a decided impact on certain Moscow underground poets of the 1960–70s. Among them were the Moscow Conceptualists Andrei Monastyrski[13] and Lev Rubinstein, whose work I will discuss in more detail in the next chapter. Monastyrski's early poetic works show a commitment to minimalist quasi-zaum verse verging on ritualistic glossolalia, as in this excerpt from a 1973 poem:

недбезность	heavennotliness
полей	of fields
нсн	nsn
влюдбинность	inpeoploveness

---

[12] Elisabeth Netzkowa is the heteronym Mnatsakanova used within the German-speaking context.

[13] Monastyrski is best known as a performance and visual artist, as well as one the main theorists of the Moscow Conceptualist movement. For a reading of his visual poetry, see Kondur (2018).

FROM BABEL TO BABBLE

холми	of hill
нсн	nsn
д` бнсн	d' bnsn
хилмо	if holl
нсн	nsn
небдезность	hovenneatliness
полей	of fields
нсн	nsn
волни	of waves
д` бнсн	d' bnsn
вилно	waves of
нсн	nsn
висне	to hang
нсн	nsn
весни	hang to
д` бнсн	d' bnsn
	(Monastyrski 2019)[14]

Similar repetitive, mantra-like techniques were characteristic of Russian avant-garde poets of the 1990s, such as Larisa Berezovchuk,[15] who uses glossolalia in her 'Ragas' cycle, particularly in the poem 'Doomed to a False Start'. Here is an example of one of these 'raga' meditations with the leitmotif 'magicians' (Berezovchuk, 1999):

1. *рица мудрые речи ведет о музыке превращений. И внемлют*
2. *шактишактишактИшак____ИшакишакишакишакишакИшак____*
3. *дом. Маг нить оставил. Маг нить оставил. Маг нить оставил.*

[...]

1. *тебя, слуга, и дорога стелется коврами на небеса._____*
2. *ТипаРватиПар____РваТипаРватиПар____РваТипаРватиПар____*
3. *Маг нить остави. Маг нить оставил. Маг нить остави. Где ти-*

[...]

---

14 I thank Rebekah Smith and Ugly Duckling Presse for sharing Andrei Monastyrski translations into English and permitting the use of these excerpts.

15 She is also a musician and author of essays about Aygi, Dragomoshchenko and other neo-modernist poets.

1. *взглядом?_____//Кто еще так любит ее?_____*
2. *вать__Шапкашактипарвать//_Шапкашактипарвать__При-*
3. *истлел льдом магнита мага. Реалист Лель истлел льдом маг-*
1. *_____//Тогда почему же она принадлежит не мне? Ведь коль-*
2. *праваи//шакаТиараТиараТиарАктиваШактиШактишакТир-*
3. *нита мага. Липа руса. Липа руса. Липа руса. Рака раг: дети - .*

Multilingual glossolalia is practiced by the poet Sergey Zavyalov,[16] in whose poems, as the critic Alexander Skidan remarked, 'the expansion of the glossa turns into a real glossolalia, and the score turns out to be designed for many voices' (2001: 55). In a cycle with the challenging title 'мокшэрзянь кирьговонь грамматат / берестяные грамоты мордвы-эрзи и мордвы-мокши', speech repeatedly strays into plurilingual incantation verging on zaum and glossolalia (Zavyalov, 2003):

> Кодамо моро минь моратано?
> Эрзянь морыне минь моратано.
> Кодамо ёвтамо минь ёвтатано?
> Эрзянь ёвтамо минь ёвтатано.
>   Какую песнь мы запоем?
> Мордовскую песню мы запоем.
>   Какую повесть мы поведаем?
> Мордовскую повесть мы поведаем.

In a poem devoted to falling snowflakes, bilingual self-translation between languages turns these languages into reverberations of sound resonances (Ibidem):

> тон марят – ты слышишь
> А телине телине   телесь ульнесь якшанзо
> А зима зима   зима эта была холодная

The minimalist current in the deformation of language was radicalised in the poetry of Anna Alchuk, reaching the greatest economy of linguistic means.[17] While in her earlier book, *Twelve Rhythmic Pauses*, written in the 1990s, poetic speech unfolded through pauses and omissions between words, in the later

---

16   Zavyalov began his poetic career in Leningrad's underground circles, alongside Arkadii Dragomoshchenko, Dmitry Golynko and others.
17   On Alchuk's poetry of language, see Schmidt (2010).

collection *NE BU* (2005), poetic language was reduced to strings of short syllables resembling musical notes (as in the line: 'побег из (тем но ты)'). Parts of words act as notes, sounding either as dotted fragments of meaning, or as particles and interjections marking the space of verse. For instance, the syllable 'но' is detached from the word 'сказано', with a space breaking the word into two lexemes: 'сказ' and 'но' ('сказа но'); conversely, the phrase 'как бы то ни было' merges into the undivided glossolalic sequence 'какбытонибыло'. Freed from the meaning created by morphological structure, word particles combine into trans-sense sequences of sounds that function as musical scales: 'в хру-ст-альном ми / ре после ля / (а фа зия)ет до темна' (Alchuk, 2005: 38). Aphasia literally controls the unfolding of verse, forcing sounds, their combinations, and the spaces-pauses between them to lay bare the illogical nature of music.

In another poetry book by Alchuk, *57577* (2004), the place of musical and rhythmic pauses is occupied by reinterpreted punctuation marks functioning as shifters of meaning within a fragmented word. Words are split and then recombined into longer chains of synthetic phrases: 'ракурс-отмерен- / рима-день-час-иначе- / ри-тм-ми-стерии', sometimes with embedded foreign language elements: 'я-там-у(з)нна-you-анну?'. The scattering of letters and syllables is associated with the image of an endless and boundless sea ('рас-сеянна-я / сле-д-за-сеянный-в-море'), echoing back the 'meaningless' and 'zero-like' sea of Alexander Vvedensky's and Konstantin Vaginov's avant-garde poetry of the absurd – the sea as an alogical 'abyss' of language.

In the 2000–2010s, the sea as a hieroglyph of all things meaningless also figured in the experimental verse of Nika Skandiaka,[18] a Russian-born poet writing in both Russian and English. The title of her cycle 'Ruins of the Sea' signals a two-fold process of dissemination– of *scattering* and of *splashing*, whereby an 'ineffable image' is assembled out of pieces and droplets: 'in the ruins of the sea / tremors of kinship' (Skandiaka, 2006a: http). In the spirit of Aygi, Mnatsakanova and Alchuk, Skandiaka uses the unusual placement of words and punctuation marks that break up speech, gravitating towards a zone beyond grammar and logic, where the utterance cancels and discredits itself, leaving 'disruptive trails' in the wake of this erasure: '(speeded up / cheered up) trails (of stars?) / distorted trails / telephone' (Ibidem). Since 'everyone left the war of things' and 'was forgetting their native language', the act of naming becomes a scattered phrase (Skandiaka, 2006b: http):

---

18   Her poems are included in the *Anthology of Contemporary Russian Women Poets* (2005), edited by Stephanie Sandler.

> winter/ (it's cold: &)/ got right
> a new night
> with a new wind wordless
> had to be named somehow
> a certain world cut in on me
> by a mirror-like, wordless

Yet, 'the right for speech' is retained, which music recovers from the rational *Logos* (Skandiaka, 2006a: http):

> & the right for speech—
> music of speech
> for the sake of binding || her constants

Music is there to save the de(ideo)logised word and restore the purity of the 'sounding sense' to the Logos. Contemporary Russian poetry perseveres in its attempts to 'catch the boat of words', following Vvedensky, who was the first to hear 'music's monotonous gait', as his *Gray Notebook* poetically testifies (2009: 007). Language-oriented poetry keeps creating newer and newer spaces of non-sense and beyonsense. In her poem dedicated to Vvedensky, who proclaimed himself the 'chinarian authority of nonsense', the contemporary Russian poet Olga Martynova calls on nonsense to 'disobey' reason (2007: http):

> All that consciousness hastily fastened and raveled
> Still in the cradle, over the pink shrunken 'I'
> How to unravel this? –
> Listen, drive me away from the logic of words,
> So I spoke to the mind in the cradle,
> Away to the nonsense of ovum and ovary –
> But the mind's disobedient
> To the baby's commands

Oscillating between the two poles of the senseless – the absurd as disintegration of language and glossolalia as the breeding of a new language of 'one's own' beyond the rational *Logos* – modern Russian poetry seems to realise in practice the dramatic utopia of Professor Dominic Matei from Mircea Eliade's short story 'Youth without Youth' – and from Francis Ford Coppola's film of the same name. In contrast to the unfortunate hero of Eliade's novella, who failed to find the origins of language in the depths of past centuries, contemporary linguocentric poets tend to seek these origins in the depths of poetic discourse, in what Khlebnikov called the 'deaf-and-dumb layers of language' a hundred years ago. By decomposing sounds, words, phrases, and languages, they contribute to the 'blowing up of linguistic silence', to use another of Khlebnikov's metaphors. From the 'poverty of language' and 'the abyss of speech' in everyday social communication, contemporary poetry makes a leap towards language's lost origin, though still looking ahead for the potentiality of the future.

CHAPTER 11

American and Russian Conceptualisms: How to Do Verse with Concepts

> The concept of a living being has the same indeterminacy as that of a language.
> LUDWIG WITTGENSTEIN

∴

> Nothing in a nonlinguistic context.
> JACKSON MAC LOW

∴

> И ВСЕ Ж ТЩЕСЛАВНЫЙ ЧЕЛОВЕЧЕ
> САМОЙ ПРИРОДЕ СДЕЛАЛ ВТЫК:
> ЯЗВИТ,
> и ЖАЛИТ,
> и КАЛЕЧИТ
> И ЯДОМ ПОТЧУЕТ – ЯЗЫК![1]
> ALEXANDER KONDRATOV

∴

In the second half of the twentieth century, Conceptualism became one of the dominant trends in contemporary art and neo-avant-garde literature. The concept, or idea, took precedence as a privileged object in the arts. Objects of the physical and cultural world, verbal descriptions of these objects, or the text-objects themselves, as well as installations, performances, and other performative genres – all of these functioned as concepts in this new artistic

---

1 A very rough literal translation of this highly expressive stanza from the poem titled 'Язык' ('Language', or 'Tongue') would be: 'And yet the human being much too vain / Told off nature itself / It mocks, / it stings, / it cripples, / it plies with poison – the tongue-language!'

practice. A concept could be exhibited, performed, or uttered. At the same time, a new trend in linguistics emerged, associated with the conceptual analysis of language. The conceptualisation of the world became a major method of scholarly research and artistic experiment within this new current of the linguistic turn. As I will argue in this chapter, this new convergence of science and art was not accidental and was based on similar methods of operating with language.

1 The Concept in Western Thought

The Latin word *conceptus* was originally an adjective meaning 'conceived'. As such, it dates back to early medieval authors such as Tertullian, Saint Augustine, and Boethius. The original meaning of the word remained relevant throughout the history of philosophical thought; the German *Begriff* and the Russian *ponyatie* were mere calques from Latin meaning 'something conceived or perceived'. It was only in the 12th century that *conceptus* began to be used as a philosophical term. It was first applied to the theory of Pierre Abélard, which *a posteriori* was called conceptualism to distinguish it from competing nominalist and realist debates in scholastic thought. According to Abélard, universals were found neither in reality nor in mere verbal expression. Just as a word itself signifies something universal about objects, so it can serve the object's predicate as signification of a concept.

Abélard's follower Duns Scotus used the term *conceptus* to signify an entity relating a word to an object. That is how *conceptus* was discussed in subsequent scholastic literature – as a mental entity ('Medium inter rem et sermonem vel vocem est conceptus', 'A concept is that which is between the thing and the verbal speech', according to Duns Scotus). To a certain extent, the concept of *conceptus* in medieval Latin corresponded to Plato's concept of the *idea* an Aristotle's concept of the *term*. In this imbricated form, it eventually entered the German philosophical lexicon several centuries later as the term *Begriff* (starting with Hegel and Kant and used as recently as in Frege and Husserl).

Before the 1950s, the philosophical term *concept* in English was only used in works on mathematical logic, where it had a specific meaning. The linguophilosophical meaning of this term was introduced by Ludwig Wittgenstein, or more precisely, by his translators into English. The first use of this kind can be found in *Tractatus Logico-Philosophicus*, where the philosopher makes a distinction between 'formal concepts', 'concepts as such' and 'concept-words'. Wittgenstein also uses it in his works on the philosophy of psychology, as well as in connection with 'language games' in works from the 1940s. It was as *concept* that the term *Begriff*[2] was translated in the English edition of *Philosophical Investigations*, published posthumously in 1953.

A few years later, the art theorist Moris Weitz, who was a Neo-Wittgensteinian, proposed a method of distinguishing art from non-art on the basis of Wittgenstein's notion of family resemblance. 'What art can be?' – this was the focal question, which looked rather like a language game at first. In Weitz' words, art may be an open concept: 'New conditions have constantly arisen and will undoubtedly constantly arise; new art forms, new movements will emerge, which will demand decisions on the part of those interested … as to whether the concept should be extended or not' (1956: 32). What is discussed here is the *concept of art*, which soon after was transformed into the *art of concepts*.

2 Concept Art in America

Henry Flynt, American philosopher and art activist, was the first to bring the term *concept* into artistic discourse. In his manifesto 'Concept Art', published in 1963, the term '*concept*' is used in inverted commas, as if unfamiliar to the world of art. The aim of the artist, Flynt claimed, is precisely to make art familiar with concepts, to put concepts into action: "Concept art' is first of all an art of which the material is 'concepts,' as the material of for ex. music is sound. Since 'concepts' are closely bound up with language, concept art is a kind of art of which the material is language' (1963: http). The transfer taking place here is intracultural – the term is explicitly borrowed from mathematics, just as the term *structure* had been earlier, in discussions of so-called 'structure art'. The recipient domain of art appropriated the term to establish a new understanding of a work of art. Flynt also stresses the *cognitive* value of 'concept art': 'Contemporary structure artists, on the other hand, tend to claim the kind of cognitive value for their art that conventional contemporary mathematicians claim for mathematics' (Ibidem).[3] It becomes clear why concept art was originally based on analytical philosophy and Wittgenstein's language games.

The aim of the new conceptual artists was to *perform*, just as a speaker performs speech acts, according to Wittgenstein and Austin. As Sol LeWitt wrote in his manifesto on Conceptual Art, 'in conceptual art the idea or concept is

---

2   A few decades earlier, Gottlob Frege's *Begriff* had also been translated into English as *concept*.
3   A decade before the 'official' establishment of conceptual art, at the end of the 1940s, the term *concept* was used by the Italian artist Lucio Fontana in the titles of his visual works (*Concetto spaziale*).

the most important aspect of the work. When an artist uses a conceptual form of art, it means that all of the planning and decisions are made beforehand and the execution is a perfunctory affair. The idea becomes a machine that makes the art' (1967: 80). Art was reframed as practical philosophy, and even as a practical philosophy of language in some Conceptualist groups, as in the activities of the British artist collective Art and Language.

It is quite logical that, when art started to do things with language, language units became constituent elements of works of art. A classic example is Joseph Kosuth's painting 'One and Three Chairs'. The canvas shows three representations of a chair in total: the object itself, its photographic image, and a dictionary entry for the word 'chair'. Artistic value is not attached to any one particular representation of the chair, but to all three elements as a whole.

Between 1965 and 2011, Kosuth created a series of neon objects representing linguistic statements of a conceptual kind. Here, the artist implements ideas from his own manifesto 'Art after Philosophy' (1969), which states that conceptual art asks questions about what art is, and language becomes the medium of creating new art. In his neon signboards, Kosuth explores the nature of the utterance through the performativisation of the utterance itself, for example, in propositions such as: 'Yes, it is so'; 'An object self-defined'; 'What does this mean?'; and 'Language must speak for itself'. Functioning as objects of art, these signs transform linguistic utterances into objects of aesthetic experience.

As we can see, conceptual art was a manifestation of another phase of the linguistic turn, this time in the domain of performative art. The logical analysis of language in the studies of Frege, Carnap, Russell, and, especially, Wittgenstein provided the impetus for the creation of a new artistic movement. To a certain extent, art took over the functions of linguistic philosophy. Metareflection about the aesthetic object and artistic process, criticism of the metalanguage of contemporary art – these were the guiding principles of the conceptual movement. In the field of American artistic writing, this conceptual turn, anticipated and largely inspired by Marcel Duchamp's verbal art, was apparent in Jackson Mac Low's performative poetry[4] as well as in John Cage's writing experiments starting with his book *Silence* (1961) and continuing with the highly conceptualist collection *Empty Words: Writings '73–'78* (1979).[5]

---

4   One of the most significant manifestations of this kind of writing was the *Anthology of Chance Operations* (Young et al., 1963), which included Henry Flynt's essay on Concept Art, as well as poem-like compositions by Mac Low and other writers/artists.
5   The term *conceptual poetry*, though, is not used in this context; in the US, it is more often applied to developments in early 21st century poetry, represented by such poets as Kenneth Goldsmith, Vanessa Place and Robert Fitterman. See Craig Dworkin's and Kenneth Goldsmith's (2011) anthology of conceptual writing.

3 The Concept in Russian Philosophy

The notion of the *concept* underwent a different semantic development in the Russian cultural and linguistic context of the 20th century. The prominent philosopher Gustav Shpet, a follower of Edmund Husserl, was one of the first Russian scholars to use the term '*концепт*' (*concept*) as distinct from the term '*понятие*' (*notion*). In his treatise *Aesthetic Fragments* (1922–1923), the 'concept' as a static notion is opposed to the 'image' as a dynamic symbol (Shpet, 2007: 223, 247, 265).[6]

Another Russian philosopher of the same generation as Shpet, Sergey Askoldov, was the first to outline a 'theory of concept' in the context of the philosophy of language. Askoldov was an idealist philosopher and also an outspoken critic of German phenomenology, especially of Husserl. His main field of inquiry was gnoseology. Criticising the notion of 'consciousness in general' and of the 'gnoseological subject', he sought to study the real process of cognition. He was much more interested in the problem of 'cognition' than the problem of 'knowledge' and wanted to concentrate on the 'pure experience' of 'individual consciousness'. This concern led him to the study of poetry, and of how consciousness manifests itself in poetic concepts.

In the 1925 article 'Form and Content in Verbal Art', Askoldov argues for distinguishing 'poetic concepts' as a category separate both from 'notion' and 'image'. He is not satisfied with the Formalist approach to studying images and devices in isolation from consciousness. Concepts, according to him, differ from vaguely defined images, but also from abstract notions as understood in philosophy. It is difficult to tell for sure where Askoldov's term *concept* originated, as he does not provide a direct reference. Three options may be possible. The most likely possibility is that he borrowed it from an encyclopaedia article about Abélard's conceptualism. Alternatively, he may have encountered the term *concept* while reading Benedetto Croce, the Italian linguist and philosopher, whose work was very popular in Russia at the time. Or he could have adopted it from Gustav Shpet's work cited above. Yet Askoldov's idea of concept is quite different from Shpet's. Both Shpet and Askoldov were ardent readers of Husserl, and both criticised him, though from different positions. Translating Husserl's *Begriff* as *концепт*, Shpet denigrates the value of the term, whereas Askoldov introduces the term *concept* in contrast to Husserl's *Begriff*.

Askoldov develops his arguments in an essay called 'The Concept and the Word' (1927), which might be considered the foundational text of concept

---

6 For Shpet's semiotics and philosophy of language, see Feshchenko (2015).

studies in Russia. The question he is preoccupied with is whether a *specific* kind of consciousness and cognition can be found in poetry. The imagery in a poem is not merely about emotions but also about concepts. Concepts are present in the depths of poetic language. Behind seemingly irrational imagery, there is cognisable meaning. However idiosyncratic poetic meanings may be, they contain a certain universality. The concept, according to Askoldov, is the carrier of the universal in the particular – an idea quite close to Abélard's scholastic conceptualism.

As if continuing the scholastic debates, Askoldov sees Husserlian *Begriffsstudien* as a variation on medieval realism. The inability to justify the existence of a multitude of concepts expressing a person's subjective view of the world is the downfall of modern realism, according to him. Nor does he agree with modern nominalists, for whom concepts are merely individual representations with no universal value.

What are the characteristic features of concepts as distinct from notions or imagery, according to Askoldov? First, concepts perform a substitutive function: 'A concept is a mental entity that substitutes in the process of thought a multitude of objects of the same kind'. He gives as an example the concept of a 'chiliagon', a polygonal figure with 1000 sides, which substitutes an infinite variety of individual chiliagons that can't be perceived as an image but can nevertheless be subject to mental calculation. The second feature of the concept is its potentiality. For example, when we assume a threatening stance against an enemy, this action opens up a range of potentialities. We might then concretise this mental entity according to our interpretations. But the concept of *threat* remains stable. And yet, this is an act of conceiving. Here, the original Latin meaning of the word *conceptus* reemerges, imbricated by the German primary meaning of the term *Konzept* as a 'project' or 'plan': 'A concept in this respect is a projective outline of a uniform mode of dealing with specific objects', Askoldov reflects. This implies the third feature of the concept – its dynamism. The concept establishes a dynamic correlation between the universal and the particular, implementing abstract ideas as concrete forms.

So far, we have seen that Askoldov's theory of concept was the result of revisiting other contexts in which the term appeared, from medieval Latin conceptualism to German *Begriffstudien*. Now, we will examine how this system of concepts acquired a specifically Russian cultural tenor, reactualising Askoldov's legacy in philosophical thought about language.

The final question Askoldov raises in his essay concerns the difference between the role of the word in scientific knowledge and artistic creativity. In the former case, the word is either a mere sign, or a scientific notion. It has, he writes, 'little or no inner affinity with its inner meanings'. The word in poetry, he continues, 'has an inner organic relation to its meaning'. In other words, Askoldov tackles the issue of the non-arbitrariness of the relation between sound and meaning. This issue was of particular interest to many Russian linguists and philosophers of language, from Alexander Potebnja and Andrey Bely to Gustav Shpet and the early Roman Jakobson. Organicism was at the core of all these conceptions. All of them used organic metaphors in describing language. Likewise, Askoldov speaks of the word as a plant that has inner and outer forms. This Russian organicist tradition was in turn largely influenced by German romanticism. Thus, Askoldov's thought builds on two asynchronical transfers from German philosophy, one negatively charged (the reception of Husserl), the other positively charged (revisiting German Romanticism and Humboldtianism). Much as in physics, where the collision between two oppositely charged particles may lead to recombination within the system, Askoldov's philosophy of the concept gave birth to a new object of study at the crossroads of intercultural transfers – the *concept*.

Askoldov's argument about the connection between cognitive (i.e., scientific) and artistic concepts was in line with the desire to overcome the boundaries of art and science, characteristic of 1920s intellectual culture in Russia. Art was understood as a kind of cognition (e.g., in Gustav Shpet's article 'Art as a Kind of Knowledge', included in (Shpet, 2007)) and poetry as a kind of philosophy (e.g., in Andrey Bely's essays on Alexander Blok). With the category of the *artistic concept* ('*художественный концепт*'), Askoldov, then, tried to bridge the generality of the scientific concept and the individuality of the poetic image. As we will see below, the conceptualisation of the word would become a link between philosophical and artistic discourses in yet another historical and cultural context – that of the art and literature of Moscow Conceptualism.

4 Moscow Conceptualist Art and Poetry

As members of the Moscow Conceptualism movement have testified, the word *concept* came to them from the West in the 1960s. Soviet artists learned about *conceptual art* from European art magazines, which sometimes landed in their hands. In the case of Russian conceptual art, we can observe an intercultural transfer, where the recipient culture inscribed the extraneous object of transfer into its own intellectual system. It took about a decade for this transfer to happen. It was a contraband transfer, we could say, as official Soviet art would not allow anything to be imported from the Western world. Yet the term *conceptual art* illegally filtered its way through Russian dissident artists.[7] The art critic Boris Groys first used the term in 1979 to refer to a specifically Russian branch of conceptual art, which he called Moscow Romantic Conceptualism. While borrowing the term from Western art, Groys was quick to clarify its limitations within the recipient context. For example, he stressed the mystical nature of the Russian version of Conceptualism, in contrast to the allegedly positivist approach of the Western version. Groys embedded the term into a specifically Russian cultural context. Characteristically, he focused on the central role of literature in Russian culture. Just as in the case of Sergey Askoldov's 'poetic, or artistic, concepts', Conceptualists implicitly revived the old medieval dispute between nominalists, realists, and conceptualists. This context was hardly relevant for the Anglo-American tradition of concept studies and concept art.

The new post-modernist artistic trend was termed *conceptual* not only because it borrowed from Western art, but also because it was reinterpreted in terms of Russian literature, philosophy, and even mysticism. For Boris Groys, Conceptualism is a radical implementation of Hegel's thesis 'Art eventually results in its own concept (Begriff)'. Russian Conceptualism is called 'romantic', in contrast to the Western version, which is rationalistic, in Groys' view. Thus, scholastic discussions of medieval philosophers proved instrumental in underpinning the Russian term 'концептуализм' as opposed, on the one hand, to official Socialist Realism, representing 'realism' in general, and on the other, to Western conceptual art as a nominalist paradigm.

In the Soviet Union and countries of the Eastern Bloc, Conceptualism manifested itself in the deideologisation of the official language of power.[8] Ordinary utterances invaded poetic texts and canvases, opposing the official discourse of Soviet authorities. Conceptualism became the most prominent artistic and literary movement of the last five decades in Russia. Moreover, to a greater extent than in the West, literature-centrism and logocentrism have played a significant role in it.

---

7   According to evidence provided by the artists themselves in Albert (2014). One piece of evidence of Russian-American contact among conceptual artists in the 1970s is the ironical correspondence between Andrei Monastyrski and John Cage, of which only Cage's response seems to have survived more or less intact (published on-line by Ekaterina Lazareva: https://syg.ma/@ekaterina-lazareva/o-poniatii-kontsieptualizma, last accessed 27.02.23).

8   For a general account of Moscow Conceptualism, see Bobrinskaya (1994), Groys (2010), Jackson (2010), Rosenfeld, (2011), Ičin (2021). Gerald Janecek's recent study (2018) provides a comprehensive analysis of Moscow Conceptualist poetry. Sylvia Sasse's book (2003) analyses the functions of speech acts in Conceptualist writing, painting, and actions.

Even in the earliest Russian Conceptualist paintings and objects, the text often occupies a leading role. A vivid example of this text-centrism is the work of the major Russian Conceptualist artist Ilya Kabakov titled 'The Fly'. It shows an insect in the center of the canvas and two comments by imaginary characters, one of them asking 'Whose fly is this?' and the other replying 'This is Nikolai's fly'. Much like in Joseph Kosuth's 'One and Three Chairs', neither the fly as a material object, nor the dialogue between characters, has independent value. They both constitute the concept of the *fly* as present in the mind of an ordinary Soviet man. Expanding on this concept, Kabakov wrote an essay titled 'The Fly as a Subject and Basis for Philosophical Discourse', which he included in the installation 'The Fly with Wings'. The essay clearly shows how the argumentation of a Conceptualist artist can be based on an ordinary concept, yet produce a discourse of language games reminiscent of late Wittgenstein (cit. in Epstein, 2010: http):

> The work presented here, the treatise 'The Fly with Wings' almost visually demonstrates the nature of all philosophical discourse – at its base may lie a simple, uncomplicated and even nonsensical object – an ordinary fly, for example. But yet the very quality of the discourse does not suffer in the least as a result of this. In this very way it is proven (and illustrated) that the idea of philosophising and its goal consists not at all in the revelation of the original supposition (if this can turn out to be an ordinary fly), but rather in the very process of discourse, in the verbal frivolity itself, in the mutual suppositions of the beginnings and ends, in the flow of connections and representations of that very thing.

As Boris Groys, the ideologist of Moscow Conceptualism, observed of this essay, Kabakov transforms the insignificant word 'fly' into a sort of joker-word, potentially applicable to anything whatsoever: 'Kabakov transforms the word 'fly' into another of these joker-words which are potentially applicable to anything whatsoever ... In the ability of an ephemeral word bereft of a noble philosophical tradition to achieve the lofty status of the words which possess this tradition we may see a historic opportunity which is also open to the fly – the opportunity to construct a fly-paradise of its own, its own world of platonic, fly-essences' (1992: http). Platonism, as we can see, appears as a generative paradigm for the conceptual mode of thinking. Concepts occupy the place of Plato's ideas, having been transferred into the domain of artistic performance. Groys even goes so far as to identify the whole Russian tradition of thought as *conceptual*.

Mikhail Epstein explains the difference between the Russian and Western schools of conceptualism as follows: 'In the West, conceptualism substitutes "one thing for another" – a real object for its verbal description. But in Russia the object that should be replaced is simply absent' (1995: 199). This argument was later reiterated by Dmitry Prigov, a prominent Moscow Conceptualist poet and artist. According to Prigov (1998: http), in Russian culture, the level of the object has traditionally been occupied by the names of objects:

> Having turned up in our context, conceptualism did not find the main character of its mysteries, since in our culture the level of the subject was traditionally occupied by nomination, or naming. And it turned out that in the Western sense, all our culture is, as it were, quasi-conceptual. The total verbalisation of the pictorial space, the increase in the number of explanatory and mystifying texts accompanying pictorial objects, worked well with the traditional prevalence of literature in Russian culture, its fundamental precondition for manifestation in any other sphere of art.[9]

This principle can be vividly illustrated with Prigov's sketches for installations known as 'For the Poor Cleaning Lady', created in the early 1990s. This series of paintings shows a big eye rising between two curtains in front of a kneeling woman. The rising of the eye is followed by the subsequent rising of the word 'ГЛАЗ', which terrifies the poor woman even more than the eye. The very word is made flesh and substitutes the object it signifies with a still more powerful effect.

The difference between Russian and Western modes of conceptualist thinking can be seen in two pictures by prominent artists of the movement. The first, by Joseph Kosuth, reproduces five boxes marked with attributes: box, cube, empty, clear, glass. These attributes refer to the real characteristics of an object: Kosuth's boxes are, indeed, a box and a cube, empty and clear and made of glass. In the second picture, by Prigov, the words 'fish', 'bird', 'tree', 'cloud' and 'man' refer to nothing but themselves. The empty baskets below them act as hollow referents. The power of the word in Prigov's version, then, may exist without reference to reality at all.

More than its American analogues, Moscow Conceptualism involved the production of many different kinds of text. Prigov alone produced several thousand poems, and a five-volume collection of his writings was recently

---

9 For Prigov's links to Russian and Western Conceptualism, see Edmond (2012), as well as the collected volume edited by Galieva (2014).

published. In the very first paintings and objects of Moscow Conceptualism, the text already plays a central role. In Ilya Kabakov's visual works, the canvases are often constituted by the utterances of typical Soviet citizens and resemble book sheets or Soviet bureaucratic documents with verse-like verbal structures.

Erik Bulatov's paintings[10] represent a kind of visual poetry made of words and their combinations and referring to the reality of Soviet society. For instance, Bulatov's canvas 'Freedom Is Freedom' ('Свобода есть свобода') is a visual interpretation of a Vsevolod Nekrasov[11] poem. The repetitive nature of the verse lines is typical of this author. The conceptual poet exploits the contradictory concept of freedom, which was used in political discourse of the time as a void signifier. Repeating this signifier several times, the poem reinforces the material texture of the word, producing pure desemanticised rhythm. The only sense the poem makes is that 'freedom is freedom'. As in every performative act, following John Austin and Emile Benveniste, the utterance makes sense only in the act of its statement *hic and nunc*. The poetic function allows the utterance to multiply itself, producing a deconstructing artistic effect. In more radical cases, this principle goes so far as to transform the abbreviated names of Soviet reality into a variation of glossolalic speech, as in this poem by Nekrasov called 'Verses in our language' (2012: 29):

СТИХИ НА НАШЕМ ЯЗЫКЕ

беseme велкесеме
гепеу энкаведе
эмгеу векапебе
эсэспе капеэсэс
цик
цека
кацо
че пе
цеу
цоб
цобе
вечека
течека

---

10   Bulatov was a member of the Sretensky Boulevard Group of Moscow Conceptualists.
11   Nekrasov was one of the leading figures of the Soviet literary underground, associated with the Lianozovo group and Moscow Conceptualism.

зепете
кегебе
а бе ве ге де её
жезеикелемене

In Russian Conceptualist poetry, the reader is faced with fragments of inner or outer speech performed as if on a stage. This principle of staging ordinary discourse is probably best realised in the poetry of Nekrasov's fellow conceptualist Lev Rubinstein. Here, the poetic text transforms into verbal performance, with utterances sporadically interrupting each other (Rubinstein, 2014: 139):[12]

> 1
> Well, what on earth is there to say?
> 2
> He knows something, but won't tell.
> 3
> Who knows, maybe you're right.
> 4
> It's good for you, and tasty too.
> 5
> At seven, by the first train car.
> 6
> It goes on about the student.
> 7
> Let's go. I'm also heading there.
> 8
> Have you decided something now?
> 9
> I rode the bus to the last stop.
> 10
> Hey, listen to what I just wrote

A later post-Soviet poem by Rubinstein titled 'Questions of literature' is composed of utterances pronounced by an unidentified persona (Idem: 331–332):

> 1
> Here I am, writing…

---

12 I thank Rebekah Smith and Ugly Duckling Presse for providing these translations of Lev Rubinstein into English and permitting the use of these excerpts.

2
I'm writing against the howling wind, the rattling window frames, the roar of surf...
3
I write: 'And then something unimaginable has begun!'
4
I'm writing against the roar of surf, the nauseating attacks of anguish, the clatter of glass...
5
I write: 'It's hard to believe what has begun here!'
6
I'm writing against the clatter of glass, the mocking glances of those nearby, the howling wind...
7
I write: 'It's impossible to describe what has begun here!'
8
Good God! What's going on?
9
Is there anyone, just one person, who could explain what this all means?
10
If yes, who is it?
11
If no, then why not?

Further in this text, the reader is faced with a set of questions posed either to them, or to the author himself, or to the text itself (Idem: 342):

99
In fact, what does all this mean?
100
And so here we are, reading.
101
We read against the howling wind, the rattling window frames, the roar of surf...

Speech fragments drawn from ordinary speech are as if forcibly incorporated into the poetic text and wondering why they find themselves there. The questions are, it seems, directed at literature as a creative mode of discourse. But nothing linguistically creative comes out of this questioning. As Boris Groys commented on Rubinstein's work in the journal *A-Я*, 'performative verbal acts reveal their illusory character and return to the text as pure literature, making nothing evident but the despair and the torment of reading' (1979: 6).

As is often the case in conceptual writing, Russian Conceptualist poets make use of found objects or found phrases, transforming them into concepts as materialised ideas. The objective nature of Conceptualist poetic language is exemplified in the 'versograms' of Dmitry Prigov (Figure 12). Versograms are visual and typographical compositions made entirely of phrases, fragments of Soviet official speeches and songs. Multiplied typographically, these verbal objects attest to the absurdity of Soviet reality. Performatives pile up, making the versogram a fractal and recursive verbal apparatus, which creates an aesthetic object out of humdrum linguistic elements.

Another Moscow Conceptualist artist-and-poet, Andrei Monastyrski, generates mantra-like poetry exploiting minimalist techniques reminiscent of the musical avant-garde. His large book-length poem *Poetic World* is composed of repetitive six-line refrains with monotone syntactic structures, which differ from each other only in minor lexical details. In most cases, only one word changes in a refrain repeated hundreds of times. Reading the poem, the reader eventually enters a state of mind whereby the increment of meaning is reduced to a minimum. Yet the discourse of the work is still perceived as poetic, although resembling shamanistic ritual. The refrains are accompanied with performative meta-commentaries, which are also part of the poem (Monastyrski, 2007: 69, 89):

> What's this
> There's nothing
> Nothing's left
> It's empty
> No answers
> That's to be expected
>
> ...
> There's nothing here
> In every way
> Used to be
> And when all's gone
> And there'll be nothing
> Except me
> Which I forget, too

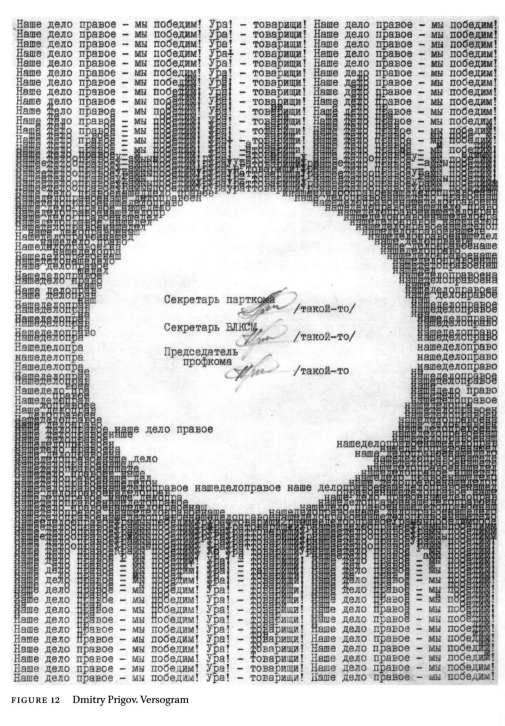

FIGURE 12   Dmitry Prigov. Versogram

The author and the poetic utterance undergo a sort of 'illocutionary suicide': the all-negative modality denies the existence of all meaning. Yet with its very denial, it produces a rhythm of presence.

Conceptualist poetry often appears as a set of material objects with seemingly no textual elements. Yet it is still deemed poetry. Such is the case with Monastyrski's work *Elementary poetry* – a set of invented objects representing a communicative phenomenon (*Finger, Tube* etc.) (Figures 13–18). Monastyrski

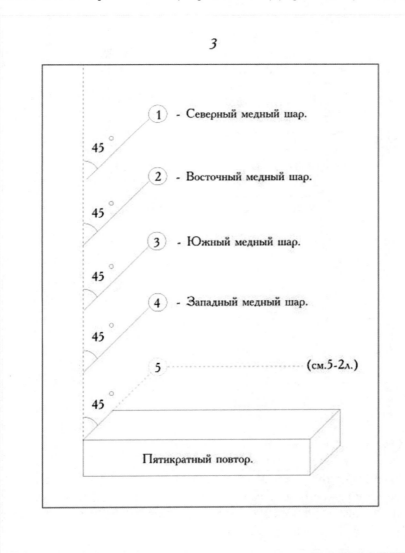

FIGURE 13   Andrei Monastyrski. From *Elementary Poetry*

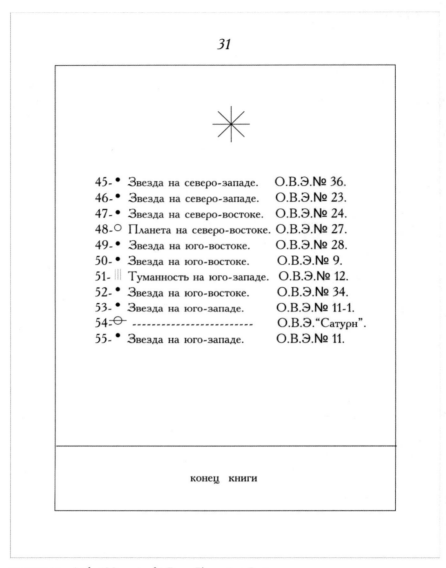

FIGURE 14   Andrei Monastyrski. From *Elementary Poetry*

calls this practice 'the poetry of action', in which words give way to pure concepts performing poetic actions while interacting with the user. Monastyrski, himself a linguistic philosopher in his own way, shows us how to do words with things, instead of doing things with words.[13]

---

13   On Monastyrski's semiotic practices, see Ioffe (2013).

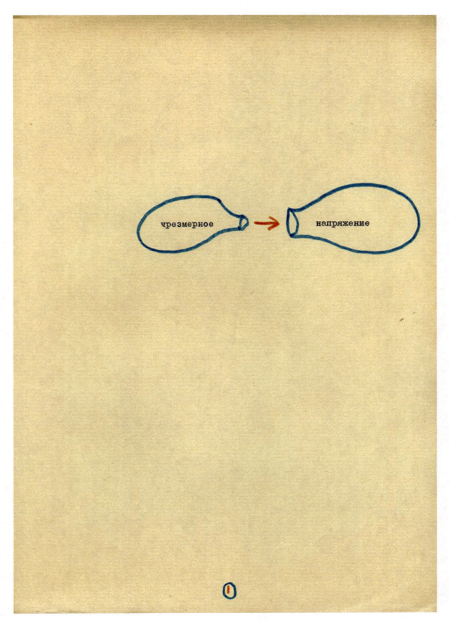

FIGURE 15   Andrei Monastyrski. From *Elementary Poetry*

Moscow Conceptualist artists considered conceptualisation an artistic method and not just a tendency in contemporary art. Conceptualism's interest in dictionaries is characteristic, for example, of Monastyrski, who compiled a dictionary of terms of the Moscow Conceptual School. In a preface to this

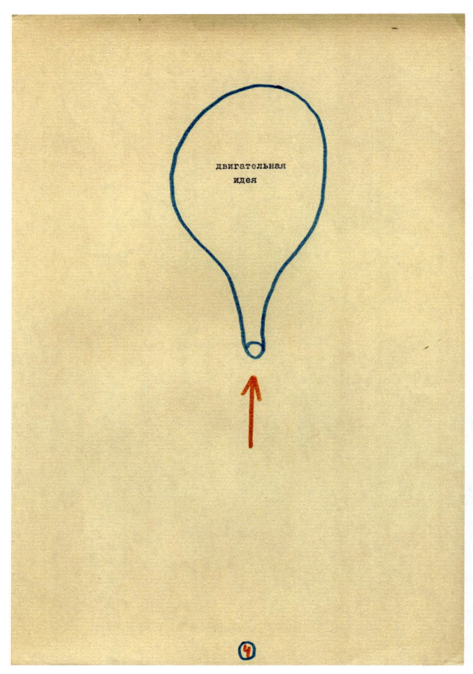

FIGURE 16   Andrei Monastyrski. From *Elementary Poetry*

AMERICAN AND RUSSIAN CONCEPTUALISMS 199

FIGURE 17   Andrei Monastyrski. From *Elementary Poetry*

FIGURE 18   Andrei Monastyrski. From *Elementary Poetry*

dictionary, he points out that 'conceptual art deals primarily with ideas (and most often with ideas of relations) and not with the world of objects and its long-established paradigms of naming' (Monastyrski, 1999: 9). Concepts are precisely these 'ideas of relations'. We will see a similar line of reasoning below, in my discussion of the conceptual analysis of language in Russian scholarly works in linguistics and semiotics of the 1990–2000s.

5 Conceptual Analysis of Language in Russian Linguistics and Semiotics

The development of a conceptual approach in Russian linguistics dates back to 1990s. This approach emerged as a result of three areas of research: firstly, the wave of cognitivism and the study of the conceptualisation of the world by means of language (influenced by American cognitive linguists such as George Lakoff, this line was developed by Elena Kubryakova, Tatyana Bulygina, Alexei Shmelev, among others); secondly, the wave of cultural linguistics as the study of language in its connection to culture (Dmitry Likhachev, Yuri Stepanov and their respective schools); and thirdly, in the logical analysis of language (Nina Arutyunova and her school, starting with her volume from 1991).

Originally, conceptual linguistics had nothing to do with the conceptual art of the 1980s. The first publications in this field made no reference to the art of concepts. The two sources for term *concept* were, firstly, the study of concepts in logic and its transfer to the study of syntax and grammar, most probably through the work of the Lithuanian philosopher of language Rolandas Pavilionis, who wrote and published works both in English and Russian; and secondly, Sergey Askoldov's theory of the concept outlined above. When Askoldov was rehabilitated after the fall of the Soviet Union, Russian linguists republished and his 1927 essay discussed above, assigning a new relevance to ideas contained in it.

Whereas structural linguistics was interested primarily in the *word* as a unit of analysis, conceptual linguistics analysed *concepts* as units of cognition in the human mind and in human culture. In his preface to the 1991 collection of articles *Cultural Concepts* (Arutyunova, 1991), Yuri Stepanov, a prominent Russian linguist and semiotician, drew a distinction between two approaches in the conceptual analysis of language: the *logical* and what he called the *sublogical*. By the sublogical analysis of concepts, he meant the study of cultural meanings beyond merely logical categories. In a later article titled 'Concept' (1997), Stepanov explored in more detail the cultural aspects of the concept, distinguishing between concept and notion as they pertain to two different fields of study – mathematical logic and cultural studies. Here is a definition of *concept* given by Stepanov: 'Concept represents a sort of conglomerate of culture in human consciousness, through the agency of which culture enters a person's mentality. Meanwhile, concept is a means by which a person – an ordinary person, not a "creator of cultural values" – enters culture, or in some cases influences it ... *Concept is a basic cell of culture in a person's mentality*'

(1997: 40). The conglomerate of culture is a central metaphor in this definition, occupying the place of a cell in human consciousness and indicative of the concept's complex and at the same time experiential nature. As opposed to *notions*, concepts are not only objects of thought but also objects of experience.

Concepts, according to Stepanov, have a multi-layered structure. Each concept has at least three strata: a basic attribute, one or several additional etymological attributes, and an inner form, which may be unconscious for the person using it, but which is expressed in the outer, verbal form. Concepts function differently in their strata for different people from the same culture. Taken together, all concepts constitute a cultural sphere related to language, what Stepanov calls 'conceptualised domains'. To analyse this area, a new research tool was introduced – the semiotics of concepts (Stepanov, 2001).

Another prominent Russian cultural scholar, Dmitry Likhachev – who had been a student of Sergey Askoldov back in the 1930s – proposed the term 'conceptosphere' to denote the conceptualised domain of Russian language and culture. In a 1993 article, Likhachev connected the problems of the *concept* and the *conceptosphere* with national culture: 'The conceptual sphere in which any national language lives', he notes, 'is constantly enriched if there are literature and cultural experiences worthy of it' (1993: 9). The word, its meanings, and the concepts behind these meanings, according to Likhachev, do not exist independently, but rather in a particular human 'ideosphere'.[14] Each person operates with an individual set of associations, shades of meaning and, by extension, individual characteristics in the potential capacities of the concept. The content of the concept, therefore, depends on the context and cultural experience of the person using the concept. The notion of the conceptosphere is especially important because it helps us understand why language is not just a means of communication, but 'a kind of concentrate of culture' (in Yuri Stepanov's terminology, concepts are 'cultural constants' (1997: 40)).

As we can see, Sergey Askoldov's theory of poetic concepts was reappropriated eighty years later and greatly expanded to become a specific field within cultural and linguistic studies. Likhachev's and Stepanov's approaches are otherwise quite different from each other. Likhachev, who introduced the term conceptosphere, was mainly interested in the study of Russian cultural concepts; whereas Stepanov, who published a dictionary of Russian concepts, was also engaged in the study of world concepts, both universal and culturally specific.

Eventually, Russian linguistic conceptology revealed its hidden affinity with conceptual art. In his later writings, Yuri Stepanov made this connection clearer by citing the work of Moscow Conceptualist artists and poets.

---

14   A similar notion, the 'semiosphere', was introduced around the same time by the Soviet semiotician Yuri Lotman.

Moreover, in the 2000s, Stepanov's essayistic writing style increasingly grew to resemble Conceptualist techniques in literature. A concept, he claimed, may even function as a specific genre across the domains of literature, the visual arts and philosophy. He often observed that concepts can be manufactured, just as we manufacture real objects. And indeed, some of the last books and essays by Stepanov may be viewed as manufactured concepts.

For example, Stepanov begins his 2007 book *Concepts* by giving a rather unacademic definition of the term concept. A concept, he claims, is a notion expanded by the context of an entire culture. He gives the example of the concept of the *queue* in Soviet times. *Standing in a queue* was a model of behaviour. Thus, Stepanov makes a list of particular phrases one could hear or say while standing in a queue. Then he shows how this concept was transferred to literature, citing Anna Akhmatova's memoirs about standing in the queue outside the Kresty prison for 17 months in Stalinist times. Each time it occurs, Stepanov adds, a concept can acquire new experiential properties, like the property of *suffering* in Akhmatova's case. That is why, he posits, a concept may not only be redefined but also reexperienced.

Instead of continuing to analyse concepts using linguistic methods, Stepanov proposes the reader experience them without resorting to descriptive analytical tools. His book ceases to be just a scholarly work and transforms into a catalogue of visual and verbal texts. He calls this manner of presentation the 'Gallery of Concepts'. For example, he reproduces René Magritte's picture of an apple alongside his own commentary or juxtaposes a painting by Van Gogh with Jacques Prévert's poems and fragments of Van Gogh's letters to his brother. A concept, in this sense, is made up of two manifestations – the textual and the visual. According to Stepanov, the concept is realised through the inner amalgamation of the picture and the caption together, as performed in the mind of the recipient – the reader-and-spectator.

The most interesting shift takes place elsewhere in the same book, when Stepanov addresses Russian Conceptualist poems. As if transferring Conceptualist techniques into this quasi-scholarly discourse, he reproduces a poetic text by Timur Kibirov.[15] What follows is a commentary to this text, discussing each line of the poem as a particular Russian concept. The commentary then continues with an autobiographical note, telling us about Stepanov's personal involvement in Kibirov's criminal prosecution in 1990, when Stepanov was asked to give an expert linguistic analysis of this poem. As he was a keen reader of Kibirov, he gave a very positive opinion to the court, and Stepanov publishes

15   A member of the Moscow Conceptualist poetic circle.

a copy of the prosecutor's letter addressed to him as evidence of just that – the poet was acquitted for lack of evidence, without any further details. What we see here is an exponential realisation of the conceptual method, which draws from the domain of art, and performs the conceptual procedures in what is supposed to be scholarly writing.

There was also a simultaneous reversal of those roles – many Russian Conceptualist artists employed quasi-scientific discourse in their performances and installations. Andrei Monastyrski often called his art actions 'research' ('исследования'), describing them as 'a combination of discourse practice and visual plastics, text and images'. In his theoretical and artistic texts, Monastyrski – who had studied philology – constantly uses linguistic, linguophilosophical or semiotic terms, such as metaphorisation, text structures, text formation, verbal event, context, sign system, post-semiosis, sense discrimination, discourse, and the like, albeit in his own idiosyncratic way.

On the subject of linguistically oriented conceptual writing, another case deserves special mention – the rare case of a Russian linguist who was also an experimental poet. This was Alexander Kondratov, whose scholarly works are well known in Russia, but whose stunning poetic oeuvre has only very recently been recovered from the archives, revealing a pre-conceptual poetics reminiscent of the better known Lianozovo group.[16] He was a virtuoso of all forms of poetic experimentation – from baroque-like visual poems to computer-generated aleatoric verse. Some of his poems could be classified as what was called Language poetry in the US due to its extensive use of linguistic terminology – for instance, in the titles of his cycles *Graphemes, Morphemes, Parts of Speech*, etc. He composed poems that laid bare certain linguistic mechanisms, as in this one about suffixation (cit. in Valieva, 2015):

Суффиксация

Афористичное, поэтическое, зрелое
Белы (ый, ое, ая, яя)
Зелен (оватый, еватый, ватый)
Желт(еющий, юющий, ующий)
-онький, енький, унький
Красноватенький, малоподвижный...
Тоскующий
желтеющий

---

16 Most of his experimental poetry was published in Kondratov (2015).

поющий
- Атенький
- Отенький
- онький!

The affinity between conceptual art and conceptual linguistics is even more striking in the case of the Russian Conceptualist artists Rimma Gerlovin and Valery Gerlovin, who in 2012 published a book titled *The Concepts*, the same title as Stepanov's semiotic study. The Gerlovins were, according to some biographical sources, the first, along with Groys, to apply the term *concept* to artistic practices in the 1960s. In a theoretical essay from the book, the Gerlovins claim that Conceptualism is just a technical tool for a deeper process of the transformation of thought: 'Basically, though it is an art phenomenon, Conceptualism is something of an ontological order. It is an intercrossing of many strata of art, philosophy, psychology, mythology, and sociology, where thinking about many principles of being is expressed in creative concepts. We can see not an image of this or that event, but its concept' (Gerlovina et al., 2012: 410). Here again, the dominant role of the word is emphasised: 'The word's potentiality consists not only in its semantic use but also in its visual form. Through syncretic creation of forms, one can synthesise a certain conceptual organum, or complex, combining the principles of literature, art, mythology, religion, philosophy, and music. The word is akin to the original creative impulse. That's why even in the canonical sense, it is the word that was "in the beginning"' (Ibidem).

The interactions between artistic and scholarly discourses analysed in this chapter were a prominent feature of post-modernist and neo-avant-garde writing. Metalinguistic reflection went hand in hand with poetic and visual experimentation. This was especially true of the Language poets as representatives of conceptual writing understood more broadly. My next chapter will address the intellectual transfers that American Language writing engaged in with Russian innovative poetries of the last century.

CHAPTER 12

Language Writing: American-Russian Poetic Transfers

I hate speech.
ROBERT GRENIER

∴

I've got a hang for langue but no truck with Parole.
CHARLES BERNSTEIN

∴

In this case, the matter of writing is language itself, understood as a system.
ARKADII DRAGOMOSHCHENKO

∴

Few paths have crossed in the history of American and Russian avant-garde poetry. Vladimir Mayakovsky's visit to America in 1925 seems to have had no direct impact on the American poetic milieu. During his visit to Soviet Russia in 1931, E.E. Cummings never got to meet his Soviet colleagues in 'leftist' poetry; Mayakovsky, Yesenin and Khlebnikov had already died by that time, David Burliuk had moved to the American continent (without ever establishing contacts with contemporary poets there), Boris Pasternak, Alexei Kruchenykh, Vassily Kamensky and other avant-garde writers had retreated to more moderate poetics due to the oppression imposed by official aesthetics. Only after World War II did the Russian poetic avant-garde – mainly represented by Mayakovsky's legacy – find footing in the active field of innovative American poetics, as is most evident in the work of Frank O'Hara[1] and

---

[1] On Mayakovsky's echoes in the work of O'Hara, see the informative article by Vroon (2020).

Allen Ginsberg.[2] The Beatniks made the first sporadic but bold attempts to establish personal ties between American and Russian alternative poetry. The visits of Allen Ginsberg to the USSR and of Evgeny Yevtushenko and Andrey Voznesensky to the United States in the 1960s and 1970s allowed the new poetic voices of the two major literary cultures to be introduced to each other in person.[3]

However, it was only in the 1980s that lasting creative networks between new Russian and American poetries started to emerge, when a number of US poets visited the Soviet Union, first informally and later in an official capacity. The majority were poets of the Language movement, invited by the Russian Metarealists. Arkadii Dragomoshchenko was at the center of these networks of American-Russian poetic transfers. Among the first invitees to Soviet Russia in the early 80s were Lyn Hejinian and Clark Coolidge, the latter coming as a jazz musician rather than a poet.[4] In 1989, these two movements – American Languagists and Russian Metarealists – joined forces to take part in a collective project whose subject was the 'poetic function of language'. Such was the title Arkadii Dragomoshchenko chose for the summer conference attended by his American colleagues, referring to an idea promoted by Roman Jakobson, who thus acted as an agent of Russian-American bilateral cultural transfer in the field of poetic linguistics and the poetry of language. Language as such, much as the Futurists' 'word as such', united the two national traditions of poetic writing within a common space of creative exchange.

The early Russian Futurists' idea of a 'poetic language' helped usher in the language bias in 1970s American writing. Another major conceptual precursor to language writing was the work of Jack Spicer, a poet of the San Francisco Renaissance, which had become a melting pot for many of the language poets. In his youth, Spicer had studied academic linguistics with the famous structuralist Zelig Harris. His career as a linguist was short-lived, but the linguistic apparatus subsequently entered his poetic work. In 1965, he published the poetry collection *Language*, parts of which were named after linguistic disciplines: morphemics, phonetics, semantics, etc. Its cover ironically appropriated the cover of the major academic journal *Language*. A famous poem from this

---

2   The transnational American-Russian aspects of Ginsberg's oeuvre are highlighted in the 2017 doctoral thesis by Dandeles.
3   Ginsberg talks about these exchanges in an interview with the Russian poet Yaroslav Mogutin: http://kolonna.mitin.com/people/mogutin/ginsberg.shtml (last accessed 27.02.23).
4   After visiting Russia in the 1980s, Clark Coolidge was working on a poem called 'Russian Nights'. Based on his trips to Saint-Petersburg he has also written two books: *This Time We Are Both* (published by Ugly Duckling Presse in 2010) and *City in Regard* (unpublished).

collection, 'Thing Language', issues a challenge to the linguisticality of poetry, taking up a problematics that would later permeate 'language writing'.[5]

In the 1970s, the Language poetry circles were starting to take shape and institutionalise themselves by way of little magazines, talks and gatherings. Several names arose on the American poetic scene whose work also dealt with language issues, though they were not part of Language poetry as such; here, we should mention Rosmarie Waldrop and Michael Palmer, whose poetics is close to linguocentric writing and is largely determined by metalinguistic reflection as the generative principle of text production.

In her doctoral thesis, which later became a book with the telling, interrogative title *Against Language?* (1971), Rosmarie Waldrop rebelled against language as a fetish, or rather, against the dictate of language. Instead, she proposed a poetics of rupture – non-linear writing that revived the experiments of Gertrude Stein. In an important later essay, 'Thinking of Follows', Waldrop describes composition as a process, and construction as a linguo-historical community. Communication across multiple languages and idioms works to destabilise language as an ideological construct: 'I do not 'use' the language. I interact with it. I do not communicate via language, but with it. Language is not a tool for me, but a medium infinitely larger than any intention' (2000: http).

Like Waldrop, Michael Palmer has done a lot to make 'language writing' possible without being formally part of the Language school. Palmer's poetic task is the radical rediscovery of the nature of the poem in its relation to the language and metalanguage in which it is created. A poetic text is thought of as a 'contingency' between language and the world it refers to (e.g., in his essay 'Poetry and Contingency', 2003). Therefore, in Palmer's texts, any reference can turn into a self-reference, a metaphor can use language as a means of assimilation, and a poetic line can be read as a proposition from linguistic philosophy and, at the same time, a performative act, as in this fragment from 'Sun', a poem later translated into Russian by the Metarealist poet Alexei Parshchikov (Palmer, 1988: http):

> Write this. We have burned all their villages
> Write this. We have burned all the villages and the people in them
> Write this. We have adopted their customs and their manner of dress
> Write this. A word may be shaped like a bed, a basket of tears or an X

---

5 See Ron Silliman's essay (1985) testifying to Spicer's impact on language-oriented poetics.

> Say this. I was born on an island among the dead. I learned language on this island but did not speak on this island. I am writing to you from this island. I am writing to the dancers from this island. The writers do not dance on this island.

With this radical orientation towards language as such, Palmer's poems assign a special function to silence at different levels of form and content. Arkadii Dragomoshchenko, who was the first to introduce Palmer to the Russian public, calls him a 'mountaineer of silence' ('альпинист тишины') (2013). Palmer always had an affinity with the Language movement and recognised the commonality of their poetic attitudes, as he notes in an interview published in Russian: 'I think we had a common goal: to erase everything and start over, to abandon the governing prescriptions and assumptions of institutionalised poetry practice and question the prevalent concepts of expressiveness, the self and the individual, and the role of the reader' (Aristov, 2013: http). In 1983, Palmer compiled a small but influential anthology, *Code of Signals*, which included both theory and poetry from authors experimenting with different modes of writing. The book opens with an epigraph about poetry as a 'code of signals' ('сигнализация') from Osip Mandelstam's *Conversation about Dante*, a choice that is itself a signal of the reception of Russian poetics in the American context.[6]

For all the decentralisation of the Language movement, historically and geographically, the school originally had two main centers – San Francisco and New York. In 1971, two poets from the West Coast, Robert Grenier and Barrett Watten, began publishing an independent poetry magazine in Iowa City under the deictic title *This*. The term *language-centered poetry* was first used in 1973 by the California-based poet Ron Silliman, who in 1970 had started publishing the language-oriented poetic bulletin *Tottel's*. In 1975, Silliman published a selection of poems by nine authors in the magazine *Alcheringa*, edited by Jerome Rothenberg, in a first attempt to present the Language poets as a circle.

On the East coast, starting in the late 1970s, Bruce Andrews and Charles Bernstein edited a newsletter named after the movement: $L=A=N=G=U=A=G=E$. As in the 1920s and 30s, experimental literature in the 1970s was mainly printed in small magazines, drawing upon the counter-cultural strategies of its precursors. Among the most active journals and publishers associated with the Language movement were Kit Robinson's *Streets and Roads*, Clark Coolidge's and Michael Palmer's *Joglars*, James Sherry's ROOF, Alan Davies'

---

[6] Both Palmer and Waldrop have had individual books translated into Russian, by Russian poets associated with language-oriented poetics.

A Hundred Posters, Bob Perelman's *Hills,* Barrett Watten's and Lyn Hejinian's *Poetics Journal,* and Lyn Hejinian's *Tuumba Press.* At the same time, the circle of authors associated with this movement was rapidly expanding. Neither the poets themselves nor scholars of their work have compiled an exhaustive list of participants. Close to a hundred different authors are more or less consistently included in this movement. Charles Bernstein (2012) prefers to talk about the 'expanded field of language writing', which also includes similar literary phenomena from around the world.

'A movement without special manifestos or official membership' – this is how the community was defined by Bob Perelman (1996: 16), who prefers the term language writing to language poetry, reflecting the multi-genre manifestations of the movement. Charles Bernstein breaks up the appellation LANGUAGE with equal signs, pointing to the egalitarianism between community members: 'L=A=N=G=U=A=G=E P=O=E=T=R=Y: a loose affiliation of unlike individuals' (2013: 124). Douglas Messerli, compiler of one of the anthologies of language writing (1987), introduced the expression *Language Poetries* into the title, indicating the plurality of poetic styles of its various authors.

Language writing is, indeed, a more accurate term for these literary practices. They are not limited to poetry, although poetic discourse is paramount. The boundaries between poetry and prose, free and 'non-free' verse, essay and treatise, theory and practice are eliminated here. Many of these texts are written and read at the same time as utterances and meta-utterances, both as poems and critical essays. The influence of French post-structuralist theory is embodied in poetic form: a critical theory of discourse is created by poetic discourse. The political meaning of such writing, within the context of Vietnam-era protest culture in the United States, is in criticising the dominant discourses, inverting everyday speech into a unique poetic language. The Russian poet Alexei Parshchikov, who was influenced by Language writing, conveyed its essence very aptly: 'Language was inherent to natural phenomena, scientific models, our body, and the forms of ideas that lived objectively in a special "reserve", as in Karl Popper's World 3. American poets were interested in language as an extension of the body, intellect, and new technologies. Michael Palmer spoke of poetry "marked by the quality of resistance and the necessary complexity, with the obligatory breakthrough and rejection, as well as exploratory forms"' (cit. in Bernstein, 2020: 399).[7] Research and academic teaching are also an important part of the public image of Language writers. Research, of course, also includes inquiry. One of the most important books

---

[7] Palmer and Parshchikov have translated each other's poems between English and Russian.

to come out of the Language school is *The Language of Inquiry* (2000) by Lyn Hejinian, in which she posits that poetic language is the language of inquiry.

Lyn Hejinian is recognised as one of the pioneers of the Language movement on the West Coast. In her essay 'Barbarism', a review of the historical context of the Language school, she points to some of the common features shared by its authors, such as the intersection of the aesthetic and ethical, the isomorphism of aesthetic and social endevours, new ways of thinking, and new relationships between the components of thought and writing (Hejinian 2000: 323):

- a poem is not an isolated autonomous rarified aesthetic object
- a person (the poet) has no irreducible, ahistorical, unmediated, singular, kernel identity
- language is a preeminently social medium the structures of language are social structures in which meanings and intentions are already in place
- institutionalised stupidity and entrenched hypocrisy are monstrous and should be attacked
- racism, sexism, and classism are repulsive
- prose is not necessarily not poetry
- theory and practice are not antithetical
- it is not surrealism to compare apples to oranges
- intelligence is romantic.

Writing as the metamorphosis of language is more important that what is written, as Hejinian's early essay 'If Written Is Writing' suggests: 'The writing emerges from within a pre-existent text of one's own devising or another's. The process is composition rather than writing' (1984: 30). In her landmark essay, 'The Rejection of Closure', Hejinian develops a theory of the 'open text', one that is 'open to the world and particularly to the reader. It invites participation, rejects the authority of the writer over the reader and thus, by analogy, the authority implicit in other (social, economic, cultural) hierarchies. It speaks for writing that is generative rather than directive' (2000: 43). A well-known example of Hejinian's work is 'The Composition of the Cell', a hybrid text that implements the principle of open structure.[8] Each numbered line is a separate statement, but the order and linearity of reading is not predetermined by

---

8 'Barbarism', 'The Rejection of Closure' and 'The Composition of the Cell', as well as many other texts by Hejinian, have been translated into Russian by Arkadii Dragomoshchenko. For many years, Arkadii and Lyn were close friends and correspondents. See more on their collaborations in Edmond (2002) and Sandler (2005). Hejinian is the author of *Oxota: A Short Russian Novel* (1991), a cycle of 270 sonnets inspired both by Alexander Pushkin's *Eugene Onegin* and the Post-Soviet Russia she saw while visiting the country in the 1990s.

numbering and sequencing. The space of the poem is restructured by the act of reading. Ludwig Wittgenstein's style of philosophical writing had a major impact on most Language poets, as well as some of their Russian counterparts such as Arkadii Dragomoshchenko, especially in his later writings, as we will see in the next chapter.

Another founding member of Language poetry, Charles Bernstein, began his career with a thesis about Wittgenstein. *Tractatus* has always served as a precedent for Bernstein's work. A typical example of this influence is his text *Artifice of Absorption*. Alexei Parshchikov, who participated in its translation into Russian and wrote a preface to it, calls it a 'treatise-like poem' or 'a learned poem'. According to Parshchikov, this text serves as a manifesto for the poetics of the author and is 'a kind of constructivist poem, where the 'real', documentary material is the poet's reflection on the meaning of the device in verbal art' (cit. in Bernstein, 2020: 400).[9] Examples of such self-reflexive manifestos can also be found in the Russian avant-garde, in texts by Igor Terentiev or Alexei Chicherin. The poetry of the Russian Futurists is perhaps the main foreign source of inspiration for Charles Bernstein, along with Osip Mandelstam, Andrey Bely, and Boris Pasternak. Bernstein translated poetry by Osip Mandelstam, as well as Khlebnikov and Kandinsky. In an interview with the Russian artist Natalia Fedorova (Bernstein, 2021), he dwells upon the affinity between Mandelstam's and Louis Zukofsky's poetics.

Of the Russian avant-garde authors, Velimir Khlebnikov is particularly significant for Language poets. For Bernstein, he worked to transcend the boundaries of language and languages in his zaum poetry and contributed to the search for a universal language. Along with Joyce, Wittgenstein, Mallarmé and Beckett, Khlebnikov, Bernstein believes, is one of the heroes of the linguistic turn in the twentieth century. Bernstein's poetry itself, however, bears little resemblance to Khlebnikov's work. There is almost no lexical creativity in it, no rationalistic attempt to create a new 'alphabet of the mind'. Rather, zaum or trans-sense is practiced through the transgression of discourse; as Ian Probstein, Bernstein's Russian translator, writes, 'this is a search for meaning hidden behind divergent stereotypes, so-called common sense or official political rhetorics' (cit. in Bernstein, 2020: 10). This is Khlebnikov read through the lens of Wittgenstein's language games and Barthes' and Foucault's discourse matrices.

Khlebnikov's traces are more visible in Ian Probstein's Russian translations of Bernstein's verse; especially in the ones that involve creative

---

9 The Russian translation of *Artifice of Absorption* was published as a separate chapbook in Moscow in 2008.

word-formation in the target language. The poem 'Fold', for instance, is translated not as 'Складка', but as 'Складень', hinting at the Russian tradition of icon painting. English tautologies like 'pet my pet' turn into root crossings of different parts of speech: 'пестую моего домашнего пестуна'; 'пытаю свою пытку'; 'вью свое вервие', etc. Non-existent but plausible and comprehensible words are also used: 'утишаю свою тихость'; 'нарекаю свое рекло'; 'распогожу свою погоду' and the like. Neologisms such as 'утвержцание' or 'транссегментальное плавание' echo Khlebnikov's principle of 'скорнение'. Bernstein's translator is doing important work on the mutual pollination of the two languages – not just a simple semantic borrowing, but a poetic transformation of a text in another language. English and Russian differ not only in their structure (analytical and synthetic), but also – in terms of poetic function – in the principle of text generation. This is especially evident in translations of Language poetry. A translator from Russian herself, Lyn Hejinian[10] explains this radical difference not only as a feature of the movement of thought, but also as the foundation of thinking itself: 'American English is a broad language with enormous horizontal freedom, and Russian is a deep language with enormous vertical freedom' (2013: 65). In interlingual English-Russian translations, the breadth of one language resonates with the depth of the other, opening up new dimensions of expressiveness.

Charles Bernstein was also influenced by the Russian avant-garde artists Kazimir Malevich, Alexander Rodchenko, and Wassily Kandinsky – both as visual artists and writers. A key term for this reception is *faktura*. For Bernstein, this is the creation of verbal objects for reflection. *Faktura* is what allows you to see form and function in their linkage, where reflecting on a poetic device becomes an implementation of the device itself. The development of the theory of *faktura* and form as such by the Russian Formalists had as much influence on Language writing as Formalist poetry itself. What Marjorie Perloff termed 'the Futurist moment', implying both the chronological (moment of time) and physical (moment of force) meanings of the term, is the 'emblem of the most radical moment of the period' (Bernstein, 2016: 64).

Robert Grenier, a Language writer from the East Coast, works with minimalist structures of poetic expression. He created a special format of publishing poetry; his *Sentences* series (1978) consists of five hundred large-format catalog cards, each containing a short poem. It appears to be a very close analogue to Lev Rubinstein's 'cards', created in the same period in Russia. This treatment of the poetic line as a sentence in itself was theorised by Ron Silliman. In his

---

10   She has translated from Russian two books by Arkadii Dragomoshchenko: *Description* (1990) and *Xenia* (1994).

book of essays *The New Sentence*, Silliman connects literary realism with bourgeois capitalism and demonstrates how this capitalism can be eradicated by the theory and practice of the 'new sentence'. The 'new sentence' as a unit of language writing was supposed to minimise the syllogistic effect expected in a work of prose through transformations in the structure, length, and position of the sentence or utterance within a text, thus reinforcing its polysemy. This is how Silliman's own poems are arranged, in particular *The Chinese Notebook*, which is built on the model of Wittgenstein's *Philosophical Investigations* with its numbered sequences of aphorisms.[11]

When it comes to Russian-American ties and transfers, one cannot underestimate the importance of Roman Jakobson's work in linguistics for Bernstein and other Language poets in the 1970s – not just because of its genetic connection to the Formalist school, which was extremely important for them, but also in its updated version, expressed in the article 'Linguistics and Poetics' (1960), which was discussed in the Transition chapter 2. Charles Bernstein noted that, among linguists, Jakobson had the most pronounced influence on him with his concept of poetic language as 'verbal language that foregrounds its material (acoustic and syntactic) features, providing an understanding of poetry as less about communicating a message than an engagement with the medium of verbal language itself' (2016: 73). The title of Barrett Watten's book of criticism, *Questions of Poetics* (2016), is characteristically a borrowing from Jakobson; namely, from his French-language monograph *Questions de poétique*.

In the 'Linguistics and Poetics' article, one of Jakobson's concerns was how the poetic function of language differs from its metalingual function (1960: http):

> It may be objected that metalanguage also makes a sequential use of equivalent units when combining synonymic expressions into an equational sentence: $A = A$ ('Mare is the female of the horse'). Poetry and metalanguage, however, are in diametrical opposition to each other: in metalanguage the sequence is used to build an equation, whereas in poetry the equation is used to build a sequence.

In poetic texts from the Language school, and especially in Bernstein's poetry, poetic and metapoetic functions are often combined within the framework of one text and even one utterance or line. This principle generates cross-cutting

---

11   *The Chinese Notebook* was translated into Russian by Viktor Mazin, a Russian philosopher and psychoanalyst, in 1997.

self-reference and metatextuality, as in the poem 'This Line' (Bernstein, 1999: 315):

> This line is no more than an
> illustration of a European
> theory. This line is bereft
> of a subject. This line
> has no reference apart
> from its context in
> this line. This line
> is only about itself.
> this line is stripped of emotion.

The magazine *L=A=N=G=U=A=G=E* frequently published essays on linguistic and semiotic topics, with titles referencing current trends in language studies, such as 'Text and Context' (1984), an essay by Bruce Andrews. Jakobson, as well as Russian Formalists such as Viktor Shklovsky and Yuri Tynianov, were instrumental for Language writers in their treatment of language as such by analogy with the word as such. The Formalists' opponents in early Soviet Russia, such as Valentin Voloshinov and Mikhail Bakhtin,[12] are also referenced in critiques of discourses as social formations. For example, Ron Silliman's manifesto-like essay 'Disappearance of the Word, Appearance of the World' criticises the transparency effect of conventional literature, where language is used instrumentally. With reference to Voloshinov's Marxist philosophy of language, Silliman calls poetry a 'philosophy of practice in language' that requires '(1) recognition of the historic nature and structure of referentiality, (2) placing the issue of language, the repressed element, at the center of the program, and (3) placing the program into the context of conscious class struggle' (1984: 131).

While American language-centered poets and theorists could easily and openly apply Russian Formalist concepts to the critique of culture, society and politics, Russian alternative poetry of the time existed in the underground. In terms of Russian counterparts to Language poetry, the first contemporaneous analogue that comes to mind is Moscow Conceptualism. Without explicitly proclaiming an orientation towards language, poets such as Andrei Monastyrski, Vsevolod Nekrasov and Lev Rubinstein were, indeed, operating with language and discourse in ways similar to those of Language writing without any knowledge of what was happening in America at that time. A somewhat

---

12   The Language poet Michael Davidson dedicated an essay (1989) to Bakhtin's theory of dialogue in discourse, applying it to poetic language.

similar figure to that of Jack Spicer – and to a certain extent, that of Jackson Mac Low – with his role in new language-oriented poetics, was the Russian linguist and poet Alexander Kondratov, discussed in the last chapter.

Marjorie Perloff has justly warned (1993) against certain oversimplifications when comparing Russian and American poetic cultures. Yet, what they definitely have in common is their orientation towards the early Russian avant-garde's critique of language as a medium of creativity. Albena Lutzkanova-Vassileva suggests that 'a parallel plotting of American Language poetry and Russian Conceptualist verses on a single stylistic, poetical graph thus manifests points of peculiar convergence via the commonality of the two with the Futurist school' (2016: 127). The scholar rightly juxtaposes Russian Conceptualism and Language poetry on the ground of their shared semiotic principle of 'sloughing off' ('отслаивание'), that is 'the process of peeling off, divesting one by one the rich semantic layers of reality, until the reader is confronted with the nothingness of pure silence, utterly unburdened by a pre-existing meaning' (Idem: 129). Charles Bernstein, in his recent talks, acknowledges the affinity of his linguistic practices with those used by Moscow Conceptualists, most notably by Rubinstein.

Despite these apparent similarities and affinities between Language poetry and Russian Conceptualism, a mutual fascination arose between the Language poets and the Metarealist circle. In 1990, two groups of poets – Alexei Parshchikov, Arkadii Dragomoshchenko, Ivan Zhdanov, Ilya Kutik and Nadezhda Konakova, on the Russian side, and Michael Palmer, Lyn Hejinian, Jean Day, Clark Coolidge, and Kit Robinson, on the American side – launched a collaborative project named 5+5. The idea was to compile an anthology of mutual translations by the authors involved. The initial translations were published in the Swedish magazine *Artes*. The anthology, however, was never published.

Michael Palmer was, along with Lyn Hejinian, most actively involved in these American-Russian poetic transfers. In an interview with Vladimir Aristov, a Russian Metarealist poet, Palmer noted (2013: http):

> How can we summarise the foundations common to us? We were all devoted to exploratory poetics and – in many ways – poetry of critical negativity and cultural resistance. Apart from the awareness of the need for exploratory poetry for the survival and renewal of culture, there was not much in common in our actual practice – which reflected our deeply different circumstances. With Aygi, Parshchikov, Khlebnikov and others, I perceived the ancient-modern resonance, which was new to me and which helped me in a new and broader understanding of the time horizons of innovative poetry. These lessons have stayed with me and deeply influenced my work.

Palmer notes in the same interview that he first met Gennady Aygi[13] in Paris in the late eighties and spent some time with him in San Francisco shortly before his death and adds that they shared an interest 'in the poetic function – or functions – of silence' (Ibidem).

The poets of the Language movement got the chance to encounter the Russian Formalist school firsthand in 1989, when four of them (Barrett Watten, Michael Davidson, Lyn Hejinian and Ron Silliman) were invited to Leningrad. They were supposed to meet with the Russian Neo-Formalist scholar Lidiya Ginzburg, whose talk 'The Historical Significance of OPOYAZ' was on the programme of the conference they attended. The conference itself was dedicated to a key Formalist concept, as reflected in its title, 'Poetic function: language, consciousness, society'. It was organised by Arkadii Dragomoshchenko, at that time the chairman of the 'creative programme' at the Soviet Cultural Foundation, which was also called 'Poetic function'.

By the late 80s, some poets of the Language movement had already visited the USSR, but this time the visit was part of a large international event. However, the main result of this conference was direct contact between representatives of the American Language school and representatives of the two leading schools of unofficial Russian poetry – Metarealism and Conceptualism.[14] However, a much greater number of Metarealists attended, among them Dragomoshchenko himself, Alexei Parshchikov, Ivan Zhdanov, Vladimir Aristov, Viktor Krivulin, and Ilya Kutik. From the Conceptualist camp, only Dmitry Prigov was present. Lyn Hejinian believes that, because of their common formal features, the two movements – Language poetry and Russian Metarealism – differed only to the extent that the American language and Western capitalism differed from the Russian language and Soviet communism. The paradigm of Metarealism turned out to be closer to Language poetry due to 'a fascination with the epistemological and perceptual nature of language-as-thinking, the belief that poetic language is a suitable tool for exploring the world, an interest in the linguistic layering of a landscape' (Hejinian, 2013: 64).

What all three groups of poets (Language poets, Conceptualists and Metarealists) shared was an interest in the relationship between language, consciousness, and society, as suggested by the title of the conference. Roman Jakobson's 'poetic function of language' related all of them to the legacy of the Russian

---

13 Palmer wrote a cycle of poems dedicated to his Russian friend Aygi, published in his book *Thread* (2011); they have recently been translated into Russian by the Aygi scholar Olga Sokolova.
14 For the foundations of these two circles, see Mikhail Epstein's pioneering 'Theses on Metarealism and Conceptualism' (1999).

avant-garde. But the problematic of the conference was more in line with the intellectual landscape of the 1980s. It is no coincidence that Dragomoshchenko decided to invite a number of prominent Soviet linguists to participate, such as Vyacheslav Ivanov, Maxim Shapir, Suren Zolyan, and some others. During these same years, the problem of consciousness came to the forefront of scientific study: in linguistics, cognitive science, conceptual analysis, linguistics of altered states of consciousness, and the theory of metaphor. The mutual interest between Conceptualist and Metarealist poets and contemporary linguistics was as topical as it was long overdue.

The conference itself was described in the book *Leningrad*, published in the US in the wake of the trip by the four Language poets in attendance. It contains many references to the legacy of Russian Formalism. The authors admit that Formalism was a 'treasure' for the theoretical aspect of the Language school. The Formal school is associated here with a uniquely Russian approach to the poem as an object. In the American tradition, Objectivism was just an episode in the work of a small group of poets (Louis Zukofsky, George Oppen, Carl Rakosi and a few others), whereas Russian theory gave birth to a whole scientific school of objectivist analysis of artistic structure: 'The unity of two projects – call them scientific and cultural – around the poetic adds up to a kind of myth of the object whose authority ultimately lies in a transcendent inherence' (Davidson et al., 1991: 37).

Barrett Watten often refers to Russian Formalism in his scholarly works (2003). He projects the concept of literariness as 'сделанность' onto modern poetics not so much as an aesthetic principle, but as an ethical imperative: 'Viktor Shklovsky's notions of the 'orchestration of the verbal material', 'defamiliarisation', and the 'semantic shift' have seemed to us thus not simply a question of art but one of ethics: the meaning of creative action in a context of some kind (literature, society) that cannot entirely be accounted for' (Davidson et al., 1991: 28). The Russian poets the Americans met in the late 1980s in the USSR seemed to defamiliarise their own tradition of defamiliarisation. In late Soviet Leningrad, the Language poets perceived the city of OPOYAZ in its 'formal contours' as a lived rather than represented experience. OPOYAZ acted as a model of a utopian marriage of the American and late Soviet avant-gardes.[15]

Charles Bernstein, too, likes to quote Viktor Shklovsky, in particular his idea of 'laying bare the device' ('обнажение приема'). The title of one of Bernstein's poems contains an explicit reference to Russian Formalism, as well as an even more explicit intertext with Marcel Duchamp: 'BALLAD LAID BARE

---

15   Jacob Edmond proposed a very suitable metaphor for this kind of convergence – 'common strangeness' – in the title of his book (2002).

BY ITS DEVICES (EVEN): A BACHELOR MACHINE FOR MLA'. The manifesto-like treatise *Artifice of Absorption* is also inspired by the Formalist concept of *device* as defamiliarisation. According to Alexei Parshchikov, this 'poem-treatise in itself is replete with a demonstration of the techniques that it describes' (cit. in Bernstein, 2020: 402). Bernstein's key term *artifice* echoes the title of Shklovsky's manifesto in English, 'Art as Device'.

The neo-formalism of the Language poets was not the result of a doctrine straightforwardly received from the Russians, but the product of cultural transfer, in which Formalist concepts reached them through a different culture and in a different chronotope. The form here was no longer the flagship of the revolution but was placed in the neo-avant-garde tradition as a countercultural criticism of art. Bernstein sometimes mocks the form: 'It is this: FORM IS NEVER MORE THAN AN EXTENSION OF MALCONTENT. There it went, flapping, more USELESSNESS' (1999: 111). Brushing aside the neo-formalists, he ironically calls his personal movement 'nude formalism' (cf. his book *The Nude Formalism*, co-authored with Susan Bee), as if Formalism had descended from Duchamp's scandalous painting as a bride stripped bare by her bachelors.

In the American tradition, Conceptualism in the narrow sense originated as a movement in the visual arts and is only indirectly associated with poetic movements. In the Russian context, these vectors were merged into one. However, this does not prevent some American literary theorists from classifying some Language poetries as a type of conceptual writing.[16]

As a concluding remark to this chapter, I would like to name additional contemporary Russian poets who have been influenced by Language writing, apart from those already mentioned: Alexander Skidan, Dmitry Golynko, Alexander Ulanov, Kirill Korchagin, Nikita Safonov, Eugenia Suslova, Ekaterina Zakharkiv, and Anna Rodionova. Characteristically, all of these authors have also translated American Language writing into Russian.[17]

Reciprocal transfers between the Russian and American literary traditions, which, as I have argued, have shaped language-centered writing over the last fifty years, are still underway. Russian translations of Language poets have appeared in recent decades in journals such as *Mitin Journal, Kommentarii, Zvezda Vostoka, Novoe Literaturnoe obozrenie*, as well as in the anthology *Contemporary American Poetry in Russian Translations* (Dragomoshchenko et al.,

---

16   For example, Marjorie Perloff places them among 'conceptual poets and their others', as the title of a conference she organised in 2008 suggests: 'Conceptual Poetry and its Others'.
17   Most of them have contributed as translators to the recently published Russian anthology of new American poetry (Probstein et al., 2022).

1995). In recent years, separate book editions of texts by Michael Palmer, Clark Coolidge, Charles Bernstein, and Rosmarie Waldrop have appeared in Russian. Some of the texts were translated for the 2013 edition of the *Translit* almanac, which was entirely devoted to the Language school and also included a number of critical articles about the movement. Language poets and their associates are still interacting with Russian poetic contexts. The two most recent examples are Charles Bernstein's collection *Sign under Test* (2020) translated into Russian by Ian Probstein, and Barrett Watten's on-going long poem *NOTZEIT*, which is being translated into Russian and receiving feedback from younger Russian poets.

Translations of New American Poetry have been appearing in Russian publications since the 1980s. Apart from the Language poets, Russian translators have also been working with some of the poets from Black Mountain College (Charles Olson, Denise Levertov, Robert Creeley, Robert Duncan) and the New York School (mostly John Ashbery). Thanks in large part to Arkadii Dragomoshchenko's interests and activities, Russian poetry has been exposed to a particular line of US innovative poetry – the Objectivist Nexus. It might seem strange that the Objectivists, who originated in the 1920–30s, only appear in the last chapters of this book. Their work should fit into the chapter about language arts of the early American avant-garde. However, my focus here is not so much on the development of Objectivism, as on its delayed but fruitful reception in late Soviet and Post-Soviet Russian experimental poetry. The next chapter, then, will explore the Objectivist stratum in American and Russian poetries, from Louis Zukofsky and Charles Olson to the new generation of Russian poets of recent decades.

CHAPTER 13

Object-Oriented Languages: American Objectivism and Contemporary Russian Poetry

> A poem is a small (or large) machine made of words.
> WILLIAM CARLOS WILLIAMS

∴

> an elementary object considers the poverty
> of logic, language, bomzhik, other
> DMITRY GOLYNKO-WOLFSON

∴

Whereas in Soviet Russia, in the late 1920s, the LEF group of writers strived for an objective 'literature of fact', and in Central Europe the circle of logical positivists led by Wittgenstein and Karnap worked toward an objective grounding for their theory of a 'transparent' and 'pure' language of science, in New York City, at roughly the same time, a young generation of poets started to publish innovative verse. For these American writers, the factography of language became the basic premise of poetry. They invented an imposing name for themselves – the 'Objectivists'.

The term *Objectivist* is primarily associated with the American poet Louis Zukofsky, a pioneer of experimental poetry in the USA. His parents were Jewish immigrants from the Russian Empire. Louis Zukofsky was born in Manhattan in 1904. His friend Whittaker Chambers, who later joined the 'objectivist nexus' (DuPlessis et al., 1999), introduced him to Marxist ideas, and, although Zukofsky always kept away from politics, he was drawn to the communist spirit coming from Eastern Europe. He dedicated his first serious poem, 'A Poem Beginning The', to his mother, and the young poet's sympathies for the Soviet experiment are discernible in that text. Ezra Pound published this poem in his magazine *Exile* in 1928. In addition, Pound asked his friend Harriet Monroe to entrust a separate issue of her influential journal *Poetry* to Zukofsky. Zukofsky's task was not just to collect impressive work by young American poets, but also to propose a name for their new literary movement.

The resulting 1931 issue of *Poetry* marked the debut of the Objectivists – a circle of poets that included, apart from Zukofsky himself, George Oppen, Carl Rakosi, Charles Reznikoff, Basil Bunting, and some others. A selection of about fifteen poems was followed by a section titled 'Commentary', which contained two of Zukofsky's programmatic texts: the first looked like a brief manifesto ('Program: 'Objectivists' 1931') and the second was an essay about Reznikoff's poetry ('Sincerity and Objectification. With Special Reference to the Work of Charles Reznikoff'). In the latter text, Zukofsky formulated the principles of poetic objectivism through case studies of individual poems.

In analysing and discussing Reznikoff's verse, Zukofsky introduced two terms that were to serve as the basic features of objectivist poetics – *sincerity* and *objectification*. The first marked a specific attitude of overarching fidelity towards words in a poem and towards facts recorded by the poem. Sincerity in writing, in Zukofsky's words, is 'the detail, not mirage, of seeing, of thinking with the things as they exist, and of directing them along a line of melody' (2000: 12).

Sincerity, Zukofsky claims, is the poet's compositional capacity; it can be detected within a single line of verse. *Objectification* is something else; it is a criterion of poetic mastery related to sincerity. It is a 'resting totality' in the reader's mind, 'the apprehension satisfied completely as to the appearance of the art form as an object' (Idem: 13). The form as 'resting totality' should be as self-sufficient as any object in the real world. Zukofsky sees objectification as a protest against depicting the visible world. He proposes instead to introduce the world's particulars and elements in all their self-containment, completeness and particularity. Sincerity and objectification are not related to Kant's 'thing-in-itself'; they are an attempt to make sense of the structures and particulars whereby things enter our perception, and with the help of which the poet can contact things and live together with them. What is meant here is a poetic practice, in which a poem is not an extension or expression of the poet's 'I', but an essence in itself, 'another created thing'.

'Mantis' is one of Zukofsky's best known Objectivist poems. The seemingly chaotic assemblage of particulars and details is in fact meticulously arranged, forming an object of the material world with all its wrinkles and contradictions, proportions and disproportions. The poem is about an insect, a mantis, which finds itself in the depths of the New York City Subway, and the particulars of this scene as perceived by the observing author. Here is an excerpt in the original and in Russian translation by Kirill Medvedev, a poet whose work also bears the imprint of the American avant-garde (Zukofsky, 2015: 104):

> Mantis! praying mantis! since your wings' leaves
> And your terrified eyes, pins, bright, black and poor
> Beg——"Look, take it up" (thoughts' torsion)! "save it!"
> I who can't bear to look, cannot touch,——You——
> You can——but no one sees you steadying lost
> In the cars' drafts on the lit subway stone.

> Богомол! молящийся богомол! раз твоих крыльев листья
> И твои испуганные глаза, булавки, яркие, черные и бедные
> Просят—«эй, возьми ее» (мыслей скрученность)! «спаси ее!»
> Я который не в силах смотреть, не могу касаться,—Вы—
> Вы можете—но никто не видит, как ты держишься, затерянная
> Под сквозняком от вагонов на подземки освещенном камне.

Even if *Objectivism* proved to be, as Zukofsky later commented, a rather accidental term encompassing a range of American avant-garde poets of the 1930s, Objectivist poetics certainly paved the way for later generations of writers. Without it, it is difficult to imagine the evolution of post-WWII American poetry, for example, the work of Charles Olson. However, Olson preferred to use the term *objectism* instead of *objectivism* in order to avoid the binary logic present in the *subjectivism/objectivism* opposition. Olson's poetry ensured the cultural transfer of Objectivist principles from Zukofsky to the Language School, and subsequently, to Arkadii Dragomoshchenko's poetics. The objectification of subjectivity is a characteristic feature of Objectivist writing, in both Olson and Dragomoshchenko.

A case in point is Dragomoshchenko's translations of Olson's poetic cycle 'The Kingfishers' (Olson, 2010: http):

> Not one death but many,
> not accumulation but change, the feed-back proves, the feed-back is the law
>
> Into the same river no man steps twice
> When fire dies air dies
> No one remains, nor is, one
>
> Не одна смерть, но много
> не собирать, но изменять, чему доказательством

обратная связь—это
закон.
Никто не войдет дважды в ту же самую реку.
Когда умирает огонь, умирает и воздух
Никому не остаться, вокруг никого

The Objectivist optics in both the original and the translation eliminates markers of subjectivity, and only impersonal pronouns are used ('no man', 'no one'). The poem reads like a sequence of inferences and impersonal utterances (Ibidem):

> Around an appearance, one common model, we grow up
> many. Else how is it,
> if we remain the same,
> we take pleasure now
> in what we did not take pleasure before? love
> contrary objects? admire and / or find fault? use
> other words, feel other passions, have
> nor figure, appearance, disposition, tissue
> the same?

> В поле зрения. Только общая матрица, мы поднимаемся
> множеством. Как же быть по-иному
> если мы остаемся теми же
> находя сейчас наслаждение там
> где его не нашли до сих пор? Любя
> противоположные вещи? восторгаясь и/или отыскивая изъяны?
> Используя другие слова, живя другими страстями
> без очертаний, облика, места, плоти
> такие же?

Further on, the personal pronoun 'we' emerges as an indefinite set subject to change in the projective space of the verse. Change is the key topic of the poem. Only change exists and persists, and subjectivity dissolves in it. 'You' becomes a thing, a stop in a 'too strong grasping' (Ibidem).

> is change, presents
> no more than itself

> And the too strong grasping of it,
> when it is pressed together and condensed,
> loses it

This very thing you are

есть изменение, оно предъявляет
не более, чем себя.

А слишком цепкое понимание,
когда оно вжато в другое, слитно,
упускает все это

Ты и есть эта вещь.

A name relevant to the discussion of American and Russian objectivist writing is Ludwig Wittgenstein, who served as a kind of agent in the transfer of objectivism as a method of writing from American to Russian poetry. Wittgenstein's ideas about logical descriptions were a significant influence on Zukofsky and a big source of inspiration for Western Conceptualist art, and later, Moscow Conceptualism.

The reactualisation of Wittgenstein's philosophy in Russian poetry took place in the 2010s, precisely within the context of 'object-oriented' writing. Two poetry books published in 2011 both contain references to Wittgenstein in their titles: Kirill Korchagin's[1] *Propositions* and Arkadii Dragomoshchenko's *Tautology*. Korchagin's poetry, however, problematises rather than develops the principles of logical positivism (the title of the poem 'In Memory of Logical Positivism' sounds characteristically ironic). There is tension between the predominantly impersonal, assertive form of the poetic statements and their rather emotional content: 'as lanterns burn in the splits between mountains / through the silence of communications / you too go to the crossing where waiting / with a parched face // blast furnaces quivering in the crevices / flipping through the uralmash book/ a scorching wind of mountain forearms / as it dozes above decrepit hollows'.[2] Wittgenstein, and the tradition of the Viennese circle connected with him, serves as a metaphor for Korchagin's verse – a type of writing approaching the style of a protocol, although what is registered is by no means an ordinary world of things, and the language used is by no means ordinary.

The Austrian philosopher was particularly influential for Dragomoshchenko, especially in his late work. For Dragomoshchenko, as well as for Wittgenstein

---

1 Korchagin is a representative of the post-conceptualist trend in contemporary Russian poetry.
2 Translated by Ainsley Morse. http://old.trans-lit.info/english.htm (last accessed 27.02.23).

and for Gertrude Stein (another author important to Arkadii) tautology is a key writing technique. The book opens with a poem titled 'Ludwig Josef Johann', dedicated to the philosopher and structured as a treatise about him (Dragomoshchenko, 2011: 15):

> Wittgenstein has long been in paradise. He's probably happy
> as the rustle surrounding him reminds him
> that the rustle around him says nothing,
> but also does not present what ought to be 'shown'.
> It is agonising, because there is no way to remember a phrase.

This is a poetics not only of the object's indefiniteness, but of the subject's, too. In this poem, the author's subjectivity is cast aside and displaced onto a third person, in this case the Austrian-British thinker.[3] Lines from Dragomoshchenko's verse read as propositions from a treatise ('Picture of a Plantation') (2011: 17):

> A tautology is not a conceivable point
> of equilibrium of values, but a description of space
> between the appearance of meaning and its expansion.
> Expansion (play by accepted rules in a craggy light)
> combined with the structure of absence.
> Absence almost is, – a necessary remainder, -
> never enough.
> Insufficiency, striving for completeness,
> encloses the subject in a sentence ...

Meanwhile, the line breaks and interruptions to the sentence structure deviate from the genre of a philosophical treatise, giving the propositions a rhythmical beat, turning them into discrete series of micro-utterances that function both as poetic innuendos ('never enough'), and as parts of a whole, as discourse fragments of overarching meaning. Interestingly, each new proposition begins from the final word of the preceding proposition. The verse sets off a chain reaction of definitions of basic concepts: expansion, absence, insufficiency and, further still, sentence, speech, form, window, sight, reading, and so on. But where and what is the subject of this poetic discourse? It seems that we are dealing with objective laws governing sentence production. The limitations of subjectivity, as we read in one of the poem's lines, are offset by introducing the

---

[3] See Evgeny Pavlov's (2015) insightful observations on this topic.

subject into the sentence, i.e., by objectivising the subject, its (or his/her) disintegration into the facts of reality and the facts of language, much like in Louis Zukofsky's Objectivist poetry. The personal deixis may emerge at times, such as the pronoun 'нас' in the same poem, this time as object rather than deixis, like all other parts of speech: 'Us – a plural pronoun, in accusative case' (Idem: 18).

Markers of personal deixis are rather common in Dragomoshchenko's early lyric poems. In his later verse, they disperse in the world of objects created by the poems. More specifically, in his last book *Tautology*, personal pronouns characteristically appear in quotes almost throughout (Idem: 21, 23, 66):

> Elusive and sleepless like 'the other'
> In whose verbal body the 'I' is frozen in a trap
>
> [...]
>
> We see how 'we' is stratified into the 'I' of time equations
> (never a single one on the road). Even if up into a sweat on the amalgam
>
> [...]
>
> (which is easier in the end:
> A 'cigarette', a 'name', a 'you', a 'film', a 'heart'?
> dictionaries are huge, revolving on the axes of oblivion

The following poem makes this idea of the objectification of deictic words even more clear (Idem: 158):

> 'I'
>   'Here'
>
> 'Now'
>
>   'You'
>
>   'There'
>
>   'Then'
>
> a probable process
> of extracting oneself

> from language
> extractable from itself
> a wandering axis
>
> floating angles

The subject, or persona, completely merges with language, the author of the text being an operator of subjectivities by linguistic means. As a poet, Dragomoshchenko seeks to, as he says, 'produce and extend subjectivity' (Idem: 205). The pronoun 'I' ceases to act as an egocentric particular, pouring into the common stream of the nominalised world: 'What's funny is – the population, which has doubled since my birth and will double by my predictable death; the four 'I's' where there was only one; the more 'I's' than there has ever been, including, perhaps, all 'I's' with the ant souls that have transmigrated into them' (Idem: 94). In the texts where deictic uses of the 'I' are present, they are discredited by the end of the poem, either by means of quotation marks, or in the form of 'non-I' ('не я'), as in this fragment (Idem: 118–119):

> I do not know what I am writing, but at the same time I know what arises in your reading.
> [...]
> Therefore, the path in the late autumn around the neighbourhood does not promise anything,
> it isn't anxious, it's simple as a bark behind which a *not-I*
>   is reflected in the *I*, like a face, melting into the hole of conception.

Entire first-person utterances can appear in quotes (Idem: 28):

> I know what I am writing, but I do not know what you are reading.
> [...]
> And 'I' exfoliates from 'I' in sight,
> Walking one step after 'I know what I am writing'.

In this case, the first line of the poem is quoted within the last one. Sometimes such sentences are provided both in quotes and italics, which defamiliarises them twice as much (Idem: 158):

> '*I am a needle in your mind*'. Childhood mercy?
>
> [...]

'I know where I am going':
>   sometimes the mistake goes through other routes

[...]

Any word turns into a name, sooner or later:
>   'I am dying'

This passion for objectivising utterances, akin to Wittgenstein's tendency in his later period, pervades most of Dragomoshchenko's later writings. Some texts read as proposition analysis, such as this poem titled 'Consideration' (Idem: 120):

> The following proposal is subject to consideration:
> 'I do not see you as a bird drinks thirst from salt'.

The objectification of subjectivity implies special attention to things as they are, to exposing their meanings, as the poet puts it in his poem 'Things Growing Shallow':

> The thing consists of doubt
> that the meaning of the word attached to it,
> merges with the elusion of meaning in the long run.
> For example: dust covering the surface of the table,
> or a burnt match, or a rusty pin,
> goodness knows when settled in the window frame.

Beside Objectivism, there are other important influences on Dragomoshchenko's oeuvre, such as Gertrude Stein, who was herself a precursor to Objectivism (cf. the title of a section of her *Tender Buttons* – 'Objects'), and the Language School poets, who were successors to the Objectivists.[4]

A similar treatment of the material world is characteristic of some other poets associated with the Metarealist movement, such as Vladimir Aristov in his cycle *Private Follies of Things*, or Alexander Skidan, who is definitely influenced by American experimental writing and Dragomoshchenko's reception of it (2009: 92–93):

---

4 See Sandler (2005) and Petrovskaya (2015) for pointed discussions of this.

    a literal translation of the final stanza
    exhaustion of the procedure
    the superfluous figure of the poet
    learning a language
    however both movements
    are morpho-syntactic unities
    besides
    so-culled culture
    imitation, again
    runs to the swing
    catches and greases
    shakes the glass without breaking it
    in accordance with the melancholia of the mountain-dwellers
    inner declension
    metric system
    euphonic condensation
    all that remains
    of an expired expression.

Skidan's cycle *Objects in Part* reveals his objectivist optics most vividly. The verse unfolds as a series of short propositions or nominative constructions. The subject is absent on the linguistic level. The poem is about actions with fragmentary utterances or linguistic terms, which transform into objects of the real world alongside other things.

The literary critic Lev Oborin designated examples of Russian object-oriented poetry of the last decade (2010s) as 'impersonal' and 'subjectless' lyric poetry, naming such authors as Kirill Korchagin, Denis Larionov, Nikita Safonov, Vladimir Lukichev, Alexandra Tsibulya, and Alexei Porvin. In poetry of this kind, Oborin writes, 'the focus of attention shifts from the figure of the speaker to what and how he/she sees and composes' (2016: http). The poet, critic, and publisher Pavel Arseniev (2017) calls this tendency 'object-oriented poetry' in his preface to an issue of the literary magazine *Translit* dedicated to this type of writing. The Russian poets who contributed to this issue include Dmitry Golynko-Wolfson, Sergej Timofejev, Yaroslava Zakharova, Darya Serenko, and some others.

Eugenia Suslova's[5] writing is one of the recent examples of subjectless, or object-centered, verse in contemporary Russian poetry. She creates poems as cognitive designs of material and mental spaces, often applying a poetics of

---

5 Suslova is also an artist and a scholar of media linguistics.

neural-network interface. In a cycle called *Access*, the tagged key words (for example the series #*DATA*, #*command*, #*attention*, #*sleep*, #*to go*, #*form*) start to perform actions in the space of a poem, which speaks for itself, or for word-objects themselves: 'Any thing, having lost / its form, is set up, / where you save it, / is opening now'. A logic structured around coincidence allows unstructured meanings and interpretations: 'I exchange warmth for forms, / accelerating my memories without order. / I want to catch their coincidence'.[6]

A similar object-oriented poetics emerges in the poetry of Alexandra Tsibulya, a laureate of the Dragomoshchenko prize. One of her poems features the image of a kingfisher, possibly alluding to Charles Olson's poetic cycle 'The Kingfishers'. The poem lacks a linguistic subject, and language acts as a 'smutter' that 'obscures' things (Tsibulya, 2019: http):

> kingfisher
> winter-born
> quasi
> offspring
> smutted by the tongue
> fog ob
> scures the hysterical
> abundance of things
> making them quiet
> endurable

Another laureate of the Dragomoshchenko prize, Nikita Safonov – who is also an electronic musician and sound scholar – also works within the Zukofsky-Oppen-Olson tradition, both in his public talks and in his poetry (2015: http):

> Into one of the shadows where
> 'Continuity' cannot be distance
> of a light print on the finger of glass
> a wave passes, receding with acceleration
> of a diverging endless edge. I have to remember
> several dates,
> or statements about the layering of disc symbols,
> which the eye reaches through hidden hands, grasping
> for a transparent branch.

---

6 Unpublished translation by Lia Na'ama Ten Brink.

Into one of the shadows of the road
you inscribe on one side a silent figure
with a torn tongue, on the other – a hole in the inscription,
dissolving notepad's awaiting. Receiving segments,
by which you can calculate the resistance of the scale,
to exclude an attempt to read the card.
Lining up in one of the dark areas
the images of illumination in the form of a treatise,
closing the pages of pictures, enlarged by themselves:
A gap remains

This poem reads as an imaginary treatise, or more precisely, as impromptu drafts for a treatise on the specifications of the world's vision. Objects undergo metamorphoses beyond the laws of physics, and the text reads as a test of the 'utterability' of particular propositions and their compatibility with the order of things. Safonov's poetic cycle *Simplification Technique: Objects* represents an elementary analysis of certain objects (iron, writing, thought, fabric, table, hole, and the like) running out, as it were, of materiality or immateriality. Any attempt to say something about a material object is interrupted by abstract notions that appear as objects entering the field of vision (Safonov, 2010: http):

So, for example, a work lying in the width of the river,
and the river does not see its bottom; (illegible) thinner than the stream
of a word scattered to the shores
always speaks only about the *body*, about another possibility of your, also different, body
strict lines of beams at the edge, indescribable (as *he* says) sound,
close not to silence, but to absence.
[...]
- You leave objectivity here to dissolve,
in this literature

The principle of his poetics is stated in the last line of this poem: 'attention is continuation of a thing, when *I* moves towards a thing'. In this type of poetry, materiality dissolves, and writing equals materiality. Object-oriented languages of new American and Russian poetic writing gravitate towards a new global paradigm in contemporary thinking – an object-oriented ontology. Language is conceptualised here as a field of actions performed by actors. The act of an utterance entering a poem is, within this framework, is a full-fledged object in itself, interacting with other objects or creatures of the world under laws no longer imposed or controlled by a demiurgic author.

CHAPTER 14

Poetry beyond Language Barriers: Contemporary 'Trans-Language' Writing in Russia and USA

> My history takes place in language. Or is it my story takes place in language.
> EUGENE OSTASHEVSKY

∴

> who turned the object on as internet
> lifting languages slightly
> NIKA SKANDIAKA

∴

We have discussed in Parts 1 and 2 of this book some cases of multilingual poetic writing from the early Russian and American avant-garde (Wassily Kandinsky, Alexander Tufanov, E.E. Cummings, Eugene Jolas). By the early 21st century, global contacts between languages and poets intensified due to the growth of communication channels and migration trajectories across the world. What interests me most in these multiple cross-cultural and cross-linguistic transactions is the encounter between Russian and English poetic languages in contemporary writing by poets writing *both* in Russian and English, poets who mainly live outside Russia but continue to use Russian in their writing alongside English and, sometimes, other languages. In this final chapter, I will consider a number of such cases, particularly those that foreground language issues in their translingual poetics. A special case of writing across languages in the history of Russian poetry is the work of Elizaveta Mnatsakanova, which was analysed in Chapter 10 of this book. Although she never used English in her poetry – and did not have anything to do with American poetry – I will address the linguistic aspects of her work once again in some detail, as they anticipate some contemporary trends in multilingual writing from the 'Russia abroad'.

When speaking about poetic bilingualism in Russian-American literary relations of the last century, scholars most often cite Vladimir Nabokov and Joseph

Brodsky. At the same time, literary bilingualism is only one type of interlingual transfer in poetry, besides other phenomena such as foreignism, heteroglossia, polyglotism, or self-translation. In recent years, the term translingualism has also proved instrumental in literary studies. The American scholar Steven G. Kellman was among the first to discuss translingualism in relation to literature, in his book *The Translingual Imagination* (2000). Translingual is the term he uses for writers who work with more than one language or a non-native language in order to mark their freedom from cultural and monolingual restrictions. Writers such as Samuel Beckett or Vladimir Nabokov, according to Kellman, can freely move between two or more linguistic identities. Another study of this kind, Sarah Dowling' book (2018), analyses poetry deliberately positioned by its authors as translingual. It is mainly concerned with postcolonial poetry, exposing the mechanisms of dominance and repression of one language by another.

Experimental poetry of the twentieth century in Russia and in the United States, despite their rich traditions, is not replete with cases of translingual writing. Perhaps the most prominent example from the early Russian avant-garde is the poetry of the artist Wassily Kandinsky, discussed in Part 1 of this book. Certain elements of experimental translingualism can also be found in the texts of Osip Mandelstam. In the history of American avant-garde poetry, translinguality is manifested to some extent in Ezra Pound's *Cantos* and in Eugene Jolas' trilingual verses.

In Russian-language poetry of the second half of the twentieth century, translingualism featured most prominently in the work of Elizaveta Mnatsakanova.[1] In Part 1 of this book, I have already discussed the multilingualism of her writing in connection with the idea of glossolalia and the magic of the word. Here, I will address more closely the experimental work of this poet, which involved multiple languages within a poem. Hers is a poetry of *trans-language*, unique within Russian poetry of the last century.

1 Elizaveta Mnatsakanova's Translingualism

Elizaveta Mnatsakanova emigrated from Moscow to Vienna in 1975. She was born into an Armenian family whose name had originally been Mnatsakanjan. The borderline position between three linguistic and poetic cultures – Russian, Armenian and Austrian-German – affected the linguistic poetics of her texts, which incorporate various national idioms into the visual-musical

---

1 However, some foreign language inclusions can be found in several significant poets of this era, such as Gennady Aygi, Vsevolod Nekrasov, Viktor Sosnora, or Arkadii Dragomoshchenko.

space of her verse. In all likelihood, the first example of language contact in the work of Mnatsakanova was her trip to Armenia in the 1960s, as a result of which she created the poetic cycle *HAYASTAN*, named for the Armenian endonym Հայաստան.[2] This cycle has not yet been published, along with other works that require access to the writer's archive.

In the titles of the handwritten books she created before moving to Austria, Mnatsakanova often included elements from foreign languages: *a daydream's book; Beim Tode zugast; Das Buch Sabeth; antigrammatical*. Her emigration to Vienna in 1975 was no accident of fate: German-language culture has always been privileged in her life and work, including Viennese classical music (especially Johann Strauss and Mozart), Austrian and German poets (among them Trakl, Rilke, Novalis, Hölderlin, and Celan) whom she translated into Russian, and contemporary poets and composers such as Hans Artmann, Gerhard Rühm, and Wolfgang Musil). In the first years of her residence in Austria, she published poetry books in German, translated her own poems into German and exhibited her artistically designed books in two languages in art galleries.

In a book written in Russian but with the German title *Beim Tode zugast*, Mnatsakanova applies translingual techniques such as quotations from European poets. A poem from the book quotes the German poet Johannes Bobrowski's 'Im Strom', which combines love lyric and biblical allusions. The phrase 'Als ich dich liebte' echoes Russian phonetics and semantics, involving the mechanism of interlingual paronymy: 'liebte' – 'либо', 'любо', 'люби'; 'dich' – 'тех' (Figure 19).

As is often the case in Mnatsakanova's verse, the poem is built like a song set to a particular tune or motif. In this case, the motif of love is performed using the elementary building blocks of two languages – deictic shifters, conjunctions, and interjections. In another poem from this cycle, the Latin word 'incognito' is embedded (in a slightly modified version, as 'inkognito') into the motif of Nikolai Gogol's 'beautiful, unknown distance' ('прекрасное далёко'), breaking down into forms that do not exist in Russian ('инко', 'тоин', 'токог'), then into semantically significant word forms 'когда', 'гнить', referencing the key theme of death for the poetic cycle (Figure 20). Processes of this kind persist in the poet's later work, with a growing tendency towards interlingual polyphony and musicalisation of the verse.

---

2   For her books she often used trilingual heteronyms, a sign of her translingual identity: the Russian *Mnatsakanova*, the German *Netzkowa* and the Armenian *Mnatsakanjan*.

```
    als ich dich liebte
ах либо ты либо я
            либо    liebte
        много
не долюбили   liebte
    liebte        либо
любят не так
ли не      там ли
  liebte
бо
  dich liebte
            dich
        не тех
            dich        dich
                dich
    люби      liebte
    мых    dich
```

FIGURE 19   Elizaveta Mnatsakanova. From *Beim Tode zugast*[3]

 The title of another book, *Das Buch Sabeth*, contains the bilingual lexeme *Sabeth*, which in Russian reads as 'testament' ('*завет*'), and in German – as an abbreviation of *Elisabeth*, the name of the poet. It is possible that the name could also refer to a rather famous 1951 radio play by the German playwright

---

3 Mnatsakanova, 1982: 36.

```
в прекрасном таком
в прекрасном моем
    inkognito
inkognitus
    inko ignotus
инко
ньи
тоин
ко
ньи
токог
ни
токог
        да бы подольше подальше бы да
            свами отвас вмоем
                прекрасном
                    таком
                    далеком
                    inkognito
дад да когда да да ког
        дада
        лекода
        леком бы таком И
            нко
        гни
            то Ин
        ко
        гнит
        о
о мне бы гнить подольше бы
свамисвами отвас от вас
        гноил и
в прекрасном далеком
                    от вас

        INKOGNITUS
```

FIGURE 20   Elizaveta Mnatsakanova. From *Beim Tode zugast*[4]

Günter Eich, in which a Raven called Sabeth discusses existential topics with a girl called Elisabeth, and their dialogue often unfolds between speech and silence. Silence is also a structuring principle in this poem by Mnatsakanova, the first in her work in which musical structures, motifs and intertexts play a

---

4 Idem: 56.

POETRY BEYOND LANGUAGE BARRIERS 237

leading role. Parts of the poem are constructed as parts of a symphony or a Catholic chorale, which is also reflected in their names. Thus, the first section bears the Latin title 'laudes', the name of a morning Catholic liturgy. In the titles of individual verses, names of psalms appear in Latin or German. Here are some of these trilingual names:
- *Laude*
- *laudemus te*
- *laudatio solemnis*
- *Stella Martis*
- *choral mit dem cantus firmus*
- *choral mit dem tenore ostinato*
- *Martialia*
- *motet (трехголосный)*
- *perpetuum mobile (choral mit dem cantus firmus)*
- *'Утоли моя печали' (lamenti)*
- *Песнь песней (Das Hohelied)*
- *Dies Irae*

Excerpts from church psalms are often used as epigraphs to parts of the poem. The epigraph to the third part is given in Russian and German, and

"УТОЛИ МОЯ ПЕЧАЛИ"

LAMENTI*

Кто плач мой
и воздыхание мое
примет аще не Ты?

Wer
sonst
als
Du?

Wem
Wem sonst   sonst
als   als
Dir?   Dir?**

FIGURE 21   Elizaveta Mnatsakanova. From *Das Buch Sabeth*[5]

---

5   Mnatsakanova, 1994: 52.

the German text is a quotation from Friedrich Hölderlin's 'Hyperion', which becomes part of the visual verse (Figure 21). The epigraph to the fourth movement is composed of fragments of the requiem 'Dies irae', from which Mnatsakanova departs, replacing the Latin 'MORS' with 'MARS', bringing together two key paronymic motifs of the poem – death and March (the calendar month) (Figure 22).

*DIES IRAE**

Dies irae, dies illa,
Solvet saeclum in favilla:
Teste David cum Sibulla.

...   ...

...   ...

MORS stupebit, et natura

...

...

Lacrimosa, dies illa ...

...

MORS stupebit

...

(Dies illa, dies illa...)
MORS stupebit...

...

MARS stupe ...

...

MARS mars
... ****

FIGURE 22   Elizaveta Mnatsakanova. From *Das Buch Sabeth*[6]

---

6   Idem: 55.

POETRY BEYOND LANGUAGE BARRIERS 239

In the first verse of *Das Buch Sabeth*, we see the Latin forms of the Catholic chorale reverberate in the Russian text. Interlingual paronymy is spread throughout the text in verbal consonances ('laudate' – 'когда-то'; 'вмарте' – 'aparte'; 'crimosa' – 'грозы') and in phono-semantic complexes ('lau' – 'лау' – 'оул'; 'март' – 'mart' – 'мерт'). Some word forms begin to echo in other languages as well ('part' – 'apart' – 'aparte' – 'à part'), further increasing the translingual tension in the text (Figure 23). The translingual decomposition of words occurs with even greater force than in her previous book, as new word formations appear out of the re-composed fragments of words: ли, не бо, бо ли, бы ли, ли бо (Figure 24).

```
                    part
                  apart
             à         part
                  aparte
            о когда-то
о когда-то                      о когда-то
    повстречались лаудамус   лаудате
         лаудате       лаудате
                   над
                   про
          улком
     гулко           узком
         узком          узким
                   la
         udate        crimosa
                   грозы
      марта    lau   в марте
              date
```

FIGURE 23   Elizaveta Mnatsakanova. From *Das Buch Sabeth*[7]

Unfolding into sound series resembling atonal music, languages sound with new meanings in Mnatsakanova's 'verbal music',[8] as syllables recombine from bilingual lexemes ('visciна': from 'oblivisci' + 'тайна'; 'тайno': from 'тайна' + 'noli') (Figure 25). The bilingual pair 'тот' – 'tot' actualises the mortality of the

---

7   Mnatsakanova, 1982: 82.
8   Sergey Biryukov's (2005) term (*словомузыка*).

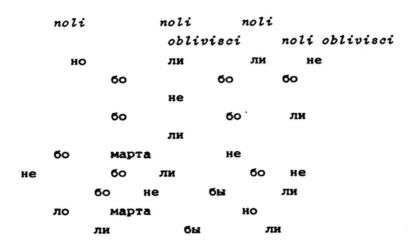

FIGURE 24   Elizaveta Mnatsakanova. From *Das Buch Sabeth*[9]

```
плетение    noli        явление       noli
тайных нитей   obli     тайное        oblivisci
жизни          visci    подспудной но   li
    жизни   noli  о цезарь      li
    тайное  obli  тайнотай      obli
    веление visciна тайно     visci
```

FIGURE 25   Elizaveta Mnatsakanova. From *Das Buch Sabeth*[10]

deictic subject (Figure 26), accompanied by the theme of death in the next fragment: 'Тот день, день гнева, ... / В золе развеет земное, / Свидетелями Давид и Сивилла / ... / Смерть и рождение оцепенеет / ... / Плачевен тот день... / ... / Смерть оцепенеет / ... / (Тот день, тот день...) / Оцепенеет смерть... / Марс оцепенеет... / ... / Марс Марс / ...' (Mnatsakanova, 1994: 110). The author's musical thinking allows the reader to listen to the poetic text across the phonetics of different languages and perceive rhythmic patterns in the minimal units of words.

---

9   Idem: 84.
10 Mnatsakanova, 1982: 84.

```
не
      о
битаем                    тот
                          март
                          to t
                          март
         в том            необитаемом
         на том           необитаемом
         того             необитаемом
         тому             необитаемом
         to t             необитаемый
         год
                          март
```

FIGURE 26   Elizaveta Mnatsakanova. From *Das Buch Sabeth*[11]

Translingualism as a poetic technique plays an important role in Mnatsakanova's magnum opus – 'Requiem: Autumn in a lazzaretto of innocent sisters'. Its first part bears the Latin title 'SEPTUAGESIMA', the name for the ninth Sunday before Easter, a day of rejoicing in Christian symbolism, thereby marking the theme of sevenfoldness, which appears in the poem in several languages. The opening lines in Latin and English introduce September, the seventh Roman month, and Septimus, the name of a male nurse in the hospital (Mnatsakanova, 2003: http):

В Лазарете Сестер Неповинных—сентябрь погибели
September. Septimus. Седьмой   гнойной
Круг на Небе Седьмом
Небо меркнет в глазах, Брат Septimus,   Брат Septimus[12]

---

11   Idem: 89.
12   Mnatsakanova, 2003: http.

Interlingual switches also accompany the motif of light in the last parts of the poem. The Latin phrase from the Catholic prayer 'Requiem Aeternam' ('Lux perpetua luceat eis') is embedded into the bilingual stream of repetitive phrases, echoing in the phonetics of two languages at once: 'веселые лейтесь лейся плоть лейся лейтесь luceat лейтесь eis лейся / лейтесь luceat лейся eis лейтесь luceat лейся плоть eis лейся' (Ibidem). The motif of eternal light from the prayer is repeated with the inclusion of the German neologism 'ewiglicht' (ewig (lich) + Licht) (Ibidem):

> святые eis святые ewig светом ewiges вечным eis
> лейтесь eis ewiges eis
> лейтесь lux luceat eis
> святитесь ewiges eis
> струитесь lux perpetua
>
> ...
>
> СМЕРТОВОЙ СВЕТОВОЙ СВЕТОВОЙ СВЕТОВОЙ LUX LICHT LUCEAT EIS
> DONA EIS EIS ewiglich eis ай, вернись, воротись, обратись, eis вернись
> Ewig LUX ewiglich ewig LICHT LUCEAT EIS LUCEAT EIS ewig LICHT EWIGLICHT EWIGLICH LUX PERPETUA ewiglich eis LUCEAT EIS LUCEAT EIS luceat eis ei

In the final passage of this long poem, the entire text resembles an anagram permeated with phono-semantic series or motifs:

> я верю! CREDO! credo PE
>   кою волною грозой я шагом я мигом я мимо resurgam волною PE
>   кою волною я верю! CREDO! приду CREDO! гряну credo PE
>   квием, реквием, упокой! requiem aeternam resurgam requiem PE
>   сургам рекою волною водою весною resurgam resurgam PE
>   чною травою resurgam рекою волною RESURGAM волною
>   я шагом я рядом resurgam я бродом я бредом
>   я с небом я светом resurgam я смертью я с веком
>   я вестью невестой из гроба resurgam восстану
>   я рядом я громом RESURGAM resurgam
>   я небом resurgam! восстану я гряну

Mnatsakanova's 'Requiem' is, therefore, a translingual poetic and musical oratorio, in which a biographical scene from a Soviet hospital is recast as a church chant based on the motifs of a Latin requiem. The multilingualism of chanted or recited phrases brings together the 'spaces of times' (a metaphor used elsewhere by Mnatsakanova herself) in a single sounding event of the text-score.

In Mnatsakanova's cycle *Metamorphosen,* the juxtaposition of the Russian and German texts and the interspersing of German phrases into the Russian text create counter-punctuation of the verse and polyphonisation in two languages. The cycle includes, among other songs, Martin Luther's hymns known from Bach's chorales. The book-length poem *Metamorphosen* is based on a sound motif from a children's song and unfolds as a musical composition modeled on Bach's suites. Verses often resemble meditations on a phrase or quotation from someone's poetic or musical work. Intertextual links with arias, romances, lyric poems, liturgies, and prayers permeate the poems. But the intertext is sonically re-orchestrated here. In *Das Buch Sabeth*, discussed earlier, the counterpoint appears more complicated: along with Slavic wedding and funeral songs in Russian, the author inscribes German prayers across the text (Mnatsakanova, 2018: 179). In the poem 'funeral kolo dance' ('надгробное коло'), three-syllable Russian verbs form a counterpoint with three-syllable German negative adjectives (Idem: 182) in a stereophonic playback of the song-text.

The last published work by Mnatsakanova, the poem 'Jelmoli', was finished in 2006. Just like 'Requiem', it is a seven-part composition. The title word 'Jelmoli' is cryptic: it sets the melody for entire sonorous fabric of the text, yet the actual identity of Jelmoli – and her variants Emilia, Elmilia, etc., mentioned in the text – remains unresolved. The poem begins with a meditation on the sound theme of this name, which takes on a variety of forms in Latin and Cyrillic script (Idem: 303, Figure 27).

The opening motif of the poem borrows from Dante's *Divine Comedy*. Part one, called 'Preghiera' in Italian, refers to the last part of the *Commedia* – the prayer to the Virgin Mary. The theme of prayer itself becomes central here, along with the theme of silence. The text incorporates quotations from Dante's opus, individual words which pass through the lines as motifs. Thus, 'dolente' resonates with 'долины', and the Russian 'домины' and 'домовины' with the Latin 'domini'. Latin phrases are translingually anagrammed: 'IN DOMINIO DOMINI / в немых домовинах'. In the last parts of the text, phrases from both the *Commedia* and from church hymns interfere with each other in four languages at once (Russian, Latin, Italian, and German). Multilingualism

ЧАСТЬ ПЕРВАЯ
PART 1

PREGHIERA
ЕЛЬМОЛИ! ЕЛЬМОЛИ! Открой книгу боли

МОЛИТВА
ЕЛЬМОЛИ, ельмоли,скажи, оттого ли JELMOLI ельмоли о молви того ли ЭЛЬМОЛИ того оттого ли
ЕЛЬМОЛИ *о молви* ELMOLI *о молви* ОТКРОЙ МНЕ
О, МОЛВИ, JELMOLI,ELMOLI,ELMILI,О, МОЛВИ,о молви ОТКРОЙ мне открой мне О МОЛВИ ЭЛЬМОЛИ

Скажи, *оттого ли* ЕЛЬМОЛИ ЭЛЬМОЛИ *открой мне* ЭЛЬМИЛЛИ *скажи мне*
того ли *тебя ли* ОТКУДА НА СЕРДЦЕ О МОЛВИ ЕЛЬМОЛИ *о молви*
давно ли *до боли* ELMOLI ELMILIE *такая остуда* EMILLI EMOLLIA
ELMOLIA ДО БОЛИ БЕЗМОЛВНО *до боли* JELMOLI *до боли откуда на сердце остуда*
О *молви Эльмолиа Откуда* БЕЗМОЛВИЕ *на сердце* *до боли* БЕЗМОЛВНО *безмолвно*
на сердце ЭЛЬМОЛИА ELMILIA JELMOLNO JELMOLIA ЭЛЬМИЛИА
того ли ЕЛЬМОЛИ *до боли* JELMOLI, ЕЛЬМОЛИ *открой мне*
ельмоли, кого ли безмолвно **EMILLI EMILIE** *откуда на сердце*
ЕЛЬМОЛИ *ответь мне* ЕЛЬМОЛИ *ответь, о* ELMOLI, *ответь,о* ELMILLI,*ответь, о* ЭЛЬМОЛИА,*откуда*

FIGURE 27   Elizaveta Mnatsakanova. From 'Jelmoli'

goes hand in hand with the polyphony of the musically structured poetic text (Idem: 324, 330, Figures 28 and 29).

The switch between languages naturally complements the polyphonic structure of verbal and musical unity in the graphic space of the page. Interlingual shifts are designed to provide access to other semiotic dimensions of the verse, both visual and audial at once. Most often, it is musical themes, leimotifs, and reminiscences that motivate the switch between idioms across the barriers between languages. Mnatsakanova's texts are constantly transmuting (to use Roman Jakobson's linguistic term) into consistently different sonic and graphic forms, into different versions of the same text, into tautological constructions of minimalist music.[13]

---

[13] Stephanie Sandler suggests the 'language sculpting' metaphor: 'Mnatsakanova's poetry creates a sound environment in which the listener is caught in a seemingly endless present: sounds repeat and recombine, and words shift as speech acts from imprecations to affirmation, from plea to prediction. In that appeal to the imagination, Mnatsakanova asks readers to join her in an experience of the senses and of the mind's capacity to bend language as if it were clay to be sculpted' (2008: 619). In her aural orientation, Sandler notes, Mnatsakanova suggests a certain affinity with the American Language poet Susan Howe. We could also extend this comparison to Gertrude Stein, especially due to the role played by incantation and repetitiveness in her texts; and to Louis Zukofsky with the professed musicality of his long poem 'A', cf. his often-quoted passage: 'I'll tell you. / About my poetics— / music / speech / An integral / Lower limit speech / Upper limit music'.

DE PROFUNDIS

De profundis clamavi ad te   Из глубины глубокой   Aus der Tiefe rufe ich
Exaudi vocem meam   зову и услышится   Meine Stimme sei für ewig
Sostinuit anima mea in   голос и светом вечным   erhöret und das Wort sei
verbo meus   светится слово   ewig Fleisch und lebe mit euch
Fleisch und lebe ewig   вечно   ewig

ET LUX PERPETUA LUCEAT EIS AMEN

L'AMOR
   ЛЮБОВЬ
      che move L' AMOR
         что видит и ведет   ЛЮБОВЬ

che move il sole
    и бег планет
и солнца путь   o grandiose stelle   и луч звезды   и луч
                                            звезды
   O LUCE ETERNA CHE SOLA IN TE SIDI,
о, вечный изначальный свет пресветлый,
o trina luce che in unica stella
oh abbondante grazia ond'io presunsi

FIGURES 28 and 29   Elizaveta Mnatsakanova. From 'Jelmoli'

Foreignisms amplify Mnatsakanova's translingualism and serve to estrange the idioethnic phenomenon of language. Mnatsakanova refers to Aristotle's theory of poetic speech as 'foreign' speech in one of her essays: 'the poet's speech in the sphere of his native language is like a foreign language, it appears a foreigner's speech to a compatriot. That is, in other words, his speech is estranged, absurdised' (1983: 103). It is no accident that this idea is cited in connection with the poetry of Velimir Khlebnikov, whose linguistic experiments are also inseparable from the musicality of his verse. Although Mnatsakanova's translingualism is of a different kind than Khlebnikov's uni-lingualism, both poets apply the Aristotelian law of poetic speech in their approach to foreignism. In the same essay on Khlebnikov, Mnatsakanova ponders: 'To what extent is the language of the poet Khlebnikov, or of any Russian poet, foreign in the sphere of his native language? What is this FOREIGNISM about? To what extent is FOREIGNISM actually FOREIGN? Isn't it, in fact, just a special manifestation of all the hidden potentials of a given language? Isn't it really a true manifestation of all the latent forces and capabilities of a given language? Haven't the ancient primordial forces of the motherland's language somehow awakened in the artist's mind?' (Ibidem).[14]

From 1975 on, Elizaveta Mnatsakanova was writing within a foreign linguistic and cultural environment, thereby making Russian a kind of foreign language for herself. It is characteristic that one of her earliest poems, 'Dedication' (1966), prophesies an exit from the Russian environment so that she can become more than just a 'Russian poet'. This exit from one culture and entry into another makes her a translingual and transmedial poet, in whose work languages sound like musical voices in a polyphonic composition.

2   Contemporary Russo-Anglophone 'Trans-Language' Writing

Emigration as a social and aesthetic prerequisite for poetic translingualism defines the poetics of Eugene (Evgeny) Ostashevsky, an English-speaking author with Russian roots. At the age of 11, he moved from Leningrad to New York, and by the time his first poems were published in the early 2000s, he had already become a fully integrated English-speaking American author. Nevertheless, the Russian stratum of his biography surfaces in his own texts and translations. Ostashevsky has published English translations of many important Russian linguo-experimental poets, such as Daniil Kharms, Alexander Vvedensky, Arkadii Dragomoshchenko, Alexei Parshchikov, Dmitry Golynko, and Alexander Skidan.

In Ostashevsky's own work, the Russian element manifests itself not only in references and allusions to Russian history and literature, but also in purely linguistic permutations of Russian vocabulary. The names of Russian poets are transmuted into English names, like Boris Pasternak, who is encoded in the title of the book *Enter Morris Imposternak, Pursued by Ironies* (2008). The process of translating Vvedensky's poetry into English creates an oscillating interlingual vibration, which reverberates in the translator's own writings. Thus, the poem 'Senselessness for Vvedensky' from his first book *Iterature* evokes the ambiguity of the national borders of the author's poetic language: either English, or Russian, or their odd mutual permutation (2005 :19): 'You've lost your ear, you can't distinguish / plosive from surd, Russian from English, / you comprehend nothing. Accept this verse then /from a Eugene trying to be a horseman'.

Ostashevsky identifies as a translingual poet. In his interviews and talks on translingual poetics, he speaks of a kind of writing where the different national

---

14   Idem: 126. See Reed (2005) for a discussion of Khlebnikov's influence on Mnatsakanova.

languages are not repulsed by each other, as in foreignisms or heteroglossia, but become parts of a hybrid multilingual entity. Inter-language transitions allow languages to find resonance in each other, permeate each other at different levels, as in the case of linguistic transfer in bilingualism. Ostashevsky invokes the metaphor of a DJ mix (*The Life and Opinions of DJ Spinoza* is the title of a 2008 poetry collection), in which different music tracks are synchronised, merged, and played back in each other.

Wittgenstein's linguistic philosophy is at play in Ostashevsky's work, as he himself acknowledges: 'As far as whether bilingualism (or, in my case, multilingualism) encourages language games, my answer is an unqualified yes. Language games make you look at language from the outside. They are a kind of meta-poetry in the way that certain logical paradoxes are a kind of meta-mathematics'. Language as such becomes a challenge for his poetic task, as an epigraph to the book about DJ Spinoza signals: 'Language is the first compromise we make'. The plurality of languages and idioms is ironically enacted in this polyphonic and polyrhythmic mix of heteroglossic fragments. The birth of speech ('mother tongue', 'Muttersprache') from the muttering glossolalia ('mutter') as a poly-language is translingually interpreted: 'She says: / t / / k / / p / /mutter babble / Her first words / are not in her Muttersprache / She walks / cries mutter / mutter mutter /Die Mutter kann nicht hören'. Brodsky rhymes with Trotsky to the tune of the paronymic similarity of the Italian 'zoccolo' ('hoof') and the Russian 'цокать' ('clatter'): 'DJ SPINOZA: It's me that stalks by the zoccolo / цокая вокруг да около / Come down softly and open your door / cause I got more rhymes than Joseph Brodsky / I got more rhymes than Leon Trotsky / Brodsky / Trotsky / Brodsky / Trotsky / La-là'.

Multilingual sound samples recall either Andrey Bely's 'language of languages', or Mallarmé's 'language within language': 'the sounds words make / as they plead for life // that's all that remains / of the language of language ...' 'Птичий язык' ('bird language') comes to the fore in another book by Ostashevsky, *The Pirate Who Does Not Know the Value of Pi* (2017), both in its Russian idiomatic sense of a secret language and coded speech, and literally – in the speech of the main character, a parrot who cannot understand in what language he is producing sounds and meanings. His interlocutor, the 'paronymic attractor' and 'linguistic alter-ego' Pirate, asks questions in the manner of Wittgenstein's language games about what kind of language the two are using to communicate (unless it is one character in two guises?). Does Parrot speak parrot? Is that his native language? Then, is it possible to speak a non-native pirate language, and vice versa? Or, perhaps, they both speak a 'private language', the possibility of which was questioned by the same Wittgenstein? A passage of the poem titled 'Discussion between P and P about native language cognitive processing' makes a direct reference to Wittgenstein. These questions represent the linguistic situation of Ostashevsky's own linguocritical writing: he writes in a transnational, transgressive dialect, which is generated by incessant linguistic switchings and shifts that evade any static identities.

Ostashevsky's Russian is an estranged kind of 'foreign Russian', as this fragment from the 'Parrot's song' lays bare: 'Попугай попугай попугай попугай / Давай попугай как следует / Извергов низвергай визг извергай / Писк испускай попугай повторяй / Припев / Попирать помаленьку / Напирать на попугая'. His poetry incorporates a lot of Russian songs, which echo in-between the English lines as a kind of cultural and linguistic background. The effect of these Russian-language inserts sometimes creates a punning Joycean burlesque: 'O half-power sickle! O cowardly dreadnought! O Battleship / Potemkin Village! Row, row, column, column, сегодня /«τὸ πᾶν», завтра не поймал!'.

In recent poems, Ostashevsky interprets this translingual situation more as a tragedy than as parody. For example, in the cycle 'Die Schreibblockade' from his book *The Feeling Sonnets* (2022), dedicated to the Siege of Leningrad, which acquires the names Letterburg and Forgettisburg in one of the poems, based on trans-linguistic punning and 'tongue-slipping':

> You have been renamed Letterburg. Lately and literally.
> For you are a littoral city and the river rhymes around your purse.
> Those who part from you place their birthplace on the tip of the tongue,
> and call it their Forgettisburg address.
> The deserts of your squares are speechless, the arch of your General Staff is arch.
> Letter-forgetter, letters are for climbing, die Buchstaben sind zum klettern.

The shifts between Russian, English, and German (Ostashevsky lives in Berlin, which adds a clear German layer to his translingual verse) continuously mirror each other here, as in the line: 'Your prospects are ladders of beech, buchene Leitern, for literature is a beech, it is wood or wode. / This wood you call бук, read book, but in the mountains чинарь, makar, and the letter, буква'. 'Бук' in Russian means 'beech' (the tree), and it is from timber that paper is made for books which contain letters ('буквы'). 'Чинарь' evidently refers to the OBERIU writers (some of whom survived the Siege of Leningrad, like Yakov Druskin, Nikolai Zabolotsky, and Igor Bakhterev) whose other group name was Chinari, stemming from an archaic Russian word meaning 'maker'. But the 'makar' following the word 'чинарь' in this excerpt not only reads as the English 'maker' but also as a Russian 'макар', which has the idiomatic meaning 'a way to do something' and at the same time refers to the Russian personal name 'Макар', in turn borrowed from the Ancient Greek 'makarios' meaning 'blessed, happy'.

The texts in this cycle represent the historical experience of an author who was born in a city that survived a tragic siege decades ago and still lives with the memory of the siege and the 'word of the siege'.[15] But the Siege also becomes a metaphor for writing itself, the stops, or blockades, one encounters while switching between languages, the gaps that get filled by alternating idioms. Thus, the Russian 'сугроб' is re-etymologised as a 'duplicate for coffin' ('Snowdrift is sugròb. A sugrob is no drift. It is an understudy for a coffin'), in order to evoke the experience of the 1942 winter of the Siege, when snowdrifts literally transformed into coffins.

Adrian Wanner (2021: 208) calls Ostashevsky's (as well as Philip Nikolaev's and Genya Turovskaya's poetics) 'an experimental style resembling the 'Language' trends in contemporary American poetics'. The poet himself does not deny his indebtedness to the Language poets. However, Russian avant-garde language-oriented poetry, from Vvedensky to Dragomoshchenko, is just as important a tradition for him. In Ostashevsky's poetic work, these two trajectories of linguistic experimentation from the last century coincide most closely and produce a new kind of Anglo-Russian translingual poetry. We might even go as far as to call this *trans-language writing*, where *trans-language*[16] means a synthetic, hybridised, or creolised idiom, and at the same time a language constantly undergoing inner self-translation, transcoding, and linguistic transfer.

Translingual strategies can also be found in the poetry of another Russian émigré writer, Nika Skandiaka, whose texts were discussed in a previous chapter. According to some sources, she has lived in Britain and, according to others, in the USA, for the past several decades. In addition to her own writing, she is a translator of Russian literature into English and English literature into Russian. Skandiaka's poetry is extremely experimental and anomalous; in it, the conventional laws of grammatical and lexical coherence all collapse. One could call her texts a poetics of *glitch*, by analogy with the style of electronic music and digital art. Verbal effects driven by errors and faults in rule-based language use predominate in this type of writing, but these failures and disruptions

---

15 On this, see the book by Irina Sandomirskaya mentioned earlier, The *Siege in the Word*, as well as the collection of Leningrad Siege poetry *The Seventh Alkaline*, compiled by the poet Polina Barskova (2020), to whom, incidentally, this cycle by Ostashevsky is dedicated. Barskova belongs to the same generation of Leningrad-born writers who emigrated to the United States in the 90s and are living in a bilingual and bicultural milieu.

16 Cf. the term *translanguaging* introduced in the 1980s in the context of first-second language acquisition theory and used extensively in pedagogy and educational research. See, for a basic account, García et al. (2014).

trigger a specific system of meaning production, as a result of which a poetic text often looks at first glance like a computer-generated verbal mess, yet close reading can reveal the poet's intentions.

Reading Skandiaka's texts, which are usually published on one of her several blogs and more often than not look like posts on a social network, one gets the impression that the author is resorting to machine translation tools and similar resources. That is, a text that seems to be written in Russian produces the effect of having been translated, or recoded, from other languages. Often, traces of this technique remain in the text: '(про мультитран) / ?спасибо за смещённый гул / за involute heart (скрученное сердце?; laudable (clappable),/ collapstible outskirts of apples (похвальная (для похлопывания),/ складная округа яблока)'. In some passages, the text itself becomes an account of the translation, both of some other text and of itself – that is, a translation of a translation, or a meta-translation – as in this verse referencing the American poet Alice Notley:

я не могу одновременно переводить стих и процесс перевода
по что со стула встает i greshit человек с турреттом иным способом чем чел без [^eto k fragmentu iz notley]
(Alice Notley, «Close to Me & Closer ...» из Grave of Light (Wesleyan: 1992), стр. 218:
Меня ... интересует, что от меня ... здесь. Тогда я смогла бы сказать тебе ... что должно
волновать там, где _ты_. Потому что – это нетрудно – они _одно_.[17]

Sometimes a text reads like a scrap from a notebook reflecting on the writing process itself, and in two languages at once:

Парщиков:
Именно эта коммуникативная реальность акцентирует мгновенную и непосредственную природу «месседжа»—все происходит у нас на глазах, в перспективе реального времени (real time) (с. 7).
yer stuff. not sure if these are the best versions ever [твои. не уверен что это лучшие из возможных версий][18]

A characteristic feature of Skandiaka's writing is transliteration in a different script, which is used to foreignise and defamiliarise the original

---

17   https://polutona.ru/premia/2007.php?show=rets46_scandiacka (last accessed 27.02.23).
18   http://www.litkarta.ru/rus/dossier/vozvr-aury/dossier_6135/ (last accessed 27.02.23).

POETRY BEYOND LANGUAGE BARRIERS

language of writing. Latin script can be transliterated into Cyrillic, and vice versa:

> цомпетитион ин гивинг уп смокинг
> акцент первого тона сердца
> жестокостойкий
> сердце зашлось / сельдяной король
> цомпетитион ин гивинг уп смокинг
> lakes known to harbor
> пёстрая лента—память?
> unknown creatures
> аттракционы, поддержка
> Only when the panther dies is it substituted completely by the 'pronoun'
> (Everett)
> more / examples of this lack (Everett)
> functioning (e.g., developing a language) under constraint
> торжественный / набор / во двор
> двуполое, двуногое без пола[19]

> [...]

> IV. 'чем меня жизнь [проявляла]»
> [ты не против, если я наш эпистолярный воспитательный detektiv
> приаттачу как часть dlja
> prokrutki?]
> Wednesday, July 21, 1999 5:37 PM
> View E-mail Message Source
> Content-Type: text/plain; format=flowed
> ja tozhe gorzhus' vashim jandlem[20]

Experimentation with different symbolic systems makes this kind of writing translingual as much as transmedial, where the text is generated, and perceived, both as a linguistic message and a programme code. The code becomes the message, and the assembly of encodings contributes to the text's translingualism based on transcoding.[21]

---

19 http://www.litkarta.ru/projects/vozdukh/issues/2006-1/skandiaka/ (last accessed 27.02.23).
20 https://polutona.ru/premia/2007.php?show=rets46_scandiacka (last accessed 27.02.23).
21 Transcoding is a notion introduced by Lev Manovich (2001) with respect to contemporary media practices involving the overlapping of codes in information transmission.

A poet of the 2010s generation who also lives in Berlin, Inna Krasnoper, is working in the wake of these translingual experiments in the poetry of the Russian diaspora. However, as opposed to Ostashevsky and Skandiaka, she uses multilingualism to explore the motor-rhythmic properties of interlingual paronymy. As a professional dancer and performer, she is interested in movement, the alternation of words at the junction of languages – Russian, German and English. These experiments, on the one hand, are in the tradition of American poetic minimalism and phonic poetry, going back to Gertrude Stein and Jackson Mac Low. On the other hand, they take up Elizaveta Mnatsakanova's translingual poetics of verbal music, as in this piece playing with Russian-English sound resonances: 'Из зума запахло другим человеком / Из иди из зума – иди по дороге // ...Chill a little – out of zoom. And then, chill a little bit more // Out of nowhere – a zoom showed up // Show me some zoom and then zoom-in (slightly) // Шел по шоу, пошел за шоу / Зашел за шоу – show me some more // Шоу some more time out of zoom – истина покажется / Истину возьми, a little bit заверни'.[22] Translanguaging is not only performed but also commented on: 'why does 'rite' sound like луч to me / i wouldn't know / let's let it be луч / a rite could be луч /and could be no лучше than no луч'. Creating this kind of poetry is a playful and plastic way of learning languages through the process of writing, as well of learning how to translate and self-translate across languages: 'took by surprise – взять за сюрприз / шариться – scuttle through / проходить между – pac-shuffle-иться / раскланяться – take a bow / ударить в грязь лицом – been there done that / всё-таки стену – gegen die wand / побегать тут и там – chop-chop /чебурек и чебурашка – been there done that'. The result of these verbal operations is a moveable language that can slip through the tiniest cracks of interlingual sounds.

Another vector of fusing Russian and American poetry of language is outlined in the work of contemporary poet Ivan Sokolov, who lives between Saint-Petersburg and San Francisco and translates Russian and American poetry. His own poetic work draws, on the one hand, upon Mnatsakanova's experiments with the space of verse on the page, and on the other, on American Language poetry with its reflexivity of poetic writing and its focus on the materiality of linguistic signs. Being essentially bilingual, Sokolov writes

---

Nika Skandiaka's poetic transcoding techniques resonate with some American modes of Language writing, such as those used by Leslie Scalapino.

22   Inna Krasnoper's texts discussed here have only been published on social media. They are used here with permission by the author.

texts in two languages at once. For example, his work 'Anne Hathaway // Энн Хэтэуэй' (2011)[23] consists of alternating parts in Russian and English and, in addition, contains translations of other texts from English into Russian, as well as what he calls 'self-translations from Russian into Russian'.

One of Sokolov's recent poems, titled 'And night took night and illumined the night' (2021), is written both in Russian and in English. In these twin versions we can observe translingual shifts that involve lexical units from multiple languages, including German and French (Figure 30):

Keeping silent in different tongues becomes an alternative to speaking in tongues. The full poetic potential of these multilingual silences and utterances is yet to be unleashed and elucidated. Trans-language writing has proved to be one of the fascinating crossovers between Russian and American innovative literature, between the two languages, and between their powerful traditions of avant-garde verbal creativity.

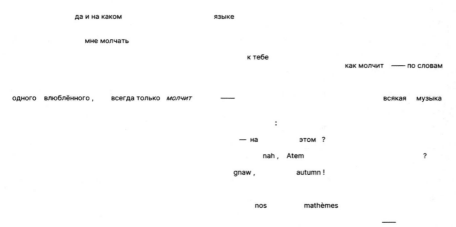

FIGURE 30   Fragment from Ivan Sokolov's poem 'And night took night and illumined the night'[24]

---

23   https://polutona.ru/?show=0410210050 (last accessed 27.02.23).
24   Published on-line in *Flagi* journal: https://flagi.media/piece/521 (last accessed 27.02.23).

Outro. Lab(-)oratory of the Logos

In the fourteen chapters of *Russian and American Poetry of Experiment: The Linguistic Avant-Garde*, as well as the introduction and two transitional essays, I have tried to bring together examples of Russian and American language-oriented experimental literature within a common framework of a *historical linguo-poetics*. This framework, guided by Roman Jakobson's efforts to bridge linguistics and poetics, allows us to analyse not only the structure of a poetic text, but also the particularities of poetic grammar, semantics, and pragmatics. In experimental poetry, we saw these linguistic dimensions radically transform and deviate from the conventional use of language in classical literature. My approach to the linguistic poetics of literary texts suggests a way to account for the *metalinguistic* coordinates of poetic creativity, that is, the intrinsic philosophies and ideologies of language contained in linguistically eccentric literary practices and theories. This has allowed me to reconstruct the historical context of language conceptualisation, common to literary evolution, developments in linguistics, and philosophical inquiry into the nature of verbal creativity.

The *turn to language*, which took place at the beginning of the 20th century, manifested itself in the emergence of theoretical linguistics as a science and in applying philosophical research to the analysis of ordinary language. Artistic processes in the early twentieth century were also characteristically focused on language issues and language experimentation. This study has pinpointed specific language techniques used in Russian and American experimental writing throughout the twentieth century, as well as corresponding methods used in linguistic research and theory of the last century.

The avant-garde literary discourses analysed in this monograph acutely problematise the status of language. As Umberto Eco testifies, 'whereas classical art violated the conventional order of language within well-defined limits, contemporary art constantly challenges the initial order by means of an extremely "improbable" form of organisation. In other words, whereas classical art introduced original elements within a linguistic system whose basic laws it substantially respected, contemporary art often manifests its originality by imposing a new linguistic system with its own inner laws' (1989: 60). The constitutive property of the experimental poetry discussed in my book is its *language experiment*, which is understood as linguistic activity aimed at the artistic development of its own aesthetic and cognitive capabilities. A language experiment is a systemic phenomenon based on a qualitative change in the original language material and the linguistic proportions of its structure, with the aim of transforming both.

This is a comparative study of two national avant-garde cultures, but also a juxtaposition of the relationships that Russian and American avant-garde poetics had with linguistic ideas of their times. I have focused on those American and Russian theories and practices of language experimentation that, though they were not in direct contact in the first half of the 20th century, may be viewed as analogous strategies of language poeticisation, in some ways radically different from their transatlantic counterparts, but in others revealing an internal typological affinity without any traces of historical kinship. In the second half of the century, transfers between the two literary traditions grew more active and more direct. We have seen this exchange, starting in the 1970s, in the case of American Language poetry, whose turn to language was the latest in a series of linguistic turns over the twentieth century initiated by Saussure, Wittgenstein and the Russian Formalists. It is in the wake of this linguistic turn that Language poetry developed in the US and was later interpreted by contemporary Russian language-oriented poetics.

The poetry of quest, revolt, and experiment that evolved in the USA beginning in the late 19th century, and in Russia in the early 20th, has engaged, for more than a century, in testing the limits and nature of language – language as such, human language, national language, and poetic language. Spanning from Walt Whitman to Charles Bernstein in American letters, and from Andrey Bely to Arkadii Dragomoshchenko in Russian literature, the idea of language as creative medium has undergone multiple transformations, reformations, revolutions, and transgressions.

In certain cases, this quest for a new language in one culture inherited the experimental spirit of the other. We see this in Whitman and Poe's avant-garde reception in the poetry of Russian Futurism, with ideas of the liberation and democratisation of language and the magic of the word as such; or the American post-WWII counterculture neo-avant-garde appropriating the poetry of the Russian avant-garde (most prominently, Mayakovsky, Khlebnikov and Mandelstam); the culmination of this creative reception being the concept of $L=A=N=G=U=A=G=E$ in the Language school – language as an arena of conflicting discourses, as a space of resistance to power and doxa, as a poetic instrument of social and ideological critique and self-critique. Finally, we see this in the cultural transfer of American Language writing techniques into the new Russian object- and language-oriented poetic experiment, from Dragomoshchenko in the 1980s to poets of the 2010s generation.

These are all cases of intercultural and interlingual cross-fertilisation of avant-garde poetries of language over the last hundred years. These processes are increasingly active nowadays, in our age of world-wide connections and social networks. Translingual poets are able to write and communicate in

Russian, English and other languages at once (as we see in the work of Eugene Ostashevsky, Nika Skandiaka and Inna Krasnoper, to name but a few), and are able to receive instant feedback to texts posted online in multiple cultural and linguistic environments and interfaces simultaneously.

At times, the trajectories of language-focused poetry in Russia and the USA have converged without clear mutual influence but with similar attitudes or intentions. For example, Eugene Jolas created his multilingual poetry and his theories of a universal 'transatlantic', or 'Euramerican' language having never heard of the Russian Futurian Velimir Khlebnikov's projects for the universalisation of language on the basis of what Khlebnikov called the 'language of the stars', or 'alphabet of the mind'; yet the ideas of both poets are charged with a common pathos and spirit. Likewise, it is unlikely that E.E. Cummings, who travelled to Soviet Russia at the twilight of the avant-garde revolution of the word, might have come across Vassily Kamensky's (mind the paronymic similarity of their two names) visual poems, which were reminiscent of Cummings' own graphic experiments. Nor did Cummings manage to meet Boris Pasternak, who was away from Moscow during his visit, or the star of the Russian avant-garde Vladimir Mayakovsky, who had died just a year before his trip. The only members of that community Cummings could meet were Mayakovsky's friends Lilya and Osip Brik, and Vsevolod Meyerhold. Mayakovsky, in his turn, did not meet any American avant-garde poets while in New York in 1925; the two poems dedicated to the 'word as radium', one by Mayakovsky and one by Mina Loy, are unlikely to have been inspired by one another, yet they bear a striking similarity in their poetics of the radioactivised word.

In all likelihood, the American poets of the interwar avant-gardes were unaware of Wassily Kandinsky's experimental verse, although his painting and art theory proved to be highly influential for much of European and American avant-garde literature. Just as the poetic work of Gertrude Stein, Louis Zukofsky and Jackson Mac Low remained unknown to the Russian reading public until recent decades. Meanwhile, as this book shows, the linguistic poetics of Gertrude Stein and Alexander Vvedensky (a Russian poet of the absurd) are in many respects typologically similar, especially in their approaches to time and language. Perhaps the only familiar aspect of Anglo-American avant-garde poetry in the Russian context of the 1910–20s was Ezra Pound's Vorticist and Imagist poetry, which was the subject of an essay by Zinaida Vengerova published in Russia in 1915. We know, also, that the trans-sense poet Alexander Tufanov quite knowingly called himself a 'Russian Vorticist'.

In the 'shimmering' traditions of language-oriented experimental poetry and poetics, the subject of this study, a crucial role was played by three great scholars who explored language from different perspectives.

The first, chronologically, was Wilhelm von Humboldt, founder of Romantic linguistics and creator of the energetic conception of language. The works of this German linguist had a profound impact on Walt Whitman's literary views and thus, indirectly, on all subsequent language-centered American literature. Humboldt's language philosophy was of paramount importance to the Russian tradition of poetic and linguistic creativity, from Andrey Bely to Velimir Khlebnikov.

The second key figure from the scholarly world was the linguist and semiotician Roman Jakobson, who played an active role in the Futurist revolution of the word and contributed to its theoretical and linguistic interpretation, and later had a major impact on both American and global linguistics, as well as on American Language writing. For some Language authors, such as Michael Palmer, Rosmarie Waldrop, or Barrett Watten, Jakobson's theory of poetic function became a significant source of inspiration, both theoretical and practical. Furthermore, Jakobson acted as an agent of intercultural transfer between the Russian poetic avant-garde (and neo-avant-garde if we think of his acquaintance Gennady Aygi) and American literary theory.

Another major theoretical influence on the poetries of language was the mighty Ludwig Wittgenstein. His *Tractatus*, published in 1922, as well as his later linguophilosophical inquiries, made a huge contribution to language-centered poetics of the post-WWII avant-garde, particularly Conceptualist art and literature and language-oriented poets such as Charles Bernstein and Arkadii Dragomoshchenko. Linguistics and philosophy of language were crucial to the artistic endeavors and 'breakthroughs into languages' – to use Khlebnikov's metaphor – of a wide variety of language-oriented poetic conceptions and practices from the late 19th century to the early 21st.

In spite of all the differences and similarities, divergences and convergences between the Russian and American strains of linguistic experimentation in poetry explored in this study, Walt Whitman's insight about America and Russia as 'so distant, so unlike' yet in 'vastest features' so 'resembling each other' holds true – and is a verifiable statement, as this study suggests – for their respective lines of language-oriented poetries. These two traditions developed independently of each other for many decades. In recent decades, they have begun to coincide and intersect, like two parallel lines in Riemann's geometry.

In an early essay from 1909, 'The Magic of Words', Andrey Bely, a pioneer of language-oriented poetry and precursor to the Formalist revolution in Russian theory and poetry, wrote: 'Humanity is alive as long as the poetry of language exists; *the poetry of the language is alive*. We are alive' (1994: 142, *emphasis original – V.F.*). By invoking a 'poetry of language', Bely emphasises language as such, capable of generating poetic speech and of word creation. But he looked even further in 'Aaron's Rod', an essay written just as the 1917 revolution was taking place, heralding a 'poetry of the word' as 'the goal of a new literature'. For him, it was no longer a question of the poeticisation of language, but of the linguistic transformation of poetry itself.

In the 1970s–1980s, American Language poets learned a lot from the early Russian avant-garde (though probably not from Andrey Bely who had not been extensively translated at that time), as well as from its leading theorists Roman Jakobson and Viktor Shklovsky. A passage from Charles Bernstein's text 'Today's Not Opposite Day' seems to precisely address these avant-gardes from distant yet neighboring continents (2001: 75):

> Four score and seven years ago our poets brought forth upon these continents a new textuality conceived in liberty and dedicated to the proposition that all meanings are plural and contextual. Now we are engaged in a great aesthetic struggle testing whether this writing or any writing so conceived and so dedicated can long endure. We are met on an electronic crossroads of that struggle. But in a larger sense we cannot appropriate, we cannot maintain, we cannot validate this ground. Engaged readers, living and dead, have validated it far beyond our poor powers to add or detract. That we here highly resolve that this writing shall not have vied in vain and that poetry of the language, by the language, and for the language shall not perish from the people.

Given that this piece was written around the year 2000, 'four scores and seven years ago' falls around 1912–1913, the very years when poetry made a 'breakthrough into languages' in Russia and the United States. The last phrase from Bernstein's quote, stylised in the manner of the Gettysburg address, amazingly also echoes Andrey Bely's century-old prophecy about the coming 'poetry of language'.

Gilles Deleuze, a great connoisseur of experimental writing, has proposed two ideas about American and Russian literature, which make an apt conclusion to this book. One of them, advanced in the essay 'On the Superiority of Anglo-American Literature', concerns the de-hierarchised, processual, and experimental nature of American literary writing. 'Experiment, never interpret ... English or American literature is a process of experimentation', he sums up (Deleuze et al., 2007: 48–49), referring to such writers as Melville, James, and Whitman. Linguistically challenging literature of the 20th century, which Deleuze elsewhere calls 'a minor literature', is, according to him, always written as if 'in a foreign language'. It is always étranger, hence, estranged – a literature of estrangement, written in an estranged or foreignised language. In his book

Essays Critical and Clinical, the French philosopher addresses a whole range of experimental, minor literatures. At the end of one of the essays, dedicated to writers who are 'stutterers in language', he surprisingly lists the names of Russian writers who 'make the language as such stutter'. Alongside Melville, Kafka and Beckett, Deleuze names Andrey Bely's 'Kotik Letaev', and, right alongside, two other Russian poets: 'Biely, Mandelstam, Khlebnikov: a Russian trinity thrice the stutterer and thrice crucified' (1998: 114). Quite tellingly, it is these three poets of the Russian literary avant-garde that are most often praised by American Language poets. Mandelstam's 'dizzying mephisto-waltz of experimentation', Khlebnikov's 'language husbandry' and Bely's 'poetry of language' remain vital to contemporary Russian-American and American-Russian transfers and exchanges within the universal *laboratory of the Logos*, this *logo-centric oratorical lab*.

Bibliography

Aarsleff, Hans. "The Context and Sense of Humboldt's Statement that Language 'ist kein Werk (Ergon), sondern eine Tätigkeit (Energeia)'." *History of Linguistics*. Ed. Eduardo Guimarães et al. Amsterdam: John Benjamins, 2007: 197–206.

Adorno, Theodor. *Aesthetic Theory*. London and Boston: Routledge and Kegan Paul, 1984.

Agamben, Giorgio. *Potentialities. Collected Essays in Philosophy*. Stanford, CA: Stanford University Press, 1999.

Albert, Jury (ed.) *Moskovskij konceptualizm. Nachalo*. Nizhnij Novgorod: Privolzhskij filial GCSI, 2014.

Alchuk, Anna. *ne BU (stihi 2000–2004 gg.)*. Moscow: Biblioteka zhurnala "Futurum ART", 2005.

Alchuk, Anna et al. *57577. Perepiska v forme tradicionnoj japonskoj pojezii*. Moscow: GNOSISLOGOS, 2004.

Alpatov, Vladimir M. *Istorija odnogo mifa: Marr i marrizm*. Moscow: Nauka, 1991.

Andrews, Bruce. "Text and Context." *The L=A=N=G=U=A=G=E Book*. Ed. Bruce Andrews et al. Carbondale: Southern Illinois Univ. Press, 1984: 31–38.

Aristov, Vladimir. "Interv'ju s Majklom Palmerom." *Inostrannaja literatura* 3 (2013): 229–232. https://magazines.gorky.media/inostran/2013/3/stihi-intervyu-esse-zapisnye-knizhki.html (last accessed 27.02.23).

Arseniev, Pavel. "#19: Ob'ektno-Orientirovannaja pojezija." *Translit* 19 (2017): 1–5.

Arutyunova, Nina D. (Ed.) *Logicheskij analiz jazyka: Kul'turnye koncepty*. Moscow: Nauka, 1991.

Askoldov, Sergey A. "Forma i soderzhanie v iskusstve slova." *Literaturnaja mysl'. Al'manah* 3 (1925): 305–314.

Askoldov, Sergey A. "Koncept i slovo." *Russkaja slovesnost'. Ot teorii slovesnosti k strukture teksta. Antologija*. Ed. Vladimir P. Neroznak. Moscow: Academia, 1997: 267–279.

Aumüller, Matthias. *Innere Form und Poetizität: Die Theorie Aleksandr Potebnjas in ihrem begriffsgeschichtlichen Kontext*. Frankfurt a. M. : Peter Lang Verlag, 2005.

Auroux, Sylvain et al. (Ed.) *La linguistique fantastique*. Paris : Denoël, 1985.

Austin, John. *How to Do Things with Words*. Oxford: At the Clarendon Press, 1962.

Averintsev, Sergey S. *Sofija – Logos. Slovar'*. Kyiv: Duh i litera, 2000.

Aygi, Gennady. *Razgovor na rasstojanii: Stat'i, jesse, besedy, stihi*. Saint-Petersburg: Limbus-Press., 2001.

Bachmann-Medick, Doris. *Cultural Turns: New Orientations in the Study of Culture*. Berlin et al.: De Gruyter, 2016.

Bakhtin, Mikhail. "Discourse in the Novel." *The Dialogic Imagination*. Ed. Michael Holquist. Austin: University of Texas Press, 1981: 259–422.

Bal, Mieke. *Endless Andness. The Politics of Abstraction According to Ann Veronica Janssens*. London: Bloomsbury, 2013.

Ball, Alan M. *Imagining America: Influence and Images in Twentieth Century Russia*. Lanham, MD: Rowman & Littlefield Publishers, Inc., 2003.

Balmont, Konstantin. *Pojezija kak volshebstvo*. Moscow: Skorpion, 1915.

Baran, Henryk. "V tvorcheskoj laboratorii Hlebnikova: o 'tetradi 1908 g.'." *Pojetika russkoj literatury nachala XX veka*. Moscow: Progress, 1993: 179–188.

Barskova, Polina. *Sed'maja shheloch'. Teksty i sud'by blokadnyh pojetov*. Saint-Petersburg: Izdatel'stvo Ivana Limbaha, 2020.

Barthes, Roland. *Writing Degree Zero*. London: Jonathan Cape, 1967.

Bartschat, Brigitte. "La réception de Humboldt dans la pensée linguistique russe, de Potebnja à Vygotskij." *Revue germanique internationale* 3 (2006) : 13–23.

Baudouin de Courtenay, Ivan A. *Ob otnoshenii russkogo pis'ma k russkomu jazyku*. Saint-Petersburg: Obnovlenie shkoli, 1912.

Baudouin de Courtenay, Ivan A. *Sbornik zadach po 'Vvedeniju v jazykovedenie', po preimushhestvu primenitel'no k russkomu jazyku*. Saint-Petersburg: Tipografija V. Bezobrazov i K (Vl. N. P. Zandman), 1912.

Baudouin de Courtenay, Ivan A. "Slovo i 'slovo'." *Den'* 49 (1914a).

Baudouin de Courtenay, Ivan A. "K teorii 'slova kak takovogo' i 'bukvy kak takovoj'." *Den'* 56 (1914b).

Baydin, Valery. "Jazykovaja utopija Velimira Hlebnikova." *Voprosy literatury* 6 (2007): 51–82.

Bely, Andrey. *Simvolizm*. M., 1910.

Bely, Andrey. "Zhezl Aarona. (O slove v pojezii)." *Skify* 1 (1917): 155–212.

Bely, Andrey. *Pojezija slova*. Petrograd: Epoha, 1922.

Bely, Andrey. *Selected Essays*. Berkeley: University of California Press, 1985.

Bely, Andrey. "O sebe kak pisatele." *Andrej Belyj: Problemy tvorchestva: Stat'i. Vospominanija. Publikacii. Sbornik*. Ed. Stanislav Lesnevskij et al. Moscow: Sovetskij pisatel, 1988: 19–24.

Bely, Andrey. *Simvolizm kak miroponimanie*. Moscow: Respublika, 1994.

Bely, Andrey. *Glossalolia*. Electronic publication, 2003: http://community.middlebury.edu/~beyer/gl/intro.html (last accessed 27.02.23).

Bely, Andrey. "Mysl' i jazyk (Filosofija jazyka A.A. Potebni)." *Semiotika i Avangard. Antologija*. Ed. Yuri Stepanov et al. Moscow: Akademicheskij project; Kultura, 2006a: 199–211.

Bely, Andrey. "Zhezl Aarona. O slove v pojezii." *Semiotika i Avangard. Antologija*. Ed. Yuri Stepanov et al. Moscow: Akademicheskij project; Kultura, 2006b: 376–426.

Bely, Andrey. *Sobranie sochinenij. Simvolizm. Kniga statej*. Moscow: Respublika., 2010.

Bely, Andrey. *Zhezl Aarona. Raboty po teorii slova 1916–1927 gg*. Moscow: IMLI RAN, 2018.

Benjamin, Walter. "On Language as Such and on the Language of Man [1916]." *Selected Writings, Volume 1, 1913–1926.* Cambridge, Mass; London: The Belknap Press of Harvard University Press, 1996: 62–74.

Benjamin, Walter. "The Task of the Translator [1923]." *Selected Writings, Volume 1, 1913–1926.* Cambridge, Mass; London: The Belknap Press of Harvard University Press, 1996: 253–263.

Benveniste, Emile. *Baudelaire.* Limoges: Lambert-Lucas, 2011.

Berdyaev, Nikolai. *The Revelation about Man in the Creativity of Dostoevsky* [1918] // http://www.berdyaev.com/berdiaev/berd_lib/1918_294.html (last accessed 27.02.23).

Berezovchuk, Larisa. *Lirika.* Saint-Petersburg: Boyanych; Blanka, 1999: http://www.vavilon.ru/texts/prim/berezovchuk1-4.html#28 (last accessed 27.02.23).

Bernstein, Charles. Interview with Natalia Fedorova // boundary 2 (2021) 48 (4). https://read.dukeupress.edu/boundary-2/article-abstract/48/4/65/232422/Interview-with-Natalia-Fedorova (last accessed 27.02.23).

Bernstein, Charles. *Ispytanie znaka: Izbrannye stihotvorenija i stat'i.* Moscow: Russkij Gulliver, 2020.

Bernstein, Charles. *My way: speeches and poems.* Chicago: University of Chicago Press, 1999.

Bernstein, Charles. *Pitch of Poetry.* Chicago: University of Chicago Press, 2016.

Bernstein, Charles. *Recalculating.* Chicago and London: University of Chicago Press, 2013.

Bernstein, Charles. "The Expanded Field of L=A=N=G=U=A=G=E." *Routledge Companion to Experimental Literature.* Ed. Joe Bray et al. London, 2012: 281–297.

Bernstein, Charles. *With Strings.* Chicago and London: University of Chicago Press, 2001.

Berry, Ellen et al. *Transcultural Experiments: Russian and American Models of Creative Communication.* New York: St. Martin's Press, 1999.

Beyer, Thomas, Jr. "Andrej Belyj's 'The Magic of Words' and The Silver Dove." *Slavic and East European Journal* 22, 4 (1978): 464–472.

Beyer, Thomas. "Andrej Belyj's Glossalolija: A Berlin Glossolalia." *Europa Orientalis*, XIV, 2 (1995): 7–25.

Birns, Nicholas. "The Three Phases of the Linguistic Turn and Their Literary Manifestations." *Partial Answers*, 15, 2 (2017): 291–313.

Biryukov, Sergey. "Pojezija: moduli i vektory. Slovomuzyka Elizavety Mnacakanovoj [2005]." *Topos. Literaturno-filosofskij zhurnal*: http://topos.ru/article/3315 (last accessed 27.02.23).

Biryukov, Sergey. "Pojeticheskij masterklass. Urok devjatyj, zaumnyj [2004]." *Topos. Literaturno-filosofskij zhurnal*: http://www.topos.ru/article/2306 (last accessed 27.02.23).

Blok, Alexander. *Sobranie sochinenij: V 8 t. T. 6.* Moscow: Goslitizdat, 1962.

Bobrinskaya, Ekaterina. *Konceptualizm.* Moscow: Galart, 1994.

Bogomolov, Nikolai A. *Russkaia literatura nachala XX veka i okkul'tizm*. Moscow: Novoe literaturnoe obozrenie, 1999.

Brandabur, Edward. "Ezra Pound and Wassily Kandinsky: A Language in Form and Color." *Journal of Aesthetic Education* 7, 2 (1973): 91–107.

Bruns, Gerald L. *Modern Poetry and the Idea of Language*. New Haven: Yale UP, 1975.

Bryson, Norman. *Vision and Painting. The Logic of the Gaze*. New Haven, CT and London: Yale UP, 1983.

Bryusov, Valery. "Sintetika pojezii." *Problemy pojetiki*. Valery Bryusov (Ed.) Moscow; Leningrad: ZiF, 1925: 9–30.

Bryusov, Valery. *Izbrannye sochinenija: V 2 t. T. 2*. Moscow: Goslitizdat, 1955.

Bugaeva, Klavdia N. *Vospominanija ob Andree Belom*. Saint-Petersburg: Izd-vo Ivana Limbaha, 2001.

Bukhshtab, Boris. "Filosofija 'zaumnogo jazyka' Hlebnikova." *Novoe literaturnoe obozrenie* 89 (2008): 44–92.

Bulgakov, Sergey N. *Filosofija imeni*. Saint-Petersburg: Nauka, 1999.

Bürger, Peter. *Theory of the Avant-Garde*. Minneapolis: University of Minnesota Press, 1984.

Burliuk, David et al. "Slap in the face to public taste." *Russian Futurism through Its Manifestoes, 1912–1928*. Ed. Anna Lawton et al. Ithaca: Cornell University Press, 1988: 51–52.

Cage, John. *Silence*. Middletown, Conn.: Wesleyan University Press, 1961.

Cage, John. *Empty Words: Writings '73–'78*. Middletown, Conn.: Wesleyan University Press, 1979.

Cassedy, Steven. *Flight from Eden: The Origins of Modern Literary Criticism and Theory*. Berkeley: University of California Press, 1990.

Cavanagh, Clare. *Lyric Poetry and Modern Politics. Russia, Poland, and the West*. New Haven: Yale University Press, 2010.

Caws, Mary A. *Manifesto: A Century of Isms*. Lincoln, Nebraska: University of Nebraska Press, 2001.

Cecire, Natalia. *Experimental: American Literature and the Aesthetics of Knowledge*. Baltimore: Johns Hopkins University Press, 2019.

Celan, Paul. *Eroded by...* (2013) // https://pierrejoris.com/blog/paul-celan/ (last accessed 27.02.23).

Celan, Paul. *Tübingen, January* (2012) // https://withoutliftingafinger.blogspot.com/2012/02/tubingen-january-by-paul-celan.html (last accessed 27.02.23).

Chernyakov, Alexey N. *Metajazykovaja refleksija v tekstah russkogo avangardizma 1910–20-h gg. Avtoref. dis. ... kand. fil. nauk*. Kaliningrad: RGU im. I. Kanta, 2007.

Chernyakov, Alexey N. "'Zaum': 'jazyk' ili 'rech'"? (Hlebnikov, Kruchenyh i drugie)." *'Doski sud'by' Velimira Hlebnikova. Tekst i konteksty: Stat'i i materialy*. Ed. Vladimir Feshchenko et al. Moscow: Tri Kvadrata, 2008.

Chomsky, Noam. *Syntactic Structures*. Berlin et al.: Mouton de Gruyter, 2002.

Clark, Elizabeth A. *History, Theory, Text: Historians and the Linguistic Turn*. Boston: Harvard University Press, 2004.

Clark, Katerina. *Petersburg: Crucible of Cultural Revolution*. Cambridge, Mass.: Harvard University Press, 1995.

Cohen, Milton A. *POETandPAINTER. The Aesthetics of E.E. Cummings's Early Work*. Detroit: Wayne State University, 1987.

Colby, Georgina (Ed.) *Reading Experimental Writing*. Edinburgh: Edinburgh University Press, 2021.

Cooke, Raymond. *Velimir Khlebnikov. A Critical Study*. Cambridge: Cambridge University Press, 1987.

Copeland, Carolyn F. *Language & Time & Gertrude Stein*. Iowa City: University of Iowa Press, 1975.

Cornwell, Neil. *James Joyce and the Russians*. London: Palgrave Macmillan, 1992.

Cummings, Edward E. *A Miscellany Revised*. New York: October House, 1965.

Cummings, Edward E. *EIMI: A Journey Through Soviet Russia*. New York and London: Liveright, 2007.

Cummings, Edward E. *Erotic Poems*. New York; London: Norton, 2010.

Cummings, Edward E. *The Enormous Room*. New York: Boni & Liveright, 1922.

Cummings, Edward E. *Complete Poems, 1904–1962*. New York: Liveright, 2013.

Dandeles, Gregory M. *AvantGardes at the Iron Curtain: A Transnational Reading of Allen Ginsberg and the Soviet Estradny Movement*. PhD Diss. in the University of Michigan, 2017.

David-Fox, Michael. *Showcasing the Great Experiment: Cultural Diplomacy and Western Visitors to the Soviet Union, 1921–1941*. Oxford: Oxford University Press, 2014.

Davidson, Michael et al. *Leningrad: American Writers in the Soviet Union*. San Francisco: Mercury House, 1991.

Davidson, Michael. "Discourse in Poetry: Bakhtin and Extensions of the Dialogical." *Code of Signals: Recent Writings in Poetics* (Ed. Michael Palmer). Berkeley: North Atlantic, 1983: 143–150.

De Certeau, Michel. "Utopies vocales: glossolalies." *Traverses* 20 (1980): 26–37.

Dekoven, Marianne. *A Different Language. Gertrude Stein's Experimental Writing*. Madison, Wis.: University of Wisconsin Press, 1983.

Deleuze, Gilles. *Essays Critical and Clinical*. London: Verso, 1998.

Deleuze G. et al. *Dialogues II*. New York: Columbia University Press, 2007.

Demyankov, Valery Z. "Jazykovye tehniki 'transfera znanija'." *Lingvistika i semiotika kul'turnyh transferov: metody, principy, tehnologii. kollektivnaja monografija*. Ed. Vladimir Feshchenko et al. Moscow: Kulturnaja Revolutsija, 2016: 61–85.

Derrida, Jacques. *Of Grammatology*. Baltimore and London: Johns Hopkins University, 1997.

Dodge, Mabel. "Speculations, or Post-Impressionism in Prose." *Arts & Decoration*, 3, 5 (1913): 172–174.

Donchin, Georgette. *The Influence of French Symbolism on Russian Poetry*. The Hague: Mouton & Co., 1958.

Dowling, Sarah. *Translingual Poetics: Writing Personhood Under Settler Colonialism*. Iowa City, Iowa: University of Iowa Press, 2018.

Dowthwaite, James. *Ezra Pound and 20th-Century Theories of Language. Faith with the Word*. New York: Routledge, 2019.

Dragomoshchenko, Arkadii. *Description*. Los Angeles: Sun & Moon Press, 1990.

Dragomoshchenko, Arkadii. *Xenia*. Los Angeles: Sun & Moon Press, 1994.

Dragomoshchenko, Arkadii. *Tavtologija*. Moscow: Novoe Literaturnoe Obozrenie, 2011.

Dragomoshchenko, Arkadii. "Frames." *Inostrannaja literature* 3 (2013): 241–242.

Dragomoshchenko, Arkadii et al. (Ed.) *Sovremennaja amerikanskaja pojezija v russkih perevodah* Ekaterinburg: Ural'skoe otdelenie RAN, 1996.

Drawicz, Andrzej. "Chlebnikov – mundi constructor." *Mir Velimira Chlebnikova: Statji. Issledovanija (1911–1998)*. Ed. Vyacheslav Vs. Ivanov et al. Moscow: Jazyki Russkoj Kultury, 2000: 490–503.

Druskin, Jakov. "Chinari." *Avrora* 6 (1989):103–115. http://www.d-harms.ru/library/chinari.html (last accessed 27.02.23).

Druskin, Jakov. *Dnevniki*. Saint-Petersburg: Akademicheskij Projekt, 1999.

Druskin, Yakov. "Zvezda bessmyslitsy." *'Sborishhe druzej, ostavlennyh sud'boju'. A. Vvedenskij, L. Lipavskij, Ja. Druskin, D. Harms, N. Olejnikov: 'chinari' v tekstah, dokumentah i issledovanijah*. Ed. Valery N. Sazhin. Vol. 1. Moscow: Ladomir, 2000: 323–416.

Duchamp, Marcel. *A l'infinitive*. New York: Cordier & Ekstrom, 1967.

Duganov, Rudolf V. *Velimir Chlebnikov: Priroda tvorchestva*. Moscow: Sovetskij Pisatel, 1990.

Dunne, John W. *An Experiment with Time*. London: A & C Black, Ltd, 1927.

DuPlessis, Rachel B. et al. (Ed.) *The Objectivist Nexus: Essays in Cultural Poetics*. Tuscaloosa: University Alabama Press, 1999.

Dvinyatin, Fedor N. "Zaumnyj Shherba: k pojetike frazy pro glokuju kuzdru." *Evrazijskoe prostranstvo: Zvuk, slovo, obraz*. Ed. Vyacheslav Vs. Ivanov. Moscow: Jazyki Slavjanskoj Kultury, 2003: 144–150.

Dworkin, Craig. "To destroy language." *Textual Practice*. 18, 2 (2004): 185–197.

Dworkin, Craig et al. (Ed.) *Against Expression: An Anthology of Conceptual Writing*. Evanston, IL: Northwestern University Press, 2011.

Dworkin, Craig. *Radium of the Word: A Poetics of Materiality*. Chicago: University of Chicago Press, 2020.

Dydo, Ulla (Ed.) *A Stein Reader*. Evanston, IL: Northwestern University Press, 1993.

Dydo, Ulla. *Gertrude Stein: The Language That Rises, 1923–1934*. Evanston, IL: Northwestern University Press, 2003.

Eco, Umberto. *The Open Work*. Cambridge, Mass: Harvard University Press, 1989.

Edmond, Jacob. *A Common Strangeness: Contemporary Poetry, Cross-Cultural Encounter, Comparative Literature*. New York: Fordham University Press, 2012.

Edmond, Jacob. "Dmitrij Prigov i mezhkul'turnyj konceptualizm," *Novoe literaturnoe obozrenie* 6 (2012): 218–245.
Eikhenbaum, Boris M. *O literature: Raboty raznyh let*. Moscow: Sovetskij Pisatel., 1987.
Enzensberger, Hans M. (Hg.) *Kursbuch 10. Dossier: Chlebnikow und andere*. Frankfurt: Suhrkamp, 1967.
Epstein, Mikhail. *After the Future. The Paradoxes of Postmodernism & Contemporary Russian Culture*. Amherst: University of Massachusetts Press, 1995.
Epstein, Mikhail. "Theses on Metarealism and Conceptualism." *Russian Postmodernism: New Perspectives on Post-Soviet Culture*. Mikhail Epstein et al. New York, Oxford: Berghahn Books, 1999: 105–112.
Epstein, Mikhail. *Slovo i molchanie. Metafizika russkoi literatury*. Moscow: Vysshaja Shkola, 2006.
Epstein, Mikhail. "The Philosophical Implications of Russian Conceptualism." *Journal of Eurasian Studies* 1, (2010): 64–71. http://www.sciencedirect.com/science/article/pii/S1879366509000098#fn11 (last accessed 27.02.23).
Epstein, Thomas. *Poetry as Apophasis; or, Vvedensky in Love*: http://obook.org/amr/library/vvedensky.pdf (last accessed 27.02.23).
Erjavec, Aleš (Ed.) *Aesthetic Revolutions and Twentieth-Century Avant-Garde Movements*. Durham; London: Duke University Press, 2015.
Ern, Vladimir F. *Bor'ba za Logos*. Moscow: Izdatel'stvo Put', 1911.
Fairley, Irene R. *E. E. Cummings and Ungrammar: A Study of Syntactic Deviance in His Poems*. Searingtown, N.Y.: Watermill Publishers, 1975.
Faryno, Jerzy. ""Antinomija jazyka" Florenskogo i pojeticheskaja paradigma "simvolizm/avangard"." *P.A. Florenskij i kul'tura ego vremeni*. Ed. Michael Hagemeister et al. Marburg/Lahn: Blaue Hörner, 1995: 307–320.
Feshchenko, Vladimir V. *Laboratorija logosa: Jazykovoj jeksperiment v avangardnom tvorchestve*. Moscow: Jazyki slavjanskix kultur, 2009.
Feshchenko, Vladimir V. "Gustav Shpet's Deep Semiotics: A Science of Understanding Signs." *Sign Systems Studies* 43, 2/3 (2015): 227–240.
Feshchenko, Vladimir V. (Ed.) *Zhivoe slovo: logos – golos – dvizhenie – zhest. Sbornik statej i materialov*. Moscow: Novoe Literaturnoe Obozrenie, 2015.
Feshchenko, Vladimir V. *Literaturnyj avangard na lingvisticheskih povorotah*. Saint-Petersburg: Izdatelstvo Evropejskogo Universiteta v Sankt-Peterburge, 2018.
Feshchenko, Vladimir V. et al. (Ed.) *'Doski sud'by' Velimira Hlebnikova. Tekst i konteksty: Stat'i i materialy*. Moscow: Tri kvadrata, 2008.
Feshchenko, Vladimir V. et al. (Ed.) *Prikljuchenija netovarishha Kemminkza v Strane Sovetov. E.E. Cummings i Rossija*. Saint-Petersburg: Izdatelstvo Evropejskogo Universiteta v Sankt-Peterburge, 2013.
Feshchenko, Vladimir V. et al. *Sotvorenie znaka. Ocherki o lingvojestetike i semiotike iskusstva*. Moscow: Jazyki Slavjanskoj Kultury, 2014.

Feshchenko, Vladimir V. (Ed.) *Transatlanticheskij avangard. Anglo-amerikanskie literaturnye dvizhenija (1910–1940). Programmnye dokumenty i teksty.* Saint-Petersburg: Izdatelstvo Evropejskogo Universiteta v Sankt-Peterburge, 2018.

Filosofov, Dmitry V. "Magija slova." *Rech'* 265 (1916): 2.

Fiveiskii, Mikhail. *Dukhovnye darovaniia v pervonachal'noi khristianskoi tserkvi: Opyt ob"iasneniia 12–14 glav pervogo poslaniia sv. Apostola Pavla k Korinfianam.* Moscow: T-vo tip. A.I. Mamontova, 1907.

Flint, Frank S. "Imagisme." *Poetry: A Magazine of Verse*, 1 (1913): 198–200.

Florensky, Pavel A. *Sochinenija. V 4 t. T. 3 (1).* Moscow: Mysl', 2000.

Flournoy, Théodore. *Des Indes à la Planète Mars.* Genève: Édition Atar; Paris: Fischbacher, 1899.

Flynt, Henry. "Essay: Concept Art." *An Anthology of Chance Operations.* Ed. La Monte Young et al. New York; London: Heiner Friedrich, 1963: unnumbered. http://www.fondazionebonotto.org/en/collection/fluxus/flynthenry/11/698.html?from=2449 (last accessed 27.02.23).

Foucault, Michel. *The Order of Things: An Archaeology of the Human Sciences.* London: Tavistock Publications Ltd., 1970.

Franken, Claudia. *Gertrude Stein, Writer and Thinker.* Münster: LIT Verlag, 2000.

Friedman, Norman. *e. e. cummings: the art of his poetry.* Baltimore: The Johns Hopkins University Press, 1960.

Friedrich, Hugo. *Struktura sovremennoj liriki. Ot Bodlera do serediny dvadcatogo stoletija.* Moscow: Jazyki Slavjanskih Kultur, 2010.

Galieva, Zhanna (Ed.) *Prigov i konceptualizm: Sbornik statej i materialov.* Moscow: Novoe Literaturnoe Obozrenie, 2014.

Gamper, Michael. *Experiment und Literatur: Themen, Methoden, Theorien.* Göttingen: Wallstein, 2010.

García, Ofelia et al. *Translanguaging: Language, Bilingualism, and Education.* New York: Palgrave MacMillan, 2014.

Gerlovina, Rimma et al. *Koncepty.* Vologda: Poligraf-Periodika, 2012.

Gilchrist, Cherry. *Russian Magic: Living Folk Traditions of an Enchanted Landscape.* Wheaton, IL: Quest Books, 2009.

Ginzburg, Lidiya. *O psihologicheskoj proze.* Leningrad: Sovetskij Pisatel, 1971.

Glazova, Elena Ju. *Metamorfoza slova. Teoreticheskaja mysl' Osipa Mandel'shtama.* Moscow: : Jazyki Slavjanskih Kultur, 2019.

Glukhova, Elena V. "Neopublikovannye risunki Andreia Belogo k "Glossolalii": Chasha Sv. Graalia." *Trudy RASH* 3 (2005): 386–408.

Gofman, Viktor. *Jazyk literatury. Ocherki i jetjudy.* Leningrad: Khudozhestvennaja Literatura, 1936.

Goodman, Felicitas. *Speaking in Tongues. A Cross-Cultural Study of Glossolalia.* Chicago: University of Chicago Press, 1972.

Goodman, Nelson. *Fact, Fiction, and Forecast*. Cambridge, Mass; London: Harvard University Press, 1983.

Gor, Gennady. "The creek sick of speech..." *Written in the Dark: Five Poets in the Siege of Leningrad*. Ed. Polina Barskova. New York: Ugly Duckling Press, 2016: 29.

Gornfeld, Alexander G. *Muki slova: Stat'i o hudozhestvennom slove*. Moscow: Kolos, 1927.

Graham, Joseph F. *Onomatopoetics: Theory of Language and Literature*. Cambridge: Cambridge University Press, 2010.

Grechko, Valerij. "Zaum' i glossolalija." *Wiener Slawistischer Almanach* 40 (1997): 39–50.

Grechko, Valerij. "Mezhdu utopiej i 'Realpolitik': Marr, Stalin i vopros o vsemirnom jazyke." *Russian Linguistics* 34, 2 (2010): 159–172.

Green, Keith. *A Study of Deixis in Relation to Lyric Poetry*. Sheffield: University of Sheffield Press, 1992.

Grenier, Robert. *Sentences*. Cambridge, Mass: Whale Cloth Press, 1978.

Grigoryev, Viktor P. *Pojetika slova*. Moscow: Nauka, 1979.

Grigoryev, Viktor P. *Budetljanin*. Moscow: Jazyki Russkoj Kultury, 2000.

Grimstad, Paul. *Experience and Experimental Writing: Literary Pragmatism from Emerson to the Jameses*. Oxford: Oxford University Press, 2015.

Groys, Boris. "Moskovskij romanticheskij konceptualizm." „*A-Ja*" 1 (1979): 3–11. http://www.mmoma.ru/press/articles/boris_grojs_moskovskij_romanticheskij_konceptualizm/ (last accessed 27.02.23).

Groys, Boris. *We Shall Be Flies (A critical response to Ilya Kabakov's installation, The Life of Flies)* (1992): https://agora8.org/BorisGroys_WeShallBeFlies/ (last accessed 27.02.23).

Groys, Boris. *History Becomes Form: Moscow Conceptualism*. Cambridge, MA: MIT Press, 2010.

Gutkin, Irina. "The Magic of Words. Symbolism, Futurism, Social Realism." *The Occult in Russian and Soviet Culture*. Ed. Bernice Glatzer Rosenthal. Ithaca, New York: Cornell University Press, 1997: 225–246.

Hacker, Andrea. *Velimir Khlebnikov's Doski Sud'by: Text, Discourse, Vision*. Unpublished Doctoral Thesis, 2002.

Hahl-Koch, Jelena, "Zametki o poezii i dramaturgii Kandinskogo." *Mnogogrannyj mir Kandinskogo*. Ed. Natalia B. Avtonomova. Moscow: Nauka, 1999: 124–130.

Han, Anna. "A. Potebnja i A. Belyj." *Andrej Belyj. Master slova – iskusstva – mysli*. Ed. John Malmstad. Bergamo: Instituto Universitario di Bergamo, 1991: 135–151.

Hansen-Löve, Aage A. "Intermedialität und Intertextualität: Probleme der Korrelation von Wort- und Bildkunst – am Beispiel der Russischen Moderne." *Dialog der Texte. Hamburger Kolloquium zur Intertextualität*. Hg. Wolf Schmid et al. Wien: Institut für Slawistik an der Universität Wien, 1983: 291–360.

Hansen-Löve, Aage A. "Am Anfang war ... das Wort. Zum Logozentrismus – à la russe." *Am Anfang war... Ursprungsfiguren und Anfangskonstruktionen der Moderne*. Hg. Eckhard Schumacher et al. München: Brill; Fink, 2008: 71–90.

Heidegger, Martin. *The Question Concerning Technology and Other Essays*. New York & London: GARLAND PUBLISHING, INC, 1977.

Hejinian, Lyn. "If Written Is Writing." *The L=A=N=G=U=A=G=E Book: Poetics of the New*. Ed. Bruce Andrews et al. Carbondale: Southern Illinois Univ. Press, 1984.

Hejinian, Lyn. *Oxota: A Short Russian Novel*. Great Barrington, MA: The Figures, 1991.

Hejinian, Lyn. *The Language of Inquiry*. Berkeley: University of California Press, 2000.

Hejinian, Lyn. "Materialy." *Translit* 13, 2013: 60–65.

Heller, Leonid. "Zamjatin: Prophète ou témoin? 'Nous autres' et les réalités de son époque." *Cahiers du Monde Russe et Soviétique* 22, 2–3 (1981): 137–165.

Heusser, Martin. *I Am My Writing: The Poetry of E. E. Cummings*. Tübingen: Stauffenburg, 1997.

Hirschkop, Ken. *Linguistic Turns, 1890–1950. Writing on Language as Social Theory*. Oxford: Oxford University Press, 2019.

Holquist, Michael et al. "Minding the Gap: Toward a Historical Poetics of Estrangement." *Poetics Today* 26, 4 (2005): 613–636.

Humboldt, Wilhelm von. *On Language: On the Diversity of Human Language Construction and Its Influence on the Mental Development of the Human Species*. Cambridge: Cambridge University Press, 1999.

Ičin, Kornelija (Ed.) *Jeto ne Moskovskij konceptualizm*. Belgrade: Izdatel'stvo filologicheskogo fakul'teta v Belgrade, 2021.

Ihde, Don. *Material Hermeneutics: Reversing the Linguistic Turn*. London: Routledge, 2021.

Iliazd. *XX vek Il'i Zdanevicha*. Moscow: Rost-Media, 2015.

Ilyin, Vladimir N. *Jesse o russkoj kul'ture*. Saint-Petersburg: Akropol, 1997.

Imposti, Gabriella E. "Poetica e teoria della lingua in Velimir Chlebnikov: Samovitoe slovo e zaum." *Studi italiani di linguistica teorica ed applicata* X (1981): 105–140.

Ioffe, Denis. "Russkaia religioznaia kritika iazyka i problema imiaslaviia (o. Pavel Florenskii, o. Sergii Bulgakov, A.F. Losev)." *Kritika i semiotika* 11 (2007): 109–173.

Ioffe, Dennis. "Andrei Monastyrski's Post-Semiosis in the Tradition of Moscow Conceptualism: Ekphrasis and the Problem of Visual-Ironic Suggestion." *Russian Literature* 74, 1–2 (2013): 255–73.

Israel, Nico. "Esperantic Modernism: Joyce, Universal Language, and Political Gesture." *Modernism/modernity* 24 (2017): 1–21.

Ivanov, Vyacheslav. "Our Language." *OUT OF THE DEPTHS (De Profundis). A Collection of Articles on the Russian Revolution*. Ed. William F. Woehrlin. Irvine, Calif.: CHARLES SCHLACKS JR., PUBLISHER, 1986: 119–124.

Ivanovich, Hristina. "Jazykovye utopii Velimira Hlebnikova." *Paul' Celan. Materialy, issledovanija, vospominanija. T. I: Dialogi i pereklichki.* Ed. Larisa Naydich. Moscow; Jerusalem: Mosty kul'tury/Gesharim, 2004: 221–243.

Ivanov-Razumnik, Razumnik V. *Tvorchestvo i kritika.* Petersburg: Kolos, 1922.

Izutsu, Toshihiko. *Language and Magic Studies in the Magical Function of Speech.* Kuala Lumpur: The Other Press, 1956.

Jackson, Mathew J. *The Experimental Group. Ilya Kabakov, Moscow Conceptualism, Soviet Avant-Gardes.* Chicago: University of Chicago Press, 2010.

Jakobson, Roman. "On Linguistic Aspects of Translation." *On Translation.* Ed. Reuben A. Brower, Cambridge, Mass: Harvard University Press, 1959: 232–239.

Jakobson, Roman. "Closing Statement: Linguistics and Poetics." *Style in Language.* Ed. Thomas A. Sebeok. New York; London: The Technology Press of Massachusetts Institute of Technology and John Wiley & Sons, Inc., 1960: 350–377.

Jakobson, Roman. *Selected Writings. Volume II: Word and Language.* Berlin et al.: Mouton, 1971.

Jakobson, Roman. *Language in Literature.* Cambridge, Mass; London: Harvard University Press, 1987.

Jakobson, Roman O. *Jazyk i bessoznatel'noe.* Moscow: Gnozis, 1996.

Jakobson, Roman O. "Moi ljubimye temy." *Roman Jakobson: Teksty, dokumenty, issledovanija.* Ed. Henryk Baran et al. Moscow: RGGU, 1999: 75–80.

Jakobson, Roman. *Budetljanin nauki: Vospominanija, pis'ma, stat'i, stihi, proza.* Moscow: Gileja, 2012.

Jakobson, Roman et al. *The Sound Shape of Language.* Berlin et al.: Mouton de Gruyter, 1987.

James, William. *The Principles of Psychology.* New York: Holt, 1890.

Janecek, Gerald. *Zaum: The Transrational Poetry of Russian Futurism.* San Diego: San Diego State University Press, 1996.

Janecek, Gerald. *Sight & Sound Entwined: Studies of the New Russian Poetry.* New York; Oxford: Berghahn, 2000.

Janecek, Gerald. "'Rekviem' Elizavety Mnacakanovoj." *Novoe literaturnoe obozrenie* 62 (2003): 272–279.

Janecek, Gerald. "Muzykal'nye processy v stihotvorenijah Elizavety Mnacakanovoj." *Hudozhestvennyj tekst kak dinamicheskaja sistema.* Ed. Natalya Fateeva et al. Moscow: Upravlenie tehnologijami, 2006: 404–416.

Janecek, Gerald. *Everything Has Already Been Written. Moscow Conceptualist Poetry and Performance.* Evanston, Illinois: Northwestern. University Press, 2018.

Jolas, Eugene. *Man from Babel.* New Haven; London: Yale University Press, 1998.

Jolas, Eugene. *Critical Writings, 1924–1951.* Evanston, Illinois: Northwestern. University Press, 2009.

Jousse, Marcel. *Études de psychologie linguistique. Le style oral rythmique et mnémotechnique chez les verbomoteurs*. Paris: Gabriel Beauchesne, 1925.

Joyce, James. "Translation into Basic English." *In Transition. Writing and Art from transition Magazine 1927–1930. A Paris Anthology*. New York et al.: Anchor Books, 1990: 137–140.

Kafka, Franz. *Parabeln und Paradoxe (Parables and Paradoxes)*. New York: Schocken Books, 1961.

Kahn, Andrew et al. *A History of Russian Literature*. Oxford: Oxford University Press, 2018.

Kamensky, Vassily. *Korabl' iz Cuvammy. Neizvestnye stihotvorenija i pojemy. 1920–1924*. Moscow: Gileja, 2016.

Kandinsky, Wassily. *Klänge*. München: Piper, 1912.

Kandinsky, Wassily. *Point and Line to Plane: Contribution to the Analysis of the Pictorial Elements*. New York: Solomon R. Guggenheim Foundation, 1947.

Kandinsky, Wassily. *Concerning the Spiritual in Art*. New York: Dover Publications, 1977.

Kandinsky, Wassily. *Sounds*. New Haven & London: Yale University Press, 1981.

Kandinsky, Wassily. *Complete Writings on Art*. Cambridge, MA: Da Capo Press, 1994.

Kandinsky, Wassily. *Zvuki*. Moscow: Kuchkovo Pole, 2016.

Kandinsky, Wassily. *O duhovnom v iskusstve. V 2 tomah*. Moscow: BuksMArt, 2020.

Karpov, Dmitry (Ed.) *Igor' Terent'ev. Levejshij iz levyh. K 120-letiju so dnja rozhdenija. Sbornik materialov*. Moscow: Gosudarstvennyj muzej Majakovskogo, 2012.

Kelbert, Eugenia. "Eugene Jolas: A Poet of Multilingualism." *L2 Journal* 7 (2015): 49–67. http://escholarship.org/uc/item/9f7486t2 (last accessed 27.02.23).

Kellman, Steven G. *The Translingual Imagination*. Lincoln: University of Nebraska Press, 2000.

Khlebnikov, Velimir. *The King of Time*. Cambridge, MA; London: Harvard University Press, 1985.

Khlebnikov, Velimir. *Collected Works. Vol. I. Letters and Theoretical Writings*. Cambridge, MA; London: Harvard University Press, 1987.

Khlebnikov, Velimir. *Collected Works. Vol. II. Prose, Plays, and Supersagas*. Cambridge, MA; London: Harvard University Press, 1989.

Khlebnikov, Velimir. *Sobranie sochinenij: V 6 t. T.3*. Moscow: IMLI; Nasledije, 2002.

Khlebnikov, Velimir. *Zangezi: Sverhpovest'*. Moscow: Boslen, 2020.

Kiefer, Klaus H. Eugene Jolas' multilinguale Poetik // *Multilinguale Literatur im 20. Jahrhundert*. Ed. Manfred Schmeling et al. Würzburg: Königshausen u. Neumann, 2002: 121–135.

Kondratov, Alexander. "Izbrannye proizvedenija." *Russian Literature* 78, 1–2 (2015): 44–507.

Kondur, Olga. "Inverted Ekphrasis: Viewing and Reading Andrei Monastyrsky's Elementary Poetry No. 2—Atlas." // *University of Toronto Art Journal* 6 (2018): 80–111.

Konovalov, Dmitry G. *Religioznyj jekstaz v russkom misticheskom sektantstve.* Sergiev-Posad: Tipografija Svjato-Troickoj Sergievoj Lavry, 1908.

Korchagin, Kirill. *Propozicii: Pervaja kniga stihov.* Moscow: Knizhnoe obozrenie (ARGO-RISK), 2011.

Kostetsky, Anatoly G. "Lingvisticheskaja teorija V. Hlebnikova." *Strukturnaja i matematicheskaja lingvistika* 3 (1975): 34–39.

Kosuth, Joseph. "Art After Philosophy: Part 3." *Studio International* 178 (1969): 212–213.

Krause, Marcus et al. (Hg.) *Literarische Experimentalkulturen: Poetologien des Experiments im 19. Jahrhundert.* Würzburg: Königshausen & Neumann, 2005.

Kristeva, Julia. *Desire in Language: A Semiotic Approach to Literature and Art.* New York: Columbia University Press, 1980.

Krzhizhanovsky, Sigizmund. *Autobiography of a Corpse.* New York: New York Review Books, 2013.

Kuhn, Thomas. *The Structure of Scientific Revolutions.* Chicago: University of Chicago Press, 1962.

Kuße, Holger et al. "Etymologie und Magie. Zur Sprachtheorie Pavel Florenskijs." *Slavische Sprachwissenschaft und Interdisziplinarität.* Nr. 1. Hg. Gerd Freidhof et al. München: Otto Sagner, 1995: 77–105.

Kustova, Galina I. "Jazykovye proekty Vjacheslava Ivanova i Andreja Belogo: filosofija jazyka i magija slova." *Vjacheslav Ivanov: Arhivnye materialy i issledovanija.* Ed. Ljudmila A. Gogotishvili et al. Moscow: Russkie Slovari, 1999: 383–411.

Kustova, Galina I."Jazykovye proekty Vjach. Ivanova i V. Hlebnikova." *Vjacheslav Ivanov — tvorchestvo i sud'ba.* Ed. Ada A. Taho-Godi et al. Moscow: Nauka, 2002: 96–107.

Lafont, Cristina. *The Linguistic Turn in Hermeneutic Philosophy.* Cambridge, Mass; London: MIT Press, 1999.

Laughlin, James. *Spearhead: 10 Years' Experimental Writing in America.* New York: New Directions, 1947.

Lauhus, Angelika. "Die Konzepzion der Sprache in der Poetik des Russischen Futurismus." *Russische Avantgarde (1907–1921).* Hg. Bodo Zelinsky. Bonn: Bouvier Verlag Herbert Grundmann, 1987: 26–52.

Levin, Gail. "Wassily Kandinsky and the American Literary Avant-Garde." *Criticism: a Quarterly for Literature and the Arts* 21, 4 (1979): 347–361.

Levinton, Georgy A. "Pojeticheskij bilingvizm i mezh#jazykovye vlijanija: (Jazyk kak podtekst)." *Vtorichnye modelirujushhie sistemy.* Ed. Yuri Lotman. Tartu, 1979: 30–33.

Lévy, Sophie S. (Ed.) *A Transatlantic Avant-Garde: American Artists in Paris, 1918–1939.* Berkeley: University of California Press, 2004.

LeWitt, Sol. "Paragraphs on Conceptual Art." *Artforum* 5, 10 (1967): 79–83.

Likhachev, Dmitry S. "Konceptosfera russkogo jazyka." *Izvestija Akademii nauk SSSR. Serija literatury i jazyka* 52, 1 (1993): 3–9.

BIBLIOGRAPHY

Lipavsky, Leonid. "Razgovory." *'Sborishhe druzej, ostavlennyh sud'boju'. A. Vvedenskij, L. Lipavskij, Ja. Druskin, D. Harms, N. Olejnikov: 'chinari' v tekstah, dokumentah i issledovanijah.* Ed. Valery N. Sazhin. Vol. 1. Moscow: Ladomir, 2000: 174–253.

Livshits, Benedikt K. "Gileja." *Russkij futurizm. Teorija. Praktika. Kritika. Vospominanija.* Ed. Vera N. Terehina et al. Moscow: Nasledie, 2000: 359–372.

Lombard, Emile. *De la glossolalie chez les premiers chrétiens et des phenomènes similaires. Etude d'exegèse et de psychologie.* Lausanne: Imprimeries réunies (S.A.), 1910.

Lönnqvist, Barbara. *Xlebnikov and Carnival. An Analysis of the Poem 'Poet'.* Stockholm: Almqvist & Wiksell International, 1979.

Losev, Alexey F. "Termin 'magija' v ponimanii P.A. Florenskogo." *Pavel A. Florenskij. Sochinenija. V 4 t. T. 3 (1).* Moscow: Mysl', 2000: 249–251.

Losonsky, Michael. *Linguistic Turns in Modern Philosophy.* Cambridge: Cambridge University Press, 2006.

Lutzkanova-Vassileva, Albena. *The Testimonies of Russian and American Postmodern Poetry.* New York: Bloomsbury Academic, 2015.

Mac Low, Jackson. *Thing of Beauty: New and Selected Works.* Berkeley: University of California Press, 2008.

Malevich, Kazimir. *Sobranie sochinenij v pjati tomah. Tom 4.* Moscow: Gileja, 2003.

Mallarmé, Stéphane. "Le Mystère, dans les Lettres, Variations sur un sujet, XI." *La Revue blanche* 78 (1896): 214–218.

Malraux, André. *La Métamorphose des dieux.* Paris: Gallimard, 1957.

Mandelstam, Osip. *Selected Essays.* Austin: University of Texas Press, 1977.

Mandelstam, Osip. "Conversation about Dante." *The Poet's Dante. Twentieth Century Responses.* Ed. Peter S. Hawkins et al. New York: Farrar, Straus and Giroux, 2001: 40–93.

Manovich, Lev. *The Language of New Media.* Cambridge, Mass.: MIT Press, 2001.

Mansanti, Céline. *La revue transition (1927–1938), le modernisme historique en devenir.* Rennes: Presses universitaires de Rennes, 2009.

Marcuse, Herbert. *The Aesthetic Dimension. Toward a Critique of Marxist Aesthetics.* Boston: Beacon Press, 1978.

Markov, Vladimir F. "O Hlebnikove (Popytka apologii i soprotivlenija)." *Grani* 22 (1954): 126–145.

Marr, Jury N. *Sochinenija. 1912–1935. Tom 1. Avtobiografii, stihotvorenija.* Moscow: Gileja, 2018.

Marshall, Alan. *American Experimental Poetry and Democratic Thought.* Oxford: Oxford University Press, 2009.

Marzaduri, Marzio. "Sozdanie i pervaja postanovka dray Janko krul' albanskaj I.M. Zdanevicha." *Russkij literaturnyj avangard: Materialy i issledovanija.* Ed. Marzio Marzaduri et al. Trento: Università di Trento, 1990: 21–32.

McMillan, Dougald. *transition: the History of a Literary Era 1927–1938*. London: Calder and Boyars, 1975.

Mencken, Henry L. *The American Language. An Inquiry into the Development of English in the United States*. New York: A.A. Knopf, 1919.

Mendelson, Maurice. *Life and Work of Walt Whitman: A Soviet View*. Moscow: Progress Publishers, 1976.

Merrington, Lyn. *Readymades Read and Made: Marcel Duchamp's linguistic strategies and jokes. Part 1. 1912–1916*. Perth: Are Press, 2019.

Messerli, Douglas (Ed.) *Language Poetries*. New York: New Directions, 1987.

Meyers, Jeffrey. "Ezra Pound and the Russian Avant-Garde." *Paideuma* 17, 2 and 3 (1988): 171–176.

Mnatsakanova, Elizaveta. *Shagi i vzdohi. Chetyre knigi stihov*. Wien: Verlag Otto Sagner, 1982.

Mnatsakanova, Elizaveta. "Hlebnikov: predel i bespredel'naja muzyka slova." *Sintaksis* 11 (1983): 101–156.

Mnatsakanova, Elizaveta. *Vita Breve. Iz pjati knig: Izbrannaja lirika*. Perm': Izd-vo Permskogo universiteta, 1994.

Mnatsakanova, Elizaveta. "Osen' v lazarete nevinnyh sester." *Novoe literaturnoe obozrenie* 6 (2003): 253–271.

Mnatsakanova, Elizaveta. *O prostranstvah vremen* [2004]: http://magazines.russ.ru/project/bely/mnatsakanova_talk.html. 2004 (last accessed 27.02.23).

Mnatsakanova, Elizaveta. *ARCADIA: Stihi. Iz lekcij. Stat'i. Jesse*. Moscow: LIA R. Jelinina, 2006.

Mnatsakanova, Elizaveta. *Novaja Arkadija*. Moscow: Novoe literaturnoe obozrenie, 2018.

Mochulsky, Konstantin. *Aleksandr Blok. Andrej Belyj. Valerij Brjusov*. Moscow: Respublika, 1997.

Monastyrski, Andrei. *Slovar' terminov moskovskoj konceptual'noj shkoly*. Moscow: Ad Marginem, 1999. https://dom-knig.com/read_333402-1 (last accessed 27.02.23).

Monastyrski, Andrei. *Pojeticheskij mir*. Moscow: Novoe literaturnoe obozrenie, 2007.

Monastyrski, Andrei. *Elementary Poetry*. New York: Ugly Duckling Presse, 2019.

Moore, Marianne. "A Penguin in Moscow: Eimi, by E. E. Cummings." *Poetry* 42 (1933): 277–281.

Muretov, Mitrofan D. "Prorochestvo i iazykogovorenie (glossolaliia) kak znameniia dlia veruiushchikh i neverov. 1 Kor. 14, 20–25." *Bogoslovskii vestnik* 7–8 (1904): 496–520.

Murphet, Julian. *Multimedia Modernism: Literature and the Anglo-American Avant-Garde*. Cambridge: Cambridge University Press, 2009.

Nänny, Max. "Iconic Dimensions in Poetry." *On Poetry and Poetics*. Ed. Richard Waswo et al. Tübingen: Gunter Narr Verlag, 1985: 111–135.

Nealon, Jeffrey. *Fates of the Performative. From the Linguistic Turn to the New Materialism*. Minneapolis: University of Minnesota, 2021.

Nekrasov, Vsevolod. *Stihi. 1956–1983*. Vologda: Biblioteka Moskovskogo Konceptualizma Germana Titova, 2012.

Netzkowa (Mnatsakanjan), Elisabeth. *Metamorphosen: 20 Veränderungen einer vierzeiligen Strophe und Finale*. Wien, 1988.

Nikitina, Svetlana. "Innovation and Multimedia in the Poetry of cummings and Mayakovsky." *CLCWeb: Comparative Literature and Culture* 11, 4 (2009): https://docs.lib.purdue.edu/clcweb/vol11/iss4/3/ (last accessed 27.02.23).

Novalis. *Notes for a Romantic Encyclopaedia (Das Allgemeine Brouillon)*. New York: State University of New York Press, 2007.

Novikov, Vladimir. "Walt Whitman v 'novom, svezhem mire' (ob odnom paradokse dialoga kul'tur)." *Obshhestvennye nauki i sovremennost'* 6 (1992): 144–152.

Oborin, Lev. "Poslednie pjat' let russkoj pojezii – kratkij obzor: kakovy tendencii, chto vazhno?" *The Question*, 2016: https://thequestion.ru/questions/77153/poslednie-pyat-let-russkoi-poezii-kratkii-obzor-kakovy-tendencii-chto-vazhno (last accessed 27.02.23).

Odoevtseva, Irina V. *Na beregah Nevy*. Washington: V. Kamkin, 1967.

Ogden, Charles K. *Debabelization. With a Survey of Contemporary Opinion on the Problem of a Universal Language*. London: K. Paul, 1931.

Ogden, Charles et al. *The Meaning of Meaning. A Study of the Influence of Language upon Thought and of the Science of Symbolism*. New York: A Harvest Book Harcourt, Brace & World, Inc., 1923.

Olender, Maurice. *Les langues du paradis. Aryens et Sémites: un couple providentiel*. Paris: Gallimard-Le-Seuil, 1989.

Olson, Charles. "Proektivnyj stih. Zimorodki." *Novoe literaturnoe obozrenie* 105 (2010): 255–273. http://magazines.russ.ru/nlo/2010/105/ol27.html (last accessed 27.02.23).

Oraić-Tolić, Dubravka. "Die Sternensprache." *Glossarium der russischen Avantgarde*. Hg. Aleksandar Flaker. Graz/Wien: Verlag Droschl, 1989: 448–455.

Oshukov, Mikhail. "Glava 12. Edward Estlin Cummings." *Amerika: Literaturnye i kul'turnye otobrazhenija*. Ed. Olga Yu. Antsyferova. Ivanovo: Ivanovskij gos. un-t, 2012: 192–210.

Oshukov, Mikhail. *Representation of otherness in literary Avant-Garde of early Twentieth century: David Burliuk's and Ezra Pound's Japan (Dissertation)*. Turku: University of Turku, 2017.

Ostashevsky, Eugene. *Iterature*. New York: Ugly Duckling Presse, 2005.

Ostashevsky, Eugene (Ed.) *OBERIU: An Anthology of Russian Absurdism*. Evanston, IL: Northwestern University Press, 2006.

Ostashevsky, Eugene. *Enter Morris Imposternak, Pursued by Ironies*. New York: Ugly Duckling Presse, 2008.

Ostashevsky, Eugene. *The Life and Opinions of DJ Spinoza*. New York: Zephyr Press, 2008.
Ostashevsky, Eugene. *The Pirate Who Does Not Know the Value of Pi*. New York: NYRB Poets, 2017.
Ostashevsky, Eugene. *The Feeling Sonnets*. New York: NYRB Poets, 2022.
Ovsyaniko-Kulikovsky, Dmitry N. *Sobrachnie sochinenij. T. VI*. Saint-Petersburg: Izdanie I.L. Ovsjaniko-Kulikovskoj, 1914.
Palmer, Michael (Ed.) *Code of Signals: Recent Writings in Poetics*. Berkeley: North Atlantic Books, 1983.
Palmer, Michael. *Sun*. Berkeley: North Point Press, 1988. https://poets.org/poem/sun (last accessed 27.02.23).
Palmer, Michael. "Poetry and Contingency: Within a Timeless Moment of Barbaric Thought." *Chicago Review* 49, 2 (2003): 65–76.
Palmer, Michael. *Thread*. New York: New Directions, 2011.
Pavlov, Evgeny. "Aleksandr Vvedensky's Rhetoric of Temporality." *New Zealand Slavonic Journal* 43 (2010): 115–130.
Pavlov, Evgeny. "Tavtologii Dragomoshhenko." *Novoe literaturnoe obozrenie* 131 (2015): 281–101.
Perelman, Bob. *The Trouble with Genius: Reading Pound, Joyce, Stein, and Zukofsky*. Berkeley, CA: University of California Press, 1994.
Perelman, Bob. *The Marginalization of Poetry*. Princeton, NJ: Princeton University Press, 1996.
Perloff, Marjorie. *The Dance of the Intellect: Studies in the Poetry of the Pound Tradition*. Cambridge: Cambridge University Press, 1985.
Perloff, Marjorie. *The Futurist Moment. Avant-Garde, Avant Guerre, and the Language of Rupture*. Chicago; London: University of Chicago Press, 1986.
Perloff, Marjorie. "Russian Postmodernism: An Oxymoron?" *Postmodern Culture* 3, 2 (1993): https://muse.jhu.edu/article/27392 (last accessed 27.02.23).
Perloff, Marjorie. *Wittgenstein's Ladder: Poetic Language and the Strangeness of the Ordinary*. Chicago: University of Chicago Press, 1996.
Perloff, Marjorie. "'Logocinéma of the Frontiersman': Eugene Jolas's Multilingual Poetics and Its Legacies." *Kunapipi* 20, 3 (1999): 145–163. http://wings.buffalo.edu/epc/authors/perloff/jolas.html (last accessed 27.02.23).
Perloff, Marjorie. *21st-Century Modernism: The "New" Poetics*. Malden, Mass; Oxford: Blackwell Publishers, 2002.
Perloff, Marjorie. "Avant-Garde Tradition and Individual Talent: The Case of Language Poetry." *Revue française d'études américaines* 103, 1 (2005): 117–141.
Perloff, Marjorie. *Unoriginal Genius: Poetry by Other Means in the New Century*. Chicago, London: University of Chicago Press, 2010.
Perloff, Marjorie. *Infrathin. An Experiment in Micropoetics*. Chicago: University of Chicago Press, 2021.

Pertsova, Natalya N. *Slovar' neologizmov Velimira Hlebnikova*. Wien; Moskau: Wiener Slawistischer Almanach, 1995.
Pertsova, Natalya N. "O 'zvezdnom jazyke' Velimira Hlebnikova." *Mir Velimira Hlebnikova: Stat'i. Issledovanija (1911–1998)*. Ed. Vyacheslav Vs. Ivanov et al. Moscow: Jazyki Russkoj Kultury, 2000: 359–384.
Pertsova, Natalya N. *Slovotvorchestvo Velimira Hlebnikova*. Moscow: Izd-vo Moskovskogo universiteta, 2003.
Peterson, Dale E. "Mayakovsky and Whitman: The Icon and the Mosaic." *Slavic Review* 28, 3 (1969): 416–425.
Petrovskaya, Elena. "Fundament—pyl'" (Zametki o pojezii A.T. Dragomoshhenko)." *Novoe literaturnoe obozrenie* 3 (2013): 267–273.
Podzemskaia, Nadia. "Art et abstraction : forme, objet, chose. Théories artistiques, linguistique et philosophie." *Ligeia* 89-90-91-92 (2009): 33–46.
Poe, Edgar A. *The Works of Edgar Allan Poe. The Raven Edition. Volume 4*. New York: P. F. Collier & Son, 1903. https://etc.usf.edu/lit2go/147/the-works-of-edgar-allan-poe/5227/the-power-of-words/ (last accessed 27.02.23).
Pogodin, Alexander L. *Jazyk, kak tvorchestvo*. Kharkiv: Tip. 'Mirnyj trud', 1913.
Polonsky, Rachel. "Translating Whitman, Mistranslating Bal'mont." *Slavonic and East European Review* 75, 4 (1997): 401–421.
Polonsky, Rachel. *English Literature and the Russian Aesthetic Renaissance*. Cambridge: Cambridge University Press, 1998.
Pomorska, Krystyna. *Russian Formalist Theory and its Poetic Ambience*. The Hague: Mouton, 1968.
Pomorska, Krystyna et al. (Ed.) *Language, Poetry and Poetics. The Generation of 1890's: Jakobson, Trubetskoy, Majakovskij*. Berlin: De Gryuter Mouton, 1987.
Potebnja, Alexander A. "Psihologija pojeticheskogo i prozaicheskogo myshlenija." *Semiotika i Avangard. Antologija*. Ed. Yuri Stepanov et al. Moscow: Akademicheskij project; Kultura, 2006: 177–198.
Pound, Ezra. "A Few Don'ts by an Imagiste." *Poetry: A Magazine of Verse* 1 (1913): 200–206.
Pound, Ezra. *Gaudier-Brzeska: A Memoir*. London: William Clowes and Sons; New York: John Lane Company, 1916.
Pozzo, Alessandra. *La glossolalie en Occident*. Paris: Les Belles Lettres, 2013.
Prigov, Dmitry A. "Chto nado znat' o konceptualizme." *Art-Azbuka. Slovar' sovremennogo iskusstva*. Ed. Maks Fray. Moscow, 1998: http://azbuka.gif.ru/important/prigov-kontseptualizm/ (last accessed 27.02.23).
Prinz, Jessica. "Words in visual art." *The Routledge Companion to Experimental Literature*. Ed. Joe Bray et al. London; N.Y.: Routledge, 2015: 323–337.
Probstein, Ian. ""I Have Beaten Out My Exile": The Perception of Ezra Pound's Poetry in Russia." *Make It New* 4, 3 (2017a): 25–48.

Probstein, Ian. *The River of Time. Time-Space, History, and Language in Avant-Garde, Modernist, and Contemporary Russian and Anglo-American Poetry.* Boston: Academic Studies Press, 2017b.

Probstein, Ian et al. (Ed.) *Ot 'Chernoj gory' do 'Jazykovogo pis'ma': Antologija novejshej pojezii SShA.* Moscow: Novoe Literaturnoe Obozrenie, 2022.

Proskurin, Sergey et al. "Voice and bodily deixis as manifestation of performativity in written texts." *Semiotica* 227 (2019): 317–374.

Quartermain, Peter. *Disjunctive poetics. From Gertrude Stein and Louis Zukofsky to Susan Howe.* Cambridge: Cambridge University Press, 1992.

Rancière, Jacques. *The Aesthetic Unconscious.* Cambridge: Polity, 2009.

Rancière, Jacques. *Aisthesis. Scenes from the Aesthetic Regime of Art.* London; New York: Verso, 2013.

Rasula, Jed et al. (Ed.) *Imagining Language: An Anthology.* Cambridge, Mass; London: The MIT Press, 1998.

Raunig, Gerald. *Art and Revolution. Transversal Activism in the Long Twentieth Century.* Cambridge, Mass: The MIT Press, 2007.

Reed, Brian. "Locating Zaum: Mnatsakanova on Khlebnikov." *Jacket* 27 (2005): http://jacketmagazine.com/27/reed.html (last accessed 27.02.23).

Revzina, Olga G. "Kachestvennaja i funkcional'naja harakteristika vremeni v pojezii A.I. Vvedenskogo." *Russian Literature* VI, 4 (1978): 397–401.

Rorty, Richard (Ed.) *The Linguistic Turn: Recent Essays in Philosophical Method.* Chicago: University of Chicago Press, 1967.

Rosenberg, Harold. *The Tradition of the New.* New York: Horizon Press Inc., 1959.

Rosenfeld, Alla (Ed.) *Moscow Conceptualism in Context.* Munich et al.: Prestel, 2011.

Rosenthal, Bernice G. (Ed.) *The Occult in Russian and Soviet Culture.* Ithaca, New York: Cornell University Press, 1997.

Ross, John R. "On Declarative Sentences." *Readings in English Transformational Grammar.* Ed. Roderick A. Jacobs et al. Waltham (Mass.): Ginn and Company, A Xerox Company, 1970: 222-272.

Rossomakhin, Andrey (Ed.) *Sverhpovest' "Zangezi": Novaja tekstologija. Kommentarij. Recepcija. Dokumenty. Issledovanija. Illjustracii.* Moscow: Boslen, 2021.

Rothenberg, Jerome (Ed.) *Revolution of the Word: A New Gathering of American Avant Garde Poetry 1914–1945.* New York: Vintage, 1974.

Rubinstein, Lev. *Compleat Catalogue of Comedic Novelties.* New York: Ugly Duckling Presse, 2014.

Russell, Bertrand. *In Praise of Idleness and Other Essays.* London: Unwin Books, 1963.

Ryan, William F. *The Bathhouse at Midnight: An Historical Survey of Magic and Divination in Russia.* University Park: Pennsylvania State University Press, 1999.

Ryklin, Mikhail. *Kommunizm kak religija: Intellektualy i Oktjabr'skaja revoljucija.* Moscow: Novoe Literaturnoe Obozrenie, 2009.

Safonov, Nikita. "Tehnika uproshhenija." *Vozduh* 4 (2010). http://www.litkarta.ru/projects/vozdukh/issues/2010-4/safonov/ (last accessed 27.02.23).

Safonov, Nikita. *Razvorot polem simmetrii*. Moscow: Novoe literaturnoe obozrenie, 2015. https://iknigi.net/avtor-nikita-safonov/96583-razvorot-polem-simmetrii-nikita-safonov/read/page-2.html (last accessed 27.02.23).

Sailer, Susan S. "Universalizing Languages: Finnegans Wake Meets Basic English." *James Joyce Quarterly* 36, 4 (1999): 853–868.

Sandler, Stephanie. "Arkadii Dragomoshchenko, Lyn Hejinian, and the Persistence of Romanticism." *Contemporary Literature* 46 (2005): 18–45.

Sandler, Stephanie. "Visual Poetry After Modernism: Elizaveta Mnatsakanova." *Slavic Review* 67, 3 (2008): 610–641.

Sandler, Stephanie. "Ajgi: Music to Name the Divine." *Russian Literature* 79–80 (2016): 61–75.

Sandomirskaya, Irina. *Blokada v slove: Ocherki kriticheskoj teorii i biopolitiki jazyka*. Moscow: Novoe literaturnoe obozrenie, 2013.

Sasse, Sylvia. *Sprech—und Sprachakte im Moskauer Konzeptualismus*. Munchen: Fink, 2003.

Saunders, Max. *Self-Impression. Life-Writing, Autobiografiction, and the Forms of Modern Literature*. Oxford: Oxford University Press, 2010.

Savchuk, Valery V. "Fenomen 'povorota' v kul'ture XX veka." *Mezhdunarodnyj zhurnal issledovanij kul'tury* 1 (2013): 93–108.

Schmidt, Henrike. "Li(?)teratura; Anna Alchuk's anagrammatic poetry." *Zeitschrift fur Slavische Philologie* 67, 1 (2010): 71–97.

Scholz, Friedrich. "Die Anfänge des russischen Futurismus in sprachwissenschaftlicher Sicht." *Poetica* 2 (1968): 477–500.

Seifrid, Thomas. *The Word Made Self. Russian Writings on Language, 1860–1930*. Ithaca; London: Cornell University Press, 2005.

Sers, Philippe. *Totalitarisme et avant-gardes : au seuil de la transcendance*. Paris: Belles Lettres, 2001.

Setz, Cathryn. *Primordial Modernism: Animals, Ideas, transition (1927–1938)*. Edinburgh: Edinburgh University Press, 2019.

Shcherba, Lev V. *Jazykovaja sistema i rechevaja dejatel'nost'*. Leningrad: Nauka, 1974.

Shklovsky, Viktor. *Zhili-byli: Vospominanija. Memuarnye zapisi. Povesti o vremeni: s konca XIX v. po 1964*. Moscow: Sovetskij Pisatel, 1966.

Shklovsky, Viktor. "On Poetry and Trans-Sense Language." *October* 34 (1985): 3–24.

Shklovsky, Viktor. *Gamburgskij schet*. Moscow: Sovetskij Pisatel, 1990.

Shpet, Gustav G. *Iskusstvo kak vid znanija. Izbrannye trudy po filosofii kul'tury*. Moscow: ROSSPEN, 2007.

Silliman, Ron. "Disappearance of the Word, Appearance of the World." *The L=A=N=G=U=A=G=E Book*. Ed. Bruce Andrews et al. Carbondale: Southern Illinois Univ. Press, 1984: 121–132.

Silliman, Ron. "Spicer's Language." *Writing/Talks*. Ed. Bob Perelman. Carbondale: Southern Illinois University Press, 1985: 166–191.

Silliman, Ron. *The New Sentence*. New York: Roof, 1987.

Simonato, Elena. *Une linguistique énergétique en Russie au seuil du XXe siècle*. Bern: Peter Lang, 2005.

Skandiaka, Nika. "Ruiny morja." *Text only* 15 (2006a): http://textonly.ru/self/?article=5708&issue=15 (last accessed 27.02.23).

Skandiaka, Nika. "Iz stihotvorenij 2005–2006 godov." *Novoe literaturnoe obozrenie* 82 (2006b): 379–385. http://magazines.russ.ru/nlo/2006/82/sk27.html (last accessed 27.02.23).

Skidan, Alexander. *Soprotivlenie poezii: Izyskanija i jesse*. Saint-Petersburg: Borey-Art, 2001.

Skidan, Alexander. "Objects in Part." *Aufgabe* 8 (2009): https://media.sas.upenn.edu/jacket2/pdf/reissues/aufgabe/J2_Reissues_Aufgabe_08_2009.pdf (last accessed 27.02.23).

Skidan, Alexander. "Trans-formation: The Poetic Machines of Alexander Vvedensky." *Floor* 3 (2015): http://floorjournal.com/2015/08/06/trans-formation-the-poetic-machines-of-alexander-vvedensky/ (last accessed 27.02.23).

Sokolov, Boris. *Vasilij Kandinskij. Jepoha velikoj duhovnosti. Zhivopis'. Poezija. Teatr. Lichnost'*. Moscow: BuksMart, 2016.

Sokolova, Olga V. "Koncepcii 'vselenskogo' i 'universal'nogo' jazyka v russkom i amerikanskom avangarde." *Kritika i semiotika* 1 (2015): 268–283.

Sokolova, Olga V. *Ot avangarda k neoavangardu: jazyk, sub#ektivnost', kul'turnye perenosy*. Moscow: Kulturnaja Revoljutsija, 2019.

Solivetti, Carla. "Lingvisticheskie prozrenija Velimira Hlebnikova." *Russian Literature* LV–I/II/III (2004): 405–429.

Spicer, Jack. *Language*. San Francisco: White Rabbit Press, 1965.

Stark, Trevor. *Total Expansion of the Letter. Avant-Garde Art and Language after Mallarmé*. Cambridge, Mass: MIT Press, 2020.

Starkina, Sofia. "Chlebnikov i lingvistika: spisok literatury." *Novoe literaturnoe obozrenie* 89 (2008): 44–92.

Starkina, Sofia. "'Uchenie o naimalah jazyka': Voprosy fonologii i morfonologii v trudah Velimira Hlebnikova." *From Medieval Russian Culture to Modernism. Studies in Honor of Ronald Vroon*. Ed. Lazar Fleishman et al. Frankfurt am Main: Peter Lang, 2012: 197–225.

Stein, Gertrude. *Portrait of Mabel Dodge at the Villa Curonia*. Firenze: Galileiana, 1912.

Stein, Gertrude. *Look at Me Now and Here I Am. Writings and Lectures 1909–1945*. Harmondsworth: Penguin Books, 1984.

Stein, Gertrude. *The Making of Americans. Being a History of a Family's Progress*. Normal, IL: Dalkey Archive Press, 1995.

Stein, Gertrude. *Writings 1932–1946*. New York: Library of America, 1998.
Stepanov, Yury S. *Konstanty: Slovar' russkoj kul'tury. Opyt issledovanija*. Moscow: Jazyki Slavjanskih Kultur, 1997.
Stepanov, Yury S. "Semiotika konceptov." *Semiotika: Antologija. Izd. 2-e.* Ed. Yuri S. Stepanov. Moscow; Akademicheskij Projekt; Ekaterinburg: Delovaja Kniga, 2001: 603–612.
Stepanov, Yury S. *Koncepty. Tonkaja plenka civilizacii*. Moscow: Jazyki Slavjanskih Kultur, 2007.
Symons, Julian. *Makers of the New: The Revolution in Literature, 1912–1939*. London: Andre Deutsch, 1987.
Tashjian, Dickran. *Skyscraper Primitives. Dada and the American Avant-Garde. 1910–1925*. Middletown, Connecticut: Wesleyan University Press, 1975.
Titarenko, Svetlana D. "Avtomaticheskoe pis'mo u Vladimira Solov'eva i Viacheslava Ivanova: arkhetipy misticheskogo soznaniia i traditsii glossolalii." *Trudy RASH* 4, 1 (2007): 147–189.
Tokarev, Dmitrii. "Escape from Utopia. The Metamorphoses of Utopian Dreams in the Russian Avant-Garde in Exile (Il'ya Zdanevich, Boris Poplavskii)." *Utopia. The Avant-Garde, Modernism and (Im)possible Life*. Ed. David Ayers et al. Berlin; Boston: De Gruyter, 2015: 411–424.
Toporkov, Andrey L. et al. "Stat'ja Aleksandra Bloka 'Pojezija zagovorov i zaklinanij' kak jezotericheskij tekst. Chast' pervaja." *Novyj filologicheskij vestnik* 1 (2021): 155–169.
Trubetskoy, Nikolaj S. *Pis'ma i zametki N.S. Trubeckogo*. Moscow: Jazyki slavjanskoj kul'tury, 2004.
Trubetskoy, Sergey N. *Sobranie sochinenij. Tom IV. Uchenie o Logose v ego istorii*. Moscow: Tip. G. Lissnera i D. Sobko, 1906.
Tsibulya, Alexandra. *Five Russian Poems*: https://www.worldliteraturetoday.org/2019/summer/five-russian-poems-aleksandra-tsibulia (last accessed 27.02.23).
Tsivyan, Tatyana V. "Hlebnikovskaja lingvistika: predvaritel'nye zametki." *Russian Literature* LV—I/II/III (2004): 65–75.
Tsur, Reuven. *Toward a Theory of Cognitive Poetics*. Brighton; Portland: Sussex Academic Press, 2008.
Tsvigun, Tatyana V. et al. "Pojeticheskie reduplikacii Aleksandra Vvedenskogo." *Slovo. ru: baltijskij akcent* 12, 4 (2021): 51–64.
Tufanov, Alexander. *K zaumi*. Petersburg: Izdanie avtora, 1924.
Tynianov, Jury N. *Literaturnaja jevoljucija: Izbrannye trudy*. Moscow: Agraf, 2002.
Uspensky, Boris A. *Ego Loquens: Jazyk i kommunikacionnoe prostranstvo*. Moscow: RGGU, 2007.
Uspensky, Fedor B. *Raboty o jazyke i pojetike Osipa Mandel'shtama*. Moscow: Iazyki slavianskoi kul'tury, 2014.
Valentine, Sarah. "Music, Silence, and Spirituality in the Poetry of Gennady Aigi." *Slavic and East European Journal* 51 (2007): 675–692.

Valentine, Sarah. *Witness and Transformation: The Poetics of Gennady Aygi*. Boston: Academic Studies Press, 2015.

Valieva, Iuliia. "Byt' – bit' – bit: tetrad' po russkomu jazyku kak porozhdajushhaja model'." *Russian Literature* 78, 1–2 (2015): 509–523.

Van Dijk, Theun. "Some Problems of Generative Poetics." *Poetics* 2, 2 (1971): 5–35.

Velmezova, Ekaterina. *Les lois du sens: la sémantique marriste*. Bern et al.: Peter Lang, 2007.

Venediktova, Tatyana D. *Obretenie golosa. Amerikanskaja nacional'naja pojeticheskaja tradicija*. Moscow: Labirint, 1993.

Vinokur, Grigorij O. "O simvolizme i nauchnoj pojetike." *Hrestomatija po teoreticheskomu literaturovedeniju. I.* Ed. Igor Chernov. Tartu: Tartuskij gosudarstvennyj universitet, 1976: 197–199.

Vinokur, Grigorij O. *Filologicheskie issledovanija: Lingvistika i pojetika*. Moscow: Nauka, 1990.

Vroon, Ronald. "Vladimir Mayakovsky and Frank O'Hara: a Reappraisal." *Studia Litterarum* 5, 3 (2020): 144–185.

Vvedensky, Alexander. *The Gray Notebook*. New York: Ugly Duckling Presse, 2009.

Vvedensky, Alexander. *Vsjo*. Moscow: OGI, 2010.

Vvedensky, Alexander. *An Invitation for Me to Think*. New York: New York Review Books, 2013.

Waldrop, Rosmarie. *Against Language?: 'Dissatisfaction with Language' as Theme and as Impulse Towards Experiments in Twentieth Century Poetry*. Berlin et al.: Mouton, 1971.

Waldrop, Rosmarie. *Thinking of Follows* [2000]: http://writing.upenn.edu/epc/authors/waldropr/thinking.html (last accessed 27.02.23).

Wanner, Adrian. *The Bilingual Muse: Self-Translation among Russian Poets*. Evanston: Northwestern University Press, 2020.

Wanner, Adrian. "Russian-English Literary Translingualism: Switching from Cyrillic to Roman across the Atlantic." *The Routledge Handbook of Literary Translingualism*. Ed. Steven G. Kellman et al. New York: Routledge, 2021: 200–210.

Warren, James P. *Walt Whitman's Language Experiment*. University Park: Pennsylvania State University Press, 1990.

Watten, Barrett. "The Turn to Language and the 1960s." *Critical Inquiry* 26, 1 (2002): 139–183.

Watten, Barrett. *The Constructivist Moment: From Material Text to Cultural Poetics*. Middletown, CT: Wesleyan University Press, 2003.

Watten, Barrett. *Questions of Poetics: Language Writing and Consequences*. Iowa City: University of Iowa Press, 2016.

Webster, Michael. "Plotting the Evolution of a "r-p-o-p-h-e-s-s-a-g-r"." *Spring. The Journal of the E.E. Cummings Society* 20 (2013): 116–143.

Weineck, Silke-Maria. "Logos and Pallaksch. The Loss of Madness and the Survival of Poetry in Paul Celan's "Tübingen, Jänner"." *Orbis Litterarum* 54, 4 (1999): 262–275.

Weitz, Morris. "The Role of Theory in Aesthetics." *The Journal of Aesthetics and Art Criticism* 15, 1 (1956): 27–35.

Welch, Michael D. "Trains to Moscow: Lewis Carroll's Russian Journal and Cummings' EIMI." *Spring. The Journal of the E.E. Cummings Society* 8 (1999): 114–121.

Weststeijn, Willem. "A.A. Potebnja and Russian Symbolism." *Russian Literature* VII (1979): 443–464.

Weststeijn, Willem. *Velimir Chlebnikov and the Development of Poetical Language in Russian Symbolism and Futurism.* Amsterdam: Rodopi, 1983.

Weststeijn, Willem. "Ajgi and Chlebnikov." *Russian Literature* 79–80 (2016): 5–12.

White, Eric. *Transatlantic Avant-Gardes: Little Magazines and Localist Modernism.* Edinburgh: Edinburgh University Press, 2013.

Whorf, Benjamin L. *Language, Thought, and Reality. Selected Writings.* New York; London: The Technology Press of Massachusetts Institute of Technology; John Wiley & Sons, Inc., 1956.

Williams, William C. "The Work of Gertrude Stein." *The Critical Response to Gertrude Stein*. Ed. Kirk Curnutt. Westport: Greenwood Press, 2000: 194–199.

Winters, Yvor. *Primitivism and Decadence: A Study of American Experimental Poetry.* New York: Arrow Editions, 1937.

Wittgenstein, Ludwig. *Tractatus logico-philosophicus.* London: Kegan Paul, Trench, Trubner & Co. Ltd., 1922.

Wittgenstein, Ludwig. *Preliminary Studies for the "Philosophical Investigations". Generally Known as the Blue and Brown Books.* Oxford: Basil Blackwell, 1958.

Wittgenstein, Ludwig. *Zettel.* Berkeley and Los Angeles: University of California Press, 1967.

Woolf, Virginia. *Orlando. A Biography.* London: Penguin Classics, 2000.

Yaguello, Marina. *Language through the Looking Glass: Exploring Language and Linguistics.* Oxford: Oxford University Press, 1998.

Yaguello, Marina. *Les fous du langage, des langues imaginaires et leurs inventeurs.* Paris: Seuil, 1984.

Young, La Monte et al. (Ed.) *An Anthology of Chance Operations.* New York; London: Heiner Friedrich, 1963.

Zamiatin, Eugene. *We.* New York: Dutton, 1924.

Zamjatin, Evgenij. *'My': Tekst i materialy k tvorcheskoj istorii romana.* Saint-Petersburg: Mir, 2011.

Zavyalov, Sergey. *Melika.* Moscow: Novoe Literaturnoe Obozrenie, 2003. http://www.vavilon.ru/texts/prim/zavyalov2-4.html (last accessed 27.02.23).

Zdanevich, Ilia. "gaROland: stihotvorenija Il'i Zdanevicha. Publikacija R. Gejro." *Vtoroj Terent'evskij sbornik.* Ed. Sergey Kudryavtsev. Moscow: Gileja, 1998a: 318–323.

Zdanevich, Ilia. "Proizvedenija gimnazicheskogo perioda". *Vtoroj Terent'evskij sbornik*. Ed. Sergey Kudryavtsev. Moscow: Gileja, 1998b: 257–268.

Zdanevich, Ilia. *Futurism i vsechestvo. 1912–1914. V 2 t.* Moscow: Gileja, 2014.

Zdanevich, Ilia. *Dom na govne: Doklady i vystuplenija v Parizhe i Berline. 1921–1926.* Moscow: Gileja, 2021.

Zholkovsky, Alexander. *Themes and Texts: Toward a Poetics of Expressiveness*. Ithaca, NY: Cornell University Press, 1984.

Zukofsky, Louis. *Prepositions +. The Collected Critical Essays*. Hanover; London: Wesleyan University Press, 2000.

Zukofsky, Louis. "Bogomol. Bogomol i interpretacija." *Translit* 17 (2015): 105–106.

Index of Names

Abélard, Pierre   181, 184–185
Adorno, Theodor   12
Agamben, Giorgio   1, 3
Akhmatova, Anna   174, 202
Alchuk, Anna   176–177
Andrews, Bruce   208, 214
Apollinaire, Guillaume   104
Aragon, Louis   125, 137
Aristotle   181, 245
Aristov, Vladimir   208, 215–216, 228
Arp, Hans   146, 149
Arseniev, Pavel   163, 229
Artmann, Hans   234
Arutyunova, Nina   200
Ashbery, John   219
Askoldov, Sergey   184–187, 200–201
Augustine   88, 181
Austin, John   164, 182, 190
Averintsev, Sergey   4
Aygi, Gennady   158, 169–171, 174–175, 177, 215–216, 233, 257

Baader, Franz   150
Bakhterev, Igor   248
Bakhtin, Mikhail   124, 134, 214
Bal, Mieke   113
Balmont, Konstantin   14, 34–35, 47
Barr, Alfred   143
Barskova, Polina   249
Barthes, Roland   6, 211
Baudelaire, Charles   32
Baudouin de Courtenay, Jan   51, 159–160
Beach, Sylvia   145
Beauzée, Nicolas   21
Beckett, Samuel   83, 149, 211, 233, 259
Bee, Susan   218
Bely, Andrey   4–5, 10–11, 19, 23–28, 31–47, 54, 58, 60–61, 69–70, 86, 101, 147–148, 170, 173–174, 186, 211, 247, 255, 257–259
Benjamin, Walter   1, 37, 131, 155, 170
Benveniste, Emile   190
Berdyaev, Nikolai   10
Berezovchuk, Larisa   175
Bergmann, Gustav   1
Bergson, Henri   83, 88

Bernstein, Charles   16, 75, 205, 208–209, 211–215, 217–219, 255, 257–258
Birns, Nicholas   6
Biryukov, Sergey   160, 172, 239
Blavatsky, Helena   33
Blok, Alexander   14, 32–34, 46, 143, 147, 186
Bobrowski, Johannes   234
Boethius   181
Böhme, Jakob   40, 42–43
Breton, André   148
Brik, Lilya   125, 127, 133, 256
Brik, Osip   24, 127, 133, 256
Brink, Lia Na'ama Ten   230
Brodsky, Joseph   233, 247
Brown, Bob   106–107
Bruns, Gerald   8
Bryson, Norman   112
Bryusov, Valery   5, 14, 24, 27
Bugaeva, Klavdia   47
Bukhshtab, Boris   29, 59, 155
Bulatov, Erik   190
Bulgakov, Sergey   4, 39
Bulygina, Tatyana   200
Bunting, Basil   221
Bürger, Peter   8, 100, 148
Burliuk, David   16, 102, 159, 163, 205
Burroughs, William   100

Cage, John   183, 187
Carroll, Lewis   132
Cassedy, Steven   5, 19, 34, 67
Cecire, Natalia   16
Celan, Paul   59, 170–171, 173, 234
Cézanne, Paul   117, 127
Chambers, Whittaker   220
Chekhov, Anton   10, 172
Chicherin, Alexei   211
Chomsky, Noam   161–164, 166
Chukovsky, Korney   14
Clark, Katerina   47
Colby, Georgina   16
Condillac, Etienne B. de   21
Cooke, Raymond   58
Coolidge, Clark   206, 208, 215, 219
Copeland, C.F.   87

Cornwell, Neil   143
Covici, Pascal   132
Creeley, Robert   219
Croce, Benedetto   21, 23, 184
Cummings, Edward E.   6, 107, 111–118, 121–143, 163–164, 205, 232, 256

Dana, Henry   126
Dante   11, 132, 208, 243
Daumal, René   83
David-Fox, Michael   125
Davidson, Michael   214, 216–217
Davies, Alan   208
Day, Jean   215
De Certeau, Michel   84
Deleuze, Gilles   258–259
Demyankov, Valery   3
Derrida, Jacques   22
Descartes, René   153
Dewey, John   3
Dickinson, Emily   113
Diderot, Denis   21
Dodge, Mabel   16, 103
Donne, John   164
Doolittle, Hilda   15, 101
Dos Passos, John   125, 128, 131
Dostoevsky, Fyodor   10, 28, 140
Dowling, Sarah   233
Dowthwaite, James   101, 155
Dragomoshchenko, Arkadii   175–176, 205–206, 208, 210–212, 215–219, 222, 224–228, 230, 233, 246, 249, 255, 257
Drawicz, Andrzej   64
Dreiser, Theodore   131
Druskin, Yakov   85–88, 91, 169–171, 248
Duchamp, Marcel   6, 8, 100, 104, 106, 108–109, 111, 183, 217–218
Duganov, Rudolf   58, 68
Duncan, Robert   219
Dunne, John W.   83, 92
Duns Scotus   181
Dvinyatin, Fedor   160
Dworkin, Craig   86, 99, 183

Eco, Umberto   254
Edmond, Jacob   217
Ehrenburg, Ilya   125–126, 139
Eich, Günter   236
Eikhenbaum, Boris   35

Eisenstein, Sergey   14, 129, 143
Eliade, Mircea   178
Eluard, Paul   155
Epstein, Thomas   93
Epstein, Mikhail   189, 216
Ern, Vladimir   4

Fabre D'Olivet, Antoine   33–34
Fainberg, Lubov   128
Fargue, Léon-Paul   146
Fedorova, Natalia   211
Filonov, Pavel   148
Filosofov, Dmitry   35–36
Fitterman, Robert   183
Fiveysky, Mikhail   43
Flint, Frank S.   101
Florensky, Pavel   4, 29–30, 36, 39
Flournoy, Théodore   42
Flynt, Henry   182–183
Fontana, Lucio   182
Foucault, Michel   6–8, 211
Frazer, Tony   74
Frege, Gottlob   181–183
Freud, Sigmund   42, 138
Friedlander, Otto   126
Friedman, Norman   116–124
Friedrich, Hugo   32
Fry, Roger   103

Gaudier-Brzeska, Henri   101
Gayraud, Régis   52
George, Stefan   155
Gerlovin, Rimma   204
Gerlovin, Valery   204
Gide, André   131
Gillespie, Abraham   107–108
Ginsberg, Allen   100, 206
Ginzburg, Lidiya   140, 216
Giuliani, Alfredo   163
Gofman, Viktor   58, 60, 64, 66
Gogol, Nikolai   10–11, 140, 234
Goldsmith, Kenneth   183
Golynko (Golynko-Wolfson), Dmitry   176, 218, 220, 229, 246
Goncharova, Natalia   125
Goodman, Nelson   79
Gor, Gennady   170
Gorky, Maksim   127, 133
Gornfeld, Alexander   38

INDEX OF NAMES

Grenier, Robert   205, 208, 212
Grigoryev, Viktor   68–69, 165
Groys, Boris   187–188, 192, 204
Gutkin, Irina   33

Hacker, Andrea   57
Halle, Morris   166
Harris, Zelig   206
Hathaway, Anne   253
Heidegger, Martin   1–2, 83, 155, 170
Hejinian, Lyn   206, 209–210, 212, 215–216
Heller, Leonid   140
Heusser, Martin   117
Himmel, Sofia   143
Hirschkop, Ken   2
Hölderlin, Friedrich   42, 170, 234, 238
Horace   21
Howe, Susan   244
Humboldt, Wilhelm von   5–6, 10, 13, 19–31, 34, 257
Husserl, Edmund   83, 95, 181, 184, 186
Huxley, Aldous   139
Hymes, Dell   162

Ilyin, Vladimir   43
Ingraham, Andrew   161
Ionesco, Eugène   83
Ivanov, Vyacheslav I.   5, 24, 26–27
Ivanov, Vyacheslav Vs.   217
Ivanov-Razumnik, Razumnik   69
Izutsu, Toshihiko   37

Jakobson, Roman   12, 31, 37, 67, 71, 96, 158–166, 170–171, 186, 206, 213–214, 216, 244, 254, 257–258
James, William   3, 42, 88, 102
Janecek, Gerald   173, 187
Jolas, Maria   151
Jolas, Eugene   6, 107, 143–157, 232–233, 256
Jousse, Marcel   146
Joyce, James   6, 83, 128–129, 132–133, 135, 137, 143, 145–148, 150, 154–155, 211

Kabakov, Ilya   188, 190
Kafka, Franz   40, 117, 259
Kamensky, Vassily   205, 256, 49
Kandinsky, Wassily   70–81, 101, 103–104, 112, 143, 211–212, 232–233, 256
Kellman, Steven G.   233

Kerner, Justinus   150
Kharms, Daniil   84, 169, 246
Khlebnikov, Velimir   5, 14–15, 28–29, 37, 46, 48, 51, 53, 55, 56–71, 83–86, 149, 152, 155, 159–160, 162, 164–165, 170–171, 179, 205, 211–212, 215, 245–246, 255–257, 259
Kibirov, Timur   202
Kiparski, Paul   166
Konakova, Nadezhda   215
Kondratov, Alexander   180, 203, 215
Konovalov, Dmitry   43, 54
Korchagin, Kirill   218, 224, 229
Kosuth, Joseph   183, 188–189
Krasnoper, Inna   252, 256
Kristeva, Julia   61
Krivulin, Viktor   216
Kruchenykh, Alexei   53, 55, 58, 86, 152, 159, 162, 205
Krylov, Ivan   174
Krzhizhanovsky, Sigizmund   133
Kubryakova, Elena   200
Kuhn, Thomas   3
Kul'bin, Nikolai   53
Kutik, Ilya   215–216

Lakoff, George   200
Larionov, Denis   229
Larionov, Mikhail   125
Lazareva, Ekaterina   187
Leiris, Michel   146
Lenin, Vladimir   133
Lessing, Gotthold   81
Levertov, Denise   219
Lewis, Wyndham   83, 103, 132
LeWitt, Sol   182
Lidin, Vladimir   126
Likhachev, Dmitry   200–201
Lipavsky, Leonid   85
Lissitzky, El   16, 143
Livshits, Benedikt   14, 29
London, Jack   138
Losev, Alexei   4, 36
Lotman, Yuri   201
Lowell, Amy   112
Loy, Mina   99, 256
Lukichev, Vladimir   229
Lurie, Vera   43
Luther, Martin   243
Lutzkanova-Vassileva, Albena   215

Lyle, Marius   107

Mac Low, Jackson   107–109, 180, 183, 215, 252, 256
Magritte, René   202
Malevich, Kazimir   9, 143, 212
Malinowski, Bronisław   37
Mallarmé, Stéphane   7–8, 32, 34, 67, 146, 150, 172, 211, 247
Malraux, André   8
Man Ray   99
Mandelstam, Osip   5, 11, 45–46, 85, 170, 208, 211, 233, 255, 259
Mann, Thomas   83
Manovich, Lev   251
Marcuse, Herbert   9
Marinetti, Filippo T.   159
Markov, Vladimir   69
Marr, Nikolai   47–48
Marr, Yuri   48
Marshall, Alan   12
Martynova, Olga   178
Marvell, Andrew   162
Marx, Karl   130, 133, 137
Matisse, Henri   102–103, 127
Mayakovsky, Vladimir   5, 14, 31, 99, 127–128, 133, 148, 162, 165, 205, 255–256
Mazin, Viktor   213
McMillan, Dougald   144–145
McTaggart, J.M.E.   82
Mead, George H.   83
Medvedev, Kirill   222
Mencken, Henry L.   150
Merrington, Lyn   109
Mersenne, Marin   153–154
Messerli, Douglas   209
Meyer, Agnes E.   104
Meyerhold, Vsevolod   127–128, 133, 256
Michaux, Henri   83, 155
Mnatsakanova, Elizaveta (Netzkowa, Elisabeth)   169, 171–174, 177, 232–241, 243–246, 252
Mochulsky, Konstantin   34
Mogutin, Yaroslav   206
Monastyrski, Andrei   174–175, 187, 193, 195–199, 203, 214
Monroe, Harriet   220
Moore, George   2, 82
Moore, Marianne   132

Morris, Charles H.   3
Morse, Ainsley   224
Muretov, Mitrofan   43
Musil, Wolfgang   234

Nabokov, Vladimir   232–233
Nänny, Max   115–116
Nekrasov, Vsevolod   190–191, 214, 233
Nikolaev, Philip   249
Notley, Alice   250
Novalis   9, 11, 32, 42, 150, 234

Oborin, Lev   229
Odoevtseva, Irina   38
Ogden, Charles   37, 154–155, 161
O'Hara, Frank   205
Olson, Charles   219, 222, 230
Oppen, George   217, 221, 230
Orwell, George   139
Oshukov, Mikhail   131
Ostashevsky, Eugene   232, 246–249, 252, 256
Ovsyaniko-Kulikovsky, Dmitry   10, 23–24

Palmer, Michael   158, 207–209, 215–216, 219, 257
Parshchikov, Alexei   207, 209, 211, 215–216, 218, 246
Pasternak, Boris   128, 205, 211, 246, 256
Pavilionis, Rolandas   200
Pavlov, Evgeny   225
Peirce, Charles S.   3, 57
Perelman, Bob   209
Perloff, Marjorie   6, 100, 111, 212, 215, 218
Pertsova, Natalia   61–62, 67
Pessoa, Fernando   155
Picabia, Francis   100, 104–105, 108, 110
Picasso, Pablo   102–103, 127, 158
Place, Vanessa   183
Plato   181, 188
Poe, Edgar A.   14, 32, 35
Pogodin, Alexander   23, 43
Popper, Karl   209
Porvin, Alexei   229
Potebnja, Alexander   5, 10, 19–21, 24–27, 31, 33–34, 43, 186
Pound, Ezra   6, 15–16, 71, 100–103, 107, 125, 129, 132, 143, 155, 220, 233, 256
Prévert, Jacques   202
Prigov, Dmitry   189, 193–194, 216

INDEX OF NAMES

Prinz, Jessica   111
Probstein, Ian   211, 219
Proust, Marcel   83
Pushkin, Alexander   28, 143, 163, 210

Quinn, John   102

Rakosi, Carl   217, 221
Rancière, Jacques   8–9, 14
Raunig, Gerald   148
Reich, Zinaida   127
Reznikoff, Charles   221
Richards, Ian   37, 161
Rimbaud, Arthur   35, 148
Robinson, Kit   208, 215
Rodchenko, Alexander   212
Rodionova, Anna   218
Rorty, Richard   1
Ross, John R.   92
Rothenberg, Jerome   100, 208
Rousseau, Jean-Jacques   22, 42
Rubinstein, Lev   174, 191, 193, 212, 214–215
Rühm, Gerhard   234
Russell, Bertrand   2, 82, 87–88, 164, 183
Ryklin, Mikhail   125

Safonov, Nikita   218, 229–231
Sakharov, Ivan   33, 46
Sandler, Stephanie   177, 244
Sandomirskaya, Irina   169, 249
Sasse, Sylvia   187
Saunders, Max   132
Saussure, Ferdinand de   1, 3, 6, 44, 161, 255
Scalapino, Leslie   252
Schmidt, Paul   58
Seifrid, Thomas   4
Serenko, Darya   229
Sers, Philippe   100
Shapir, Maxim   217
Shcherba, Lev   6–7, 11, 77, 160–161
Sherry, James   208
Shklovsky, Viktor   5, 15, 28, 36, 43, 50–51, 53–54, 56, 85, 92, 101, 158, 214, 217–218, 258
Shmelev, Alexei   200
Shpet, Gustav   5, 30, 184, 186
Silliman, Ron   207–208, 212–214, 216
Skandiaka, Nika   177–178, 232, 249–250, 252, 256

Skidan, Alexander   85, 176, 218, 228–229, 246
Skriabin, Alexander   112
Słowacki, Juliusz   45, 54
Smith, Rebekah   175, 191
Smith, Hélène   42
Sokolov, Ivan   252–253
Sokolova, Olga   143, 216
Soloviev, Vladimir   43
Sosnora, Viktor   233
Spicer, Jack   206–207, 215
Stark, Trevor   8
Starkina, Sofia   59
Stein, Gertrude   6, 15–16, 82–83, 87–90, 92, 94–96, 99–100, 102–103, 107, 111–112, 129, 146, 149, 163, 207, 225, 228, 244, 252, 256
Stenich, Valentin   128
Stepanov, Nikolai   68
Stepanov, Yuri   200–202, 204
Stieglitz, Alfred   102, 104
Stramm, August   155
Strauss, Johann   234
Suslova, Eugenia   218, 229

Terentiev, Igor   55, 161, 211
Tertullian   181
Timofejev, Sergej   229
Tolstoy, Leo   13, 162
Tretyakov, Sergey   127
Triolet, Elsa   125, 127
Trubetskoy, Nikolai   165
Trubetskoy, Sergey   4
Tsibulya, Alexandra   229–230
Tsvetaeva, Marina   44
Tufanov, Alexander   48–49, 51, 232, 256
Turgenev, Ivan   13
Turovskaya, Genya   249
Twain, Mark   131
Tynianov, Yuri   56–57, 69, 214
Tzara, Tristan   83

Ulanov, Alexander   218
Uspensky, Boris   162

Vaginov, Konstantin   169, 177
Valentine, Sarah   171
Van Dijk, Theun   166
Van Gogh, Vincent   127, 202
Vengerova, Zinaida   15, 256

Vertov, Dziga   14
Veselovsky, Alexander   21, 34
Vinokur, Grigory   38, 58, 69
Vishnevsky, Vsevolod   128
Voloshinov, Valentin   214
Vossler, Karl   5, 10, 21, 24
Voznesensky, Andrey   206
Vvedensky, Alexander   82–96, 169–172, 177–178, 246, 249, 256

Wagner, Richard   147
Waldrop, Rosmarie   207–208, 219, 257
Wanner, Adrian   249
Warren, James   12–13
Watten, Barrett   2, 16, 208–209, 213, 216–217, 219, 257
Waugh, Linda   37, 165
Webb, Beatrice   131
Webern, Anton   171
Webster, Michael   124
Weitz, Moris   182
Weststeijn, Willem   58
Whitehead, Alfred   83, 88
Whitman, Walt   12–15, 113, 164, 255, 257–258
Whorf, Benjamin   95, 164
Williams, William C.   92, 107, 220

Wittgenstein, Ludwig   1–2, 82, 84, 88, 93, 164, 180–183, 188, 211, 213, 220, 224–225, 228, 247–248, 255, 257
Woolf, Virginia   79
Wright, Emily   73, 124

Yesenin, Sergei   133, 205
Yevtushenko, Evgeny   206

Zabolotsky, Nikolai   248
Zadkine, Ossip   128
Zakharkiv, Ekaterina   218
Zakharova, Yaroslava   229
Zamyatin, Yevgeny   130, 138–142
Zavyalov, Sergey   176
Zayas, Marius de   104–105
Zdanevich, Ilia (Iliazd)   15, 45, 50–56, 84, 104, 150, 152
Zdanevich, Kirill   50
Zhdanov, Ivan   215–216
Zhirmunsky, Vladimir   24, 165
Zholkovsky, Alexander   166
Zola, Emile   10
Zolyan, Suren   217
Zorn, Max   163
Zoshchenko, Mikhail   143
Zukofsky, Louis   155, 211, 217, 219–222, 224, 226, 230, 244, 256

Index of Terms

abstraction   11, 72–74, 77–78, 81, 101, 146, 161, 184–185, 231
absurd   6, 12, 68, 83–85, 162, 171, 177–178, 256
   Absurdism   12
   alogism   84, 86, 169, 171
   nonsense   6, 31, 54, 84, 87, 171, 178
   senselessness   119, 160, 178, 246
Acmeism   11
adjective   94, 163, 181, 243
adverb   94, 96
aesthetic regime   8
aestheticism   26, 113
aesthetics   9–10, 19, 25, 71, 205
alphabet   5, 34–35, 48, 51, 61–63, 65, 67, 81, 111, 211, 256
anomaly   55, 159–162, 164, 249
   vs. norm   2, 96, 147–148, 159, 164, 166
antinomy   22, 25, 27, 29, 36
aphasia   42, 177
apophaticism   2, 169–170
Art and Language   183
article   119–120, 130, 134
avant-garde   1, 6, 8–10, 12–14, 16–17, 28, 44, 47, 53–54, 56, 71, 74, 83–84, 99–100, 102, 104, 106–107, 111, 124, 138, 143–144, 147–148, 156–159, 171, 205, 211–212, 217–219, 233, 254, 256–259
   American   6, 15, 99–100, 104, 106–107, 111, 128, 145, 155, 219, 222, 232–233, 255–256
   art   8, 90, 155
   avant-gardism   8, 100, 128
   creativity   5, 30, 72, 83
   experiment   5, 29, 86, 102
   literature   5–6, 144, 146, 256
   mentality   12
   poetics   171, 255
   poetry   83, 96, 163, 177, 205, 233, 255–256
   Russian   5–6, 8, 12, 14, 16, 44, 54, 56, 83, 86, 100, 111, 127, 148, 175, 205, 211–212, 215, 233, 249, 255–256, 258
   transatlantic   100, 157
   writing   97, 146, 169, 205

babble   169–170, 173, 247

Babel   6, 39–40, 45, 47, 49, 100, 135, 144, 146, 154, 156, 169–171
   Tour de Babel   40
   Trou de Babel   40
Basic English   154–155
Beatniks   100, 206
bilingualism   74–77, 176, 232–233, 235, 239, 242, 247, 249, 252
bitextuality   71–72, 74, 78, 81

capitalism   139, 213, 216
Chinari   84–87, 169, 171, 178, 248
Christianity   4, 34, 36, 41–43, 48, 86, 147, 241
   Catholic   237, 239, 242
   Orthodox   4–5, 36, 43
code   61, 66, 71, 73, 80, 118, 130, 137, 208, 247, 251
   decoding   124, 162
   encoding   130, 140, 246, 251
   recoding   72, 80–81, 250
   transcoding   249, 251–252
cognition   12, 27, 58, 60, 88, 182, 184–186, 200, 217, 229, 248, 254
communication   1, 23, 27, 37, 55, 66, 71, 84, 93, 107, 144, 150, 153–154, 159, 164, 170, 179, 195, 201, 207, 213, 224, 232, 247, 255
communism   125–127, 130–131, 133, 136, 139, 216, 220
composition   16, 69, 77–78, 81–82, 114, 132, 138, 145, 160, 172–173, 183, 193, 207, 210, 221, 243, 246
   recomposition   116, 138
   vs. decomposition   5, 63, 85, 170, 239
concept   1–10, 12, 14, 16, 20–21, 23, 25–30, 32, 36, 38, 43, 45, 52–53, 56, 59–63, 80–81, 83, 86–87, 89, 93, 95–96, 101, 107–108, 112, 118, 145, 147, 153, 155, 180–182, 184–188, 190, 193, 196, 199–204, 208, 214, 216–218, 225, 255
   conceptology   201
   conceptosphere   201
   concept studies   187
   conceptual analysis   200, 217
   conceptualisation   2, 62, 82, 96, 122, 181, 186, 197, 200, 254
   poetic   187

Conceptualism   108, 123, 180–181, 183–191, 193, 195, 197, 201–204, 215, 217–218, 224, 257
   conceptual art   111, 182–183, 186–187, 199, 201, 204
   conceptual poetry   86, 106, 183, 187, 190, 218
   conceptual writing   183, 187, 193, 203–204, 218
   Moscow Conceptualism   174, 186–190, 193, 197, 202, 214–216
   post-conceptualism   224
Cubism   102, 127, 141
Cubo-Futurism   11, 16, 50

Dadaism   50, 54, 104, 111, 113, 125
Debabelisation   154–155
deixis   226, 113, 117, 226
   bodily   112–113
   deicticality   113
   deictics   113, 115, 123, 208, 226–227, 234, 240
descriptivism   149
dialogue   12, 65, 70, 93, 135–136, 141, 169, 188, 236
dictionary   62, 111, 149, 155, 163, 183, 197, 199, 201, 226
dystopia   130, 138–141

ekphrasis   72
   auto-ekphrasis   78–79
energeia   10, 19, 21–22, 26, 29–30, 43
   vs. ergon   19, 21–22, 26
Enlightenment   21, 153
everyday language   10, 16, 53, 60, 66, 95, 166
   everyday communication   179
   everyday speech   164, 209
   ordinary language   66, 96, 254
   ordinary communication   84
   ordinary discourse   191
   ordinary speech   20, 102, 192
   ordinary utterance   187
experiment   5, 8–12, 23, 26, 29, 42, 47, 62, 69, 82–83, 86, 101–102, 107–108, 113, 123–124, 136, 139, 142–144, 148, 154–155, 157, 159–160, 162, 183, 207, 220, 233, 252, 255–256, 258
   artistic   11, 56, 155
   experimental aesthetics   10

experimental art   6, 12, 16
experimental grammar   88, 122
experimentalism   10, 111–112
experimental linguistics   12, 30
experimental literature   10, 12, 15–16, 83, 145, 147, 208, 259
experimental novel   10
experimental philology   26
experimental poetics   10, 123
experimental poetry   35, 83, 99, 145, 154, 203, 219, 233, 246, 254, 256
experimental verse   113, 145, 177, 256
experimental writing   12, 16, 52, 101, 147, 228, 254, 258
experimentation   6, 8–9, 11–12, 13, 26, 83, 107, 158, 203–204, 251, 258–259
   grammatical   122
   interlingual   31, 143, 150
   lexical   11
   linguistic   11, 56, 74, 83, 87, 136, 145, 149, 161–162, 245, 249, 257
   literary   11, 16, 23, 38, 83, 102
   poetic   23, 42, 59, 69, 96, 108, 161, 255
   see also language experiment
Expressionism   155

factuality   132, 138
faktura   212
folklore   31–32, 34, 37, 162
foreign language   49, 135–136, 174, 177, 233–234, 245–246, 258
foreignism   233, 245, 247
form vs. content   7, 24–25, 32, 36, 43, 64, 79, 81, 184, 208, 218, 224
Formalism   6, 64, 184, 212, 218
   Russian   4, 10, 15, 28, 35–36, 38, 43, 56, 101, 158, 159, 165–166, 212–214, 217–218, 255, 257
   Neo-Formalism   216, 218
free verse   12, 101, 171, 209
Futurism   5, 8, 12, 14–16, 23, 28–30, 35–36, 43, 45, 48–51, 53–56, 58, 60, 70, 81, 101, 113, 146, 148–149, 155, 158–163, 170–171, 206, 211–212, 215, 255, 257
   Neo-Futurism   158, 170

generativism   161, 164, 166
gesture   14, 40–41, 115, 121, 146

INDEX OF TERMS

glossolalia 31, 33, 36, 38–39, 42–50, 54–56, 84, 150, 170–171, 173–178, 233, 247
    gift of tongues 39, 45, 47–48
    glossolalic speech 42, 48, 190
    grapholalia 45, 54, 56
    speaking in tongues 39, 43–45, 48, 170, 253
grammar 5, 7, 11, 21, 25, 33, 60, 67, 72, 81, 88–89, 92, 94–95, 122, 136–138, 148–149, 159–164, 166, 177, 200, 249
    agrammatism 85, 164
    grammaticality 162–163
    poetic grammar 82–83, 90, 96, 164, 254

heteroglossia 67, 124, 135, 233, 247
Humboldtianism 10, 19, 23–24, 27–30, 38, 43, 186
hybridisation 124, 130, 132, 134–138, 141, 151, 210, 247

iconicity 3, 57, 61, 113, 115–116, 123
ideology 101, 136, 170, 187, 207, 254–255
idiom 156, 207, 244, 247, 249
    national 144, 149, 171, 233
Imagism 15, 100–101, 256
Imiaslavites 36
incantation 32, 33, 37, 103, 149, 176, 244
indexicality 113, 115–118, 123
inner form 21, 26, 73, 201
interculturality 144, 186, 255, 257
interjection 177, 234
interlinguality 31, 61, 74, 76, 135, 150, 171, 212, 233–234, 239, 242, 244, 246, 252, 255
intermediality 71, 73–74
    intersemiotic translation 71–72, 78, 80–81
    transmutation 71–72
language as such 58, 206, 208, 214, 247, 255, 257, 259
language experiment 5, 12–13, 15, 57–58, 60, 64, 66, 68–69, 103, 111, 254–255
language game 88, 109, 181–182, 188, 211, 247
language of art 8, 23, 71–72, 79
language of the future 15, 62, 66–67, 146, 150
language project 47, 59, 69

Language writing 111, 166, 204–207, 209, 212–214, 218, 232, 246, 249, 252–253, 255, 257

language-centered writing 113, 144, 208, 214, 218, 257
Language movement 206, 208, 210, 216
language-oriented poetry 13, 54, 101, 111, 123, 157, 155–156, 178, 207–208, 215, 249, 254–256
Language poetry 1, 6, 203, 207, 209, 211–212, 214–216, 218, 252, 255
LEF 131, 143, 220
Leninism 141
lexeme 170, 177, 239
lexis 11, 73, 85, 90, 94, 136–138, 149, 160, 181, 193, 211, 249, 253
linguistic activity 21, 153, 254
linguistic creativity 23, 27–30, 34, 43, 60, 145, 149, 159, 166, 171, 257
    language creation 5, 24, 69
    language creativity 8, 60, 155
linguistic ideas 20, 24, 50, 59, 161, 255
linguistic material 9, 11, 161
    negative linguistic material 11
linguistic philosophy 2, 183, 207, 247
linguistic poetics 21, 38, 101, 160, 165, 233, 254, 256
    historical linguo-poetics 254
    linguo-poetics 164
linguistic theory 8, 10, 13, 21, 23–24, 37, 44, 59
    theory of language 1, 19, 13, 23–25, 33, 50, 59–60, 163–164, 166
linguistic turn 1–6, 8, 20, 72, 155–156, 181, 183, 211, 255
    the return of language 4, 8
    turn to language 2–3, 6, 97, 254–255
    turn to Logos 20
literature of fact 131, 220
living word 6, 26, 45–46, 51
    living language 6, 11, 55, 159
    living speech 6, 22
logical connection 89, 92–94, 170
logocentrism 4–5, 187
logology 5
logos 4–5, 20, 29, 34, 45, 60, 84, 87, 143, 145, 147, 151, 156, 169–172, 174, 178, 254, 259

Marxism 127, 132, 133, 136, 214, 220
message 37, 74, 113, 158, 165, 213, 251
metalanguage 1, 3, 102, 183, 207, 213
metalinguistic reflection 204, 207, 254

metalinguistics   204, 207, 254
metaphor   5, 24, 34, 40, 61, 70, 133–134, 141, 146–147, 156, 179, 186, 201, 203, 207, 217, 224, 243–244, 247, 249, 257
Metarealism   206–207, 215–217, 228
migration   100–101, 144, 157–158, 232
   emigration   234, 246
minimalism   6, 16, 174, 176, 193, 212, 244, 252
Modernism   2, 8, 12–15, 42, 71, 82–83, 97, 100, 102, 125, 129, 132, 138, 140–141, 146
morpheme   48–49, 136, 170–171, 203, 206
morphology   11, 51, 90, 137, 149, 160, 177
multilingualism   39, 45, 135, 143–144, 146, 150–151, 153, 155–156, 170, 176, 232–233, 243, 247, 252–253, 256
   polyglotism   144, 150, 233
musicality   130, 172, 244–245
mysticism   31, 34, 38, 187

naming   33, 177, 189, 199
nominalism   181, 185, 187
narrative   80, 83, 130–132, 133, 140–141
native language   174, 177, 245, 247
Neo-Avant-Garde   100, 163, 166–167, 170, 180, 204, 218, 255, 257
Neo-Futurism   158, 170
neologism   23, 25, 38, 47, 76, 120, 136–137, 141, 212, 242
noun   74, 94–96, 113, 122

OBERIU   84–86, 169–170, 248
Objectivism   155, 217, 219–224, 226, 228–229
   objectification   221–222, 226, 228
   objectism   222
   object-oriented language   220, 231
   object-oriented ontology   231
   object-oriented poetics   230
   object-oriented poetry   229
   object-oriented writing   224
occultism   31, 33–34
OPOYAZ   35, 216–217
origin of language   7, 22, 25–26, 42, 146, 153, 178
orthography   15, 50, 52, 55

part of speech   118, 203, 212, 226
paradigm   3, 159, 187–188, 199, 216, 231
paronymy   76, 85, 234, 238–239, 247, 252, 256
particle   55, 68, 170, 173, 177, 186

Pentecostal myth   39–41, 45
performativity   2, 3, 13, 78, 112–113, 116–117, 123, 164, 180, 183, 190, 193, 207
philosophy of language   4–5, 20, 23–24, 27–28, 30, 33–34, 37, 57, 59, 70, 164, 183, 184, 214, 257
philosophy of the name   4, 30, 36, 39
phonetics   43, 48–49, 206, 234, 240, 242
poetic function of language   158–59, 164, 190, 206, 212, 213, 216, 257
poetic language   2, 6, 8, 12–15, 20, 33, 44–46, 56, 59–61, 67, 82, 85, 96, 100–102, 132, 136, 149, 159–160, 164–166, 170–172, 177, 185, 193, 206, 209–210, 213–214, 216, 232, 246, 255
   poetic discourse   123, 170, 178, 209, 225
   poetic speech   10, 19–20, 31–32, 36, 52, 66, 69, 85, 116, 166, 172, 176, 245, 257
poetic text   21, 26, 70, 74, 92, 115, 118, 123, 151, 164, 187, 191–192, 202, 207, 213, 240, 244, 250, 254
poetic theory   20, 43, 50
poetic utterance   159, 164, 169, 172, 195
politics   125–126, 214, 220
polyphony   52, 104, 234, 243–244, 246, 247
positivism   1, 6, 10, 144, 149, 187, 220, 224
Post-Conceptualism   224
Post-Modernism   123, 167, 187, 204
Post-Symbolism   44
pragmatics   3, 81, 115, 122, 254
Pragmatism   3
proletarianism   126, 128, 141, 143
pronoun   74, 94, 118, 119, 120–122, 130, 134, 223, 226–227, 251
propaganda   14, 125–126, 128, 131–132
proposition   8, 78, 183, 207, 224–225, 228–229, 231, 258
prose vs. poetry   11, 20–21, 23, 210
proto-language   40, 47–48, 111
punctuation   35, 80, 113, 159, 171, 177, 243

realism   185, 187, 213
   Socialist Realism   187
repetition   16, 31, 73–74, 89–92, 103, 175, 190, 193, 242, 244
revolution   3, 8–9, 15, 47, 125, 127, 144–145, 147–148, 150, 156, 159, 218, 257
   aesthetic   9
   artistic   81

INDEX OF TERMS

in art   8, 125, 147–148
in poetic language   11–12, 82
linguistic   9, 150, 158
logosophical revolution   5
October   27, 129, 138, 147, 101, 128, 147, 258
of language   5, 8, 143–148, 155
of the sign   81
of the word   8, 14, 81, 86, 146–148, 256–257
scientific   3
rhythm   11, 14, 23, 32, 44, 47, 73–74, 76, 85, 94, 101, 103, 146, 148, 176–177, 190, 195, 225, 240, 247, 252
Romanticism   8, 10, 42, 186

self-reference   8, 78, 207, 214
self-translation   72, 74, 77, 81, 176, 233, 249, 252–253
semantics   6, 43, 56, 67, 114–115, 118, 136, 206, 234, 254
semiotics   1, 3, 5, 57, 61, 71–73, 78, 80–81, 86, 112–113, 116, 120, 135, 160, 184, 196, 200–201, 203–204, 214–215, 244, 257
sentence   4, 80, 92, 96, 111, 141, 162–163, 212–213, 225–227
seriality   83, 89, 92, 95
shifter   118–119, 121, 177, 234
sign   3–4, 14, 23, 33, 51–52, 57, 61, 64, 69–72, 80–81, 85–86, 102, 111, 113, 116, 123, 150, 174, 183, 185, 209, 219, 252
verbal   33, 61, 71–72
sign system   1, 5–6, 71–73, 155, 160, 203
signification   22, 65, 115, 181
silence   80, 86, 118, 169, 171, 179, 183, 208, 215–216, 236, 243, 253
Silver Age   13, 20, 24, 35
socialism   126, 128, 131, 137–138, 187
society   7, 9, 130, 133–134, 139, 141, 147, 150, 170, 190, 214, 216–217
sound poetry   33, 116, 163, 156, 172
sound writing   38, 45, 47, 52, 55
speech act   78, 182, 187, 244
spelling   50–52, 137, 159
Stalinism   84, 138, 141, 169, 174, 202
structuralism   149, 165, 206, 209
structure   1, 14, 20–21, 26, 32, 55, 58, 66, 68, 85, 92, 95, 117, 138, 141, 146, 149, 154, 158, 160–162, 165, 171–172, 177, 182, 190, 193, 201, 203, 210, 212–214, 217, 221, 225, 236, 244, 254

subjectivity   7, 117–118, 120, 222–223, 225, 227–228
Surrealism   8, 54, 83, 125, 148, 166, 210
syllable   32, 52, 67, 177, 239, 243
symbol   5, 25–26, 34–35, 37, 42–43, 57, 61, 80, 86, 113, 154, 184
Symbolism   12, 15, 17, 24–28, 31–35, 44, 54, 60, 61, 67, 69, 113, 147, 241
French   32, 34, 67
Russian   5, 10, 14, 23–24, 27, 30–32, 34, 38
synaesthesia   77, 112, 154
syntax   6, 76, 85, 90, 94, 114–115, 148–149, 160–162, 193, 200, 213

tautology   73, 89–90, 212, 224–226, 244
temporality   68, 82–83, 87, 91, 93–96
tense   73, 83, 92–93, 95, 126, 136
terminology   51, 53, 72, 165, 201, 203
totalitarianism   84, 124, 130, 140–141, 169
authoritarianism   139, 170
transatlantic poetics   100
transfer   12, 32, 116, 136, 158, 164, 182, 186, 200, 204, 213, 218, 224, 233, 255, 259
cultural   36, 186, 206, 218, 222, 255, 257
linguistic   76, 247, 249
poetic   205–206, 215
transformation   9, 22–23, 28, 42, 57, 60, 65, 86–88, 153, 166, 204, 212–213, 255, 258
translation   3, 14–15, 23,49, 57–58, 71–75, 77–78, 80–81, 84, 93, 104, 111, 129, 133, 139–140, 154–155, 171, 173, 175–176, 180, 191, 211–212, 215, 218–219, 222–230, 246, 250, 253
translingualism   233, 241, 245, 246, 251
trans-language writing   232, 233, 246, 249, 253
translingual poetry   249
transmutation   71–72
travelogue   124, 129, 132–133, 138, 142
typography   16, 52, 80–81, 107, 116, 193

underground   174, 176, 190, 214
understanding vs. non-understanding   93–94
universal language   39, 44, 47, 61, 64, 143, 145, 150, 153–155, 211
artificial language   29, 40, 155
auxiliary language   154–155
utopia   42, 44, 47, 54, 59, 84, 107, 139, 178, 217

utterance   2, 4, 88, 113–115, 123, 134–135, 139, 146, 159, 163–164, 169–170, 172, 177, 183, 187, 190–191, 195, 209, 213, 223, 225, 227–229, 231, 253

verb   60, 73–74, 89, 92, 94–96, 112, 118, 126, 130, 134, 243
verbal art   58, 99, 104, 111, 158, 165, 183–184, 211
   language art   99, 104, 111, 219
verbal magic   14–15, 31, 34–37, 42, 172, 174
   magic of language   15, 32, 34
   magic of the word   31, 35–36, 47, 233, 255
visual poetry   106, 122, 174, 190
   concrete poetry   116
vocabulary   23, 33, 61, 72–73, 76, 103, 137, 155, 159, 246
voice   45, 47, 68, 78, 84, 104, 113, 115, 126, 156, 171, 173, 206, 246

Vorticism   15, 101–102, 256
Vsechestvo   52

word as such   5, 15, 26, 28, 53, 58, 60, 92, 159, 206, 214, 255
word creation   5, 29, 64, 69–70, 86, 129, 139, 257
World War II   15, 107–108, 150, 156–157, 166–167, 170, 205, 222, 255, 257
writing system   15, 45, 49, 50–51, 55, 62

yazykovodstvo   57

zaum   31, 36, 43, 48–54, 56, 58, 64, 84, 86, 151, 160, 172, 174, 176, 211
   beyonsense   58, 62, 64–65, 68, 178
   trans-sense   48, 52–56, 58, 84, 151, 159, 177, 211, 256
zvukoslovie   31, 39